TAIWAN

DIPLOMATIC HANDBOOK

International Business Publications, USA
Washington, DC, USA-Taiwan

TAIWAN
DIPLOMATIC HANDBOOK

Editorial content: International Business Publications, USA

Editor-in-Chief: Dr. Igor S. Oleynik
Editor: Natasha Alexander

Published by
International Business Publications, USA
P.O.Box 15343, Washington, DC 20003
Phone: (202) 546-2103, Fax: (202) 546-3275.
E-mail: rusric@erols.com

UPDATED ANNUALLY

We express our sincere appreciation to all government agencies and international organizations which provided information and other materials for this handbook

Databases & Information: International Business Publications, USA
Cover Design: International Business Publications, USA

International Business Publications, USA. has used its best efforts in collecting, analyzing and preparing data, information and materials for this unique handbook. Due to the dynamic nature and fast development of the economy and business environment, we cannot warrant that all information herein is complete and accurate. IBP does not assume and hereby disclaim any liability to any person for any loss or damage caused by possible errors or omissions in the handbook.
This handbook is for individual use only. Use this handbook for any other purpose, included but not limited to reproducing and storing in a retrieval system by any means, electronic, photocopying or using the addresses or other information contained in this handbook for any commercial purposes requires a special written permission from the publisher.

2007 2nd Edition Updated Reprint International Business Publications, USA
ISBN 0-7397-5905-1

For customer service and information, please contact:

in the USA: International Business Publications, USA
    P.O.Box 15343, Washington, DC 20003
    Phone: (202) 546-2103, Fax: (202) 546-3275.
    E-mail: rusric@erols.com

Printed in the USA

For additional analytical, marketing, investment and business opportunities
information, please contact
Global Investment & Business Center, USA
(202) 546-2103. Fax: (202) 546-3275. E-mail: rusric@erols.com

TAIWAN
DIPLOMATIC HANDBOOK

TABLE OF CONTENTS

- **STRATEGIC AND DEVELOPMENT PROFILES** 8
  - COUNTRY OVERVIEW 8
    - *ECONOMIC OVERVIEW* 9
    - *Geography* 9
    - *People* 10
    - *Government* 12
    - *Economy* 15
    - *Communications* 16
    - *Transportation* 17
    - *Military* 18
    - *Transnational Issues* 18
- **IMPORTANT INFORMATION FOR UNDERSTANDING TAIWAN** 19
  - PROFILE 19
  - PEOPLE 20
    - *Education* 20
    - *Languages* 20
    - *Religions* 20
    - *Culture* 21
  - HISTORY 21
  - ADMINISTRATION 22
    - *Principal Leaders* 23
  - POLITICAL CONDITIONS 24
    - *Political Parties* 25
    - *Taiwan and the Mainland* 26
  - ECONOMY 27
    - *Foreign Trade* 27
    - *Agriculture* 28
    - *Economic Outlook* 28
    - *DEFENSE* 28
  - TAIIWAN FOREIGN POLICY: CURRENT TRENDS 29
    - *Foreign Policy Making Orientation* 30
    - *General Situation of ROC Foreign Relations* 31
    - *Diplomatic Allies in Europe* 32
    - *ROC-US relations* 33
    - *ROC-Japan relations* 33
    - *ROC-ROK relations* 34
    - *ROC-Europe relations* 34
  - OVERVIEW OF EU - TAIWAN RELATIONS 34
    - *Cross-straits relations* 35
    - *Announcement of the establishment of the European Economic and Trade Office in Taiwan by the European Commission - 10 March 2003* 35

For additional analytical, marketing, investment and business opportunities information, please contact
Global Investment & Business Center, USA
(202) 546-2103. Fax: (202) 546-3275. E-mail: rusric@erols.com

Interview with Chris Patten, "European Voice", 23 January 2003 .... *36*
ROC's relations with countries without diplomatic ties *37*
ECONOMY 39
Foreign Trade *39*
Agriculture *40*
Economic Outlook *40*

THE U.S. AND TAIWAN RELATIONS: BASIC INFORMATION 42

MILESTONES IN U.S.-TAIWAN RELATIONS 43
PENTAGON REPORT ON IMPLEMENTATION OF TAIWAN RELATIONS ACT (U.S. REAFFIRMS COMMITMENT
TO TAIWAN'S DEFENSIVE CAPABILITY) 46
Report to Congress Pursuant to Public Law 106-113 .... *47*
*EXECUTIVE SUMMARY OF REPORT TO CONGRESS ON IMPLEMENTATION OF THE TAIWAN
RELATIONS ACT* *47*
GAPS IN KNOWLEDGE REGARDING THE PRC-TAIWAN MILITARY BALANCE *49*
GEORGE W. BUSH ON TAIWAN: SELECTED STATEMENTS 52
President Welcomes China, Taiwan into WTO *52*
President Signs Bills *52*
US-TAIWAN SECRET TALKS ON ARMS SALE: ANALYSIS 53
CONGRESSIONAL TAIWAN CAUCUS FOUNDED 56
Senate passes Taiwan-into-the-WHO resolution *56*
REPORT TO CONGRESS PURSUANT TO PUBLIC LAW 106-113 57
*EXECUTIVE SUMMARY OF REPORT TO CONGRESS ON IMPLEMENTATION OF THE TAIWAN
RELATIONS ACT* *57*
GAPS IN KNOWLEDGE REGARDING THE PRC-TAIWAN MILITARY BALANCE *59*
The Content and Structure of a PRC-Taiwan Assessment *59*
Shaping and deterrence *61*
Contingency outcomes *61*
Where are the Gaps in Knowledge? *61*
PERSPECTIVES ON CROSS-STRAIT RELATIONS: CHALLENGES AND OPPORTUNITIES 62
The Military Balance *63*
Economic Relations *65*
Systems in Transition *67*
Directions for the Future *68*
MANAGING U.S.-TAIWAN RELATIONS: 20 YEARS AFTER THE TAIWAN RELATIONS ACT 69
Background of the TRA *70*
Rocky Start: 1979-1980 .... *71*
II. Assessment of the TRA *73*
III. Setbacks of the TRA *75*
IV. Lessons For Future U.S.-Taiwan Relations *77*
Taiwan Arms Sales - DSAA Fiscal Year Series (Dollars in Thousands) *85*

IMPORTANT DOCUMENTS DEFINING US – TAIWAN RELATIONS 87

U.S.-TAIWAN RELATIONS 87
TAIWAN RELATIONS ACT Public Law 96-8 96th Congress *90*
THE JOINT U.S.-CHINA COMMUNIQUE, SHANGHAI, February 27, 1972 .... *96*
U.S.-PRC JOINT COMMUNIQUE, August 17, 1982 .... *99*
CONGRESSIONAL TESTIMONIES AND STATEMENTS ON US-TAIWAN RELATIONS 101
DAS SUSAN SHIRK TESTIMONY ON TAIWAN RELATIONS ACT AT 20 .... *101*
On the 20th Anniversary of the Taiwan Relations Act: U.S. Anchor Interests Across the Taiwan Strait *107*
Strengthening U.S.-Taiwan Relations: Confidence-Building and Building Confidence *110*
Sen. Torrecelli Introduces Resolution Supporting Peaceful and Democratic Future for Taiwan *112*

**For additional analytical, marketing, investment and business opportunities
information, please contact
Global Investment & Business Center, USA
(202) 546-2103. Fax: (202) 546-3275. E-mail: rusric@erols.com**

Unofficial Ties with Free Taiwan	*113*
U.S. Lawmakers Say Taiwan Deserves Unwavering Support	*114*
Sec. of State Powell Praises Taiwan	*115*
Taipei-Washington Ties Better Than Ever: President	*117*
TAIWAN RELATIONS ACT -- HON. JOHN B. LARSON (Extensions of Remarks - April 10, 2002)	118
NEW TRENDS IN TAIWAN DIPLOMACY	119
NGOs give Taiwanese a voice to the world	*119*
POLITICAL AND GOVERNMENT SYSTEM	**123**
CHEN SHUI-BIAN, TENTH-TERM PRESIDENT OF THE REPUBLIC OF CHINA	123
STRUCTURE OF THE GOVERNMENT	127
EXECUTIVE	127
Functions	*128*
Special Powers	*128*
The Office of the President	*129*
THE NATIONAL ASSEMBLY	130
Delegates	*130*
FIVE GOVERNMENT BRANCHES	131
Executive Yuan	*131*
Executive Yuan Council	*132*
Ministries and Other Organizations	*132*
Relationship with the Legislative Yuan	*132*
Relationship with the Judicial Yuan	*133*
Relationship with the Examination Yuan	*133*
Relationship with the Control Yuan	*133*
Prosecutorial Arm	*133*
LEGISLATIVE YUAN	134
Functions and Powers	*134*
JUDICIAL YUAN	135
EXAMINATION YUAN	135
Civil Service	*135*
CONTROL YUAN	136
PROVINCIAL GOVERNMENT	136
Special Municipality Government	*136*
Taipei City Government	*137*
City Councils	*137*
Reinvention of Government	*137*
FOREIGN RELATIONS	138
Obstruction	*139*
Multilateralism	*139*
The UN Issue	*139*
Economic Organizations	*140*
Humanitarian Aid	*141*
BILATERAL RELATIONS	141
US TAIWAN RELATIONS	*142*
OVERSEAS CHINESE	143
Overseas Chinese Affairs Commission	*143*
Major Destinations for ROC Emigrants	*143*
THE STATUS OF A DIVIDED CHINA	144
Unification Guidelines	*145*
Statute Governing Relations	*146*
Organizational Structures	*146*
Cross-strait Consultations	*147*

**For additional analytical, marketing, investment and business opportunities
information, please contact
Global Investment & Business Center, USA
(202) 546-2103. Fax: (202) 546-3275. E-mail: rusric@erols.com**

Defining Cross-strait Relations *148*
Unofficial Exchanges *149*
Indirect Trade *150*
Policy toward Hong Kong and Macau *150*
NATIONAL DEFENSE 151
Budgetary Reduction Trend *151*
Command Structure *152*
Ministry of National Defense *152*
General Staff Headquarters, MND *152*

STUDYING COUNTRY THROUGH THE CONSTITUTION **154**

CONSTITUTIONAL DEVELOPMENT 154
Enactment and Fundamental Features *154*
CONSTITUTION 154
CHAPTER I. GENERAL PROVISIONS 154
CHAPTER II. RIGHTS AND DUTIES OF THE PEOPLE 154
CHAPTER III. THE NATIONAL ASSEMBLY 155
CHAPTER IV. THE PRESIDENT 157
CHAPTER V. ADMINISTRATION 158
CHAPTER VI. LEGISLATION 159
CHAPTER VII. JUDICIARY 160
CHAPTER VIII. EXAMINATION 161
CHAPTER IX. CONTROL 161
CHAPTER X. POWERS OF THE CENTRAL AND LOCAL GOVERNMENTS 162
CHAPTER XI. SYSTEM OF LOCAL GOVERNMENT 164
Section 1. The Province *164*
Section 2. The Hsien *165*
CHAPTER XII. ELECTION, RECALL, INITIATIVE AND REFERENDUM 165
CHAPTER XIII. FUNDAMENTAL NATIONAL POLICIES 166
Section 1. National Defense *166*
Section 2. Foreign Policy *166*
Section 3. National Economy *166*
Section 4. Social Security *167*
Section 5. Education and Culture *168*
Section 6. Frontier Regions *168*
CHAPTER XIV. ENFORCEMENT AND AMENDMENT OF THE CONSTITUTION 169

TRAVELING **169**

US STATE DEPARTMENT SUGGESTIONS 169
GETTING THERE 171
GETTING AROUND 172
ACCOMMODATION 173
MONEY 174

SUPPLEMENTS **175**

TAIWAN SECURITY ENHANCEMENT ACT (S. 693) 175
STRATEGIC GOVERNMENT AND BUSINESS CONTACTS 181
TAIWAN INFORMATION OFFICES NI NORTH AMERICA 181
1. U.S. Trade Related Contacts *183*
Washington-Based Country Contacts *184*
2. AmCham and/or Bilateral Business Councils *185*
3. Trade or Industry Associations *185*
4. Public Agencies *185*

**For additional analytical, marketing, investment and business opportunities information, please contact
Global Investment & Business Center, USA
(202) 546-2103. Fax: (202) 546-3275. E-mail: rusric@erols.com**

- 5. Market Research Firms (Partial Listing) 186
- 6. Commercial Banks (Partial Listing) 186
- **KEY ECONOMIC INDICATORS** 187
- **TAIWAN: RECENT DEVELOPMENTS AND U.S. POLICY CHOICES** 188
  - *SUMMARY* 188
  - *MOST RECENT DEVELOPMENTS* 189
  - *BACKGROUND AND ANALYSIS* 189
  - *Economic and Political Issues* 195
  - *Political Liberalization* 196
  - *LEGISLATION* 198
  - *CHRONOLOGY* 198
- **WASHINGTON-TAIPEI RELATIONS AND THE ROC'S PRAGMATIC DIPLOMACY** 201
- **INTERNATIONAL CONFERENCE ON UNITED STATES -- TAIWAN RELATIONS: TWENTY YEARS AFTER THE TAIWAN RELATIONS ACT** 206
  - *Beijing-Taipei-Washington Relations: Opportunities and Risks* 206
  - *The Taiwan Relations Act and US-Taiwan Military Relations* 212
  - *Improving the Nature and Quality of Bilateral Trade Relations between Taiwan and the United States with the TRA* 220
  - *The Trade Relationship Between Taiwan and the U.S. Since the Taiwan Relations Act* 232
  - *The National Committee on American Foreign Policy's Project on U.S.-China Policy and Cross-Strait Relations* 250

For additional analytical, marketing, investment and business opportunities information, please contact
Global Investment & Business Center, USA
(202) 546-2103. Fax: (202) 546-3275. E-mail: rusric@erols.com

STRATEGIC AND DEVELOPMENT PROFILES

COUNTRY OVERVIEW

Capital	Taipei (de facto) Nanking (de jure)[1] 25°02′N 121°38′E
Largest city	Taipei
Official language	Mandarin (Guóyǔ)
Government	Semi-presidential system
- President	Chen Shui-bian
- Vice President	Annette Lu
- Premier	Su Tseng-chang
Establishment	Xinhai Revolution
- Declared	October 10, 1911
- Established	January 1, 1912
- Relocation to Taiwan	December 7, 1949
Area	
- Total	35,980 km² (137th) 13,892 sq mi
- Water (%)	10.3
Population	
- 2006 estimate	23,036,087 (47th[2])
- Density	635/km² (14th[2]) 1,658/sq mi
GDP (PPP)	2005 estimate
- Total	$631.2 billion (16th)
- Per capita	$27,600 (24th)
HDI (2003)	0.910 (high) (25th if ranked[3])
Currency	New Taiwan Dollar (NT$) (TWD)
Time zone	CST (UTC+8)
Internet TLD	.tw
Calling code	+886

The **Republic of China** (**R.O.C**) is a state in East Asia. It was formerly the national government of all China. However, it lost control of the mainland to the People's Republic of China (PRC) as a result of the Chinese Civil War in 1949, and since then its administration has been restricted to the island groups of Taiwan (Formosa), the Pescadores, Kinmen, and Matsu. Over subsequent decades, the Republic of China has been commonly referred to as "**Taiwan**", and since the late 1970's the name "**China**" has been increasingly used to refer to the People's Republic of China. For political reasons, the Republic of China is commonly referred to as "**Chinese Taipei**" in international organizations.

The ROC was established in 1912, replacing the last Chinese dynasty - the Qing - and ending over 2,000 years of imperial rule in China. It is thus the oldest surviving republic in East Asia. The rule of the Republic of China in Mainland China was scarred by warlordism, Japanese invasion as a predecessor to World War II, and civil war. Major fighting in the civil war ended in 1950 with the

---

For additional analytical, marketing, investment and business opportunities information, please contact
Global Investment & Business Center, USA
(202) 546-2103. Fax: (202) 546-3275. E-mail: rusric@erols.com

Communist Party of China (CPC) in control of most of Mainland China, and the ROC in control of Taiwan and several offshore islands (Kinmen, Penghu, and Matsu). The CPC proclaimed a new state, the People's Republic of China (PRC) in Beijing in 1949. The Republic of China on Taiwan continued to regard itself as the sole and legitimate government of all of China. This was a claim recognized by most states until the late 1970's.

Starting in 1928, the Republic of China was ruled by the Kuomintang (KMT) as an authoritarian dictatorship. In the 1950's and 1960's, the KMT took steps to reform the economy by reducing corruption and reforming land policies which coincided with a period of great economic growth despite the constant threat of war and civil unrest. The political climate changed in the 1980's and 1990's as the government actively pursued a transition to a democratic system, beginning with the first direct presidential election in 1996 and culminating in the 2000 election of President Chen Shui-bian, the first non-KMT president elected.

Population: 22.1 million, heavily concentrated along the West coast
Area: 14,000 square miles (slightly larger than Maryland and Delaware combined)
Major Cities: Taipei (Capital), Kaohsiung, Taichung, Tainan
Major Religions: Mixture of Buddhist, Confucian, and Taoist 93%, Christian 4.5%, other 2.5%
Languages: Mandarin (official), Taiwanese (Min), Hakka Chinese dialects
Ethnic Groups: Taiwanese, 84%; mainland Chinese, 14%; aborigine, 2%
Armed Forces: Army, 240,000; Air Force, 68,000; Navy, 68,000

ECONOMIC OVERVIEW

Currency: New Taiwan Dollar (NT$)
Gross Domestic Product): $282 billion
Real GDP Growth Rate : 4.9%; : 5.8%
Inflation Rate (consumer prices): 1.2%; : 1.7%
Unemployment Rate : 3.1%
Total Reserves, Non-Gol: $99.7 billion
Current Account Balance : $8.1 billion
Merchandise Exports : $115.3 billion
Merchandise Imports : $100.6 billion
Merchandise Trade Surplus: $14.7 billion
Major Exports: Textile products, electrical machinery & apparatus, machinery, chemicals & allied products, iron & steel, plastic articles
Major Imports: Crude oil, capital goods, consumer goods, agricultural and industrial raw materials
Major Trading Partners: United States, Japan, Europe, Hong Kong (China)

Background: In 1895, military defeat forced China to cede Taiwan to Japan, however it reverted to Chinese control after World War II. Following the communist victory on the mainland in 1949, 2 million Nationalists fled to Taiwan and established a government that over five decades has gradually democratized and incorporated the native population within its structure. Throughout this period, the island has prospered to become one of East Asia's economic "Tigers." The dominant political issue continues to be the relationship between Taiwan and China and the question of eventual reunification.

GEOGRAPHY

Location: Eastern Asia, islands bordering the East China Sea, Philippine Sea, South China Sea, and Taiwan Strait, north of the Philippines, off the southeastern coast of China
Geographic coordinates: 23 30 N, 121 00 E

**For additional analytical, marketing, investment and business opportunities information, please contact
Global Investment & Business Center, USA
(202) 546-2103. Fax: (202) 546-3275. E-mail: rusric@erols.com**

Map references: Southeast Asia

Area:
total: 35,980 sq km
land: 32,260 sq km
water: 3,720 sq km
note: includes the Pescadores, Matsu, and Quemoy

Area - comparative: slightly smaller than Maryland and Delaware combined
Land boundaries: 0 km
Coastline: 1,566.3 km

Maritime claims:
exclusive economic zone: 200 nm
territorial sea: 12 nm

Climate: tropical; marine; rainy season during southwest monsoon (June to August); cloudiness is persistent and extensive all year
Terrain: eastern two-thirds mostly rugged mountains; flat to gently rolling plains in west

Elevation extremes:
lowest point: South China Sea 0 m
highest point: Yu Shan 3,997 m

Land use:
arable land: 24%
permanent crops: 1%
permanent pastures: 5%
forests and woodland: 55%
other: 15%

Irrigated land: NA sq km
Natural hazards: earthquakes and typhoons

Environment - current issues: air pollution; water pollution from industrial emissions, raw sewage; contamination of drinking water supplies; trade in endangered species; low-level radioactive waste disposal

Environment - international agreements:
party to: none of the selected agreements
signed, but not ratified: none of the selected agreements

PEOPLE

Population: 22,191,087

Age structure:
0-14 years: 22% (male 2,485,421; female 2,292,901)
15-64 years: 70% (male 7,869,939; female 7,629,195)
65 years and over: 8% (male 1,013,074; female 900,557)

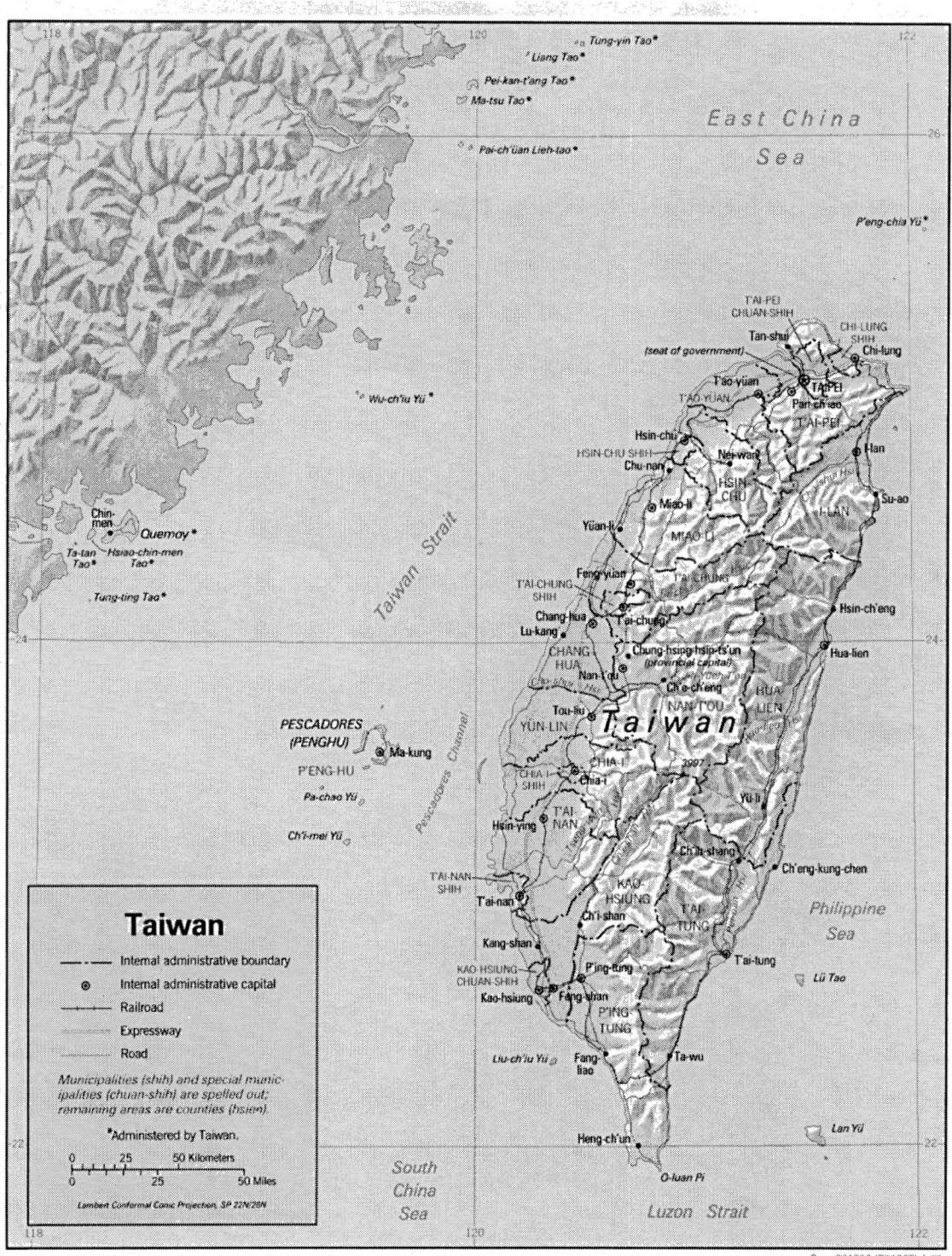

Natural resources: small deposits of coal, natural gas, limestone, marble, and asbestos

Population growth rate: 0.81%
Birth rate: 14.42 births/1,000 population
Death rate: 5.91 deaths/1,000 population
Net migration rate: -0.38 migrant(s)/1,000 population

Sex ratio:
at birth: 1.08 male(s)/female
under 15 years: 1.08 male(s)/female
15-64 years: 1.03 male(s)/female
65 years and over: 1.12 male(s)/female
total population: 1.05 male(s)/female

Infant mortality rate: 7.06 deaths/1,000 live births

Life expectancy at birth:
total population: 76.35 years
male: 73.62 years
female: 79.32 years

Total fertility rate: 1.76 children born/woman

Nationality:
noun: Chinese (singular and plural)
adjective: Chinese

Ethnic groups: Taiwanese (including Hakka) 84%, mainland Chinese 14%, aborigine 2%
Religions: mixture of Buddhist, Confucian, and Taoist 93%, Christian 4.5%, other 2.5%
Languages: Mandarin Chinese (official), Taiwanese (Min), Hakka dialects

Literacy:
definition: age 15 and over can read and write
total population: 86% (1980 est.); note - literacy for the total population has reportedly increased to 94%
male: 93%
female: 79%

GOVERNMENT

Country name:
conventional long form: none
conventional short form: Taiwan
local long form: none
local short form: T'ai-wan

Data code: TW
Government type: multiparty democratic regime headed by popularly elected president
Capital: Taipei

Administrative divisions: since in the past the authorities claimed to be the government of all China, the central administrative divisions include the provinces of Fu-chien (some 20 offshore islands of Fujian Province including Quemoy and Matsu) and Taiwan (the island of Taiwan and

the Pescadores islands); note - the more commonly referenced administrative divisions are those of Taiwan Province - 16 counties (hsien, singular and plural), 5 municipalities* (shih, singular and plural), and 2 special municipalities** (chuan-shih, singular and plural); Chang-hua, Chia-i, Chia-i*, Chi-lung*, Hsin-chu, Hsin-chu*, Hua-lien, I-lan, Kao-hsiung, Kao-hsiung**, Miao-li, Nan-t'ou, P'eng-hu, P'ing-tung, T'ai-chung, T'ai-chung*, T'ai-nan, T'ai-nan*, T'ai-pei, T'ai-pei**, T'ai-tung, T'ao-yuan, and Yun-lin; the provincial capital is at Chung-hsing-hsin-ts'un
note: Taiwan uses the Wade-Giles system for romanization

National holiday: National Day, 10 October (1911) (Anniversary of the Chinese Revolution)
Constitution: 1 January 1947, amended in 1992, 1994, and 1997
Legal system: based on civil law system; accepts compulsory ICJ jurisdiction, with reservations
Suffrage: 20 years of age; universal

Executive branch:
Taiwan--NDE

President	CHEN Shui-bian
Vice President	Annette LU
Pres., Executive Yuan (Premier)	Frank HSIEH
Vice Pres., Executive Yuan (Vice Premier)	
Sec. Gen., Executive Yuan	Arthur IAP
Pres., Control Yuan	Fredrick CHIEN
Pres., Examination Yuan	YAO Chia-wen
Pres., Judicial Yuan	WENG Yueh-sheng
Pres., Legislative Yuan	WANG Jin-pyng
Min. of Economic Affairs	HO Mei-yueh
Min. of Education	TU Cheng-sheng
Min. of Finance	LIN Chuan
Min. of Foreign Affairs	Mark CHEN
Min. of Health	CHEN Chien-jen
Min. of Interior	SU Jia-chyuan
Min. of Justice	SHIH Mao-lin
Min. of National Defense	LEE Jye
Min. of Transportation & Communications	LIN Ling-san
Min. Without Portfolio	HU Sheng-cheng
Min. Without Portfolio	LIN Yi-fu
Min. Without Portfolio	LIN Sheng-Fong
Min. Without Portfolio	KUO Yao-chi
Min. Without Portfolio	CHEN Chi-mai
Min. Without Portfolio	LIN Ferng-ching
Min. Without Portfolio	FU Li-yeh
Chmn., Agricultural Council	LEE Ching-lung

For additional analytical, marketing, investment and business opportunities information, please contact
Global Investment & Business Center, USA
(202) 546-2103. Fax: (202) 546-3275. E-mail: rusric@erols.com

Chmn., Atomic Energy Council	OUYANG Min-sheng
Chmn., Central Election Commission	CHANG Masa
Chmn., Consumer Protection	YEH Chu-lan
Chmn., Cultural Affairs	CHEN Chi-nan
Chmn., Economic Planning & Development Council	HU Sheng-cheng
Chmn., Fair Trade Commission	HWANG Tzong-leh
Chmn., Labor Affairs Council	CHEN Chu
Chmn., Mainland Affairs Council	Joseph WU
Chmn., Mongolian & Tibetan Affairs Commission	HSU Chih-hsiung
Chmn., National Council on Physical Fitness & Sports	CHEN Chuan-show
Chmn., National Palace Museum	SHIH Shou-chien
Chmn., National Science Council	WU Mau-kuen
Chmn., National Youth Commission	CHENG Li-chiun
Chmn., Overseas Chinese Affairs Commission	CHANG Fu-mei
Chmn., Public Construction Commission	KUO Yao-chi
Chmn., Research Development & Evaluation Commission	YEH Jiunn-rong
Chmn., Veterans Affairs Commission	KAO Hua-chu
Representative to the US	David LEE
Governor, Central Bank of China	PERNG Fai-nan

Legislative branch: Legislative Yuan (225 seats - 168 elected by popular vote, 41 elected on basis of proportion of islandwide votes received by participating political parties, eight elected from overseas Chinese constituencies on basis of proportion of island-wide votes received by participating political parties, eight elected by popular vote among aboriginal populations; members serve three-year terms); National Assembly (300 seat nonstanding body; delegates nominated by parties and elected by proportional representation six to nine months after Legislative Yuan calls to amend Constitution, impeach president, or change national borders) - see note
note: as a result of constitutional amendments approved by National Assembly in June 2005, number of seats in legislature will be reduced from 225 to 113 beginning with election in 2007; amendments also eliminated National Assembly thus giving Taiwan a unicameral legislature
elections: Legislative Yuan - last held 11 December 2004 (next to be held in December 2007); National Assembly - last held 14 May 2005; dissolved in June 2005
election results: Legislative Yuan - percent of vote by party - DPP 38%, KMT 35%, PFP 15%, TSU 8%, other parties and independents 4%; seats by party - DPP 89, KMT 79, PFP 34, TSU 12, other parties 7, independents 4; National Assembly - percent of vote by party - DPP 42.5%, KMT 38.9%, TSU 7%, PFP 6%, others 6.6%; seats by party - DPP 127, KMT 117, TSU 21, PFP 18, others 17

Judicial branch: Judicial Yuan, justices appointed by the president with the consent of the National Assembly

Political parties and leaders: Chinese New Party or CNP [CHOU Yang-sun]; Democratic Progressive Party or DPP [LIN Yi-hsiung, chairman]; Kuomintang or KMT (Nationalist Party)

[LIEN Chan, acting chairman]; Taiwan Independence Party or TAIP [CHENG Pang-chen]; other minor parties

Political pressure groups and leaders: Taiwan independence movement, various business and environmental groups
note: debate on Taiwan independence has become acceptable within the mainstream of domestic politics on Taiwan; political liberalization and the increased representation of opposition parties in Taiwan's legislature have opened public debate on the island's national identity; advocates of Taiwan independence oppose the ruling party's traditional stand that the island will eventually reunify with mainland China; goals of the Taiwan independence movement include establishing a sovereign nation on Taiwan and entering the UN; other organizations supporting Taiwan independence include the World United Formosans for Independence and the Organization for Taiwan Nation Building

International organization participation: APEC, AsDB, BCIE, ICC, IOC, WCL, WTrO (applicant) **Diplomatic representation in the US:** none; unofficial commercial and cultural relations with the people of the US are maintained through a private instrumentality, the Taipei Economic and Cultural Representative Office (TECRO) in the US with headquarters in Taipei and field offices in Washington and 12 other US cities

Diplomatic representation from the US: none; unofficial commercial and cultural relations with the people on Taiwan are maintained through a private corporation, the American Institute in Taiwan (AIT), which has its headquarters in Rosslyn, Virginia (telephone: [1] (703) 525-8474 and FAX: [1] (703) 841-1385) and offices in Taipei at #7 Lane 134, Hsin Yi Road, Section 3, telephone [886] (2) 2709-2000, FAX [886] (2) 2702-7675, and in Kao-hsiung at #2 Chung Cheng 3d Road, telephone [886] (7) 224-0154 through 0157, FAX [886] (7) 223-8237, and the American Trade Center at Room 3207 International Trade Building, Taipei World Trade Center, 333 Keelung Road Section 1, Taipei 10548, telephone [886] (2) 2720-1550, FAX [886] (2) 2757-7162
Flag description: red with a dark blue rectangle in the upper hoist-side corner bearing a white sun with 12 triangular rays

ECONOMY

Economy - overview: Taiwan has a dynamic capitalist economy with gradually decreasing guidance of investment and foreign trade by government authorities. In keeping with this trend, some large government-owned banks and industrial firms are being privatized. Real growth in GDP has averaged about 8% during the past three decades.

Exports have grown even faster and have provided the primary impetus for industrialization. Inflation and unemployment are low; the trade surplus is substantial; and foreign reserves are the world's third largest. Agriculture contributes 3% to GDP, down from 35% in 1952. Traditional labor-intensive industries are steadily being moved off-shore and replaced with more capital- and technology-intensive industries.

Taiwan has become a major investor in China, Thailand, Indonesia, the Philippines, Malaysia, and Vietnam. The tightening of labor markets has led to an influx of foreign workers, both legal and illegal. Because of its conservative financial approach and its entrepreneurial strengths, Taiwan suffered little compared with many of its neighbors from the Asian financial crisis in 1998-99. Growth in 2000 should pick up a bit from 1999, backed by expansion in domestic consumption, exports, and private investment.

GDP: purchasing power parity - $357 billion

GDP - real growth rate: 5.5%
GDP - per capita: purchasing power parity - $16,100
GDP - composition by sector:
agriculture: 3%
industry: 33%
services: 64%
Population below poverty line: 1%
Household income or consumption by percentage share:
lowest 10%: NA%
highest 10%: NA%
Inflation rate (consumer prices): 0.4%
Labor force: 9.7 million
Labor force - by occupation: services 55%, industry 37%, agriculture 8%
Unemployment rate: 2.9%
Budget:
revenues: $36.82 billion
expenditures: $40.53 billion, including capital expenditures of $NA
Industries: electronics, petroleum refining, chemicals, textiles, iron and steel, machinery, cement, food processing
Industrial production growth rate: 7.5%
Electricity - production: 133.586 billion kWh
Electricity - production by source:
fossil fuel: 65.91%
hydro: 7.84%
nuclear: 26.25%
other: 0%
Electricity - consumption: 124.235 billion kWh
Electricity - exports: 0 kWh
Electricity - imports: 0 kWh

Agriculture - products: rice, corn, vegetables, fruit, tea; pigs, poultry, beef, milk; fish

Exports: $121.6 billion (f.o.b.)
Exports - commodities: electronics, electric and machinery equipment 52%, metals, textiles, plastics, chemicals
Exports - partners: US 26%, Hong Kong 21%, Europe 18%, Japan 10%, Singapore 3%
Imports: $101.7 billion (c.i.f)
Imports - commodities: electronics, electric and machinery equipment 45%, minerals, precision instruments
Imports - partners: Japan 27%, US 18%, Europe 16%, South Korea 6%, Malaysia 4%
Debt - external: $35 billion (September 1999)
Economic aid - recipient: $NA
Currency: 1 New Taiwan dollar (NT$) = 100 cents
Exchange rates: New Taiwan dollars per US$1 - 31.395 (yearend 1999), 32.216 (1998), 32.052 (1997), 27.5 (1996), 27.5
Fiscal year: 1 July - 30 June (up to FY98/99); 1 July 1999 - 31 December 2000 for FY00; calendar year

COMMUNICATIONS

Telephones - main lines in use:	13.615 million

Telephones - mobile cellular:	22.17 million
Telephone system:	*general assessment:* provides telecommunications service for every business and private need *domestic:* thoroughly modern; completely digitalized *international:* country code - 886; satellite earth stations - 2 Intelsat (1 Pacific Ocean and 1 Indian Ocean); submarine cables to Japan (Okinawa), Philippines, Guam, Singapore, Hong Kong, Indonesia, Australia, Middle East, and Western Europe
Radio broadcast stations:	AM 218, FM 333, shortwave 50
Television broadcast stations:	29 (plus two repeaters)
Internet country code:	.tw
Internet hosts:	3,838,383
Internet users:	13.21 million

TRANSPORTATION

Railways:
total: 2,481 km (519 km electrified)
narrow gauge: 2,481 km 1.067-m

Highways:
total: 34,901 km
paved: 31,271 km (including 538 km of expressways)
unpaved: 3,630 km
Pipelines: petroleum products 3,400 km; natural gas 1,800 km
Ports and harbors: Chi-lung (Keelung), Hua-lien, Kao-hsiung, Su-ao, T'ai-chung
Merchant marine:
total: 175 ships (1,000 GRT or over) totaling 4,944,166 GRT/7,710,891 DWT
ships by type: bulk 45, cargo 33, combination bulk 1, container 69, petroleum tanker 17, refrigerated cargo 8, roll-on/roll-off 2
Airports: 38
Airports - with paved runways:
total: 35
over 3,047 m: 8
2,438 to 3,047 m: 9
1,524 to 2,437 m: 8
914 to 1,523 m: 7
under 914 m: 3
Airports - with unpaved runways:
total: 3
1,524 to 2,437 m: 1
under 914 m: 2
Heliports: 2

MILITARY

Military branches: Army, Navy (includes Marines), Air Force, Coastal Patrol and Defense Command, Armed Forces Reserve Command, Combined Service Forces
Military manpower - military age: 19 years of age
Military manpower - availability:
males age 15-49: 6,554,373
Military manpower - fit for military service:
males age 15-49: 5,017,643
Military manpower - reaching military age annually:
males: 201,413
Military expenditures - dollar figure: $8.042 billion
Military expenditures - percent of GDP: 2.8%

TRANSNATIONAL ISSUES

Disputes - international: involved in complex dispute over the Spratly Islands with China, Malaysia, Philippines, Vietnam, and possibly Brunei; Paracel Islands occupied by China, but claimed by Vietnam and Taiwan; claims Japanese-administered Senkaku-shoto (Senkaku Islands/Diaoyu Tai), as does China

Illicit drugs: considered an important heroin transit point; major problem with domestic consumption of methamphetamines and heroin

---

**For additional analytical, marketing, investment and business opportunities information, please contact
Global Investment & Business Center, USA
(202) 546-2103. Fax: (202) 546-3275. E-mail: rusric@erols.com**

IMPORTANT INFORMATION FOR UNDERSTANDING TAIWAN[1]

PROFILE

NAME: Taiwan

Geography
Area: 35,967 sq. km. (13,887 sq. mi.).
Cities (2006): *Capital*--Taipei (pop. 2.6 million). *Other cities*--(Kaohsiung 1.5 million), Taichung (1.0 million).
Terrain: Two thirds of the island is largely mountainous with 100 peaks over 3,000 meters (9,843 ft.).
Climate: Maritime subtropical.

People
Population (July, 2006 est.) 23.0 million.
Annual growth rate (2006 est.): 0.61%.
Languages: Mandarin Chinese (official), Taiwanese, Hakka.
Education: *Years compulsory*--9. *Attendance* (2005)--99.4%. *Literacy* (2005)--97.3 %.
Health: *Infant mortality rate* (2006 est.)--0.63%. *Life expectancy* (2006 est.) male 74.67 yrs.; female 80.47 yrs.
Work force (2006 est.):10.6 million.

Political Establishment
Type: Multi-party democracy. There are four major parties forming two alliances known as Pan-Blue and Pan-Green. The Pan-Blue includes the Kuomintang (KMT) and the People First Party (PFP). The Pan-Green includes the Democratic Progressive Party (DPP) and the Taiwan Solidarity Union (TSU). The Pan-Blue coalition holds a slight majority of seats in the Legislative Yuan (LY).
Constitution: December 25, 1946; last amended 2005.
Branches (Yuan): Executive, Legislative, Judicial, Control, Examination.
Major political parties: Democratic Progressive Party (DPP); Kuomintang (KMT or Nationalist Party); People First Party (PFP); Taiwan Solidarity Union (TSU).
Suffrage: Universal over 20 years of age.
Central budget proposed (FY 2007): $50.8 billion.
Defense proposed (2007): 18.7 % of entire budget.

Economy
GNP: $364 billion.
Real annual growth rate (2006 est.): 4.3%.
Per capita GNP (2006): $16,024.
Unemployment (Jan-Aug. 2006) 3.9%.
Natural resources: Small deposits of coal, natural gas, limestone, marble and asbestos.
Agriculture (1.7% of GDP): *Major products*--pork, rice, fruit and vegetables, sugarcane, poultry, shrimp, eel.
Services: (73.3% of GDP). Industry (25.0% of GDP): *Types*--electronics and computer products, chemicals and petrochemicals, basic metals, machinery, textiles, transport equipment, plastics,

---
[1] US State Department Profile

For additional analytical, marketing, investment and business opportunities information, please contact
Global Investment & Business Center, USA
(202) 546-2103. Fax: (202) 546-3275. E-mail: rusric@erols.com

machinery.

Trade (2005): *Exports*--$198 billion: electronics, optical & precision instruments, information and communications products, textile products, basic metals, plastic and rubber products. *Major markets*--U.S. $29 billion, PRC and Hong Kong $78 billion, Japan $15 billion. *Imports*--$183 billion: electronics, optical & precision instruments, information & communications products, machinery & electrical products, chemicals, basic metals, transport equipment, crude oil. *Major suppliers*--Japan $46 billion, PRC $20 billion, U.S. $21 billion. (Note: 2005 trade figures are revised because Taiwan began early this year to include re-exports in its exports and re-imports in its imports. End Note.)

PEOPLE

Taiwan has a population of 22.8 million. More than 18 million, the "native" Taiwanese, are descendants of Chinese who migrated from Fujian and Guangdong Provinces on the mainland, primarily in the 18th and 19th centuries. The "mainlanders," who arrived in Taiwan after 1945, came from all parts of mainland China. About 370,000 aborigines inhabit the mountainous central and eastern parts of the island and are believed to be of Malayo-Polynesian origin. Of Taiwan's total population, approximately one million, or 4.4%, currently reside in Mainland China.

EDUCATION

A 9-year public educational system has been in effect since 1979. Six years of elementary school and 3 years of junior high are compulsory for all children. About 93.5% of junior high graduates continue their studies in either a senior high or vocational school. Taiwan has an extensive higher education system with more than 150 institutions of higher learning. Each year, over 100,000 students attempt to enter higher education institutes; about 75% of the candidates are admitted to a college or university. Opportunities for graduate education are expanding in Taiwan, but many students travel abroad for advanced education. In FY 2006, over 16,000 U.S. student visas were issued to Taiwan passport holders.

LANGUAGES

A large majority of people in Taiwan speak Mandarin Chinese, which has been the medium of instruction in the schools for more than five decades. Native Taiwanese and many others also speak one of the Southern Fujianese dialects, Min-nan, also known as Taiwanese. Recently there has been a growing use of Taiwanese in the broadcast media. The Hakka, who are concentrated in several counties throughout Taiwan, have their own distinct dialect. As a result of the half-century of Japanese rule, many older people also can speak Japanese. The method of Chinese romanization most commonly used in Taiwan is the Wade-Giles system. In 2002, Taiwan authorities announced adoption of the pinyin system also used on the Mainland to replace the Wade-Giles system, but its use is not consistent throughout society, often resulting in two or more romanizations for the same place or person.

RELIGIONS

According to Taiwan's Interior Ministry figures, there are about 11.2 million religious believers in Taiwan, with more than 75% identifying themselves as Buddhists or Taoists. At the same time, there is a strong belief in Chinese folk religion throughout the island. These are not mutually exclusive, and many people practice a combination of the three. Confucianism also is an honored school of thought and ethical code. Christian churches have been active on Taiwan for many

---

For additional analytical, marketing, investment and business opportunities information, please contact
Global Investment & Business Center, USA
(202) 546-2103. Fax: (202) 546-3275. E-mail: rusric@erols.com

years, and today, the island has more than 600,000 Christians, a majority of whom are Protestant.

CULTURE

Taiwan's culture is a blend of its distinctive Chinese heritage and Western influences. Fine arts, folk traditions, and popular culture embody traditional and modern, Asian, and Western motifs. One of Taiwan's greatest attractions is the Palace Museum, which houses over 650,000 pieces of Chinese bronze, jade, calligraphy, painting, and porcelain. This collection was moved from the mainland in 1949 when Chiang Kai-shek's Nationalist Party (KMT) fled to Taiwan. The collection is so extensive that only 1% is on display at any one time.

HISTORY

Taiwan's aboriginal peoples, who originated in Austronesia and southern China, have lived on Taiwan for 12,000 to 15,000 years. Significant migration to Taiwan from the Chinese mainland began as early as A.D. 500. Dutch traders first claimed the island in 1624 as a base for Dutch commerce with Japan and the China coast. Two years later, the Spanish established a settlement on the northwest coast of Taiwan, which they occupied until 1642 when they were driven out by the Dutch. Dutch colonists administered the island and its predominantly aboriginal population until 1661. The first major influx of migrants from the Chinese mainland came during the Dutch period, sparked by the political and economic chaos on the China coast during the Manchu invasion and the end of the Ming Dynasty.

In 1664, a Chinese fleet led by the Ming loyalist Cheng Ch'eng-kung (Zheng Chenggong, known in the West as Koxinga) retreated from the mainland and occupied Taiwan. Cheng expelled the Dutch and established Taiwan as a base in his attempt to restore the Ming Dynasty. He died shortly thereafter, and in 1683, his successors submitted to Manchu (Qing Dynasty) control. From 1680, the Qing Dynasty ruled Taiwan as a prefecture and, in 1875, divided the island into two prefectures, north and south. In 1887 the island was made into a separate Chinese province.

During the 18th and 19th centuries, migration from Fujian and Guangdong provinces steadily increased, and Chinese supplanted aborigines as the dominant population group. In 1895, a weakened Imperial China ceded Taiwan to Japan in the Treaty of Shimonoseki following the first Sino-Japanese war.
During its 50 years (1895-1945) of colonial rule, Japan expended considerable effort in developing Taiwan's economy. At the same time, Japanese rule led to the "Japanization" of the island, including compulsory Japanese education and forcing residents of Taiwan to adopt Japanese names.

At the end of World War II in 1945, Taiwan reverted to Chinese rule. During the immediate postwar period, the Nationalist Chinese (KMT) administration on Taiwan was repressive and corrupt, leading to local discontent. Anti-mainlander violence flared on February 28, 1947, prompted by an incident in which a cigarette seller was injured and a passerby was shot to death by Nationalist authorities. The island-wide rioting was brutally put down by Nationalist Chinese troops, who killed thousands of people. As a result of the February 28 Incident, the native Taiwanese felt a deep-seated bitterness toward the mainlanders. For 50 years the KMT authorities suppressed accounts of this episode in Taiwan history. In 1995 a monument was dedicated to the victims of the "2-28 Incident," and for the first time, Taiwan's leader, President Lee Teng-hui, publicly apologized for the Nationalists' brutality.

**For additional analytical, marketing, investment and business opportunities information, please contact
Global Investment & Business Center, USA
(202) 546-2103. Fax: (202) 546-3275. E-mail: rusric@erols.com**

Starting before World War II and continuing afterwards, a civil war was fought on the mainland between Chiang Kai-shek's KMT government and the Chinese Communist Party led by Mao Zedong. When the civil war ended in 1949, 2 million refugees, predominately from the Nationalist government, military, and business community, fled to Taiwan. In October 1949 the People's Republic of China (PRC) was founded on the mainland by the victorious communists. Chiang Kai-shek established a "provisional" KMT capital in Taipei in December 1949. During the 1950s, the KMT authorities implemented a far-reaching and highly successful land reform program on Taiwan. They redistributed land among small farmers and compensated large landowners with commodities certificates and stock in state-owned industries. Although this left some large landowners impoverished, others turned their compensation into capital and started commercial and industrial enterprises. These entrepreneurs were to become Taiwan's first industrial capitalists. Together with refugee businessmen from the mainland, they managed Taiwan's transition from an agricultural to a commercial, industrial economy.

Taiwan has developed steadily into a major international trading power with nearly $381 billion in two-way trade (2005) and the world's 17th largest economy. Taiwan's accession to the World Trade Organization in 2002 has expanded its trade opportunities and further strengthened its standing in the global economy. Tremendous prosperity on the island has been accompanied by economic and social stability. Chiang Kai-shek's successor, his son Chiang Ching-kuo, began to liberalize Taiwan's political system, a process that continued when President Lee Teng-hui took office in 1988. The direct election of Lee Teng-hui as president in 1996 was followed by opposition Democratic Progressive Party candidate Chen Shui-bian's election victory in March 2000. Chen was re-elected in March 2004 in a tightly contested election.

ADMINISTRATION

The authorities in Taipei exercise control over Taiwan, Kinmen, Matsu, the Penghus (Pescadores) and several other smaller islands. Taiwan is divided into counties, provincial municipalities, and two special municipalities, Taipei and Kaohsiung. At the end of 1998, the Constitution was amended to make all counties and cities directly administered by the Executive Yuan. From 1949 until 1991, the authorities on Taiwan claimed to be the sole legitimate government of all of China, including the mainland. In keeping with that claim, when the Nationalists moved to Taiwan in 1949, they re-established the full array of central political bodies, which had existed on the mainland. While much of this structure remains in place, the authorities on Taiwan in 1991 abandoned their claim of governing mainland China, stating that they do not "dispute the fact that the PRC controls mainland China."

The first National Assembly, elected on the mainland in 1947 to carry out the duties of choosing the President and amending the constitution, was re-established on Taiwan when the KMT moved. Because it was impossible to hold subsequent elections to represent constituencies on the mainland, representatives elected in 1947-48 held these seats "indefinitely." In June l990, however, the Council of Grand Justices mandated the retirement, effective December 1991, of all remaining "indefinitely" elected members of the National Assembly and other bodies.

The second National Assembly, elected in 1991, was composed of 325 members. The majority were elected directly; 100 were chosen from party slates in proportion to the popular vote. This National Assembly amended the Constitution in 1994, paving the way for the direct election of the President and Vice President the first of which was held in March 1996. In April 2000, the members of the National Assembly voted to permit their terms of office to expire without holding new elections. The National Assembly elected in May 2005 voted to abolish itself the following month, leaving Taiwan with a unicameral legislature. The President is both leader of Taiwan and Commander-in-Chief of its armed forces. The President has authority over four of the five administrative branches (Yuan): Executive, Control, Judicial, and Examination. The President appoints the President of the Executive Yuan, who also serves as the Premier. The Premier and the cabinet members are responsible for government policy and administration.

The main lawmaking body, the Legislative Yuan (LY), was originally elected in the late 1940s in parallel with the National Assembly. The first LY had 773 seats and was viewed as a "rubber stamp" institution. The second LY was not elected until 1992. The third LY, elected in 1995, had 157 members serving 3-year terms, while the fourth LY, elected in 1998, was enlarged to 225 members. The LY has greatly enhanced its standing in relation to the Executive Yuan and has established itself as a major player on the central level. With increasing strength, size, and complexity, the LY now mirrors Taiwan's recently liberalized political system. In the 1992 and 1995 elections, the main opposition party--the Democratic Progressive Party (DPP)--challenged the half-century of KMT dominance of the Legislature. In both elections, the DPP won a significant share of the LY seats, leaving only half of the LY seats in the hands of the KMT. In 2001, the DPP won a plurality of LY seats – 88 to KMT's 66, PFP's 45 seats, TSU's 13, and other parties' 13. In the December 2004 LY election, the Pan-Blue coalition won a slender majority of 114 of the 225 seats (later increased to 115) compared to the Pan-Green coalition's 101 (later reduced to 111 and 97 seats, respectively, of the 220 occupied seats).

In 1994, when the National Assembly voted to allow direct popular election of the President, the LY passed legislation allowing for the direct election of the Governor of Taiwan Province and the mayors of Taipei and Kaohsiung Special Municipalities. These elections were held in December 1994, with the KMT winning the Governor and Kaohsiung Mayor posts, and the DPP's Chen Shui-Bian winning the Taipei Mayor's position. In 1998, the KMT's Ma Ying-jeou wrestled back control of the mayorship of Taipei from Chen Shui-bian, and DPP leader Frank Hsieh defeated the KMT incumbent to become Mayor of Kaohsiung. Additionally, in a move to streamline the administration, the position of elected Governor and many other elements of the Taiwan Provincial Government were eliminated.

The Control Yuan (CY) monitors the efficiency of public service and investigates instances of corruption. The 29 Control Yuan members are appointed by the President and approved by the National Assembly; they serve 6-year terms. In recent years, the Control Yuan has become more activist, and it has conducted several major investigations and impeachments. Since December 2004, however, the pan-Blue dominated LY has refused to approve the new slate of CY members proposed by President Chen, leaving the CY inactive.

The Judicial Yuan (JY) administers Taiwan's court system. It includes a 16-member Council of Grand Justices (COGJ) that interprets the constitution. Grand Justices are appointed by the President, with the consent of the National Assembly, to 9-year terms.

The Examination Yuan (EY) functions as a civil service commission and includes two ministries: the Ministry of Examination, which recruits officials through competitive examination, and the Ministry of Personnel, which manages the civil service. The President appoints the President of the Examination Yuan.

PRINCIPAL LEADERS

President--Chen Shui-bian
Vice President--Annette Lu (Lu Hsiu-lien)
Premier--Su Tseng-chang
Vice Premier--Tsai Ing-wen
Legislative Yuan President--Wang Jin-pyng

**For additional analytical, marketing, investment and business opportunities information, please contact
Global Investment & Business Center, USA
(202) 546-2103. Fax: (202) 546-3275. E-mail: rusric@erols.com**

Judicial Yuan President--Weng Yueh-sheng
Defense Minister--Lee Jye
Foreign Minister--James Huang (Huang Chih-fang)
Minister of Justice--Shih Mao-lin
Mainland Affairs Council Chairperson--Joseph Wu (Wu Chao-hsieh)
Government Information Office Minister--Cheng Wen-tsan
Cabinet Spokesperson--Cheng Wen-tsan

POLITICAL CONDITIONS

Until 1986, Taiwan's political system was effectively controlled by one party, the Kuomintang (KMT), the chairman of which was also Taiwan's President. As the ruling party, the KMT was able to fill appointed positions with its members and maintain political control of the island.

After 1986, the KMT's hold on power was challenged by the emergence of competing political parties. Before 1986, candidates opposing the KMT ran in elections as independents or "nonpartisans." Before the 1986 island-wide elections, many "nonpartisans" grouped together to create Taiwan's first new political party, the Democratic Progressive Party (DPP). Despite the official ban on forming new political parties, Taiwan authorities did not prohibit the DPP from operating, and in the 1986 island-wide elections, DPP and independent candidates captured more than 20% of the vote. In 1987, President Chiang Ching-kuo lifted the emergency decree, which had been in place since 1948 and which had granted virtually unlimited powers to the President for use in the anti-communist campaign. This decree provided the basis for nearly four decades of martial law under which individuals and groups expressing dissenting views were dealt with harshly. Expressing views contrary to the authorities' claim to represent all of China or supporting independent legal status for Taiwan was treated as sedition. Since ending martial law, Taiwan has taken dramatic steps to improve respect for human rights and create a democratic political system. Almost all restrictions on the press have ended, restrictions on personal freedoms have been relaxed, and the prohibition against organizing new political parties has been lifted. Lee Teng-hui succeeded Chiang Ching-kuo as President when Chiang died on January 13, 1988.

The Civic Organizations Law passed in 1989 allowed for the formation of new political parties, thereby legalizing the DPP, and its support and influence increased. Lee was elected by the National Assembly to a 6-year term in 1990, marking the final time a President was elected by the National Assembly. In the 1992 Legislative Yuan elections, the DPP won 51 seats in the 161-seat body. While this was only half the number of KMT seats, it made the DPP's voice an important factor in legislative decisions. Winning the Taipei mayor's position in December 1994 significantly enhanced the DPP's image. The DPP continued its strong showing in the 1995 LY race, winning 45 of the 157 seats to the KMT's 81. In 1996, Lee Teng-hui was elected President and Lien Chan Vice President in the first direct election by Taiwan voters. In the November 1997 local elections, the Democratic Progressive Party (DPP) won 12 of the 23 county magistrate and city mayor contests to the Kuomintang (KMT)'s 8, outpolling the KMT for the first time in a major election. In the 2001 LY elections, the DPP won a plurality of seats for the first time.

In March 2000, DPP candidate Chen Shui-bian became the first opposition party candidate to win the presidency. His victory resulted in the first-ever transition of the presidential office from one political party to another, validating Taiwan's democratic political system. In a hotly contested election on March 20, 2004, President Chen Shui-bian was re-elected by 50.1% of the popular vote to a second term. The election was marred by a shooting incident the day before the election during which President Chen and his running mate Vice President Annette Lu were slightly wounded. While the opposition contested the results, it was the first time that the DPP had won an outright majority in an island-wide election.

The March election also included a "defensive referendum." Historically, the issue of referenda has been closely tied to the question of Taiwan independence, and thus has been a sensitive issue in cross Strait relations. There were two referenda before the voters on March 20. The first asked in light of the PRC missile threat whether Taiwan should purchase anti-missile systems. The second asked whether Taiwan should adopt a "peace framework" for addressing cross Strait differences with the PRC. However both referenda failed to obtain support from over 50% of registered voters, as required to be valid.
President Chen Shui-bian called for major constitutional reforms by 2006 – later changed to 2008 – aimed at further reducing layers of government, and making other structural changes aimed at improving governance. The People's Republic of China has accused Chen of using the constitution issue to move Taiwan towards independence. Chen pledged, however, in his May 20, 2004 inaugural address not to use constitutional reform to alter the constitution's approach to Taiwan's status vis-à-vis China.

The final National Assembly passed a set of constitutional amendments in June, 2005 that will halve the number of LY seats from 225 to 113 and create single-member legislative election districts beginning with the next legislative election scheduled for 2007. The constitutional revisions also abolished the National Assembly and provided for the public to confirm or reject future constitutional amendments passed by the LY. President Chen has called for "Round Two" of constitutional revision focusing on the form of government (presidential or parliamentary, 5-branch or 3-branch) and on human, labor, and aborigine rights. He has pledged not to include independence or name change in his proposed constitutional revisions.

In the December 2004 Legislative election, the ruling DPP won a plurality with 89 of the 225 seats, gaining 2 seats more than it did in 2001. The opposition KMT won 79 seats, or 11 more than it did in 2001. The KMT's "pan-Blue" coalition partner, the PFP, won only 34, 12 fewer than it won in 2001, while the DPP's partner, TSU won 12 seats. The New Party won one seat. The ruling "pan-Green" coalition's inability to secure a majority has left the LY in virtual gridlock since the election. The KMT won a landslide victory in December 2005 local elections, however, winning 14 of the 23 city mayor and county magistrate races to the ruling DPP's 6.

POLITICAL PARTIES

In addition to the KMT (described above in 'History' and 'Political Conditions'), there are three other major parties. The DPP, membership is made up largely of native Taiwanese, and its platform includes outspoken positions on some of the most sensitive issues in Taiwan politics. For example, the DPP maintains that Taiwan is an entity separate from mainland China, in contrast to the KMT position that Taiwan and the mainland, though currently divided, are both part of "one China." In sharp contrast to the tenets of both KMT and PRC policy, a number of ranking DPP officials openly advocate independence for Taiwan.

The People First Party (PFP) was formed in the wake of the March 2000 presidential election, composed of former KMT members who supported former KMT Taiwan Provincial Governor James Soong's presidential bid. PFP and KMT subsequently formed the "Pan-Blue" Alliance to oppose the DPP government. Former KMT President Lee Teng-hui, in turn, broke with the KMT and formed the pro-independence Taiwan Solidarity Union (TSU) in 2001. The TSU, which advocates changing Taiwan's official name and completely replacing the 1947 constitution, allied itself with the DPP as part of the ruling "Pan-Green" alliance.

TAIWAN AND THE MAINLAND

Despite differences between Taiwan and the PRC, contact between the two sides of the Taiwan Strait has grown significantly over the past decade. Taiwan has continued to relax restrictions on unofficial contacts with the PRC, and cross-Strait interaction has mushroomed. In January 2001, Taiwan formally allowed the "three mini-links" (direct trade, travel, and postal links) from Quemoy and Matsu Islands to Fujian Province and permitted direct cross-strait trade in February 2002. Cross-Strait trade has grown rapidly over the past 10 years. China is Taiwan's largest trading partner, and Taiwan is China's fifth largest. Estimates of Taiwan investment on the mainland, both officially approved by Taiwan authorities and investment made by Taiwan firms through third parties, start from $100 billion, making Taiwan and Hong Kong the two largest investors. This trade runs heavily in Taiwan's favor and continues to grow, providing another engine for the island's economy. The trend in cross-Strait economic interaction is one of steady growth with, so far, only temporary setbacks due to political factors such as the PRC's March 2005 passage of an Anti-Secession Law. In August 2001, President Chen accepted the recommendation of the Economic Development Advisory Council to set aside the "no haste, be patient" policy of the Lee administration and replace it with an "active opening, effective management policy." However, in January 2006, President Chen reversed the policy to "active management, effective opening." In February 2003, Taiwan and the PRC agreed to allow Taiwan carriers to fly non-stop via Hong Kong or Macao to bring Taiwan residents on the mainland home for the Lunar New Year holiday. The two sides agreed to conduct Lunar New Year charter flights again in 2005, with flights operated by both Taiwan and P.R.C. carriers flying over, but not having to land in, Hong Kong or Macau. The two sides agreed on an expanded series of Lunar New Year charter flights in January-February 2006, and in June 2006 regularized these charter flights to include the other 3 major holidays - Dragon Boat festival, Mid-Autumn festival and January 1 New Year.

The development of semiofficial cross-Strait relations has been halting. Prior to April 1993, when talks were held in Singapore between the heads of two private intermediary organizations--Taiwan's Straits Exchange Foundation (SEF) and the PRC's Association for Relations Across the Taiwan Strait (ARATS)--there had been some lower-level exchanges between the two sides of the Strait.

The April 1993 SEF-ARATS talks primarily addressed technical issues relating to cross-Strait interactions. Lower-level talks continued on a fairly regular basis until they were suspended by Beijing in 1995 after President Lee's U.S. visit. Unofficial exchanges resumed in 1997 through informal meetings between personnel of the two sides' unofficial representative organizations. Direct SEF-ARATS contacts resumed in April 1998, and SEF Chairman Koo Chen-fu visited the mainland in October 1998. A planned visit by ARATS Chairman Wang Daohan to Taiwan in the fall, however, was postponed following statements made by then-President Lee Teng-hui that relations between the PRC and Taiwan should be conducted as "state-to-state" or at least as "special state-to-state relations." Since his May 20, 2000 inauguration, President Chen has called for resuming the cross-Strait dialogue without any preconditions.

President Chen has stated that such talks should be conducted in the spirit of the 1992 Hong Kong talks, a reference to a meeting the two sides held to discuss how to handle political barriers to cross-Strait interaction. ThePRC has responded that the Chen administration must acknowledge that the two sides reached a consensus that there is only "one China" before any dialogue can be restarted. In his May 20, 2004 inaugural address, President Chen recognized the PRC's insistence on "one China" but stopped short of endorsing the concept. He called for a new "Cross-Strait Framework for Peace and Stability" and enhanced political, economic, and social exchanges between the two sides. In the face of the "one China" recognition obstacle and Taiwan's resentment over the PRC's March 2005 "Anti-Secession Law," Taipei and Beijing have been cautiously feeling each other out on a series of smaller, intermediary steps, including cross-

Strait cargo and passenger charter flights, sale of Taiwan agricultural products in the PRC, and PRC tourists visiting Taiwan. The United States has welcomed and encouraged the cross-Strait dialogue as a process which contributes to a reduction of tension and to an environment conducive to the eventual peaceful resolution of the outstanding differences between the two sides. The United States believes that differences between Taipei and Beijing should be resolved by the people on both sides of the Strait themselves. The United States has consistently stated that its abiding interest is that the process be peaceful.

ECONOMY

Through nearly five decades of hard work and sound economic management, Taiwan has transformed itself from an underdeveloped, agricultural island to an economic power that is a leading producer of high-technology goods. In the 1960s, foreign investment in Taiwan helped introduce modern, labor-intensive technology to the island, and Taiwan became a major exporter of labor-intensive products. In the 1980s, focus shifted toward increasingly sophisticated, capital-intensive and technology-intensive products for export and toward developing the service sector. At the same time, the appreciation of the New Taiwan dollar (NT$), rising labor costs, and increasing environmental consciousness in Taiwan caused many labor-intensive industries, such as shoe manufacturing, to move to the Chinese mainland and Southeast Asia. Taiwan has transformed itself from a recipient of U.S. aid in the 1950s and early 1960s to an aid donor and major foreign investor, especially in Asia.

Taiwan is now a creditor economy, holding the world's third largest stock of foreign exchange reserves ($261 billion as of August 2006). Although Taiwan enjoyed sustained economic growth, full employment, and low inflation for many years, in 2001, the combination of the slowing global economy, weaknesses in parts of the financial sector, and sagging consumer and business confidence in the government's economic policymaking resulted in the first recession since 1952. The economy began to recover in 2002, but the outbreak of severe acute respiratory syndrome (SARS) slowed growth to 3.4% in 2003. The world economic upturn drove growth in 2004 to 6.1%. However, slower world growth in 2005, higher energy prices and interest rates, and excess inventory dragged 2005 growth to 4%. Continued expansion of exports will sustain Taiwan's economic growth above 4% in 2006 and 2007.

FOREIGN TRADE

Foreign trade has been the engine of Taiwan's rapid growth during the past 50 years. Taiwan's economy remains export-oriented, so it depends on an open world trade regime and remains vulnerable to fluctuations in the world economy. The total value of trade increased more than five-fold in the 1960s, nearly ten-fold in the 1970s, and doubled again in the 1980s. The 1990s saw a more modest, slightly less than two-fold, growth. In the first half of the 2000's, exports grew 60%. Export composition changed from predominantly agricultural commodities to industrial goods (now 98%). The electronics sector is Taiwan's most important industrial export sector and is the largest recipient of U.S. investment. Taiwan became a member of the World Trade Organization (WTO) as a special customs territory in January 2002.

Taiwan firms are the world's largest supplier of computer monitors and leaders in PC manufacturing. Textile production, though of declining importance as Taiwan loses its competitive advantage in labor-intensive markets, is another major industrial export sector. Imports are dominated by raw materials and capital goods, which account for more than 90% of the total. Taiwan imports coal, oil and gas to meet most of its energy needs. Reflecting the large Taiwan investment in the mainland, China supplanted the United States as Taiwan's largest trade partner in 2003. In 2005, China (including Hong Kong) accounted for over 26% of Taiwan's total trade and almost 40% of Taiwan's exports. Japan was Taiwan's second-largest trading partner with 16% of total trade, including 25% of Taiwan's imports.

The U.S. is now Taiwan's third-largest trade partner, taking 15% of Taiwan's exports and supplying 11.6% of its imports. Taiwan is the United States' eighth-largest trading partner; Taiwan's two-way trade with the United States amounted to $56 billion in 2004 and rose 1% to $57 billion in 2005. Imports from the United States consist mostly of agricultural and industrial raw materials as well as machinery and equipment. Exports to the United States are mainly electronics and consumer goods. The United States, Hong Kong, the PRC, and Japan account for nearly 61.4% of Taiwan's exports, and the United States, Japan, and the PRC provide almost 50% of Taiwan's imports. As Taiwan's per capita income level has risen, demand for imported, high-quality consumer goods has increased. The U.S. trade deficit with Taiwan in 2003 was $14 billion, fell slightly to $13 billion in 2004, and leveled off to $13 billion in 2005. The lack of formal diplomatic relations with all but a score of its trading partners appears not to have seriously hindered Taiwan's rapidly expanding commerce, but has made free trade agreements extremely difficult to pursue. Taiwan maintains trade offices in nearly 100 countries with which it does not have official relations. Taiwan is a member of the Asian Development Bank, the WTO, and the Asia-Pacific Economic Cooperation (APEC) forum. Taiwan is also an observer at the OECD. These developments reflect Taiwan's economic importance and its desire to become further integrated into the global economy.

AGRICULTURE

Although only about one-quarter of Taiwan's land area is arable, virtually all farmland is intensely cultivated, with some areas suitable for two and even three crops a year. However, increases in agricultural production have been much slower than industrial growth. Agriculture only comprises about 1.7% of Taiwan's GDP. Taiwan's main crops are rice, sugarcane, fruit, and vegetables. While largely self-sufficient in rice production, Taiwan imports large amounts of wheat, corn, and soybeans, mostly from the United States. Poultry and pork production are mainstays of the livestock sector and the major demand drivers for imported corn and soybeans. Rising standards of living have led to increased demand for a wide variety of high-quality food products, much of it imported. Overall, U.S. agricultural and food products account for more than 30% of Taiwan's agricultural import demand. U.S. food and agricultural exports total about $2.5 billion annually, making Taiwan the United States' sixth-largest agricultural export destination. Taiwan's agricultural exports include frozen fish, aquaculture and sea products, canned and frozen vegetables, and grain products. Taiwan's imports of agricultural products have increased since its WTO accession in 2002, and it is slowly liberalizing previously protected agricultural markets.

ECONOMIC OUTLOOK

Taiwan now faces many of the same economic issues as other developed economies. With the prospect of continued relocation of labor-intensive industries to countries with cheaper work forces, Taiwan's future development will have to rely on further transformation to a high technology and service-oriented economy. In recent years, Taiwan has successfully diversified its trade markets, cutting its share of exports to the United States from 49% in 1984 to 15% in 2005 and 2006. However, a significant proportion of Taiwan's rapidly growing exports to the PRC are ultimately dependent on consumer demand in the U.S. Taiwan firms are increasingly acting as management centers that take in orders, produce them in Taiwan, the Mainland or South East Asia and then ship the final products to the U.S. Taiwan's accession to the WTO and its desire to become an Asia-Pacific "regional operations center" are spurring further economic liberalization.

DEFENSE

For additional analytical, marketing, investment and business opportunities information, please contact
Global Investment & Business Center, USA
(202) 546-2103. Fax: (202) 546-3275. E-mail: rusric@erols.com

In proportion to its population, Taiwan still maintains a large military establishment accounting for 15.3% of the central budget and 2.1% of GDP in FY 2006. However, the defense budget as a proportion of GDP has shrunk significantly over the past decade from about 22.5% of the central budget and 4% of GDP in 1994. (Taiwan has pledged to increase its military spending to 3% of GDP. In the proposed 2007 central budget proposal, military expenditures would increase to 19% of the total central budget, or between 2.6% and 2.85% of GDP.) The military's primary mission is the defense of Taiwan against the PRC, which is seen as the predominant threat and which has not renounced the use of force against Taiwan. Taiwan's armed forces were reduced as part of a reform initiative from 1997 to 2001, going from about 450,000 to 385,000, with further reductions since then bringing the total force level down to just under 300,000. Registered reservists reportedly totaled 3,870,000 in 1997. Conscription remains universal for qualified males reaching age 18.

Taiwan's armed forces are equipped with weapons obtained primarily from the United States. In recent years, however, Taiwan also has procured some weapons from other Western nations and has stressed military "self-reliance," which has resulted in the growth of indigenous military production in certain fields. Taiwan's legislature is currently debating the approval of defense budget proposals to purchase defensive weapons systems the U.S. agreed to sell Taiwan in 2001 and earlier. The proposals would provide funds to purchase the Patriot Advanced Capability (either PAC-3 or PAC-2 upgraded) missile defense system, P-3C maritime patrol aircraft, and diesel-electric submarines. These systems would give Taiwan key capabilities in missile defense and anti-submarine warfare to remedy vulnerabilities in countering the PRC's accelerated military modernization. Taiwan adheres to the principles of the nuclear Non-Proliferation Treaty and has stated that it does not intend to produce nuclear weapons.

TAIIWAN FOREIGN POLICY: CURRENT TRENDS

The People's Republic of China replaced Taiwan at the United Nations in 1971, and Taiwan's diplomatic position eroded, as many countries changed their official recognition from Taipei to Beijing. In mid-2000, Taiwan had formal diplomatic ties with 29 countries.

At the same time, Taiwan has cultivated informal ties with most countries to offset its diplomatic isolation and to expand its economic relations. A number of nations have set up unofficial organizations to carry out commercial and other relations with Taiwan. Between its official overseas missions and its unofficial representative and/or trade offices, Taiwan is represented in 149 countries. Recently, Taiwan has lobbied strongly for admission into international organizations such as the United Nations. The P.R.C. opposes Taiwan's membership in such organizations, most of which require statehood for membership, because Beijing considers Taiwan to be a province of China, not a separate sovereign state.

PLACE: Foreign and Overseas Chinese Affairs Committee, Legislative Yuan
SPEAKER: Foreign Minister Dr. Hung-mao Tien

Mr. Chairman, Committee members, ladies and gentlemen:
It is a great honor for me to brief your distinguished Committee on our foreign policy for the first time since the formation of the new administration. I take this opportunity to pay my respects and express my appreciation to all members of the Committee for your assistance in expanding our diplomatic space and for the input of your insightful suggestions into our foreign policy making. I will now report to you on the international circumstances of our foreign diplomacy during the last

few months, our foreign diplomacy ideals and means, and on our future international relations and foreign diplomacy perspective. Your comments are most welcomed! .

1. Foreword

With the presidential inauguration on May 20, we witnessed the first democratic alternation of political parties in power in the ROC's constitutional history. Taiwan thus formally entered into the era of party politics, which is a great historic achievement in the development of our democracy. The international community has widely recognized the maturity of our democracy; it has hailed the ROC as a new democracy in Asia that can serve as beacon of hope for 1.3 billion Chinese and a role model for mainland China's future democratization.
The Republic of China is an independent sovereign state that has made outstanding political and economic achievements. As a matter of course, it should have the right to establish normal diplomatic relations with other countries and to join international organizations and activities. The ROC government will thus continue to actively promote our comprehensive pragmatic diplomacy in order to expand its international survival space and development. It will also assume its international responsibilities by sharing its unique growth experience and economic strength with the entire world, thus feeding back its share to the international community. .

Even though the PRC constitutes the main obstacle to the smooth conduct and development of our foreign diplomacy, we do not intend to play a "zero-sum" game with her. We are willing to improve dialogue with the PRC through all available channels based on the principles of reciprocity, mutual benefit, reason and dignity. By demonstrating our good intentions, they may come to realize that both sides can forsake disagreements so as to create a "win-win" situation, hence contributing together to world peace, stability and development.

FOREIGN POLICY MAKING ORIENTATION

The purposes of implementing our pragmatic diplomacy are to maintain the sovereignty and dignity of the ROC, to ensure its survival and development, and to guarantee the safety and benefits its citizens deserve from the international community. In facing the PRC's severe diplomatic pressure, the ROC needs to pool the strengths of the government and of the civilian sectors and promote "peoples' diplomacy" avenues that can best allow us to fully participate in international organizations, as well as allow us to fully promote our pragmatic diplomacy. The ROC's foreign policy will use "continuity" and "stability" to consolidate relations with nations with which it shares diplomatic ties, enhance the substantial relations it has with nations with which it shares no diplomatic ties, and seek to actively participate in international organizations and activities. In addition, I would like to propose the three concepts of "democracy-based diplomacy", "civilian-based diplomacy" and "public opinion-based diplomacy" that will serve in strengthening the promotion of our comprehensive pragmatic diplomacy objectives.

1. The Principle of "Democracy-based Diplomacy"

In recent years, the international community has praised our country's democratic development and achievements, and the measures that we have adopted to guarantee and protect human rights have been recognized by people all over the world. Democracy and freedom are the ideals and lifestyle that we uphold. They constitute an important strength in preserving our national security. Any system or action that violates democracy or human rights can be seen as a threat to our survival. Democracy and human rights are the two sides of a same coin, especially in this post-cold war era where civilized nations attach great importance to human life and human rights. This trend has gradually brought the international community to give human rights precedence over the concept of sovereignty, and we therefore should promote "human rights diplomacy" and "democracy-based diplomacy". By cooperating with international human rights organizations and democratic institutions to assist members of the international society in improving human rights situations, we then would contribute in creating an international environment conducive to democracy and peace. The ROC can thus elevate its international image and status, which will in turn help reinforce the legitimacy of our participation in international activities.

2. The Principle of "Civilian-based Diplomacy"

The ROC's civilian sector has enormous vitality and unlimited human and material resources. If the government can fully cooperate with it and make the best use of all available resources to carry out its foreign affairs tasks, we would gain immense momentum for multi-level, multi-faceted and diversified diplomacy. Encouraging the participation of the civilian sector would also increase people's understanding and support of our foreign policy, as well as help us reach a common consensus on our foreign affairs. In practical terms, the government will actively develop "the second track" mechanisms of exchange and dialogue. This practice will help the civilian sector's participation in international non-governmental organizations and activities, and help the conduct of diplomatic activities between cities, academic institutions, political parties, think tanks and businesses. This use of the resources of the whole people will significantly expand our country's participation and presence in the international community.

3. The Principle of " Public Opinion-based Diplomacy"

A responsible government or administration should base its policy making on democratic principles and on the respect of public opinion. Any policy that does not follow public opinion will not win the genuine support of the people and will not succeed. Hence, the government should fully grasp public opinion and take it as an important reference in policy-making. Practically speaking, we need to establish a mechanism of communication between the government and civil society and encourage people to use it to input their suggestions and creativity into our foreign policy process. This will give people a greater sense of participation as well as a sense of mission and accomplishment. It will also in turn allow the government to win more popular support and raise the nation's overall ability to realize its foreign policy objectives. In view of the above, MOFA is planning to conduct opinion polls targeting MOFA colleagues and the general public to obtain their views on a variety of foreign affairs issues. We will then combine all opinions and suggestions on how to expand our international space, and these will serve as a basis to review and improve our foreign policy.

GENERAL SITUATION OF ROC FOREIGN RELATIONS

Next I would like to report to you on the three main directions of our foreign diplomacy, which are "consolidating our relations with diplomatic allies", "promoting substantial relations with nations having no diplomatic relations with the ROC", and "actively participating in international organizations".

1.Consolidating relations with diplomatic allies

The bilateral relations we hold with our diplomatic allies are not only a mainstay of the preservation of our sovereignty in the international community, they also constitute an important force in support of the ROC's participation in international organizations. The ROC currently has 29 diplomatic allies, five in Asia, two in Europe, eight in Africa and 14 in the Americas. President Chen Shui-bian stressed "continuity" and "stability" in our foreign policy both during the meeting arranged by the Ministry of Foreign Affairs with ambassadors stationed in the ROC, and when receiving congratulatory delegations after his inauguration. The ROC government will not only honor all the present treaties, agreements and cooperation projects signed with the other nations, but also, on the basis of existing foundations, reinforce cooperation with its diplomatic and friendly allies.

Central and South American Diplomatic Allies:
About half of our diplomatic allies are in Central and South America and the Caribbean region. They constitute one of the most important support of the ROC in the international community. The ROC has strengthened its exchanges and cooperation with all of these countries through exchanges of visits between high-ranking officials, encouraging businesses to invest in the region, and technical assistance, etc.

After gaining observer status at the Central American Parliament and at the Forum of Speakers of Central American Parliaments, we also obtained observer status in the System of Integration of Central America (SICA) on February 1, 2000. This is very helpful to the promotion of our bilateral and multilateral relations in the region's countries.

Diplomatic Allies in Africa
Eight African countries have diplomatic ties with the ROC. Currently, the annual trade volume between the ROC and the whole of Africa is only US$1.6 billion. There is thus tremendous potential and space for further development of bilateral and substantive relations.

In order to strengthen our relations with African diplomatic allies, the ROC government has held commercial exhibitions, provided business information services, improved investment regulations, and encouraged ROC business investments in friendly countries. To help economic development in the region, the ROC government also combines the use of private charities and medical personnel to assist in improving the public health and medical services of these countries. We further provide them with agricultural technology and skills training in the hope of both consolidating our relationships and reviving the local economies.

DIPLOMATIC ALLIES IN EUROPE

Since the ROC and the Republic of Macedonia established diplomatic relations in January 1999, the two sides have exchanged visits of high-ranking officials many times, and a variety of cooperation projects will be carried out in phases according to the provisions of agreements signed by the two sides. Last month, the Ministry of Foreign Affairs of the Republic of Macedonia formally notified the ROC to recommend a candidate for the post of Ambassador according to the provisions of the Vienna Convention, and this process is presently under way.

With respect to our relations with the Holy See, communication channels between the ROC embassy and the Secretariat for Relations with States of the Holy See are working smoothly. As to the rumor about the possible establishment of diplomatic ties between the PRC and the Holy See, our ministry is closely watching the development of the relations between Beijing and the Vatican. It is also checking on the validity of the rumor through a variety of channels. According to my understanding, during the past two decades the Holy See has hoped to be able to tend to the 10 million Catholics in China, and the PRC and the Holy See kept contact through a variety of indirect channels. In the short term, there will still be some disagreements between the PRC and the Holy See on the issues of religious freedom and the appointment of archbishops. The ROC has always attached great importance to religious freedom and enthusiastically participated in international charity activities. We share the values and ideals of the Holy See, and on this basis the new government will do its best to consolidate its relations with the Vatican.

Diplomatic Allies in the Asia Pacific:
The ROC has five diplomatic allies in the Asia-Pacific region. They often speak in support of the ROC in various international organizations and meetings. Among these diplomatic allies, the Republic of Palau established diplomatic relations with the ROC on December 29, 1999. Palau

strongly supports the ROC's participation in the international community and the two sides are developing relations based on the principles of equality and reciprocity. Palau President Kumio Nakamura and Nauru President Bernard Dowiyogo came to attend the presidential inauguration of May 20. Various diplomatic allies also sent senior officials such as governor-generals, foreign affairs ministers, or other high-ranking official to come to the ROC to convey their congratulations. This underscores the cordial relations the ROC has with friendly nations in the region.

2.Promoting substantive relations with nations having no diplomatic ties with the ROC
Most countries only maintain non-official relations with our country because of the actual international political influence bearing on them. Yet in view of its economic clout and brilliant democratic achievements, the international community cannot ignore the existence of the ROC. We currently maintain close economic, cultural and technical cooperation relations with more than 150 countries sharing no diplomatic ties with us. We have 97 representative offices in 63 countries, and among them, 13 offices use the title of the Republic of China while 84 use the title of Taipei.

ROC-US RELATIONS

The ROC and the US share common values and ideals, and the Ministry of Foreign Affairs has always attached great importance to promoting its substantive relations with the US. It keeps close contacts with the US Congress, administration, academic institutions, think tanks and media, as well as with important people from its business circles.

The US Congress has always been friendly to us and has recently passed in succession a variety of acts in favor of the ROC, including acts in support of the upholding our military security and of our rights to participate in international organizations. In January of this year, the US House of Representatives passed the "Taiwan Security Enhancement Act" with an overwhelming majority of 341 votes to 70 votes which underscores the US' support for strengthening the ROC's security.

As to the US administration's upholding of its "one China" policy, the relation with Taiwan do remain based on the "Taiwan Relations Act". After the PRC announced its "White Paper on the Principle of One China and Taiwan Question", the White House, the State Department, and the Defense Department all quoted provisions of the "Taiwan Relations Act" to express their positions. They declared that any use force or any threat to use of force to solve the cross-Strait issue will be of grave concern to the United States, and repeatedly publicly asked the PRC to exercise self-control. All of these show the US administration's concern over to the ROC's security.

After the formation of our new government, Americans of all circles said that the content of President Chen Shui-bian's inaugural address as well as our democratic achievements were conducive to the development of constructive cross-Strait dialogue. Although the US clearly said that it will not play the role of mediator between the two sides, it nevertheless will remain engaged in helping to create an environment for cross-Strait dialogue in order to insure the peace and stability of the Asia Pacific region. Our government will continue to strengthen its substantial ties with the US in order to maintain Taiwan's peace and security.

ROC-JAPAN RELATIONS

At present, our relations with Japan are stably developing. Japan has improved its visa treatment toward ROC citizens for the second consecutive year. In addition, both sides have reached agreements on increasing flights, the clearance of customs, and the transfer of technology. Moreover, from a geopolitical point of view, Japan is very concerned about peace in the Taiwan

Strait. Although Japan held summits with the PRC in 1998 and in 1999, it did not make any new pronouncement on the so-called "Taiwan Question" that were derogative to the ROC. Judging from Japan's responses to the PRC's publication of the "White Paper on the Principle of One China and Taiwan Question", the result of the presidential election, and to President Chen Shui-bian's inaugural speech, Japan's position of hoping that the two sides solve cross-Strait issues through peaceful means remains unchanged. The ROC government will continue to strengthen its interaction with all sectors of Japan to further enhance mutual understanding and exchanges.

ROC-ROK RELATIONS

When he received a South Korea's Kyung Nam University delegation headed by its president, President Chen said that the two countries ought to improve bilateral relations. He suggested that they need to take a pragmatic attitude and raise contact levels before discussing the reopening of air links and the promotion of economic cooperation. The Kim Dae Jung administration has repeatedly expressed its willingness to improve substantive ties with Taipei. Our government welcomes such statements and hopes that South Korea will soon promote exchange of visits between high-ranking officials to enhance mutual understanding and conduct talks on the basis of equality and reciprocity so as to effectively solve problems of traffic links and other economic issues.

ROC-EUROPE RELATIONS

The ROC has maintained close contact with major European countries in the areas of trade, culture, technology, education, tourism and navigation. The two sides have enjoyed close substantive relations with frequent visits by high-ranking government officials. Up to now, 11 countries including the Netherlands, the United Kingdom, France, Germany, Italy, Denmark, Sweden, the Czech Republic, Poland, Hungary and Spain have set up semi-official institutions in Taiwan staffed with professional diplomats from their respective governments. With regards to our relations with the European Union, the European Commission has made it a priority to set up an EC office in Taiwan. The European Parliament has also passed several resolutions in support of our bid to join international organizations.

Following our presidential election, the European Parliament adopted an urgent resolution on April 14. Apart from complimenting us for our democratic achievements and requesting Beijing to solve cross-strait issues peacefully, the resolution also "called on EU Member States and the Commission to step up their relations with Taiwan with a view to securing better representation for Taiwan in international fora (including the WTO) and to open a European Commission Representative office in Taipei". The adoption of this resolution underscores the European Parliament's support for Taiwan's democratic development and security.

Although North European nations have always kept a neutral stance in international affairs, it is worth noting that they have spared no efforts in supporting democracy. As the North European nations advocate highly of freedom and human rights, we should strengthen our interaction with this region to gather more support from foreign countries.

OVERVIEW OF EU - TAIWAN RELATIONS

Taiwan is an important trading partner, and is the EU's third or fourth largest trading partner in Asia, after Japan, the People's Republic of China and sometimes Korea. The EU encourages the healthy flow of trade and investment between Europe and Taiwan, and therefore strongly supported Taiwan's accession to WTO. Taiwan, as the "Separate Customs Territory of Taiwan, Penghu, Kinmen and Matsu" (or "Chinese Taipei"), joined the world trade body on 1 January 2002.

For additional analytical, marketing, investment and business opportunities information, please contact
Global Investment & Business Center, USA
(202) 546-2103. Fax: (202) 546-3275. E-mail: rusric@erols.com

The European Commission holds annual consultations with Taiwan, alternately in Brussels and Taipei, which cover all relevant aspects of the relationship. The last round of Consultations took place in Taipei in June 2005.

On 10 March 2003, the European Commission established a permanent presence on the island, through the opening of its 'European Economic and Trade Office'. The Office, whose establishment had been a Commission priority for some time, will contribute to the strengthening of communications with the Taiwanese authorities and other economic and social interlocutors, and will promote opportunities for collaboration in areas of mutual interest.

The EU pursues a "One China" policy and recognises the Government of the People's Republic of China as the sole legal government of China. However, it recognises Taiwan as an economic and commercial entity, has solid relations with Taiwan in non-political areas and maintains exchanges in various technical fields, such as economic relations, science, education and culture. In line with the EU's "One China" policy, the European Economic and Trade Office will not be engaged in relations of a diplomatic or political nature.

CROSS-STRAITS RELATIONS

The EU supports the peaceful resolution of differences between Taiwan and the People's Republic of China, rejecting the use or threat of force. It urges both sides to resume constructive dialogue, and to eschew dogmatic positions. The EU insists that any arrangement between Beijing and Taipei can only be achieved on a mutually acceptable basis, with reference also to the wishes of the Taiwanese population.

The EU believes that increasing economic integration between the People's Republic of China and Taiwan, to be further strengthened now that both sides have entered into WTO, can make a substantial contribution to creating a more favourable climate for resumption of dialogue and eventual resolution of the question of Taiwan.
You can visit the European Commission's External Relations website at:
http://ec.europa.eu/comm/external_relations/taiwan/intro/index.htm

ANNOUNCEMENT OF THE ESTABLISHMENT OF THE EUROPEAN ECONOMIC AND TRADE OFFICE IN TAIWAN BY THE EUROPEAN COMMISSION - 10 MARCH 2003

The European Commission has opened an office in Taipei, Taiwan. The move will strengthen relations between the EU and Taiwan in areas such as trade, investment, economic co-operation, research and education. Commenting on the event, Commissioner for External Relations Chris Patten said, "The opening of the European Economic and Trade Office in Taipei confirms the steady development of commercial ties between the European Union and Taiwan. The volume of our bilateral trade and investment flows makes Taiwan an important economic partner for the EU. We look forward to the strengthening of this partnership".

With the Office in Taipei, the European Commission will, for the first time, establish a permanent presence on the island. Mr Brian McDonald has been appointed by the European Commission as Head of Office.

The Office will mainly cover economic and trade relations, economic co-operation as well as cultural and information activities. It will contribute to the strengthening of communications with the Taiwanese authorities and other economic and social partners as well as promoting and boosting opportunities for collaboration in areas of mutual interest. In line with the EU's "One China" policy, the Office will not be engaged in relations of a diplomatic or political nature.

The decision to open the Office in Taiwan forms part of the European Union's new strategy for Asia, the core objective of which is to promote the EU's presence in the region, as Enlargement of the Union makes it an ever more significant global player.

The establishment of a local presence in Taiwan has been a Commission priority for some time. This was confirmed in the Commission's Communication of 3 July 2001. It also in line with the objective of reinforcing the EU's presence and raising its profile across Asia, reaffirmed in the Commission's Asia Communication of 4 September 2001.

INTERVIEW WITH CHRIS PATTEN, "EUROPEAN VOICE", 23 JANUARY 2003

'ONE CHINA' POLICY CAN STILL ACCOMMODATE EU RELATIONS WITH TAIWAN

Do you accept criticism that you and the EU have turned your backs on Taiwan in favour of China?

Absolutely not - and I cannot see where European Voice has got this strange idea from. It's not the view of the Taiwanese authorities, by the way. We rightly stick to the principle of 'One China' - but that doesn't mean we are any the less engaged with Taiwan, which is an important economic partner of the EU. On an institutional level, we are about to open a new office in Taiwan: not obviously a sign that we are turning our backs. People have been asking us to do this for years. Next month, the office will open.

What is the EU doing to encourage Taiwan's membership of the international community – for example the United Nations (UN), World Health Organisation (WHO) and so on?

We pushed very strongly for Taiwan's membership of the WTO – an organisation that is important for both Taipei and Beijing.

Our position has long been to support Taiwan's membership in other international organisations, where there is a sufficient added value, economic or otherwise, to justify it, and where the organisation's statutes allow it.

The WHO has its own rules, and is only open to states. But we are happy with others to see whether Taiwan could be more involved in the WHO's work in a different way, because we recognise Taiwan is increasingly active in international aid and health issues.

What will be the goal of the new EU office in Taipei?

It will be an economic and trade office, and it will cover the full range of areas where we have a relationship with Taiwan, including science, technology and education. The office will not, obviously, have diplomatic status, and will not engage in political issues.

Cynics say the presence of Commission officials there is more to help ensure that Taiwan meets the terms of its WTO obligations than anything else. Do you reject this?

Of course, implementation of WTO is an important consideration, but our relations with Taiwan are not limited to ensuring that Taiwan lives up to its WTO commitments.

We are opening an office because Taiwan is our 3rd biggest trading partner in Asia, and, like the 12 EU Member States who also have trade offices in Taiwan, we think it is important to maintain good relations on the ground.

We need to make progress on trade and investment, economic and scientific cooperation and create the conditions for increased regional and global prosperity. WTO membership is an important facet of this. It is crucial to make the new Round of negotiations under the Doha Development Agenda a success. It is not an exaggeration to say that the future of free global trade depends on this. We want to work closely with all like-minded partners to achieve this goal, and Taiwan is definitely a part of this effort.

What could Taiwan itself offer to foster more support from the international community?

Taiwan has impressed the international community, with its successful transition to democracy, and with the impressive economic prosperity it has achieved.

At the same time, of course, the vast majority of countries sensibly follow a 'One China' policy.

Do you believe there is a genuine military threat from the Chinese against Taiwan? How is the EU dealing with this issue?

The situation is indeed of concern to the EU. We are firmly opposed to the use or threat of force across the Taiwan straits, and we have said so consistently. Nobody can be interested in yet another regional arms race. It is up to both sides to refrain from taking steps, or making statements, that increase tensions.

We also think that increasing economic interaction and cooperation between China and Taiwan will help create a more favourable climate between them. Their accession to the WTO should make a positive difference. Both sides should make full use of the channels of communications that the WTO offers.

Overall, how would you evaluate EU-Taiwan relations?

I think our relations are good. There is no reason why this positive trend should not continue. Our office in Taiwan should contribute to this.

Moving forward, in the medium term do you see any further developments beyond the current status quo? Do you think Taiwan will ever get the recognition it yearns for?

The issue of Taiwan's relations with China can only be resolved by the two sides. Economic integration should help to bring them closer, provided that it is seen as an opportunity, not a threat.

But it must be complemented by the resumption of dialogue. I personally believe that both sides should put aside entrenched positions to make this possible.

There are some signs of a growing maturity on both sides in handling this sensitive relationship, and that should be welcome to all friends of Asia.

ROC'S RELATIONS WITH COUNTRIES WITHOUT DIPLOMATIC TIES

In terms of our relations with Southeast Asian nations, Taiwanese investments in this region topped US$40 billion during the past decade. Taiwan has become a major investor in Southeast Asia. Nevertheless, due to Beijing's obstruction we have not been able to join this region's security mechanism. In the future, our government will strengthen its interaction with Southeast Asian nations and take the initiative to establish a dialogue mechanism with them via Track Two or Track Three diplomatic channels so as to step up mutual exchanges and cooperation.

As for our ties with nations of West Asia, we are focusing on setting up more offices in Russia, concluding the ROC-Russia air agreement at the earliest possible date, and maintaining sound interaction with the oil-producing countries of the Middle East.

In recent years, Central and East European nations have conducted political and economic reforms and begun talks to join the EU. Noting that these countries have great potential to become important players in the international arena, we will enhance our efforts to strengthen our relations with Central and East European nations as well as the Baltic states.

In terms of our relations with the third world nations, we will actively promote the Taiwan Experience to assist in the economic development of these nations based on our sincerity to contribute to the international community. We hope to take further steps to develop friendly ties with these countries on the basis of reciprocity and mutual benefit.

3. Active participation in international organizations and related activities

At present, we have official member status in 16 inter-governmental international organizations and 970 international non-governmental organizations. A total of 30 NGOs have set up headquarters or secretariats in Taiwan. From the second half of 1999 to the end of April 2000, we hosted or participated in 951 NGO meetings as well as joined 384 non-governmental international activities. It is our long-term goal to join the United Nations. At present, our goals are to actively participate in other functional and regional international organizations, to assist domestic private organizations in joining NGOs, and to promote our legal rights and status in the international organizations that we have already joined.

Our application to become a member of the United Nations is closely related to our status and rights in the international community. In the past six years, our applications to join the UN failed to be included in the UN's General Assembly's plenary agenda due to Beijing's obstruction. However, in pursuit of our national interests, the new administration will continue to promote our bid to join the UN. Meanwhile, we will seek various channels to join or sponsor the activities of UN special agencies.

With regards to our bid to join the World Health Organization, we have, as of May 2000, applied to become an observer with the WHO for four consecutive years. However, Beijing's obstruction prevented our case from being included in the WHA's plenary agenda. Since this case greatly affects the personal health, public health and national interests of our people, my ministry has mapped out mid and long-term work plans to promote our case in European and North American countries. We will continue to urge the participation of the civilian sector in the WHO bid campaign.

After years of hard work, our application to join the World Trade Organization has reached the final stage. In terms of bilateral procedures, we have completed bilateral negotiations with 26 members that requested talks with us. To date, only Hong Kong has yet to sign an agreement with us. In terms of multilateral procedures, the WTO has called for ten working group meetings and three unofficial working group meetings on our application. We have yet to conclude the last working group meeting before our working group report and accession protocol are adopted. Once the General Council accepts our application, we will proceed to complete the ratification and deposition procedures and then become a full member. However, Beijing has repeatedly stressed that it should enter the WTO ahead of Taipei. Thus the majority of WTO members delayed our case because of Beijing's attitude. After Beijing signed agreements with the US and the EU, it still needs to complete bilateral talks with five members. The US House of Representatives approved granting China Permanent Normal Trade Relations on May 24, and the Senate is expected to vote on this issue in the near future. We expect smoother progress on Beijing's accession to the WTO. My Ministry will keep on watching closely the progress of

Beijing's accession and continue requesting support from WTO members to allow Taiwan to join this organization at the earliest possible date.

As a major trade partner and investor in East Asia, the ROC has always played an active role in various APEC activities. Last September, our proposal entitled "Economic Revitalization through Start-up Companies and Venture Capital" was incorporated in the joint statement of APEC's Ministerial Meeting. Our government then gathered opinions from various sectors to map out relevant working points which were reported and adopted by the first senior officials' meeting this year. In May 2000, my ministry held a seminar on venture capital and representatives from 15 members attended this meeting in Taiwan. We are presently planning another seminar on related issues in October of this year and will report the results of our research to the APEC annual economic leaders' meeting and its annual ministerial meeting in November. Our future goal is to increase our participation in the group's meetings and activities

ECONOMY

Through nearly five decades of hard work and sound economic management, Taiwan has transformed itself from an underdeveloped, agricultural island to an economic power that is a leading producer of high-technology goods. Taiwan is now a creditor economy, holding one of the world's largest foreign exchange reserves of more than $100 billion in 1999. Despite the Asian financial crisis, the economy continues to expand at about 5% per year, with virtually full employment and low inflation. The population also enjoys an annual average income equal to U.S. $13,152 .

In the 1960s, foreign investment in Taiwan helped introduce modern, labor-intensive technology to the island, and Taiwan became a major exporter of labor-intensive products. In the 1980s, focus shifted toward increasingly sophisticated, capital-intensive and technology-intensive products for export and toward developing the service sector. At the same time, the appreciation of the New Taiwan dollar (NT$), rising labor costs, and increasing environmental consciousness in Taiwan caused many labor-intensive industries, such as shoe manufacturing, to move to the Chinese mainland and Southeast Asia.

Taiwan has transformed itself from a recipient of U.S. aid in the 1950s and early 1960s to an aid donor and major foreign investor, especially in Asia. Private Taiwan investment in the P.R.C. is estimated to total more than $30 billion, and Taiwan has invested a comparable amount in Southeast Asia.

FOREIGN TRADE

Foreign trade has been the engine of Taiwan's rapid growth during the past 40 years. Taiwan's economy remains export-oriented, so it depends on an open world trade regime and remains vulnerable to downturns in the world economy. The total value of trade increased more than five-fold in the 1960s, nearly 10-fold in the 1970s, and doubled again in the 1980s. The 1990s has seen a more modest, slightly less than two-fold, growth. Export composition has changed from predominantly agricultural commodities to industrial goods (now 98%). The electronics sector is Taiwan's most important industrial export sector and is the largest recipient of U.S. investment.

Taiwan is the world's largest supplier of computer monitors and is a leading PC manufacturer. Textile production, though of declining importance as Taiwan loses its competitive advantage in labor-intensive markets, is another major industrial export sector. Imports are dominated by raw materials and capital goods, which account for more than 90% of the total. Taiwan imports most of its energy needs.

The United States is Taiwan's largest trading partner, taking 25% of Taiwan's exports and supplying 17% of its imports. Taiwan is the U.S.'s seventh-largest trading partner and eigth-largest export market. In 1999, Taiwan's two-way trade with the U.S. amounted to about U.S. $54.3 billion. Imports from the U.S. consist mostly of agricultural and industrial raw materials. Exports to the U.S. are mainly electronics and consumer goods.

The United States, Hong Kong (including indirect trade with the P.R.C.), and Japan account for two-thirds of Taiwan's exports, and the U.S. and Japan provide 45% of Taiwan's imports. As Taiwan's per capita income level has risen, demand for imported, high-quality consumer goods has increased. This trend has driven imports to rise faster than exports and has cut into Taiwan's global trade surplus. Another important factor in the substantial increase in Taiwan's imports has been industrial upgrading, which has pushed up imports of capital goods, raw materials, parts, and components. Taiwan's l999 trade surplus with the United States was $16.1 billion, a significant amount, but a decline from a high of $17 billion in 1987.

The lack of formal diplomatic relations with all but 29 of its trading partners appears not to have seriously hindered Taiwan's rapidly expanding commerce, and Taiwan is currently the world's 14th-largest trading economy. Taiwan maintains trade offices in more than 60 countries with which it does not have official relations. Taiwan is a member of the Asian Development Bank, and it is engaged in negotiations to join the World Trade Organization (WTO) as a special customs territory. In 1991 Taiwan, under the name "Chinese Taipei," became a member of the Asia-Pacific Economic Cooperation (APEC) forum. These developments reflect Taiwan's economic importance and its desire to become further integrated into the global economy.

AGRICULTURE

Although only about one-quarter of Taiwan's land area is arable, virtually all farmland is intensely cultivated, with some areas suitable for two and even three crops a year. However, increases in agricultural production have been much slower than industrial growth. Agriculture only comprises about 269% of Taiwan's GDP. Taiwan's main crops are rice, sugar cane, fruit, and vegatables.

Although self-sufficient in rice production, Taiwan imports large amounts of wheat, mostly from the United States. Meat production and consumption are rising sharply, reflecting a rising standard of living. Taiwan has exported large amounts of frozen pork, although this was affected by an outbreak of hoof and mouth disease in 1997. Other agricultural exports include fish, aquaculture and sea products, canned and frozen vegetables, and grain products. Imports of agriculture products are expected to increase due to the approaching WTO accession, which will open previously protected agricultural markets.

ECONOMIC OUTLOOK

Taiwan now faces many of the same economic issues as other developed economies. With the prospect of continued relocation of labor-intensive industries to countries with cheaper work forces, Taiwan's future development will have to rely on further transformation to a high technology and service-oriented economy. In recent years, Taiwan has successfully diversified its trade markets, cutting its share of exports to the U.S. from 49% in 1984 to 25% in l999. Taiwan's dependence on the U.S. market should continue to decrease as its exports to Southeast Asia and the P.R.C. grow and its efforts to develop European markets produce results. Taiwan's bid to join the WTO and its desire to become an Asia-Pacific "regional operations center" are spurring further economic liberalization.

**For additional analytical, marketing, investment and business opportunities information, please contact
Global Investment & Business Center, USA
(202) 546-2103. Fax: (202) 546-3275. E-mail: rusric@erols.com**

THE U.S. AND TAIWAN RELATIONS: BASIC INFORMATION

On January 1, 1979, the United States changed its diplomatic recognition from Taipei to Beijing. In the U.S.-P.R.C. Joint Communiqué that announced the change, the United States recognized the Government of the People's Republic of China as the sole legal government of China and acknowledged the Chinese position that there is but one China and Taiwan is part of China. The Joint Communiqué also stated that within this context the people of the United States will maintain cultural, commercial, and other unofficial relations with the people on Taiwan.

On April 10, 1979, President Carter signed into law the Taiwan Relations Act (TRA), which created domestic legal authority for the conduct of unofficial relations with Taiwan. U.S. commercial, cultural, and other interaction with the people on Taiwan is facilitated through the American Institute in Taiwan (AIT), a private nonprofit corporation. The Institute has its headquarters in the Washington, DC, area and has offices in Taipei and Kaohsiung. It is authorized to issue visas, accept passport applications, and provide assistance to U.S. citizens in Taiwan. A counterpart organization, the Taipei Economic and Cultural Representative Office in the United States (TECRO), has been established by the Taiwan authorities. It has its headquarters in Taipei, the representative branch office in Washington, DC, and 11 other Taipei Economic and Cultural Offices (TECO) in the continental U.S. and Guam.

Following derecognition, the United States terminated its Mutual Defense Treaty with Taiwan. However, the United States has continued the sale of appropriate defensive military equipment to Taiwan in accordance with the Taiwan Relations Act which provides for such sales and which declares that peace and stability in the area are in U.S. interests. Sales of defensive military equipment also are consistent with the 1982 U.S.-P.R.C. Joint Communiqué. In this communiqué, the United States stated that "it does not seek to carry out a long-term policy of arms sales to Taiwan" and that U.S. arms sales would "not exceed, either in qualitative or in quantitative terms, the level of those supplied in recent years," and that the U.S. intends "gradually to reduce its sale of arms to Taiwan." The P.R.C., in the 1982 communiqué, stated that its policy was to strive for a peaceful resolution of the Taiwan question.

U.S. commercial ties with Taiwan have been maintained and have expanded since 1979. Taiwan continues to enjoy Export-Import Bank financing, Overseas Private Investment Corporation guarantees, normal trade relations (NTR) status, and ready access to U.S. markets.

In recent years, U.S. Government economic dealings with Taiwan have focused on expanding market access for American goods and services. AIT has been engaged in a series of trade negotiations, which have focused on protection of intellectual property rights, and issues relating to Taiwan's accession to the WTO. In February 1998, the U.S. completed a bilateral market access agreement with Taiwan, an important step forward in Taiwan's WTO accession process.

Maintaining diplomatic relations with the P.R.C. has been recognized to be in the long-term interest of the United States by six consecutive administrations; however, maintaining strong, unofficial relations with Taiwan also is in the U.S. interest. The United States is committed to these efforts because they are important for America's global position and for peace and stability in Asia. In keeping with its one-China policy, the U.S. does not support "two Chinas," "one China, one Taiwan," or Taiwan independence. Nor does the United States support Taiwan's efforts to become a member of the UN or other organizations in which membership is limited to states. The U.S. does support Taiwan's membership in other appropriate international organizations, such as the APEC forum and the Asian Development Bank, in which statehood is not a requirement for membership. In addition, the U.S. supports appropriate opportunities for Taiwan's voice to be heard in organizations where its membership is not possible.

MILESTONES IN U.S.-TAIWAN RELATIONS

February 27, 1972 — Signing of the Shanghai Communiqué

President Nixon and Chairman Mao agree on "one China" policy, but leave considerable ambiguity. The U.S. "acknowledges" – but does not itself endorse – the formula "that all Chinese on either side of the Taiwan Strait maintain there is one China and Taiwan is a part of China." The statement remains the guiding principle of U.S. policy toward Taiwan.

January 1, 1979 — U.S. recognizes People's Republic of China

President Carter switches diplomatic recognition from Taiwan to the PRC. Taiwan's diplomatic isolation begins.

April 10, 1979 — Passage of Taiwan Relations Act

Congress approves the Taiwan Relations Act, which remains in effect today. Among other things, it provides that the U.S. will sell Taiwan defensive arms. The act includes an important clause saying that the U.S. would view military assault by the PRC a matter of grave concern. It also states that nothing in the TRA should be construed as favoring Taiwan's exclusion from international organizations.

1982 — Reagan's "Six Assurances"

As he prepares to participate in a joint communiqué with Beijing, President Reagan addresses the issue of arms sales to Taiwan, giving Taiwan what would become known as the "Six Assurances." The first of these says that the U.S. would not agree to a specific date for terminating arms sales to Taiwan. The second says that the U.S. would not consult with the PRC concerning specific sales decisions.

September 28, 1986 — Formation of principal opposition party

The Democratic Progressive Party is born. Though it is technically illegal at the time, officials look the other way. The DPP, at least nominally, favors independence for Taiwan. Within two years, formation of competing parties is legalized. Today, more than 75 political parties exist on Taiwan.

July 15, 1987 — End of martial law

Taiwan accelerates its march toward democracy with the official end of martial law.

**For additional analytical, marketing, investment and business opportunities information, please contact
Global Investment & Business Center, USA
(202) 546-2103. Fax: (202) 546-3275. E-mail: rusric@erols.com**

November 2, 1987 — Cross-strait visits permitted

For the first time in nearly 40 years, Taiwan permits its citizens to travel to the mainland to visit friends and relatives. Today, more than one million Taiwanese do so annually.

January 1, 1988 — Free press comes to Taiwan

The ban on the founding of new newspapers on the island ends. Today, residents can choose from more than 350 newspapers.

May 1, 1991 — Taiwan constitutional reform

Taiwan reforms its Constitution, providing for direct election of legislators and rescinding its claim of sovereignty over the mainland.

May 27, 1992 — Second constitutional reform

Further constitutional reforms include requirement that the president and vice president be elected directly by the people of Taiwan.

April 27-29, 1993 — Cross-strait talks begin in Singapore

Taiwan negotiator Koo Chen-fu and PRC negotiator Wang Daohan meet for the first time. They produce agreements on transportation and mail issues, and formally agree to continue dialogue.

June 1995 — PRC ends talks

Protesting an unofficial visit to the United States by Taiwan President Lee Teng-hui, the PRC unilaterally suspends cross-strait talks.

March 1996 — China conducts missile tests in Taiwan Strait

The PRC's military maneuvers are designed to intimidate Taiwan on the eve of its first direct presidential election. President Clinton sends two aircraft carrier groups, comprising nearly 30 warships, to the region, raising U.S.-Sino tensions to their highest level in more than two decades.

March 23, 1996 — Lee elected president

In the first democratic elections in a Chinese society in 5,000 years, Lee Teng-hui is elected President, winning a four-way race with more than 54 percent of the vote. Before this election, Lee succeeded Chiang Ching-kuo to the position of president when Chiang died suddenly in January 1988.

February 21, 1998 — U.S. and Taiwan sign bilateral market treaty

The American Institute in Taiwan and the Taiwan Economic and Cultural Representative Office – the U.S. and Taiwan representative organizations – completed a bilateral market access agreement, an important step forward in Taiwan's efforts to join the World Trade Organization.

June 30, 1998 — President Clinton endorses "three no's"

In Shanghai during a 10-day tour of mainland China, President Clinton becomes the first American leader to embrace explicitly the PRC position on Taiwan: no independence, no "two Chinas," and no membership in international organizations that require statehood.

October 14-19, 1998 — Resumption of cross-strait talks

Taiwan negotiator Koo Chen-fu travels to Beijing for the first face-to-face dialogue with Wang Daohan in five years.

February 1999 — Pentagon report details PRC missile build-up

A Pentagon report describes a massive missile build-up by the PRC on the coast facing Taiwan and predicts that the PRC will be able to "overwhelm" Taiwan within five years. The study is a rare official admission in Washington that the military balance is tilting in favor of Beijing.

July 9, 1999 — President Lee's "state-to-state" relations comment

In a radio interview, President Lee says that Taiwan and the PRC have a "special state-to-state" relationship. He points out that "one China" is a future prospect rather than a current reality. Beijing reacts angrily, threatening military reprisals. The U.S. signals displeasure with Lee, pressing him to back down.

February 1, 2000 — House passes TSEA

By a bipartisan vote of 341 to 70, the U.S. House of Representatives overwhelmingly supports the Taiwan Security Enhancement Act. The act strengthens the ability of the U.S. to fulfill the defense and security mandate of the 1979 Taiwan Relations Act.

February 21, 2000 — China issues "Taiwan white paper"

One the eve of Taiwan's presidential elections, Beijing issues a white paper on Taiwan. The 11,000-word document states that further delays by Taiwan on the question of reunification could lead to war, and it criticizes the U.S. for interfering in China's "internal affairs" by selling advanced weapons systems to Taiwan.

February 24, 2000 — Clinton and "the assent of the people of Taiwan"

President Clinton uses carefully crafted remarks to elaborate on the long-standing U.S. policy that differences between Beijing and Taiwan must be settled without military coercion. Clinton says: "the issues ... must be resolved peacefully and with the assent of the people of Taiwan." The significant phrase – "with the assent of the people of Taiwan" – demonstrates U.S. recognition that Taiwan's democracy must be a decisive factor in the cross-strait question.

March 18, 2000 — Chen elected president

Democratic Progressive Party candidate Chen Shui-bian is elected president, representing a major milestone in Taiwan's democracy. It is the nation's first peaceful transfer of power to an opposition party and the consolidation of democracy.

October 10, 2000 — Congress passes PNTR for China

Congress passes H.R.4444, granting permanent normal trade relations to the People's Republic of China and paving the way for U.S. support of the PRC's accession to the WTO.

October 24, 2000 — Congress passes Taiwan notification provision

Congress passes a measure requiring the President to consult on a classified basis with congressional leaders prior to its annual arms talks with Taiwan. It is one of the key provisions of the TSEA, which was never voted on in the Senate. The important provision reasserts congressional oversight over U.S. arms sales to Taiwan – a congressional role guaranteed by the TRA but often overlooked by the President.

PENTAGON REPORT ON IMPLEMENTATION OF TAIWAN RELATIONS ACT (U.S. REAFFIRMS COMMITMENT TO TAIWAN'S DEFENSIVE CAPABILITY)

Although the People's Republic of China (PRC) "claims that Taiwan is an inalienable part of China and has reserved the right to use force to unify Taiwan with the mainland," the U.S. position is that "any effort to determine the future of Taiwan by other than peaceful means, including boycotts or embargoes, [is] a threat to peace and security of the Western Pacific area and of grave concern to the U.S.," according to a report summary released by the Department of Defense.

The Department of Defense published an unclassified summary of the "Report to Congress on Implementation of the Taiwan Relations Act," which assesses the security situation in the Taiwan Strait, December 19.

In accordance with the Taiwan Relations Act (TRA), the United States actively monitors the security situation in the Taiwan Strait in order to adequately provide Taiwan with a "sufficient self-defense capability" consistent with U.S. security policy toward the region.

"The United States takes its obligation to assist Taiwan in maintaining a self-defense capability very seriously," the summary says. "This is not only because it is mandated by U.S. law in the TRA, but also because it is in our own national interest. As long as Taiwan has a capable defense, the environment will be more conducive to peaceful dialogue, and thus the whole region will be more stable."

According to the report summary, the United States supplies Taiwan with military hardware and addresses non-hardware capabilities -- including organizational issues and training -- to enhance Taiwan's capacity to absorb new military technologies.

In order to determine the appropriate defense mechanisms Taiwan needs, U.S. officials have focused on assessing the military options they believe Beijing might exercise against Taiwan, according to the report summary.

Possible scenarios include an invasion of Taiwan via air or sea; a blockade of Taiwan's commerce; or air or missile strikes on Taiwan's population, military assets or economic infrastructure.

"The fundamental question for assessment is whether the military balance is or is not satisfactory in relation to those U.S. goals," the report summary says.

The report summary acknowledged gaps in knowledge regarding the PRC-Taiwan military balance, but noted that "any assessment of a military balance would by its nature have major unresolved uncertainties."

Following are the texts of the introduction to and the executive summary of the report:

REPORT TO CONGRESS PURSUANT TO PUBLIC LAW 106-113

Public Law 106-113, an act making consolidated appropriations for the fiscal year ending September 30, 2000, states that the "Office of Net Assessment in the Office of the Secretary of Defense, jointly with the United States Pacific Command, shall submit, through the Under Secretary of Defense (Policy), a report to Congress no later than 270 days after the enactment of this Act which addresses the following issues:

(1) A review of the operational planning and other preparations of the United States Department of Defense, including but not limited to the United States Pacific Command, to implement the relevant sections of the Taiwan Relations Act since its enactment in 1979; and

(2) A review of evaluation of all gaps in relevant knowledge about the People's Republic of China's capabilities and intentions as they might affect the current and future military balance between Taiwan and the People's Republic of China, including both classified United States intelligence information and Chinese open source writing. The report shall be submitted in classified form, with an unclassified summary."

The report, submitted in response to Public Law 106-113, addresses relevant sections of the Taiwan Relations Act and gaps in knowledge regarding the current and future security situation in the Taiwan Strait. Specifically, the report addresses U.S. provision of defense articles and services to meet Taiwan's legitimate defense needs, U.S. capacity to respond to the use of force against Taiwan, and challenges associated with assessing the security situation in the Taiwan Strait.

EXECUTIVE SUMMARY OF REPORT TO CONGRESS ON IMPLEMENTATION OF THE TAIWAN RELATIONS ACT

The TRA stipulates that "the United States will make available to Taiwan such defense articles and services in such quantity as may be necessary to enable Taiwan to maintain a sufficient self-defense capability." The TRA states that "the President and Congress shall determine the nature and quantity of such defense articles and services based solely upon their judgment of the needs of Taiwan, in accordance with procedures established by law." The TRA further asserts that "such determination of Taiwan's defense needs shall include review by United States military authorities in connection with recommendations to the President and the Congress." Section 2(b) states:

It is the policy of the United States to consider any effort to determine the future of Taiwan by other than peaceful means, including by boycotts or embargoes, a threat to the peace and security of the Western Pacific area and of grave concern to the United States; to provide Taiwan with arms of a defensive character; and to maintain the capacity of the United States to resist any resort to force or other forms of coercion that would jeopardize the security, or the social or economic system, of the people of Taiwan.

For additional analytical, marketing, investment and business opportunities information, please contact
Global Investment & Business Center, USA
(202) 546-2103. Fax: (202) 546-3275. E-mail: rusric@erols.com

The United States takes its obligation to assist Taiwan in maintaining a self-defense capability very seriously. This is not only because it is mandated by U.S. law in the TRA, but also because it is in our own national interest. As long as Taiwan has a capable defense, the environment will be more conducive to peaceful dialogue, and thus the whole region will be more stable. The United States actively monitors the security situation in the Taiwan Strait, and provides articles and services to Taiwan to ensure it can maintain a sufficient self-defense capability. This section of the report will discuss these activities in more detail.

In assessing Taiwan's defense needs, the Department of Defense has dedicated significant resources over the past two decades to monitoring the security situation in the Taiwan Strait. We have an active unofficial dialogue with Taiwan's defense authorities to better understand their current capabilities and future requirements. Additionally, through engagement with the People's Republic of China (PRC), and dialogue with the People's Liberation Army (PLA), we gain clearer insights into Chinese military capabilities and intentions. We continue to improve our efforts in all areas to assess the security situation in the Taiwan Strait.

Through provision of carefully selected defensive articles and services, we have helped Taiwan maintain a sufficient capacity to defend itself. Among the defensive systems Taiwan has acquired from the U.S. in recent years are F-16 fighters, Knox-class frigates, M-60A tanks, and the Modified Air Defense System -- a Patriot system derivative.

We continually reevaluate Taiwan's defense posture to ensure that we make available to Taiwan such items as will provide a sufficient self-defense capability. Our arms sales policy aims to enable Taiwan to maintain a self-defense capability, while also reinforcing regional stability. We avoid introducing capabilities that would go beyond what is required for Taiwan's self-defense.

As part of our policy to ensure that we provide appropriate defensive capability to Taiwan, President Clinton in 1994 initiated a policy review that, among other things, expanded our non-hardware programs with Taiwan. These programs focused on such areas as defense planning, C4I, air defense, maritime capability, anti-submarine warfare, logistics, joint force integration, and training. These non-hardware programs serve multiple purposes. Functional non-hardware initiatives address many of the shortcomings in Taiwan's military readiness that were identified in the February 1999 DoD Report to Congress on the Security Situation in the Taiwan Strait. They allow Taiwan to better integrate newly acquired systems into its inventory and ensure that the equipment Taiwan has can be used to full effectiveness. These initiatives provide an avenue to exchange views on Taiwan's requirements for defense modernization, to include professionalization and organizational issues, and training. Exchanges and discussions enhance our ability to assess Taiwan's longer term defense needs and develop well-founded security assistance policies. Such programs also enhance Taiwan's capacity for making operationally sound and cost effective acquisition decisions, and more importantly, to use its equipment more effectively for self-defense.

The TRA obliges us to maintain the United States' capacity to resist any resort to force or coercion that would jeopardize the security of Taiwan. This obligation is consistent with America's overall strategy in the region, our commitment to peace and stability, and our regional military posture. The Administration's commitment to maintaining approximately 100,000 troops in the region for the foreseeable future is well-known and widely appreciated throughout the region. The presence of 100,000 U.S. military personnel represents the capabilities of the U.S. Eighth Army and Seventh Air Force in Korea, III Marine Expeditionary Force and Fifth Air Force in Japan, and the U.S. Seventh Fleet.

For additional analytical, marketing, investment and business opportunities information, please contact
Global Investment & Business Center, USA
(202) 546-2103. Fax: (202) 546-3275. E-mail: rusric@erols.com

As has repeatedly been stated publicly, it is the policy of the United States to consider any effort to determine the future of Taiwan by other than peaceful means, including boycotts or embargoes, a threat to the peace and security of the Western Pacific area and of grave concern to the U.S. We demonstrated our commitment to maintaining regional peace and stability in the Taiwan Strait by deploying two carrier battle groups to the region in response to provocative PRC missile exercises in 1996.

GAPS IN KNOWLEDGE REGARDING THE PRC-TAIWAN MILITARY BALANCE

This section of the report discusses gaps in our knowledge regarding the current and future security situation in the Taiwan Strait. By describing what a net assessment of the military balance in the Taiwan Strait would include and how it would be structured it suggests what kinds of gaps in our knowledge are most important. It should be noted that any assessment of a military balance would by its nature have major unresolved uncertainties.

THE CONTENT AND STRUCTURE OF A PRC-TAIWAN ASSESSMENT

An assessment of the PRC-Taiwan balance would begin with an attempt to delineate the subject matter, i.e., who are the relevant parties, and what are the plausible contingencies of interest. The focus of an assessment depends on its intended audience. In an assessment for U.S. defense planners, we need to identify the U.S. goals at stake in this situation, and determine how to measure the adequacy of the military balance in view of those goals. A second section of the assessment would describe and compare key trends and asymmetries in the military capabilities of the parties to the balance. A third section would assess whether U.S. peacetime objectives -- deterring conflict and shaping the behavior of the parties -- are adequately served by the balance of capabilities. A fourth section would assess the likely outcome of conflict if deterrence fails, including both the immediate military result and the broader political effects of that result. Two more sections would summarize major findings and formulate the key strategic management issues that the assessment raises for top Defense officials. Since these final sections would mainly draw out implications from the earlier sections, the discussion of knowledge gaps in this report will be organized around the first four topics mentioned.

DEFINING THE PRC-TAIWAN BALANCE

The PRC claims that Taiwan is an inalienable part of China and has reserved the right to use force to unify Taiwan with the mainland if Taiwan declares independence, if Taiwan is occupied by a foreign country, if it acquires nuclear weapons, or if Taiwan indefinitely refuses the peaceful settlement of cross-Strait reunification through negotiation. U.S. policy opposes any use of force to settle this dispute. A net assessment must therefore focus on the military options that Beijing might exercise against Taiwan, and on the military capabilities relevant to the contingencies that those options would create. In addition to the forces of the PRC and Taiwan, we would need to consider the role of U.S. forces in deterring the use of force or in assisting Taiwan if deterrence fails. The Soviet Union was in the past another relevant actor, initially as an ally of the PRC and later as a competing focus of Chinese military attention. The possibility of a coinciding military crisis on the Korean peninsula would also shape PRC and U.S. calculations. Other regional countries should also figure in the analysis, at least insofar as their reactions to a Taiwan contingency would be important to China and the United States.

It appears that several broad classes of military contingency are possible. First, the PRC could launch an invasion of Taiwan (or an offshore island), using amphibious or other sea or air transported forces. Second, Beijing could try to impose a blockade on Taiwan's commerce as a means of coercing political concessions. Third, the PRC could try to coerce Taiwan by means of air or missile strikes on Taiwan's population, military assets, or economic infrastructure. Associated with each of these options would be some Chinese strategy for avoiding, discouraging, forestalling, or reacting to a possible U.S. intervention on Taiwan's side.

An assessment of the military balance for U.S. defense planners must begin from actual or assumed U.S. goals. The fundamental question for assessment is whether the military balance is or is not satisfactory in relation to those U.S. goals. The overarching U.S. goal is to avoid any use or threat of force to resolve differences in the Taiwan Strait. Thus, our goals include that the PRC be persuaded against or deterred from attacking or threatening attack, that if a threat is made it is unavailing, and that if an attack is made it is unsuccessful. In the latter case, our goal would be that Taiwan defend itself without outside assistance -- or, as a fallback, that it defend itself long enough to permit outside assistance, and that the combination of Taiwan and U.S. forces defeat a PLA attack on Taiwan, should the U.S. decide to intervene.

Moreover, we have goals associated with the outcome of any conflict, apart from the primary goal of defending Taiwan against unprovoked attack. We would want any U.S. intervention to reassure other allies and friends and discourage other aggressions, strengthening or at least not weakening our future military relations in the region. Finally, we seek to avoid in peacetime the erosion of our capacity to assist Taiwan in the future.

From this starting point, an assessment would identify and analyze the trends and asymmetries that may change or affect our ability to achieve these goals given the variety of possible Chinese military operations; and then focus specifically on the adequacy of deterrence and the likely outcome of any conflict if deterrence fails.

TRENDS AND ASYMMETRIES

To assess the present and future military balance, we need to depict trends in those military capabilities most decisive for each of the conflict scenarios. Ideally, we would want to judge how each scenario would play out if it happened today, or some time in the next 5 or 10 or 20 years. Given the difficulty of making any absolute judgment on likely war outcomes, it is useful to determine at least the direction of any change in the situation: are China's or Taiwan's relative capabilities for these various scenarios getting better or worse? Accordingly, we would want to trace trends in capabilities over the past 20 to 40 years, as well as project those trends into the future.

A starting point is to track changes over time in the number, technical quality, and stationing of each party's weapons and equipment, including ground, air, sea, amphibious, air defense and missile forces. For the PRC and the United States, judgments would be needed on which part of the country's overall force could or would play a timely part in a Taiwan scenario; for Taiwan, all available forces would be considered likely to be engaged. We would also need to describe trends in each side's training, exercises, doctrine, and logistics, looking for indications of relative change in capability or changes in the kinds of military operations envisioned or emphasized. Training and doctrine will be important indicators of the actual competence of each side's military forces. For the United States, we would need to consider trends in forward deployment and basing patterns, airlift and sealift capabilities, and the political context that makes U.S. intervention more or less likely in fact, and more or less likely in the PRC's perception. Trends in other countries are also relevant, such as the shift over time from a Soviet-Chinese alliance, to a Soviet-Chinese competition, to a post-Soviet Russia with reduced military forces.

The focus of a study of trends would be to track relative changes in a manageable number of military capabilities that appear most important for deterrence and war outcomes. While tracing the development over time of each of these capabilities or competitions (e.g., "air vs. air defense"), we would also need to consider whether the list of which capabilities are most important is itself changing. We also need to identify changes over time in the vulnerabilities of each side that might facilitate the other side's operations.

Asymmetries to be considered are important differences between the forces, doctrines, geographical and political situations, and strategic and political calculations of the several parties to this conflict. Such asymmetries, some of which are obvious in the PRC-Taiwan case, strongly affect how a military "balance" between dissimilar actors should be assessed.

SHAPING AND DETERRENCE

To judge whether the military balance adequately deters Beijing, we need to understand how the Chinese authorities assess the situation. Whether or not we or a hypothetical observer would think the consequences of their initiating a blockade, invasion, or strikes against Taiwan are promising or discouraging is not really sufficient for our purposes if China's rulers see it differently. Similarly, our ability to influence Taiwan's security posture depends on understanding their assessments, including their assessments of our -- and of China's -- likely behavior and capabilities.

CONTINGENCY OUTCOMES

We cannot expect to predict confidently the outcome of a military conflict. The best approximation would be to consider systematically a range of plausible scenarios, relying on war gaming and experienced military analysts to judge the likely outcome given the forces, levels of training, and operational methods of all parties. We would want to game the conflict that follows from each presumed Chinese operational plan (invasion, blockade, strike) not only for the present situation, but for the forces we project for the future; and the games should be repeated, with different players who would test a variety of operational plans and options.

WHERE ARE THE GAPS IN KNOWLEDGE?

For each of the major topics of assessment just outlined, there are a number of more specific subjects on which better information would be very useful. In some cases, we are unlikely ever to obtain exactly the information we would want. If some knowledge gaps cannot be corrected, it is at least advantageous to be aware that they exist. In general, three kinds of gaps stand out.

First, we need to know more about how the authorities in the PRC and Taiwan view their military and political situation -- in order to identify the most important conflict scenarios and hence the capabilities central to them; in order to assess whether the balance of forces adequately deters Chinese attack and reassures Taiwan; and in order to understand how both sides' calculations of priority, risk, and military capability would shape the course and outcome of a conflict. We are unlikely to be able to replicate their precise views on this military balance, but we probably can learn much more about both sides' ideas about statecraft, their approaches to the use of force, their perceived vulnerabilities, and their preferred operational methods, as well as about the political and military organizations that produce military assessments and plans. Second, as might be predicted, we are less knowledgeable about things that are less visible or tangible -- training, logistics, doctrine, command and control, special operations, mine warfare -- than we are about airplanes and surface ships. Third, although we can identify emerging methods of warfare that appear likely to be increasingly important in the future -- particularly missiles and information warfare-we cannot confidently assess how each side's capabilities will develop or the interaction of measures and countermeasures that these emerging military competitions will generate.

GEORGE W. BUSH ON TAIWAN: SELECTED STATEMENTS

PRESIDENT WELCOMES CHINA, TAIWAN INTO WTO

Statement by the President: Ministerial Decision to Admit the People's Republic of China and Taiwan Into the World Trade Organization

Ministerial Decision to Admit the People's Republic of China and Taiwan into the World Trade Organization

I welcome the unanimous decisions made this week by trade ministers meeting in Doha, Qatar to admit the People's Republic of China and Taiwan into the World Trade Organization (WTO). I believe that the entry of China and Taiwan into the WTO will strengthen the global trading system and expand world economic growth.

China, with more than 1.2 billion people and a one trillion dollar annual gross domestic product, is one of the fastest growing economies in the world. Taiwan is the world's 16th largest economy. The decision in Doha -- reached following many years of negotiations -- marks a formal agreement by the 142 members of the WTO on the steps that China and Taiwan must take to open their markets as WTO members. Taking these steps will introduce greater competition into both economies and mean that both follow the same trade rules as the United States and other trading partners. This, in turn, will generate greater trade and investment that will bring benefits to businesses, consumers, and workers in all of our economies.

I am confident that China's entry into the WTO will bring other benefits to China beyond the expected economic benefits. WTO membership, for example, will require China to strengthen the rule of law and introduce certain civil reforms, such as the publication of rules. In the long run, an open, rules-based Chinese economy will be an important underpinning for Chinese democratic reforms.

China and Taiwan now face the challenge of implementing their WTO commitments. The United States stands ready to work constructively with both economies to assist them in meeting the challenges of implementation. We also look forward to the great benefits we know that greater trade will bring to all our peoples.

PRESIDENT SIGNS BILLS

Statement by the Press Secretary

On Thursday, April 4, 2002, the President signed into law:

H.R. 1499, "District of Columbia College Access Improvement Act of 2002" which expands the eligibility criteria for tuition assistance for District of Columbia residents under the District of Columbia College Access Act of 1999;

H.R. 2739, which authorizes the Secretary of State to initiate a plan to endorse and obtain observer status for Taiwan at the May 2002 annual summit of the World Health Assembly;

For additional analytical, marketing, investment and business opportunities information, please contact
Global Investment & Business Center, USA
(202) 546-2103. Fax: (202) 546-3275. E-mail: rusric@erols.com

H.R. 3985, which authorizes certain binding arbitration disputes regarding the leasing of reservation lands of the Gila River Indian Community in Arizona to be under the jurisdiction of Federal courts rather than tribal courts.

US-TAIWAN SECRET TALKS ON ARMS SALE: ANALYSIS[2]

US President George W. Bush's February China visit has pushed China-US relations a step forward. However, inharmonious chord has arisen recently in the United States. The US government, on one hand, held the fourth China-US arms control symposium with the Chinese side in Washington, on the other hand, invited Tang Yiau-min, the "defense minister" of Taiwan to go to the United States to attend the so-called "US-Taiwan defense meeting" and quickened its step of arms sale to Taiwan.

With regard to the matter of US invitation to Taiwan's "defense minister" to visit the United States, Chinese Foreign Ministry spokesman Kong Quan pointed out on March 7 that the Chinese side had made serious representations with and lodged serious protest against the US side. On that same day, Chinese Assistant Foreign Minister Zhou Wenzhong was ordered to summon US Ambassador to China Clark Randt, making serious representations with the US government.

Representations between China and the United States concerning this matter have not come to an end. On March 9, the American "Los Angeles Times" divulged a shocking news: The United States has directed its nuclear weapon at China! The report says it has tried to obtain a copy of the secret report of the US Defense Department, which had been forwarded to US Congress on January 8 this year. The report indicates that the Bush administration has instructed US military to draw up a plan for launching nuclear attack under special circumstances and has prepared, when necessary, to use nuclear weapons against at least seven countries, including China. These seven countries are China, Russia, Iraq, the Democratic People's Republic of Korea (DPRK), Iran, Libya and Syria. The report lists three possibilities for the use of nuclear weapons: First, attacking the targets by which the enemy can resist the non-nuclear attack; second, retaliating the enemy's attacks launched with nuclear and biochemical weapons; and third, coping with the special circumstance arising from contingencies. The "special circumstance" mentioned in the report includes conflicts in the Taiwan Straits. Although the US Defense Department spokesman denied the report about the United States aiming its nuclear weapons at China and other countries, he admitted that the secret report did exist. These practices on the part of the US government cannot but arouse China's high vigilance.

Heated disputes appeared between China and the United States at the arms control conference. From March 4 to 5, China and the United States, in accordance with the schedule, held the fourth China-US conference on armament control, disarmament and prevention of proliferation.

Personnel attending the seminar were of a high ranking, chief representative of the Chinese side was Liu Jieyi, director of the Arms Control Department of the Chinese Foreign Ministry; chief representative of the US side was an assistant Secretary of State in charge of the issue concerning a halt to the spread of weapons. According to a US media report, the topic for discussion at the conference is highly sensitive, which include topics on strategic stability, missile defense and the prevention of weapon proliferation. The sponsor repeatedly indicated that this was a civil regular conference with a very strong academic atmosphere, and it was not negotiation or consultation between governments of the two countries. However, shortly after the conclusion of Bush's China visit, what is more, since the seminar was attended by officials of both sides, so this meeting received the high attention of the two countries.

At the two-day seminar, both sides mainly expressed their own opinions. Both sides agreed that

---

[2] PRC Assesment

"the proliferation of massive lethal weapons should be checked", however, on the most sensitive question concerning US arms sale to Taiwan, representatives of both side had serious differences, a scene of heated disputes appeared for sometime at the venue. Representative of the Chinese side repeatedly stressed that US arms sale to Taiwan belonged to the topic of "armament control" and time and again expressed his opposition to US arms sales to Taiwan and interference in China's internal affairs. But representative of the US side, harping on the same old tunes, claimed that US arms sale to Taiwan was carried out in accordance with the "Taiwan Relations Act" and so "cannot and should not be confused with the issue concerning the proliferation of China's weapons".

US Lets Taiwan's "Defense Minister" Visit America

Precisely at the time when US and Chinese representatives were discussing matters concerning non-proliferation of weapons, the United States invited Taiwan's "defense minister" to go to the country to discuss the question related to US arms sale to Taiwan, so the US act is self-contradictory.

The "US-Taiwan defense summit meeting" was sponsored by the "US-Taiwan Business Council" composed of American firms selling weapons to Taiwan, and received assistance from several arms dealers. Senior US officials, including Carlucci, chairman of "US-Taiwan Business Council" and former US defense secretary; Paul Wolf-fowitz, current US deputy defense secretary; J. A. Kelly, assistant secretary of state in charge of East Asian affairs and Sorensen, an official in charge of arms sale for the air and army force as well as vice-chairman of the Lockheed and Martin companies and other munitions merchants, all delivered speeches at the meeting which was therefore called the first "bilateral meeting" of extremely large scale and high specification ever held since the "severance of diplomatic relations" between the United States and Taiwan in 1979.

Since Taiwan leader Chen Shuibian was anxious to further give himself up to the United States which, in turn, was also eager to further strengthen bilateral military cooperation, the "US-Taiwan Business Council" invited "defense minister" Tang Yiau-min who holds real power in Taiwan to attend the meeting. US State Department formally issued on March 6 a "service visa" to Tang Yiau-min who therefore became the first "defense minister" of the Taiwan authorities to pay a formal visit to the United States over the past 20-odd years since the "severance of diplomatic ties" between the United States and Taiwan. Reports say that, according to the schedule decided through discussion between the United States and Taiwan, Tang Yiau-min had started off from Taipei on March 9 to attend the meeting. With the said "service visa", Tang can give open speeches, participate in various activities and jointly attend the seminar with US officials. Taiwan authorities therefore played this up, claiming that this was a "major breakthrough made in the diplomatic and military exchanges between Taiwan and the United States".

Nevertheless, the matter concerning Tang's America visit did not evoke much reaction in the United States. Although Tang holds a high position in Taiwan, his name is completely strange to ordinary American people, so there are not many people showing interest in him. Furthermore, the United States treated the matter with a low-key as far as possible, not wanting to arouse the attention of the outside world. US Defense Department spokesman Davis deliberately avoided mentioning the fact about Deputy Defense Secretary Wolf-fowitz attending the meeting, he only said that the Defense Department officials attended the meeting in an "nonofficial capacity". The sponsor even adopted confidential measures, not only Tang's activities in the United States were kept secret, agenda of the meeting was not made known to the public, journalists were not allowed to cover the meeting.

But news about the matter quickly spread throughout Taiwan Island. Since the agenda of the meeting concerned US arms sale to Taiwan, so when the "Legislative Yuan" questioned Tang whether he was going to discuss matters concerning arms purchase in the United States and whether there were any behind-the-scene deals, Tang said that he was not to be accompanied by any "foreign ministry" staff in his American visit, and no "official visits" were arranged, and that the main purpose of his US trip was "to publicize Taiwan's defense policies among US arms dealers and to win recognition and support from international friends". Hard pressed, Tang was at last compelled to say with raised voice, "I go to the United States in the capacity of defense minister, I will absolutely not discuss the matter of arms purchase, still less privately meet with arms dealers".

However, it is already an indisputable fact that Taiwan authorities are actively strengthening their military exchanges with the United States and seeking to purchase advanced US weapons. At present, the form of US arms sale to Taiwan has been diversified and procedures have become more simple and convenient. The United States has promised that Taiwan can raise the demand for arms purchase from America at any time from now on. The United States has also decided to deliver a batch of new weapons to Taiwan ahead of schedule. The United States decided to sell four "Kidd-class destroyers to Taiwan last year, which were planned to be delivered in four-six years, but in order to allow Taiwan troops to carry out their "ocean operational plan" as soon as possible, America decided to deliver two "Kidd" destroyers to Taiwan in 2004. In February this year, Taiwan authorities raised the demand for buying 30 long bow-shaped attacking helicopters . Sources say that the US Defense and Security Cooperation Agency has left this matter of arms purchase to be handled by the US army, and the matter will be put to discussion and will likely be passed quickly.

Striking a "balance" between the Chinese mainland and Taiwan aims to seek a "balance" between the left- and right-wingers in the United States.
The Bush administration was recently in intimate terms with Taiwan, this causes people to doubt whether its China policy is going to be changed. But some experts in contacts with our correspondents stationed in the United Nations headquarters said that superficially, the Bush administration's policy toward China appeared to be somewhat capricious, and this precisely reflected the characteristic of the policy-maker's intention to strike a "comprehensive balance" and give consideration to the interests of various quarters. No wonder that some experts said this is a "policy" without policy. A university professor said that if Bush wants to be re-elected for the second term, he must consider the political requirements of various quarters, and that resembling a puddle mixer, Bush is good at integrating different viewpoints, he, of course, needs to balance the interests of various quarters in handling relations with China. On other issues, he may be somewhat gentle, he needs to give consideration to the life-wingers and the middle-of-the-roaders, he appears to be tougher in his attitude toward the Taiwan issue, so that he can give more reflection of the viewpoints of the right-wing of the Republicans, to show the difference between the Republicans and the Democrats in their relations with China. Such basic principle actually has remained unchanged since Bush took office.

Another university professor who once worked in the US National Information Office said that the hard liners in the Bush administration are likely to overdo in dealing with the Taiwan or other sensitive issues, and supporters of Taiwan may also take Taiwan's interests into account at the expense of the stability of China-US relations. It can thus be seen that the problem arises mainly from among some people in the Bush administration, in dealing with the US-Taiwan ties, they ignore the interest of China-US relations and push an extreme policy. However, damaging China-US relations will naturally result in harming US national interests, this is precisely what the Bush administration needs to consider prudently.

CONGRESSIONAL TAIWAN CAUCUS FOUNDED

On 9 April 2002, eighty-five members of the US House of Representatives established the Congressional Taiwan Caucus, a bi-partisan group, which will help increase the awareness of issues impacting the relations between the US and Taiwan.

The group will focus on "the concrete steps that Congress can take to enhance and strengthen this important economic, political, cultural and strategic relationship," Congressman Robert Wexler said at the official launch of the caucus. "The caucus will also serve as a forum to educate members of Congress on issues affecting US-Taiwan relations as well as play a constructive role in monitoring and supporting peaceful cross-strait discussions between Taipei and Beijing," he said.

"Finally, the caucus will serve as a medium by which legislators from the United States and Taiwan can formally exchange ideas and policy concerns," Wexler said. He said the group does not have plans at present to initiate Taiwan-related legislation, although finding ways to help Taiwan's bid to participate in international organizations is expected to be a priority.

"Members of the caucus will seek the administration's endorsement of Taiwan's participation in the World Health Organization," said co-founder Sherrod Brown. "With the creation of the Congressional Taiwan Caucus, I am confident we will accomplish our goals and establish Taiwan as an active member of the international community," he said. The other two co-founders are Dana Rohrabacher and Steve Chabot. A group of legislators from Taiwan, led by Trong Chai, were present at the launch in the Capitol.

Prior to the press conference where the caucus was announced, a meeting was held to discuss its future direction. The caucus is led by four joint chairmen, and three of them — Sherrod Brown, a Democrat; Steve Chabot, a Republican; and Dana Rohrabacher, also a Republican — took part in the meeting.

Rohrabacher said that the US has been preoccupied with its war against terror following the Sept. 11 attacks, but to achieve the goal of long-term national security, other threats must not be ignored. He went on to say that stability in Taiwan and the Pacific region is in the long-term interest of the US, and that the Taiwanese experience sets a good example for the future development of China.

Chabot said that Taiwan, one of its most loyal allies, is special to the US. He continued to say that Taiwan is the US' seventh largest trading partner and the 14th largest trading nation in the world, and that the Taiwan caucus would in future do its utmost to promote US-Taiwan relations.

SENATE PASSES TAIWAN-INTO-THE-WHO RESOLUTION

On 19 March 2002, the U.S. Senate on Wednesday passed by two-thirds vote a resolution urging the Bush administration to support Taiwan's bid to rejoin the World Health Organization as an observer. An amendment to Public Law 107-10, House Resolution 2739 was passed by the U.S. House of Representatives in December 2001.

On 4 April 2002, President Bush signed the Bill into law. The bill authorizes the Secretary of State to initiate a United States plan to endorse and obtain observer status for Taiwan at the annual week-long summit of the World Health Assembly in May 2002 and asks the Secretary of State to submit a written report on the plan to Congress within 14 days after the Act's enactment.

For additional analytical, marketing, investment and business opportunities information, please contact
Global Investment & Business Center, USA
(202) 546-2103. Fax: (202) 546-3275. E-mail: rusric@erols.com

Minister of Foreign Affairs Eugene Chien conveyed his gratitude to the U.S. Congress and the European Parliament for their staunch support of this, the country's latest bid to gain WHO observer status.

Taiwan was forced to leave the WHO in 1972 after 24 years as a full member and cofounder of the international health body when the PRC was granted China's seat in the United Nations. Since then, Beijing has adamantly opposed Taiwan's entry to any international organization for which statehood is a membership requirement.

In 1997 Taiwan began to lobby for observer status in the health body, arguing that the health of the 23 million people living on the island should take precedence over political semantics and international one-upmanship. This effort has been defeated six times due to pressure from China.

In related news, a Taipei-based newspaper reported that several members of the ruling Democratic Progressive Party are calling on Beijing to support this latest effort to join the organization. "Supporting Taiwan's WHO bid would serve as the best icebreaker for cross-strait relations," said DPP Legislator Lai Ching-teh of his entreaty to Beijing. Not unexpectedly, Beijing refused.

REPORT TO CONGRESS PURSUANT TO PUBLIC LAW 106-113

Public Law 106-113, an act making consolidated appropriations for the fiscal year ending September 30, 2000, states that the "Office of Net Assessment in the Office of the Secretary of Defense, jointly with the United States Pacific Command, shall submit, through the Under Secretary of Defense (Policy), a report to Congress no later than 270 days after the enactment of this Act which addresses the following issues:

> (1) A review of the operational planning and other preparations of the United States Department of Defense, including but not limited to the United States Pacific Command, to implement the relevant sections of the Taiwan Relations Act since its enactment in 1979; and
>
> (2) A review of evaluation of all gaps in relevant knowledge about the People's Republic of China's capabilities and intentions as they might affect the current and future military balance between Taiwan and the People's Republic of China, including both classified United States intelligence information and Chinese open source writing. The report shall be submitted in classified form, with an unclassified summary."

The report, submitted in response to Public Law 106-113, addresses relevant sections of the Taiwan Relations Act and gaps in knowledge regarding the current and future security situation in the Taiwan Strait. Specifically, the report addresses U.S. provision of defense articles and services to meet Taiwan's legitimate defense needs, U.S. capacity to respond to the use of force against Taiwan, and challenges associated with assessing the security situation in the Taiwan Strait.

EXECUTIVE SUMMARY OF REPORT TO CONGRESS ON IMPLEMENTATION OF THE TAIWAN RELATIONS ACT

The TRA stipulates that "the United States will make available to Taiwan such defense articles and services in such quantity as may be necessary to enable Taiwan to maintain a sufficient self-defense capability." The TRA states that "the President and Congress shall determine the nature and quantity of such defense articles and services based solely upon their judgment of the needs of Taiwan, in accordance with procedures established by law." The TRA further asserts that "such determination of Taiwan's defense needs shall include review by United States military authorities in connection with recommendations to the President and the Congress." Section 2(b) states:

> It is the policy of the United States to consider any effort to determine the future of Taiwan by other than peaceful means, including by boycotts or embargoes, a threat to the peace and security of the Western Pacific area and of grave concern to the United States; to provide Taiwan with arms of a defensive character; and to maintain the capacity of the United States to resist any resort to force or other forms of coercion that would jeopardize the security, or the social or economic system, of the people of Taiwan.

The United States takes its obligation to assist Taiwan in maintaining a self-defense capability very seriously. This is not only because it is mandated by U.S. law in the TRA, but also because it is in our own national interest. As long as Taiwan has a capable defense, the environment will be more conducive to peaceful dialogue, and thus the whole region will be more stable. The United States actively monitors the security situation in the Taiwan Strait, and provides articles and services to Taiwan to ensure it can maintain a sufficient self-defense capability. This section of the report will discuss these activities in more detail.

In assessing Taiwan's defense needs, the Department of Defense has dedicated significant resources over the past two decades to monitoring the security situation in the Taiwan Strait. We have an active unofficial dialogue with Taiwan's defense authorities to better understand their current capabilities and future requirements. Additionally, through engagement with the People's Republic of China (PRC), and dialogue with the People's Liberation Army (PLA), we gain clearer insights into Chinese military capabilities and intentions. We continue to improve our efforts in all areas to assess the security situation in the Taiwan Strait.

Through provision of carefully selected defensive articles and services, we have helped Taiwan maintain a sufficient capacity to defend itself. Among the defensive systems Taiwan has acquired from the U.S. in recent years are F-16 fighters, Knox-class frigates, M-60A tanks, and the Modified Air Defense System--a Patriot system derivative.

We continually reevaluate Taiwan's defense posture to ensure that we make available to Taiwan such items as will provide a sufficient self-defense capability. Our arms sales policy aims to enable Taiwan to maintain a self-defense capability, while also reinforcing regional stability. We avoid introducing capabilities that would go beyond what is required for Taiwan's self-defense.

As part of our policy to ensure that we provide appropriate defensive capability to Taiwan, President Clinton in 1994 initiated a policy review that, among other things, expanded our non-hardware programs with Taiwan. These programs focused on such areas as defense planning, C4I, air defense, maritime capability, anti-submarine warfare, logistics, joint force integration, and training. These non-hardware programs serve multiple purposes. Functional non-hardware initiatives address many of the shortcomings in Taiwan's military readiness that were identified in the February 1999 *DoD Report to Congress on the Security Situation in the Taiwan Strait*. They allow Taiwan to better integrate newly acquired systems into its inventory and ensure that the equipment Taiwan has can be used to full effectiveness. These initiatives provide an avenue to exchange views on Taiwan's requirements for defense modernization, to include professionalization and organizational issues, and training. Exchanges and discussions enhance our ability to assess Taiwan's longer term defense needs and develop well-founded security assistance policies. Such programs also enhance Taiwan's capacity for making operationally sound and cost effective acquisition decisions, and more importantly, to use its equipment more effectively for self-defense.

The TRA obliges us to maintain the United States' capacity to resist any resort to force or coercion that would jeopardize the security of Taiwan. This obligation is consistent with America's overall strategy in the region, our commitment to peace and stability, and our regional military posture. The Administration's commitment to maintaining approximately 100,000 troops in the region for the foreseeable future is well-known and widely appreciated throughout the region. The presence of 100,000 U.S. military personnel represents the capabilities of the U.S. Eighth Army and Seventh Air Force in Korea, III Marine Expeditionary Force and Fifth Air Force in Japan, and the U.S. Seventh Fleet.

As has repeatedly been stated publicly, it is the policy of the United States to consider any effort to determine the future of Taiwan by other than peaceful means, including boycotts or embargoes, a threat to the peace and security of the Western Pacific area and of grave concern to the U.S. We demonstrated our commitment to maintaining regional peace and stability in the Taiwan Strait by deploying two carrier battle groups to the region in response to provocative PRC missile exercises in 1996.

GAPS IN KNOWLEDGE REGARDING THE PRC-TAIWAN MILITARY BALANCE

This section of the report discusses gaps in our knowledge regarding the current and future security situation in the Taiwan Strait. By describing what a net assessment of the military balance in the Taiwan Strait would include and how it would be structured it suggests what kinds of gaps in our knowledge are most important. It should be noted that any assessment of a military balance would by its nature have major unresolved uncertainties.

THE CONTENT AND STRUCTURE OF A PRC-TAIWAN ASSESSMENT

An assessment of the PRC-Taiwan balance would begin with an attempt to delineate the subject matter, i.e., who are the relevant parties, and what are the plausible contingencies of interest. The focus of an assessment depends on its intended audience. In an assessment for U.S. defense planners, we need to identify the U.S. goals at stake in this situation, and determine how to measure the adequacy of the military balance in view of those goals. A second section of the assessment would describe and compare key trends and asymmetries in the military capabilities of the parties to the balance. A third section would assess whether U.S. peacetime objectives—deterring conflict and shaping the behavior of the parties—are adequately served by the balance of capabilities. A fourth section would assess the likely outcome of conflict if deterrence fails, including both the immediate military result and the broader political effects of that result. Two more sections would summarize major findings and formulate the key strategic management issues that the assessment raises for top Defense officials. Since these final sections would mainly draw out implications from the earlier sections, the discussion of knowledge gaps in this report will be organized around the first four topics mentioned.

**For additional analytical, marketing, investment and business opportunities information, please contact
Global Investment & Business Center, USA
(202) 546-2103. Fax: (202) 546-3275. E-mail: rusric@erols.com**

DEFINING THE PRC-TAIWAN BALANCE

The PRC claims that Taiwan is an inalienable part of China and has reserved the right to use force to unify Taiwan with the mainland if Taiwan declares independence, if Taiwan is occupied by a foreign country, if it acquires nuclear weapons, or if Taiwan indefinitely refuses the peaceful settlement of cross-Strait reunification through negotiation. U.S. policy opposes any use of force to settle this dispute. A net assessment must therefore focus on the military options that Beijing might exercise against Taiwan, and on the military capabilities relevant to the contingencies that those options would create. In addition to the forces of the PRC and Taiwan, we would need to consider the role of U.S. forces in deterring the use of force or in assisting Taiwan if deterrence fails. The Soviet Union was in the past another relevant actor, initially as an ally of the PRC and later as a competing focus of Chinese military attention. The possibility of a coinciding military crisis on the Korean peninsula would also shape PRC and U.S. calculations. Other regional countries should also figure in the analysis, at least insofar as their reactions to a Taiwan contingency would be important to China and the United States.

It appears that several broad classes of military contingency are possible. First, the PRC could launch an invasion of Taiwan (or an offshore island), using amphibious or other sea or air transported forces. Second, Beijing could try to impose a blockade on Taiwan's commerce as a means of coercing political concessions. Third, the PRC could try to coerce Taiwan by means of air or missile strikes on Taiwan's population, military assets, or economic infrastructure. Associated with each of these options would be some Chinese strategy for avoiding, discouraging, forestalling, or reacting to a possible U.S. intervention on Taiwan's side.

An assessment of the military balance for U.S. defense planners must begin from actual or assumed U.S. goals. The fundamental question for assessment is whether the military balance is or is not satisfactory in relation to those U.S. goals. The overarching U.S. goal is to avoid any use or threat of force to resolve differences in the Taiwan Strait. Thus, our goals include that the PRC be persuaded against or deterred from attacking or threatening attack, that if a threat is made it is unavailing, and that if an attack is made it is unsuccessful. In the latter case, our goal would be that Taiwan defend itself without outside assistance—or, as a fallback, that it defend itself long enough to permit outside assistance, and that the combination of Taiwan and U.S. forces defeat a PLA attack on Taiwan, should the U.S. decide to intervene.

Moreover, we have goals associated with the outcome of any conflict, apart from the primary goal of defending Taiwan against unprovoked attack. We would want any U.S. intervention to reassure other allies and friends and discourage other aggressions, strengthening or at least not weakening our future military relations in the region. Finally, we seek to avoid in peacetime the erosion of our capacity to assist Taiwan in the future.

From this starting point, an assessment would identify and analyze the trends and asymmetries that may change or affect our ability to achieve these goals given the variety of possible Chinese military operations; and then focus specifically on the adequacy of deterrence and the likely outcome of any conflict if deterrence fails.

TRENDS AND ASYMMETRIES

To assess the present and future military balance, we need to depict trends in those military capabilities most decisive for each of the conflict scenarios. Ideally, we would want to judge how each scenario would play out if it happened today, or some time in the next 5 or 10 or 20 years. Given the difficulty of making any absolute judgment on likely war outcomes, it is useful to determine at least the direction of any change in the situation: are China's or Taiwan's relative capabilities for these various scenarios getting better or worse? Accordingly, we would want to trace trends in capabilities over the past 20 to 40 years, as well as project those trends into the future.

A starting point is to track changes over time in the number, technical quality, and stationing of each party's weapons and equipment, including ground, air, sea, amphibious, air defense and missile forces. For the PRC and the United States, judgments would be needed on which part of the country's overall force could or would play a timely part in a Taiwan scenario; for Taiwan, all available forces would be considered likely to be engaged. We would also need to describe trends in each side's training, exercises, doctrine, and logistics, looking for indications of relative change in capability or changes in the kinds of military operations envisioned or emphasized. Training and doctrine will be important indicators of the actual competence of each side's military forces. For the United States, we would need to consider trends in forward deployment and basing patterns, airlift and sealift capabilities, and the political context that makes U.S. intervention more or less likely in fact, and more or less likely in the PRC's perception. Trends in other countries are also relevant, such as the shift over time from a Soviet-Chinese alliance, to a Soviet-Chinese competition, to a post-Soviet Russia with reduced military forces.

The focus of a study of trends would be to track relative changes in a manageable number of military capabilities that appear most important for deterrence and war outcomes. While tracing the development over time of each of these capabilities or competitions (e.g., "air vs. air defense"), we would also need to consider whether the list of which capabilities are most important is itself changing. We also need to identify changes over time in the vulnerabilities of each side that might facilitate the other side's operations.

Asymmetries to be considered are important differences between the forces, doctrines, geographical and political situations, and strategic and political calculations of the several parties to this conflict. Such asymmetries, some of which are obvious in the PRC-Taiwan case, strongly affect how a military "balance" between dissimilar actors should be assessed.

SHAPING AND DETERRENCE

To judge whether the military balance adequately deters Beijing, we need to understand how the Chinese authorities assess the situation. Whether or not we or a hypothetical observer would think the consequences of their initiating a blockade, invasion, or strikes against Taiwan are promising or discouraging is not really sufficient for our purposes if China's rulers see it differently.

Similarly, our ability to influence Taiwan's security posture depends on understanding their assessments, including their assessments of our—and of China's—likely behavior and capabilities.

CONTINGENCY OUTCOMES

We cannot expect to predict confidently the outcome of a military conflict. The best approximation would be to consider systematically a range of plausible scenarios, relying on war gaming and experienced military analysts to judge the likely outcome given the forces, levels of training, and operational methods of all parties. We would want to game the conflict that follows from each presumed Chinese operational plan (invasion, blockade, strike) not only for the present situation, but for the forces we project for the future; and the games should be repeated, with different players who would test a variety of operational plans and options.

WHERE ARE THE GAPS IN KNOWLEDGE?

**For additional analytical, marketing, investment and business opportunities information, please contact
Global Investment & Business Center, USA
(202) 546-2103. Fax: (202) 546-3275. E-mail: rusric@erols.com**

For each of the major topics of assessment just outlined, there are a number of more specific subjects on which better information would be very useful. In some cases, we are unlikely ever to obtain exactly the information we would want. If some knowledge gaps cannot be corrected, it is at least advantageous to be aware that they exist. In general, three kinds of gaps stand out.

First, we need to know more about how the authorities in the PRC and Taiwan view their military and political situation—in order to identify the most important conflict scenarios and hence the capabilities central to them; in order to assess whether the balance of forces adequately deters Chinese attack and reassures Taiwan; and in order to understand how both sides' calculations of priority, risk, and military capability would shape the course and outcome of a conflict. We are unlikely to be able to replicate their precise views on this military balance, but we probably can learn much more about both sides' ideas about statecraft, their approaches to the use of force, their perceived vulnerabilities, and their preferred operational methods, as well as about the political and military organizations that produce military assessments and plans. Second, as might be predicted, we are less knowledgeable about things that are less visible or tangible— training, logistics, doctrine, command and control, special operations, mine warfare—than we are about airplanes and surface ships. Third, although we can identify emerging methods of warfare that appear likely to be increasingly important in the future—particularly missiles and information warfare—we cannot confidently assess how each side's capabilities will develop or the interaction of measures and countermeasures that these emerging military competitions will generate.

PERSPECTIVES ON CROSS-STRAIT RELATIONS: CHALLENGES AND OPPORTUNITIES

On September 15, 2000, the Center for National Policy (CNP) and the Taipei Economic and Cultural Representative Office (TECRO) held a meeting on the topic of cross-Strait relations. The participants at the meeting included current and former policy-makers, legislators, academics, and policy analysts from both the United States and Taiwan. The discussions were off the record, and all participants spoke on a personal basis.

The meeting was organized around panels that discussed military, economic, and political aspects of cross-Strait relations, as well as prospects for the future. Among the numerous observations that were made, a few key points can be summarized here.

> · There was widespread consensus that any military confrontation between the Republic of China on Taiwan (ROC) and the People's Republic of China (PRC) would likely be damaging to Taiwan in some respects, whatever the outcome, and should be avoided. It is in the interests of both sides to settle their differences through dialogue and diplomacy.
>
> · World Trade Organization (WTO) membership for the ROC and PRC may forge new links, processes, and opportunities for discussion between the two. There is hope that the WTO will contribute to economic development and democratization in China. At the same time, just as the WTO will affect China, China will have an effect on the further development of the WTO.
>
> · Taiwan's democratization has had a great impact both within the ROC and internationally. An increasing sense of a distinct Taiwanese identity both poses new issues for US policy, and

also has widened the base of American political support for Taiwan.

· Further dialogue between the ROC and PRC would help the two sides confront issues of democracy, equality, sovereignty and security. Talks will not necessarily bring quick results, but they can help both sides find common ground and address their differences constructively.

What follows is a summary of the discussion at a meeting cosponsored by the Center for National Policy (CNP) and the Taipei Economic and Cultural Representative office (TECRO), held in Washington, DC, on September 15, 2000, on the topic of cross-Strait relations. The participants at the meeting included current and former policy-makers, legislators, academics, and policy analysts from both the United States and Taiwan. The discussions were off the record, and no individual remarks have been attributed to the speakers here.

The meeting sought to examine the full spectrum of cross-Strait relations as well as steps for future policy. To spur discussion, CNP commissioned papers that addressed the military, economic, and political aspects of cross-Strait relations. Paper abstracts were distributed to the group before the meeting, and at the event each author presented a summary of his ideas. The abstracts are posted on this website. These presentations were followed by remarks from one or two previously designated discussants. After these remarks, the floor was open for discussion among the entire group. The presentations based on the papers were not off the record, but the response to the papers are treated confidentially, and only a summary of views are presented here.

The meeting began with a few brief introductory remarks. One participant noted at the outset that tensions in the cross-Strait relationship constitute one of the most pressing issues facing the world today. It was suggested that the off the record format would allow for the sort of candid talk needed to reach an innovative solution. This speaker also noted that it was important that the meeting would not only include policy-makers, scholars, and other analysts, but legislators as well, allowing the group to include the perspectives of those who understand the challenges of acting in the public domain.

THE MILITARY BALANCE

The first panel of the day began with a presentation of the cross-Strait military balance by Dennis Blasko, of International Technology and Trade Associates. Mr. Blasko surveyed various assessments of cross-Strait military relations, which display a range of views on two related issues: the state of the cross-Strait military balance and the level of need for US intervention should conflict erupt. Some analysts suggest that the PRC is building a force that will soon have the capacity to overtake the Taiwanese militarily. Other analysts disagree, arguing that that in the foreseeable future, there is little chance of the PRC being able to mount a successful invasion of Taiwan. From the perspective of US policy, the question of which of these two assessments are more correct poses implications for whether, how, and when the US might be called on to become involved in ensuring the security of the ROC. The presenter noted that the US Department of Defense findings fall in the middle of the range of views on this issue.

Blasko then considered the discrepancy between the sizes of the Chinese and Taiwanese military forces. He observed that, technically, there is a 6:1 personnel ratio in favor of the PRC, but he argued that quantitative considerations should be supplemented with an appreciation of equipment quality, geographic factors, and the different requirements for fighting an offensive or defensive battle. He also noted that a substantial portion of those the PRC counts as military personnel are in administrative support, and would not normally be included in a balance assessment.

Turning to the issue of weapons purchases, Blasko noted that Israel has been a major supplier of arms to Taiwan, sending a great deal of technology to the ROC in cases where the US hesitated to send similar equipment. Further, neither Chinese nor Taiwanese official statistics include all foreign arms purchases. Over the past ten years, the US has provided $20 billion in weapons support and training to Taiwan, compared to $10 billion in similar support from Russia to China. Blasko questioned whether the Taiwanese military could absorb more equipment, given a limited supply of pilots and junior naval officers.

Blasko said that that despite media speculation to the contrary, a US Department of Defense report recently found that China would be unlikely to choose to attempt an amphibious invasion of Taiwan. The People's Liberation Army (PLA) would more likely attempt a decapitating attack using special operations forces and information warfare in the hope that Taiwan would capitulate before the US could respond. The PLA has few weapons suited to such an attack, but Blasko reminded the participants that the PLA has the capability to develop innovative solutions to difficult problems.

Then Blasko reflected on the proposed Taiwan Security Enhancement Act (TSEA), which would call for closer coordination between the US and ROC militaries and more technology transfer from the US to the ROC. He argued that much of what the TSEA seeks could be accomplished without an act of Congress. He noted that Taiwanese cadets are currently training in US military academies, and that senior Taiwanese officers do come to the US to confer with their counterparts. In addition, he argued, it would be better for the Taiwanese to maintain and operate currently available equipment more effectively than to purchase new technology. Instead of seeking to pass TSEA, he said, the US Congress should reaffirm the provisions of the Taiwan Relations Act.

In closing, Blasko said that both the PRC and ROC know that US and Taiwanese forces together could repel a Chinese attack, but that it would be better for everyone to de-emphasize the military component of cross-Strait relations and to focus on a political resolution. Whether or at what point the PRC might overtake Taiwan militarily, and whatever appropriate US response should be to prevent the conflict from occurring, he argued, it is important to prospects for stability in the region for both the PRC and ROC to provide leadership and to work toward compromise in settling their differences.

Following this presentation, there was an exchange of views on the cross-Strait military balance and the best possible course for US and Taiwanese policies. There was broad agreement on the importance of the political and psychological dimensions of cross-Strait relations in addition to military considerations. No one argued that a Chinese invasion is likely to take place any time soon. Instead, the consensus view was that the PRC is most likely to engage in a battle of nerves with Taiwan, building up its military capability and maintaining the capacity to intimidate Taiwan with improvements to its missile force.

There also was consensus supporting Blasko's argument about the need for a political solution to cross-Strait tensions, as opposed to a military one. It was noted, however, that prospects for such a solution remain unclear, and there were no concrete suggestions for how Taiwan and the PRC would reach agreement on how to settle their differences.

**For additional analytical, marketing, investment and business opportunities information, please contact
Global Investment & Business Center, USA
(202) 546-2103. Fax: (202) 546-3275. E-mail: rusric@erols.com**

Despite these areas of consensus, there was a good deal of debate among the participants. In particular, several meeting attendees argued that TSEA would help enhance Taiwan's security by reaffirming United States support for Taiwan, by ensuring better communication between the US and Taiwanese militaries, and by providing the means whereby Taiwan would be able to obtain additional military hardware and benefit from training from the United States.

Another significant group of meeting participants held a different view of TSEA, arguing that the Taiwan Relations Act provides adequately for Taiwan's security, and that further US legislation would only serve to provoke the PRC and lessen the security of Taiwan. According to this view, Taiwan has received and is receiving enough military assistance from the United States to deter a Chinese attack, and even in the unlikely event of a Chinese attack, the PRC would be unable to gain control of the island.

This disagreement unearthed different perceptions of US policy toward Taiwan. Some participants expressed concern about what they characterized as a US policy of calculated "strategic ambiguity" toward Taiwan, in which the US refuses to delineate the conditions under which it would defend Taiwan against Chinese attack so as to restrain the Taiwanese from acting provocatively while deterring the Chinese from acting aggressively. They argued that the US should abandon this approach in favor of a more explicit security guarantee to, or perhaps even an alliance with, Taiwan.

In opposition to this view, a number of participants argued that there is little that is ambiguous about US policy. They cited the decision to send two US aircraft carriers to the region in 1996 when the PRC launched missiles into the sea near Taiwan as clearly not ambiguous. In this view there are few serious analysts or policy-makers, including those in China, who doubt that the US would come to Taiwan's aid if it were subject to a Chinese attack. They cautioned against a more formal security guarantee on the grounds that such a move would provoke the Chinese, or could even encourage Taiwan to provoke China unnecessarily.

One policy-maker summed up implications of a potential US-China military conflict by citing the saying that "when the elephants fight, the grass gets trampled." It was suggested that the need to avoid such a situation is essential and obvious, but it is also the case that the differences that could potentially lead to such a conflict are unlikely to come to resolution any time soon. Instead of looking for a quick fix, this speaker offered the view that, over time, through dialogue and diplomacy, China and Taiwan can gradually work out their differences and find a mutually acceptable solution.

ECONOMIC RELATIONS

The meeting's second panel featured a presentation by Tse-Kang Leng, of the Institute of International Relations at National Chengchi University, that considered the effect of globalization and the potential impact of World Trade Organization (WTO) membership on cross-Strait relations. In particular, Leng focused on the interaction between state and society, pointing to a divergence between Taiwan business firm behavior and state policy in relation to the PRC. He noted that the Taiwanese business community negotiates with both its home country and with the PRC. In general, he suggested that businesses try to stay out of politics, focusing on opportunities to produce revenue on both sides of the Strait. He cautioned against thinking of cross-Strait economic relations solely in terms of the bilateral Taiwan-China relationship. Instead, he suggested, it would be wise to consider global interaction involving the broader world economy.

Leng then considered the impact of cross-Strait economic relations on Taiwan's national security. In the past, he noted, the Taiwanese government employed tools such as capital controls, limits on technology transfers, limits on the transfer of personnel, and a predefined division of labor to maintain Taiwan's independence as an economic entity. The use of these means showed that Taiwan was attempting to resist some of the trends associated with globalization. Now, however, Leng said, the Taiwanese government appears to be embracing globalization. Instead of focusing on the control of international economic flows, the Taiwanese are trying to benefit from them. He offered as an example current ROC efforts to improve technological innovation and global management practices. He noted there is still discussion about how to regulate imports from the mainland, however, and how quickly to negotiate the "three links," which consist of postal, communication, and transportation ties.

Turning to the issue of WTO membership for Taiwan, Leng outlined the challenges and opportunities he sees as involved in joining the organization. Submitting to WTO practices will subject Taiwanese firms to increased competition from multinational corporations and businesses based in the PRC. Leng pointed out that most Taiwanese firms are either small or medium sized businesses, many of which fear the result of direct competition with larger foreign firms. Further, he suggested that WTO membership would force Taiwan to lift restrictions on international investment and other flows, making the island accommodate capital and personnel from the mainland and elsewhere.

Leng argued, despite these challenges for Taiwan, WTO membership for both the PRC and ROC should increase political stability across the Strait, providing a good channel for ROC-PRC interaction and making it possible to integrate Taiwanese business interests with domestic development in the PRC. The WTO can serve as a mechanism to "de-bilateralize" ROC-PRC negotiations. While Leng cautioned against excessive optimism, he suggested that the opening and widening of multiple channels across the Strait could result in a situation of complex interdependence that would benefit both Taiwan and China.

The discussion following this presentation focused on the issue of potential WTO membership for China and Taiwan. Several participants considered whether WTO membership would result in domestic change in China. Some argued that it would produce greater openness and freedom for the Chinese people. Others agreed with Leng that WTO participation could serve to stabilize the cross-Strait relationship. It was suggested that WTO membership could generate opportunities for both Taiwan and China by creating new constituencies for peace, empowering different actors in each country, and by changing the political dynamic.

Several participants discussed other potential benefits of WTO membership for both Taiwan and China. In the view of these participants, by joining the institution, Taiwan should gain economically through increased trade and investment, and politically by achieving increased international recognition. The ROC and PRC also should benefit from the opportunity to discuss their differences in a multinational forum. Economics is one of the few bright spots in cross-Strait relations, in this view, and to the extent that WTO membership benefits the region's economy, it could spur economic growth for all.

Other members of the group were more cautious, either questioning whether the WTO would have much of an effect on China, considering possible negative consequences of PRC WTO membership, or positing that China could have more of an effect on the WTO than the international organization is likely to have on it.

Some participants suggested that the WTO could actually contribute to cross-Strait friction by creating new arguments between Taiwan and China. For example, at present there is uncertainty

For additional analytical, marketing, investment and business opportunities information, please contact
Global Investment & Business Center, USA
(202) 546-2103. Fax: (202) 546-3275. E-mail: rusric@erols.com

about Taiwan's likely status within the WTO. Recent statements from the PRC indicate that they believe that Taiwan should not be permitted to join the organization on the same status as sovereign nation-states.

A few participants pointed to another potential problem resulting from China's reliance on foreign direct investment, noting that if the PRC continues to attract significant amounts of international capital, including capital from Taiwan, it could result in higher borrowing costs for Taiwanese businesses.

SYSTEMS IN TRANSITION

The third panel of the day began with a presentation by Taifa Yu, of the University of Northern Iowa, detailing political developments in Taiwan, and highlighting the role played by rising perceptions of Taiwanese national identity. Yu said that, along with the growth of the Taiwanese economy and the transition to democracy, a rising sense of Taiwanese identity has been one of the most significant changes in Taiwan in the past 50 years. He said that political leaders often encourage nationalist sentiment as a means of consolidating power or in order to mobilize resources for military action. But, in Taiwan's case, he argued, nationalist sentiments have risen more organically from the situation in which Taiwan finds itself. He traced the rise of the current sense of Taiwanese identity to a reaction to diplomatic setbacks the ROC suffered in the 1970's.

Yu emphasized that there is a close relationship between a sense of Taiwanese identity and the idea of an independent Taiwan. To illustrate the importance of the rise of Taiwanese identity he offered a number of developments he believes are related to it: Taiwan's transition to democracy, the legitimization of an independence movement, polarization between native Taiwanese and mainland-born politicians, and tensions in the cross-Strait relationship. He suggested that a growing sense of Taiwanese identity complicates resolution of the cross-Strait dispute, and makes the "one China" framework increasingly problematic. He closed by offering the view that a growing sense of a separate and distinct Taiwanese political identity will continue to play an important role in Taiwanese politics.

Following this presentation, one participant questioned whether he was talking about ethno-nationalism, suggesting instead that Taiwanese identity is more of a civic nationalism based on political contingency. Others offered differing views of the precise origin of the Taiwanese identity. One group of participants held that Taiwanese nationalism has been primarily a reaction to the behavior of the PRC, while others suggested both Chinese nationalism in the PRC and Taiwanese nationalism in the ROC were products of a reaction to the Kuomintang (KMT). Participants also suggested other reasons for Taiwanese nationalism, including a reaction to colonial rule, and domestic forces within the island. It was suggested that this debate has implications for how one might expect the Taiwanese people to react to threatening behavior from the PRC. If Taiwanese identity is at all related to pressure from the PRC, for example, additional pressure from the mainland would likely bolster Taiwanese nationalism.

It was further argued that the debate about Taiwanese identity has implications for ROC behavior. If Taiwanese nationalism were to contribute to the transition to democracy and to economic growth in Taiwan, then most observers would welcome its further development. However, if Taiwanese nationalism were to contribute instead to overtly chauvinistic Taiwanese behavior, then a rise of nationalistic fervor in Taiwan could provoke China, hinder the development of democracy in China, and potentially result in the loss of support from the US.

On the subject of US support for Taiwan, more than one participant noted that Taiwanese democratization has led to increased interest in the US Congress. Growing arguments for weapons sales to the ROC, for allowing senior Taiwanese leaders to travel to the US, and for increased contact with senior ROC officials can all be traced to an appreciation of Taiwan's transition to popular rule. Several participants suggested that further democratization in China would aid the effort to resolve cross-Strait tensions peacefully.

Questions of democratization, in turn, raised issues of legitimacy. Several members of the group referred to what they see as problems of legitimacy on both sides of the Strait, problems that are affecting the way political leaders are dealing with the cross-Strait relationship.

DIRECTIONS FOR THE FUTURE

The meeting's last panel featured personal statements reflecting on the future of cross-Strait relations. Representative C.J. Chen, of the Taipei Economic and Cultural Representative Office, noted that China has been divided into two parts since 1949, and that for nearly 40 years, cross-Strait relations had a distinctly adversarial tone. However, he said that since 1987, political and economic changes in the ROC have led to a significant shift in its attitude and its channels of communication with the PRC have expanded. Besides some changes that have eased tensions in the cross-Strait relationship somewhat, however, he suggested fundamental differences remain between the two sides. As a key example, he pointed to the fact that, while refusing to renounce the use of force to achieve unification, Beijing still insists that Taiwan accept a subordinate status.

Chen said, on the question of cross-Strait relations, that Taiwan has essentially three basic options: unification with the PRC, declaration of independence, or continuation of the status quo. Polls over the last decade show that the majority of the people on Taiwan prefer to maintain Taiwan's status quo for the time being and they want a peaceful, secure, and stable future. He said that Taiwan's government trusts the people to make rational decisions in their own best interests. Any change has to take this into account.

Chen then discussed the current state of cross-Strait relations. He said President Chen Shui-bian's new government has actively sought to resume dialogue with Beijing through institutions that were used in the past, and it is convinced that wisdom, creativity and sincerity on both sides can eventually bring about breakthroughs and improvements in the normalization of cross-Strait relations. He laid out the basic principles that the ROC believes should govern the talks: that both sides should be able to deal with cross-Strait issues on the basis of democracy, equality, and peace. But, he said, Beijing authorities want Taipei first to accept, as a condition for talks, the position that Taiwan is part of "One China" –which they define as the "People's Republic of China"—and their "one country, two systems" formula, downgrading Taiwan to a status like that of Hong Kong and Macau. He said that approach doesn't't respect the aforementioned three principles, nor does it make room for principles of human rights and free choice by a self-respecting people.

By contrast, Chen emphasized, President Chen Shui-bian has made it clear that his government has no preconditions for resuming talks, nor does he believe there should be any preconditions. If Beijing returns to that same spirit of "dialogue, exchange, and shelving of disputes," that both sides agreed to years ago, Chen indicated representatives from both sides could meet again and talk about anything.

Finally, Chen said that he appreciates that the US understands and respects Taiwan's determination to honor the people's freedom of choice in such matters. He noted that not only the US government, but also both major political parties in the US have stated that any final resolution to the cross-Strait situation must be made with the consent of the people on Taiwan. Chen emphasized that Taiwan is appreciative of the efforts that the US government has been making in encouraging and persuading Beijing to resume dialogue with Taipei. He said that Taiwan hopes the US will play more of an active and constructive role as a stabilizer and balancer across the Strait, providing the impetus for dialogue and practical incentives for reconciliation. Chen also noted that a peaceful settlement of the issues and maintenance of regional stability and prosperity are broadly shared interests. He said the way the issues involved are managed, improved and resolved may well be the most challenging task we all have to face in the future.

Next, Richard Bush, managing director of the American Institute in Taiwan, presented his personal views regarding cross-Strait relations. He observed that the day's discussions had dealt with the particular factors that affect the context in which transactions between Taipei and Beijing take place. Such military, economic and political factors matter, he said, but sooner or later the two governments will have to create broader frameworks of action (or fail to act altogether) and live with the results. He focused on what he sees as two core substantive issues framing cross-Strait relations.

First, he discussed the issue of sovereignty. He suggested that the PRC is offering "one country – two systems", or "Hong Kong plus"; and that this is not acceptable to Taiwan because the island would only have home rule, but the PRC would remain the exclusive sovereign. Taiwan, he said, wants Beijing to acknowledge that the governing authorities in Taiwan would possess a measure of sovereignty within the context of any unified China. This includes an internal element, the exclusive right to rule the territory that is under its jurisdiction, and an external element, Taiwan's right to have a greater international role. Bush argued that conceptually unification is not necessarily inconsistent with Taiwan having sovereignty. He pointed out that both Taipei and Beijing face challenges in addressing the issue of unification for the future. Taipei must determine what conceptions of China the people of Taiwan would be comfortable with. Beijing must decide if there are conceptions of unification that it could accept where Taiwan could be a sovereign part of a unified China.

Another core framing issue Bush posed is security. He noted the PRC is modernizing its military capability, and Taiwan has a significant force as well. This raises a number of questions: How will these assets factor in to a new political equation? How will the parties deal with the sense of insecurity these military forces create? Are there confidence-building measures that could reduce Taiwan's sense of insecurity? US policy, Bush said, is that the two sides need to work out mutually acceptable answers to these questions. He said the US will not get involved in mediating between the two sides. US attention is focused on process, the need for a peaceful resolution, and an outcome that people can accept. In his view, the US "one China policy" can accommodate a variety of solutions. He said that it is important that dialogue be resumed because it can reduce risks while creating momentum to clarify misunderstandings, find common ground, and grapple constructively with differences.

MANAGING U.S.-TAIWAN RELATIONS: 20 YEARS AFTER THE TAIWAN RELATIONS ACT

The United States has severed diplomatic relations with the Republic of China for twenty years. The Taiwan Relations Act (TRA) was enacted in 1979 to preserve and promote commercial, cultural and other relations between the United States and Taiwan. It has been instrumental in maintaining peace, security, and stability in the Taiwan Strait since its enactment.

Joseph S. Nye, Jr., former Assistant Secretary for International Security Affairs of the U.S. Defense Department, has observed that historically the rise and fall of great powers are often accompanied by great instability in international state systems.[1] The international power structure in East Asia today is marked by the rise and fall of great powers. The Soviet Union collapsed and North Korea's future remains uncertain. Japan's role is evolving and China's power is rising.

The Taiwan-Strait Crises of 1995-1996 demonstrates that peace and stability in this region can no longer be taken for granted. According to a Pentagon report, the PRC now has 150-200 ballistic missiles aimed at Taiwan. North Korea's August 1998 missile launch and the nuclear tests conducted by Indian and Pakistan in May 1998 also add new challenges and complications for the United States.

Taiwan's most significant vulnerability is its limited capacity to defend against the growing arsenal of Chinese ballistic missiles. The Taiwan Relations Act states that "it is the policy of the United States ... to consider any effort to determine the future of Taiwan by other than peaceful means, including by boycotts or embargoes, a threat to the peace and security of the Western Pacific area and of grave concern to the United States." The Act also provides explicit language that the U.S. will make available defense articles and defense services in such quantities as may be necessary for Taiwan to maintain a sufficient self-defense capability. It is time to evaluate Taiwan's self-defense needs.

This study reviews the background, provisions, ambiguities and implementation of the Taiwan Relations Act (TRA) of 1979, followed by analysis of causes of the March 1996 crisis, and lessons for future U.S.-Taiwan relations.

BACKGROUND OF THE TRA

On November 26, 1974, Secretary of State and Assistant to the President for National Security Affairs, Henry A. Kissinger, met with the PRC Vice Premier Deng Xiaoping on the normalization issue. Kissinger proposed that a liaison office in Taiwan be maintained after U.S.-China normalization. The United States would accept Beijing as the legal government of China, withdraw recognition from Taiwan, break diplomatic relations with Taiwan, and withdraw U.S. troops from Taiwan. But the U.S. would like to keep the defense treaty with Taiwan as assurances of peaceful reintegration; however, Kissinger acknowledged that the defense treaty would have no international status after the normalization of relations. <3>

Vice Premier Deng told Kissinger that "it would not be possible for us to accept this method of normalization. It still looks as if you need Taiwan." Secretary of State Kissinger replied: No, we do not need Taiwan. That is not the issue. What we would like to achieve is the disassociation from Taiwan in steps, in the manner we have done until now.<4>

On December 15, 1978, President Jimmy Carter announced the establishment of full diplomatic relations with the PRC. The U.S. gave Taiwan one year's notice to terminate the Mutual Defense Treaty in accordance with Article 10 of the Treaty. The U.S.-ROC defense treaty expired at the end of December, 1979. The U.S. was not allowed to establish a liaison office in Taiwan after normalization with the PRC. Nor did the Carter Administration receive a firm commitment from Beijing not to use military force to attack Taiwan.<5> The Carter Administration considered China a "strategic imperative"; thus, it was not particularly concerned about the fate of Taiwan. It was generally believed at that time that Taiwan would soon be absorbed by the PRC.<6> The Republic of China government would have no choice but to agree to reunification on PRC terms.<7>

Taiwan was only given seven hours notice. The U.S. Congress was not consulted in the normalization agreement. In July 1978, the U.S. Senate had passed an amendment to the'

International Security Assistance Act by the unanimous 94-0 roll call vote that called on the President to consult with the Senate before taking any action to terminate the 1954 Mutual Defense Treaty with the Republic of China. The Dole-Stone amendment was later approved in a House-Senate conference meeting, making it a resolution of the full Congress.

Offended by the lack of a security guarantee for Taiwan in the normalization agreement, Congress took an active role in drafting the Taiwan Relations Act. On January 29, 1979, the Carter Administration sent a bill (S.245) to Congress providing for the conduct of unofficial U.S.-Taiwan relations (Appendix1). It contained a basic economic, cultural and functional framework, but did not have any provision on Taiwan's security guarantee, arms sales, or the privileges and immunities of unofficial organs. Congress found it unacceptable; Senator Frank Church, Chairman of the Foreign Relations Committee, believed that the bill was Awoefully inadequate to the task, ambiguous in language, and uncertain in tone.<8> After numerous hearings, Congress added many provisions in order to maintain continuing political and defense relationships between the U.S. and Taiwan. The Taiwan Relations Act (Public Law 96-8) was adopted by Congress on March 29, 1979, and was signed into law by President Carter on April 10, 1979 (Appendix2).

The Taiwan Relations Act is unique. The United States never broke relations with an ally, either before or after its passage. On December 19, 1978, President Carter stated in an interview that ATaiwan will no longer be a nation in the view of our own country.<9> The Republic of China government was no longer formally recognized by the United States; however, the Taiwan Relations Act, providing a new and unprecedented legal arrangement, has managed to maintain virtually all U.S.-Taiwan relationships that had existed before its passage.

The so-called American Institute in Taiwan (AIT) was created to take over all functions of former U.S. embassy and consular services in Taiwan. The "Coordination Council for North American Affairs (CCNAA)" was established to serve as a counterpart of the AIT. All treaties and agreements between the U.S. and the ROC, except the Mutual Defense Treaty, have continued in force. Section 4 of the Taiwan Relations Act declares that "the absence of diplomatic relations or recognition shall not affect the application of the laws of the United States with respect to Taiwan"; "whenever the laws of the United States refer or relate to foreign countries, nations, states, governments, or similar entities, such terms shall include and such laws shall apply with such respect to Taiwan." This section of the TRA, according to one authority, effectively wipes out all the international legal consequences of U.S. de-recognition of the Republic of China. <10>

In order to continue providing Taiwan with enriched uranium for nuclear power reactors, the U.S. continued to consider the ROC a "friendly government." For purposes of the U.S. Immigration and Nationality Act, the ROC continued to be treated as a country separate from the PRC.<11> U.S. investors in Taiwan continued to receive insurance protections under the U.S. Overseas Private Investment Council (OPIC). In addition, Washington and Taipei also reached an agreement to grant privileges and immunities to the CCNAA and the AIT for their personnel.<12> The Taiwan Relations Act also confirmed Taiwan=s continued eligibility under the U.S. Arms Export Control Act, the U.S. Export-Import Bank Act, the U.S. Foreign Assistance Act of 1961, and other U.S. legislation.<13>

ROCKY START: 1979-1980

The Taiwan Relations Act, adopted by the Congress at the end of March, 1979, was very different from the original bill (S.245) proposed by the Carter Administration. President Carter had considered vetoing the Act,<14> but decided otherwise because the TRA had been approved by more than two-thirds of the Congress (339-50 in the House and 85-4 in the Senate) and thus his veto would have been overridden.

Beijing, of course, did not like the TRA. On April 19, 1979, Vice-Premier Deng Xiaoping told a visiting delegation of the U.S. Senate Foreign Relations Committee that China was not satisfied with the TRA. President Carter indicated that when he executed the TRA, he would comply with the U.S.-PRC normalization agreements; China was watching the future behavior of the United States.<15>

The PRC secretly protested to the United States on April 28, 1978. It was revealed by the Chinese source that the U.S. Embassy in Beijing replied to the Chinese protest on July 6, 1979, as follows:

The United States shall comply with various understandings reached with the People's Republic of China on establishing diplomatic relations. The Taiwan Relations Act finally adopted by the Congress does not comply with the wishes of the [U.S.] government in every detail; however, it provides full discretionary authority to the President in dealing with [difficult] situations and enables the President to implement this Act in a manner fully consistent with the normalization formula. It is on that basis that the President signed this bill and made it law. The United States Government has ensured that the language used in this Act will not impair the understanding reached with your government or compel our government to take action deviating from such understanding.<16>

The process of adjustment to unofficial U.S.-Taiwan relations was rather complicated at the beginning. According to Charles T. Cross, the first Taipei Director of AIT (1979-1981), Deputy Secretary of State Warren Christopher had given him a brief instruction: Taiwan shouldn't do anything that would obstruct our relationship with the PRC.<17> Assistant Secretary for East Asian Affairs Richard Holbrooke, on the other hand, offered Cross an informal instruction: Atry to make the new set-up work but don=t ask for anything (i.e., changes in the arrangements) because we can't help.<18>

Cross relied on two basic principles to determine his own approach to AIT: first, productive and wide-ranging relations with the PRC were important to the U.S. and the rest of East Asia?including Taiwan?and that these were of the first priority; second, the 1978 U.S.-PRC Normalization Agreements provided adequate arrangements for good relations.<19> Cross's main challenge as AIT Director in Taipei was to avoid the appearance of doing official business while actually carrying it out in practice.<20> AIT's staff of career diplomats were not fully prepared for the multiplying administrative complexities, the required subtleties, the circumspection, and the constant attention to the details of unofficialty. <21>

The Carter Administration unilaterally developed guidelines on how U.S. Government personnel, AIT, and the CCNAA were to interact with each other to conduct "unofficial" relationship. The guidelines contained matters that included meetings, contacts, travel, correspondence, and terminology, among others.<22> Natale H. Bellocchi, Chairman of the AIT from 1990 to 1995, believed that these guidelines were costly and inefficient. They served the purpose of keeping the relationship, in appearance at least, as unofficial. None were mentioned in the TRA, but once established, they set a precedent, which, whenever one was changed, became an issue between Washington and Beijing.<23>

Charles T. Cross pointed out that the initial problems derived from the natural irritations that Taiwan officials felt with respect to the symbolic character of the rules.<24> Unfortunately, the people in Taiwan chafed at these symbols; the more publicity aroused by the symbolic details of unofficialty, the more strictly AIT had to apply them, and, consequently, the less chance there was to change them publicly.<25>

Director Cross had tried to persuade the Carter and Reagan Administrations to allow AIT to have some operating flexibility, but gained little support. Cross found that the Reagan Administration especially was responsive to PRC pressures over arms sales to Taiwan for what Secretary of State Alexander Haig, Jr. called the ASoviet Imperative.<26>

II. ASSESSMENT OF THE TRA

The TRA has provided a legal framework for the continuation of commercial, cultural, and other relations between the U.S. and Taiwan. It has stood the test of time. Trade between the United States and Taiwan has grown spectacularly over the last 20 years. In 1979, bilateral trade stood at a mere US $9.2 billion. In 1998, the figure was US $51.2 billion (see Table 1).<27> Taiwan is now America's the seventh largest trading partner. In 1998, Taiwan imported US $18.15 billion American goods and services; the PRC, on the other hand, has only imported US $14.25 billion. <28>

Meanwhile cultural relations between the U.S. and Taiwan have also been steadily expanding. In 1997, people in Taiwan made more than 588 thousand trips to the United States. More than 30 thousand students from Taiwan are currently studying in the United States. Scientific, technological and cultural exchanges have also been frequent. There are currently 117 bilateral treaties, agreements or memorandums of understanding between Taiwan and the United States. <29>

Section 2(c) of the TRA reaffirms "the preservation and enhancement of the human rights of all the people on Taiwan." After the U.S. severed diplomatic relations with the Republic of China, Taipei had tightened up its security forces against political dissidents for fear of domestic instability.

Table 1. United States - Taiwan Trade
(Figures in billions of U.S. Dollars)

Year	Total	U.S. Exports	U.S. Imports	U.S. Deficit
1979	9.2	3.3	5.9	2.6
1980	11.2	4.3	6.9	2.6
1981	12.4	4.3	8.1	3.8
1982	13.3	4.4	8.9	4.5
1983	15.9	4.7	11.2	6.5
1984	19.8	5.0	14.8	9.8
1985	22.4	4.7	17.7	13.0
1986	26.8	5.5	21.3	15.8
1987	33.8	7.4	26.4	19.0
1988	38.4	12.1	26.3	14.2

For additional analytical, marketing, investment and business opportunities information, please contact
Global Investment & Business Center, USA
(202) 546-2103. Fax: (202) 546-3275. E-mail: rusric@erols.com

1989	35.6	11.3	24.3	13.0
1990	34.2	11.5	22.7	11.2
1991	36.2	13.2	23.0	9.8
1992	39.9	15.3	24.6	9.3
1993	41.3	16.2	25.1	8.9
1994	43.8	17.1	26.7	9.6
1995	48.2	19.3	28.9	9.6
1996	48.4	18.5	29.9	11.4
1997	53.0	20.4	32.6	12.2
1998	51.2	18.1	33.1	14.9

Sources: United States Department of Commerce, International Trade Administration; United States Department of Commerce News, Washington, D.C., February 19, 1999, p.19.

The so-called 1979 Kaohsiung incident and trials, the murder of Lin Yi-hsiung's mother and twin daughters, Professor Chen Wen-cheng's death in 1981 and Henry Liu's murder in 1984, combined to cause great concern within the U.S. government and Congress. Congress had conducted a series of hearings to examine human rights violations and political developments in Taiwan. <30>

The ROC government was criticized for the ban on new political parties, martial law and the ban on certain publications. Taiwan's record on human rights has gradually improved since the mid-1980s. Martial law was lifted in July 1987. The ban on travel by residents of Taiwan to mainland China was abolished in November 1987. Restrictions on publishing newspapers and the ban on new political parties were removed in 1988 and 1989, respectively. The ROC has become a democratic country with direct election of the president in 1996. Taiwan is now a model of consolidating democracy with a free press, free elections, stable democratic institutions, and human rights protections. Thus Taiwan has gained more support and respect in the United States through its peaceful transformation to democracy.

The main purpose of the TRA is to help maintain peace, security, and stability in the Western Pacific. Section 2(b)(4) of the TRA considers any effort to determine the future of Taiwan by other than peaceful means, including by boycotts or embargoes, a threat to the peace and security of the Western Pacific area and of grave concerns to the United States. The TRA asserts that it is the policy of the U.S. to maintain American capability to resist any resort to force or other forms of coercion that would jeopardize the security, or the social or economic system, of the people on Taiwan. The TRA has provided a favorable and stable environment for the people on Taiwan to develop its economy and democracy.

Continuing U.S. arms sales to Taiwan also add to Taiwan's confidence in its dealing with the PRC. In September 1992, President George Bush decided to sell 150 F-16 aircraft to Taiwan. Seven months later, Dr. Koo Chen-fu, Chairman of the Strait Exchange Foundation(SEF), had first meeting with Mr. Wang Daohan, Chairman of the Association of Relations across the Taiwan Straits(ARTAS) in Singapore. U.S. arms sales have contributed to maintaining peace and stability in the Taiwan Strait and to creating an atmosphere conducive to the improvement of cross-strait relations, including dialogue.<31>

For additional analytical, marketing, investment and business opportunities information, please contact
Global Investment & Business Center, USA
(202) 546-2103. Fax: (202) 546-3275. E-mail: rusric@erols.com

III. SETBACKS OF THE TRA

In retrospect, the TRA undoubtedly has played a very important role in Taiwan's security and domestic political developments. There is room, however, for further improvements. Simply put, the U.S. has not lived up to either the letter or the spirit of the TRA. Indeed, during the past 20 years, there were several setbacks in the implementation of the TRA. Notable among them were: (1) the August 17, 1982 Communique; (2) the 1994 Policy Review to ban visits to the U.S. of Taiwan's top leadership; and (3) the recent "Three No's Pledge" by the U.S. to the PRC. Each setback merits brief analysis.

(1)The August 17, 1982 Communique

Sections 3(a) and 3(b) of the TRA set forth the provisions for implementing arms transfers by stating in 3(a) that the U.S. "*will* make available to Taiwan such defense articles and defense services in such quantity as may be *necessary* to enable Taiwan to maintain *sufficient* self-defense capability" (italics supplied). The ambiguity of the italicized words prompts the question of who decides what arms are necessary or sufficient for Taiwan's security. Section 3(b) appears to supply the answer, as follows:

(b) The President and the Congress *shall* determine the nature and quantity of such defense articles and services based *solely* upon their judgment of the needs of Taiwan, in accordance with the procedures established in by law. Such determination of Taiwan's defense needs shall include review by United States' military authorities in connection with recommendations to the President and the Congress.

The italicized sections in (a) and (b) above appear to unambiguously posit sole responsibility for determinining Taiwan's security needs in the United States -- namely U.S. military authorites, the President and the Congress -- without any regard to participation by PRC authorities. However, at the behest of the PRC, the August 17, 1982 Communique stated the intention of "the United States Government....to reduce gradually its sales of arms to Taiwan, leading over a period of time to a final resolution." The PRC interpreted this phrasing as implying the complete termination of U.S. arms sales to Taiwan over a period of time,[32] whereas President Ronald Reagan considered "final resolution" to apply to the Taiwan issue generally and not in particular to U.S. arms sales.[33]

Senator John Glenn, Chairman of the East Asia and Pacific Affairs Committee when the TRA became law, flatly stated that in his opinion the August 17 Communique "does undermine the spirit and intent of the TRA." He explained:

Now, because we anticipate the PRC would pressure us to end or limit Taiwan arms sales, we provided in the act's framework for the executive branch to resist such pressures... The communique.discards that very carefully crafted framework, the heart of the TRA, in favor of an arms sale formulation negotiated under Chinese threats of retrogression of United States-PRC relations.[34]

Beijing has continued to pressure Washington to reduce and eventually to terminate U.S. arms sales to Taiwan. Meanwhile, the August 17 , 1982 Communique has failed to put the arms sales issue to rest; instead this issue remains a main core of tensions between Washington and Beijing. The conclusion is inescapable, therefore, that whatever stability and security of Taiwan has been provided by the TRA remains jeopardized by the August 17, 1982 Communique.

**For additional analytical, marketing, investment and business opportunities information, please contact
Global Investment & Business Center, USA
(202) 546-2103. Fax: (202) 546-3275. E-mail: rusric@erols.com**

The Carter Administration insisted on continuing arms sales to Taiwan after the U.S.-PRC normalization in 1979 because: (1) arms sales to Taipei would give Taiwan more confidence in its defense capability against the People's Republic of China. Thus, Tiawan would not be panic or seek radical solutions, such as considering the nuclear option that would be contrary to United States interests; (2) continued arms sales to Taiwan could reduce suspicions and doubts from other U.S. allies about U.S. reliability in keeping its defense commitments in Asia; and (3) if Taiwan remained strong militarily, the PRC would be less likely to launch an attack on Taiwan.

Thus, continuing arms sales to Taiwan could provide the United States with more leverage in its conduct of foreign policy. This equation has not changed; therefore, in compliance to the Taiwan Relations Act, the United States should continue to ensure Taiwan has adequate means of self-defense (for details of U.S. arms sales to Taiwan, see Appendix 3).

(2)The 1994 Ban of Visits to the U.S. of Taiwan's Top Leadership

In September 1994, the U.S. State Department completed its first thorough review of U.S. policy toward Taiwan since 1979.[35] The Clinton Administration made some policy adjustments toward Taiwan. Under the new Taiwan policy, visits to the U.S. by Taiwan's top leaders (president, vice-president, premier, and vice-premier) would be forbidden, but they would allowed to make transit stops in the U.S. when necessary. Between 1979 and 1994, Taiwan's vice-president and premier had visited the U.S. in private capacities and had been treated with dignity by U.S. administrations. The 1994 policy adjustment clearly proved a step backward, in light of the Taiwan Strait Crisis of 1995-1996 that was actually rooted in this policy change.

From 1994 to 1995, the Clinton administration repeatedly assured China that Taiwan President Lee Teng-hui would not be admitted to the United States. However, responding to pressure from the Congress, Clinton reversed that decision in May 1995 and allowed President Lee to enter the United States. The Chinese authorities were enraged at what they saw as a broken U.S. promise, and the military exercises and missle "test firings" off Taiwan's shores soon followed. Had Clinton made no such assurance to China, the crisis could have been avoided.

Another setback was the 1994 policy change that allows meetings between high-level Taiwan officials and U.S. officials to take place in U.S. government offices, excluding the White House, the State Department, and the Old Executive Office Building, whereas AIT or other U.S. officials who visit Taiwan are permitted to meet Taiwanese officials in Taiwan's government offices. From Taiwan's perspective, these new policy stipulations are manifestly inequitable and is tantamount to more loss of face and unfair treatment of Taiwan's officials.

(3)Clinton's Three No's Pledge to the PRC

Another setback is represented by President Clinton's October 1997 meeting with Jiang Zemin in Washington when Clinton made the so-called "Three No's Pledge" to the PRC, promising (1) not to support Taiwan's independence; (2) not to support "Two Chinas" or "One China, One Taiwan"; and (3) not to support Taiwan's membership in any international organization based on statehood. These three pledges were repeated by Secretary of State Madeleine Albright during her visit to Beijing in April 1998. Clinton publicly reiterated this pledge in Shanghai on June 30, 1998.

A different tune was sounded by AIT Chairman Richard Bush's immediate reassurance to the Taiwan people who unabashedly said: "the United States policy toward Taiwan, in all its elements, remains the same today as it was before the summit." This was soon followed, in a *Newsweek* interview, by Secretary of State Madeleine Albright who reportedly asserted that "the president said exactly the kind of thing that previous presidents have said. I think there's an over-interpretation here. We have been for peaceful dialogue. The authorities on Taiwan understand the one-China policy and the need for peaceful cross-straits dialogue."<36>

The wording of the Shanghai Communique of 1972 is clear:" The United States acknowledges that all Chinese on either side of the Taiwan Strait maintain there is but one China and Taiwan is a part of China. The United States Government does not *challenge* that position. "The U.S. never recognizes or endorsed Beijing's position regarding Taiwan; it simply "acknowledged" it. This is a subtle but important distinction. In the two later communiques, the U.S. continues to *acknowledge* "the Chinese position that there is but one China and Taiwan is part of China," but it never *supports* this notion.

According to Nat Bellocchi, from 1979 to 1995, "it was standard policy by all who dealt with the PRC and Taiwan, that the U.S. does not respond to questions of support or non-support of independence."<37> So, at least in this sense, Bellocchi believed that Clinton's Three No's statement does represent a change of policy from the past.<38>

Futhermore, there is no statement at all in the three communiques about forbidding Taiwan's participation in international organnization. In fact, Section 4(d) of the TRA specifically states: "Nothing in this Act may be construed as a basis for supporting the exclusion or expulsion of Taiwan from continued membership in any international financial insititution or any other international organization." Still, Clinton maintains that his public statement that the United States will not support Taiwan's membership in any international organization based on statehood is nothing new. The Clinton Administration has conveninetly "over-interpreted" the three communique with the PRC in an attempt to portray his statements as entirely harmless and inoffensive. The claim made by the Clinton Administration that nothing has changed is deceptive and overly simplistic. The U.S. policy toward Taiwan has changed, albeit subtly, clearly to Taiwan's disadvantage.

The Clinton Administration may believe that stating acceptance of Beijing's position on these issues somehow will discourage China's leaders from acting rashly over Taiwan as they did in 1996. However, the opposite is more likely because the White House is allowing Beijing to drag it step by step into increasingly explicit support of China's agenda toward Taiwan while reducing Washington's room for maneuver in asserting its own long-range interests.

Kent Wiedemann, the Deputy Assistant Secretary of State for East Asian and Pacific Affairs, testified at a 1995 hearing by the House International Relations Committee that the United States should support Taiwan's participation in the United Nations only if Taiwan and China reach an agreement on that issue. He stated, "we should not seek to insert the United States into the middle of this issue."<39>

However, the "Three No's Pledge" changes this question. With the third pledge, the United States in a way forcecloses the possibility of Taiwan's membership in the United Nations and other international organizations comprised of sovereign states. By doing so , the United States has inserted itself into the issue at the expense of Taiwan's interests.

Some U.S. policy-makers may believe making these kinds of concessions to China will stabilize cross-strait relations. What they fail to realize, however, is the more rash promises the United States makes to China, the greater the likelihood that one of these promises will have to be broken when it clashes with other policy considerations.

IV. LESSONS FOR FUTURE U.S.-TAIWAN RELATIONS

**For additional analytical, marketing, investment and business opportunities information, please contact
Global Investment & Business Center, USA
(202) 546-2103. Fax: (202) 546-3275. E-mail: rusric@erols.com**

In his book *Why Nations Go to War*, John G. Stoessinger observed that the most important single precipitating factor in the outbreak of war is mis-perception.<40> Distorted views of the adversary's intentions and character often help to precipitate a conflict. One of the major causes of the Taiwan Crisis of 1995-1996 was Beijing's mis-perception of Washington and Taipei's motives. In addition, Washington's mismanagement of the decision to allow President Lee's private visit to the U.S. and Taipei's miscalculation of Beijing's reactions also contributed to the outbreak of the crisis.<41> In order to maintain peace and prevent conflict in the Taiwan Strait, it is appropriate here to draw some lessons from the past twenty years.

Lesson No. 1: Taiwan should remain aware that exploitation of TRA ambiguities by different U.S. administrations foster situational and/or inconsistent applications of TRA.

As we have observed, various divergent interpretations of the TRA have greatly complicated the issue of U.S. arms sales to Taiwan, thus putting Taiwan security at risk. Two major ambiguities, here discussed, concern different interpretations of the roles of the President and Congress in implementing the TRA.

The first ambiguity arises from the TRA's provision that "the President and the Congress shall determine" weapons transfers to Taiwan, which suggests an greater-than-normal congressional role. On the one hand, the U.S. Supreme Court held in 1936, concerning the issue of U.S. arms sales to South American countries, that the President had sweeping authority in the field of foreign affairs -- that the President alone had the constitutional power to speak or listen as a representative of the nation in its external relations.<42> On the other hand, on November 8, 1979, Congressman Robert Lagomarsino told Deputy Secretary of State Warren Christopher, at a House Foreign Affairs Committee hearing, "As the [TRA] states...this body and specifically this committee take a direct interest in the nature and quantity of arms sold to Taiwan and intend to be a full partner in any decision made on this matter.<43>

Regardless of the TRA language that imputes shared decision-making by Congress and the President over the issue of arms sales to Taiwan, the Carter Administration -- by referring to the TRA language that decisions about arms sales to Taiwan be made "in accordance with procedures established by law" -- proceeded to exclude Congress from the process altogether. According to Natale H. Bellocchi, former AIT chairman, the Carter Administration established a process for considering and then either approving or rejecting specific requests from Taiwan. Congress was notified only after the process was complete and the U.S. commitment, or rejection, had already been conveyed to Taiwan. Congressional objections did not prevail, and decisions regarding U.S. arms sales to Taiwan thereafter have been exclusively made by the President.<44>

The second TRA ambiguity, exploited by U.S. administrations to exclude Congressional participation, concerns Section 3(c) of the TRA which provides:

The President is directed to inform the Congress promptly of any *threat* to the security or the social or economic system of the people on Taiwan and any *danger* to the interests of the United States arising therefrom. The President and the Congress shall determine, in accordance with constitutional processes, appropriate action by the United States in response to any such *danger*. [italics supplied]

Over the past 20 years, the United States -- according to Bellocchi -- has avoided ever using the TRA's key operating word "threat" in describing any situation regarding activities in the Taiwan Strait.<45>

During the 1995-1996 missile crisis, for example, the Clinton Administration labeled PRC's missile tests as "irresponsible," but the word "threat" was not used. Moreover, Assistant Secretary of State Winston Lord described the tests as constituting "psychological warfare" against Taiwan and as "risky and provocative," but were not tantamount to a prelude to an attack on Taiwan. Although the Clinton Administration in March 1996 deployed two U.S. carriers to the waters near Taiwan "to monitor the activities of Chinese forces,[46] Secretary of Defense William Perry interposed: "We do not believe China plans to attack Taiwan. We do not expect military conflict there." And he added: "Nevertheless, we are increasing our naval presence in the region as a precautionary measure. [47]

The word "threat" again was avoided, and hence the necessity to inform Congress thereby was obviated. Despite the U.S. dispatch of the two carriers, the U.S. set a precedent of handling a Taiwan Strait crisis that circumvented participation by the Congress as seemingly directed by Section 3(c) of the TRA.

Lesson No. 2: The U.S. should not make to any country any promise that is against its fundamental national values.

In September 1994, the State Department announced the ban of to the U.S. of Taiwan's top leadership. Beijing argued that if someone visits, in whatever capacity, who is called the President of an entity, that would make an official visit.[48] Unfortunately the Clinton Administration went along with Beijing's position. In 1994-1995, senior U.S. officials had continued to assure the PRC that permitting a Lee visit would be inconsistent with U.S. unofficial ties with Taiwan. The administration's position was reiterated on April 17,1995 by Warren Christopher at a meeting in New York with Foreign Minister Qian Qichen.[49]

Secretary of State Christopher also indirectly warned Qian that the administration had so far been unsuccessful in arguing its case to Congress. Christopher told Qian that "many people in Congress, including good friends of Beijing, do not understand why a visit to the *alma mater* to pick up an honorary degree would have to be seen as official in nature.... The mood in the country was such that the administration position was not receiving overwhelming accolades," said Christopher.[50] Christopher's remark was intended as a veiled hint that a policy reversal was in the offing. But the hint was probably lost on Foreign Minister Qian.[51]

In 1972 and 1975, Presidents Nixon and Ford visited Beijing officially while recognizing the Republic of China on Taiwan as the legal government of China. At that time the PRC leaders did not think these visits were violations of the one-China principle. If official visits of U.S. Presidents to Beijing did not violate unofficial U.S.-PRC relations, then why should a private visit of President Lee be charged as a violation of unofficial ties between Washington and Taipei?

As a leader of democratic countries, the United States has always treasured the freedom of travel. The Clinton Administration should never have made any promises to Beijing to ban visits to the U.S. by Taiwan's top leadership. Any U.S. promise abroad, which is against its fundamental national values, would never enjoy the support of the American people. Without the support of the American public and Congress, the United States, like any other democratic nation, cannot long sustain its promises abroad. The Taiwan Crisis was rooted in a broken promise. The U.S. decision-makers should avoid making the same mistake in the future.

Lesson No. 3: The U.S. should slow down while making a U-turn.

In May 1995, the Clinton Administration's way of handling President Lee's visit suggests deep flaws. Leaders in Beijing were furious over Clinton's reversal of Lee's visit because Washington suddenly made a U-turn without giving any warning or prior preparation to the PRC.

In an interview with *Newsweek* in October 1995, President Jiang Zemin revealed that Beijing was stunned because Washington had flip-flopped on whether to grant a visa to President Lee. Jiang said:

After we got information that Lee Teng-hui was going to visit Cornell University, we raised this issue officially before the State Department of the United States. Secretary of State [Warren] Christopher firmly replied that if Lee Teng-hui's visit took place, it would represent [a] violation of the joint U.S. - Sino communiques. However, after seven or eight days, all of a sudden, the White House announced the decision allowing Lee Teng-hui to make the visit, and they said that it was consistent with the principles enshrined in the communiques. According to a Chinese proverb, with one turn of the hand you can produce clouds, with another turn of the hand you can produce rain. What I mean is, they always have a justification. They think they are always right .... This is a hegemonic act. This is not the right way to treat others as equals.<52>

On May 9-11, 1995, President Clinton visited Moscow to commemorate the 50th anniversary of V-E Day. Clinton and Jiang met but did not hold formal talks. Jiang pointed out in another interview that he chatted with Clinton in Moscow, but did not sense that a drama was in store for Beijing that is the visit of Lee Teng-hui to Cornell.<53>

Foreign Minister Qian Qichen felt betrayed by Clinton's reversal and made similar remarks in a statement issued by the PRC on March 23, 1995:

The U.S. administration has stated on many occasions that to allow Lee Teng-hui's visit to the United States would be inconsistent with the unofficial nature of U.S. - Taiwan relations. Until recently, the spokesperson of the U.S. State Department has said that a visit by a person of Lee Teng-hui's title, whether or not the visit were termed "private," would unavoidably be seen as changing the unofficial nature of U.S.- Taiwan relationship and would endanger one of the critical underpinnings of its unofficial relationship with Taiwan on the one hand and its official relationship with the PRC on the other. The sound of these remarks had barely subsided when the U.S. administration suddenly made a U-turn. Does the administration have any regard for its international credibility when it goes back on its own words on such a major issue of principle?<54>

In brief, leaders in Beijing felt humiliated by Clinton's U-turn decision. The dispute coincides with a period of uncertainty over the leadership succession in the PRC. Jiang, apparently under pressure from hard-liners, felt compelled to make a strong response to Clinton's turnaround on President Lee's visit. "The question of Taiwan is a highly sensitive issue for the Chinese people. If any Chinese leader yielded on this question, he could not face the 1.2 billion Chinese people," Jiang said.<55>

In 1992, President Bush had handled the reversal of F-16 sales to Taiwan very differently. President Bush made a U-turn; the PRC was very unhappy with Bush's decision. But it did not lead to a major political confrontation between Beijing and Washington. Why?

In June 1992, President Bush rejected Taipei's request to purchase the F-16 aircraft. On July 29, General Dynamics, the maker of the F-16, announced that it would have to lay off 5,800 workers by 1994. In a radio interview the following day, President Bush said he was taking "a new look" at

---

For additional analytical, marketing, investment and business opportunities information, please contact
Global Investment & Business Center, USA
(202) 546-2103. Fax: (202) 546-3275. E-mail: rusric@erols.com

the possibility of selling F-16s to Taiwan.<56> On August 5, some 200 U.S. Congressmen signed a petition urging President Bush to approve F16 sales to Taiwan to save American jobs. [57]

On September 2, 1992, President Bush announced the selling of 150 F-16A and F-16B aircraft to Taiwan. Domestic politics may have dictated the timing of Bush's announcement, but the sale was also the result of a careful policy review concerning the military balance between Beijing and Taipei.

The Bush Administration was concerned about the PRC's growing military expenditures, its purchase of advanced Sukhoi-27 warplanes from Russia, and its expansive territorial claims in the South China Sea.<58> The Bush Administration did not think the sale violated any of the existing bilateral agreements with the PRC because the U.S. could no longer provide the logistical support necessary to keep Taiwan's F-5E and F-104 aircraft flying. It was therefore necessary to support a somewhat newer fighter or provide none at all.<59>

According to Douglas H. Paal, former Senior Director of Asian Affairs of the National Security Council (NSC), the Bush Administration handled the reversal of F-16 sales to Taiwan issue very carefully so as to mute Beijing's reaction. President Bush sent high-level personal diplomatic and military emissaries, led by Assistant Secretary for State for East Asian and Pacific Affairs William Clark, to Beijing to explain the bilateral justification and military implications of the sale. Bush also invited a well-placed Chinese official, who was visiting the U.S. before the decision's announcement, to the White House and explained the decision to him personally.<60> In addition, the Bush Administration decided to close out four cases of suspended Foreign Military Sales (FMS) to the PRC, which was part of the sanctions imposed by President Bush against China in June 1989. High level visits to the PRC were resumed as well, with the trip of the U.S. Commerce Secretary Barbara Franklin.

The four suspended programs covered by this decision involved an avionics upgrade for the Chinese F-8 aircraft, equipment for a munitions production line, four anti-submarine torpedoes, and two artillery-locating radars. The Bush Administration believed that "continuing to hold aging items after a 32-year suspension hinders rather than helps U.S. efforts to promote cooperative PRC behavior in a range of areas."[61] The decision was formally announced by the State Department on December 22, 1992.

Beijing, of course, strongly opposed the F-16 sale. Vice Foreign Minister Liu Huaqui summoned Ambassador J. Stapleton Roy and lodged a strong protest, accusing Washington of violating the August 17, 1982 U.S.-China Joint Communique. The PRC press, on the other hand, denounced the F-16 sale decision with terms like "short-sighted," "perfidious," "lying," and "treacherous," and threatened a terrible setback and cooling in U.S.-PRC relations.<62>

Beijing's actual retaliation, however, was minimal. The PRC briefly delayed several import deals C notably for commercial aircraftCfrom the U.S., but that was about all.<63> On September 28, 1992, President Bush vetoed a congressional bill (H.R. 5318) that put conditions on the renewal of China's MFN status for 1993-1994.[64] Beijing warmly welcomed Bush's action. In spite of the F-16 sale to Taiwan, George Bush was still Beijing's best friend in Washington.<65>

Later, under the Clinton Administration, Beijing began to link the non-proliferation issue with the F-16 sale. When the Clinton Administration asked the PRC for talks about its sale of M-11 missiles to Pakistan, Beijing replied that it would do so only if the U.S. agreed to discuss the F-16 sale.<66> In a March 1,1994 interview, Shen Guofeng, Deputy Director of the information Department at the PRC Ministry of Foreign Affairs, said: "when the United States talks about non-proliferation, the U.S. should take note of its arms sales to Taiwan."<67> Nevertheless, the F-16 sale to Taiwan did not lead to a political crisis between Washington and Beijing during the Bush Administration.

The Clinton Administration should learn from the Taiwan Strait crisis of 1995-1996. It should avoid making a fast U-turn in the future. It should slow down and give warnings to all passengers on board.

Lesson No. 4: Beijing's military actions toward Taiwan increase fears of the "China threat" and thwarts its unification goal.

The Clinton Administration has repeatedly stated that the U.S. policy toward China is "comprehensive engagement."[68] Leaders in Beijing, however, believe Washington has a long-term strategy of containment. It holds that U.S. Government officials are basically opposed to the rising power of China and are taking a variety of measures in various policy areas, including Taiwan, in order to "hold back" and weaken China's power. [69]

Secretary of Defense William Perry has stated in 1995 that containment would only provoke reflexive and intractable Chinese opposition to U.S.-led security initiatives in the U.N. and other multilateral bodies. If the United States were to adopt a containment policy toward the PRC, Perry believes that all of these results are not only possible, but they are probable.[70] For the same reason, if the PRC believes the U.S. is containing her, she may react in reflexive and intractable ways⊂the "China threat" may become real.

Winston Lord pointed out in 1995 that there is a growing perception in some quarters of the PRC that the U.S. is trying to foster an independent Taiwan as part of an effort to "contain" China.[71] The U.S. decision to allow President Lee Teng-hui to visit Cornell University has reinforced PRC suspicions that Washington had decided to "contain" China in a new cold war in Asia. Beijing's sharp reactions, including widely publicized military exercises and ballistic missile tests near Taiwan, have increased fears of the "China threat" and strengthened the hands of those U.S. officials who are deeply suspicious of, or hostile to, the PRC government.[72]

China's reactions to President Lee's U.S. visit dampened the enthusiasm of some countries, including Japan and the European Community, to follow the U.S. lead in granting greater recognition to Taiwan's government and leaders. China's missile firings and ground, air, and naval exercises were supposed to make Taiwanese think twice about President Lee, but they did not intimidate voters in Taiwan. In March 1996, President Lee won 54% of the vote in a four-way race. In addition, the missile exercises off Taiwan's coast in March 1996 attracted more than 700 reporters from all over the world to Taiwan. The ROC's first Presidential election was thrust into the international spotlight, to Beijing's surprise.

Leaders in Beijing may believe military threats and diplomatic pressures are its best tools for dealing with pro-independence advocates in Taiwan. But according to public opinion polls, Beijing's missile threats had actually prompted more support for independence in Taiwan. In 1994-1995, before Beijing's missile threats, more of the Taiwanese public favored unification than independence (see Table 2). After PRC's first missile exercise in July 1995, support for unification has gradually decreased in Taiwan. In March 1996, for the first time, more Taiwanese favored independence (18%) than unification (15%), although the majority of those polled (more than 40%) still favored the status quo. Leaders of the PRC should learn that military threats against Taiwan increase fears of the "China threat" and thwart its goal of unification.

Lesson No. 5: Agreements to resolve conflicts have no effect if they are not observed.

Experience suggests that the United States' disposition has been to negotiate or support agreements to resolve major conflicts, regardless of their efficacy or consequences over time that nullified them. Thus, Henry Kissinger was lauded for the Paris Peace Accord between the North and South Vietnam of 1973, then considered a major breakthrough; yet, thereafter this so-called agreement proved meaningless, the war continued, and North Vietnam won the war in 1975.

Similarly, the 1992 Basic Agreement between North and South Korea on Reconciliation, Nonagression, and Exchange and Cooperation, declaring the "denuclearization" of the Korean Peninsula, though strongly supported by the United States, proved unavailing. As Kissinger, himself, was to warn after the Paris Agreement faltered:

No settlement is self-enforcing. It is not possible to write an agreement whose terms, in themselves, guarantee its performance.Any agreement will last if the hostility of the parties is thereby lessened, if the parties have an incentive to observe it, and/or if the parties pay a penalty for breaking it.If those three conditions are not met, no matter what the terms of the agreement, there is a tendency toward erosion.<73>

Regardless of U.S. disavowals of interference in the resolution of differences between Taiwan and the PRC, a recent statement by Assistant Secretary of State Stanley Roth that "thinking" about "interim agreements" might contribute to cross-strait dialogue suggests a continuing U.S. disposition in support of agreements regardless of Kissinger's caveats. <74>

According to the Mainland Affairs Council of Taiwan's Executive Yuan, over 205 "relaxing measures" on cross-strait relations since 1987 have resulted in cultural and educational exchanges, personnel visits, and economic relations between Taiwan and the PRC. Nevertheless, the Council has charged the PRC with breaking at least 25 promises from 1993 to 1997.<75> In view of current tensions and anxieties aroused by the menace of PRC missile threats, now may be a time for developing more confidence-building or peace-advancing measures as conditions precedent to achieving any meaningful agreements.

Lesson No. 6: The U.S.-Taiwan-PRC triangular relationship should be conditioned by regional and global strategic considerations.

With the demise of the USSR, and the end of the Cold War, the PRC's regional and global strategy has been to foster a balanced multipolar world in place of its perception of an unbalanced unipolar world dominated by the U.S. as the sole global superpower.

Regionally, for example, the PRC has initiated trade and diplomatic relations with South Korea while acting as a constraint on North Korea bellicosity. Perhaps more important, the PRC has sought to forge comprehensive partnerships or cooperative relations one-by-one with other important countries -- as for example Britain, Germany and France in Europe, and Pakistan, Japan and all ASEAN countires in Asia -- while engaging in constructive strategic relationships with the preeminently powerful Russia and the United States.

Table 2. Attitudes toward Independence or Unification in Taiwan, 1994-1997

Date	Unification(%)	Independence(%)	Status Quo(%)
1994.07.07	26	17	34
1995.02.08	23	15	40

For additional analytical, marketing, investment and business opportunities information, please contact
Global Investment & Business Center, USA
(202) 546-2103. Fax: (202) 546-3275. E-mail: rusric@erols.com

1995.07.14	20	15	42
1995.07.21	20	14	46
1995.08.14	19	15	44
1995.11.24	19	12	45
1996.01.29	17	14	49
1996.02.28	17	14	45
1996.03.08	16	17	46
1996.03.11	17	16	46
1996.03.22	15	18	46
1996.09.13	19	19	42
1996.12.05	19	21	45
1997.01.30	19	20	41
1997.04.04	17	17	45
1997.05.31	16	21	44
1997.06.28	16	20	43
1997.07.02	19	24	43

Source: Public Opinion Center of the United Daily, *United Daily*, July 4, 1997, p.2
(Percentages of respondents answering "no opinion" or "no answer" are not shown.)

The essence of PRC's "great power diplomacy" is apparent, namely to reduce, if not to isolate, the influence of the United States in world affairs. To the extent that this PRC strategy becomes successful, the U.S. influence and dominance in East Asia is bound to be mitigated, thus vitally affecting Taiwan's security.

Lesson No. 7: Promotion of Taipei's international status always carries risks.

Taiwan cannot expect the U.S. administration to take the initiative in upgrading relations; it must take a proactive stance. Examples of developments brought about by Taipei's pressure on Washington are abundant: U.S. support of Taiwan's standing in the Asian Development Bank (ABD); support for Taiwan in the Asia-Pacific Economic Cooperation (APEC) in 1991; support for Taiwan's observer status in the General Agreement on Tariffs and Trade (GATT) in 1992; the sale of 150 FX fighter planes to Taiwan in 1992; high-level interchanges between U.S. and Taiwan leaders, including U.S. Trade Representative Carla Hills and Secretary of Transportation Federico F. Pena's visits to Taiwan in 1992 and 1994, respectively.

The PRC will always oppose attempts to upgrade relations between Washington and Taipei. Promotion of Taipei's international status, therefore, always carries risks. In 1981-1982, for example, Taiwan wanted to purchase FX fighter planes, and in return saw the United States-PRC Joint Communique issued on August 17, 1982, which restricted arms sales to Taiwan.[76] In 1994, Taipei endeavored to win permission from Washington for President Lee's private visit to the U.S.; the State Department, instead, announced policy adjustments toward Taiwan in

September 1994, which forbid visits to the U.S. by Taiwan's top leadership. Taipei must bear in mind that any significant request is always discussed openly in Washington within the context of Beijing-Washington-Taipei relationships, and such discussion always carries risks.

The Republic of China has become an emerging democracy, the people in Taiwan demand that their leaders take concrete actions to upgrade the ROC's international status. If U.S. interests are well served by supporting democracy and human rights abroad, as the Clinton Administration and most Americans believe, such support must entail treating the ROC and its leaders with respect and dignity. The United States should continue to play an active role in Asia and be willing to exercise leadership and develop a coherent policy to promote freedom and democracy in this region. The time has come for the U.S. to take a truly balanced approach toward Beijing and Taipei.

Leaders in Beijing should realize that the use of force against Taiwan is counterproductive and will severely damage its own interests and thwart its unification goal. Disputes between Beijing and Taipei should be resolved through peaceful means. The Taiwan Strait Crisis of 1995-1996 has eased, but Washington-Beijing-Taipei relations remain in a delicate state. In order to prevent future crises from happening, leaders in Washington, Beijing, and Taipei should reexamine their own role in the crisis and draw lessons from the events of the past twenty years.

TAIWAN ARMS SALES - DSAA FISCAL YEAR SERIES (DOLLARS IN THOUSANDS)

Year	Total Sales Agreements	Total Sales Deliveries	FMS Agreements	FMS Deliveries	Commercial Exports Deliveries
1950	1	-	1	-	-
1967	14,362	4,320	14,362	4,230	-
1973	204,241	66,264	204,241	66,264	6,001
1977	140,542	142,224	140,542	142,224	46,140
1978	324,514	134,178	423,514	134,178	73,637
1979	547,205	180,751	547,205	180,751	44,547
1980	480,601	210,373	480,601	210,373	57,770
1981	310,525	373,425	310,525	373,425	66,731
1982	501,546	386,374	501,546	386,374	75,000
1983	628,749	386,803	628,749	386,803	85,000
1984	693,577	298,327	693,577	298,327	70,000
1985	679,391	337,308	679,391	337,308	54,463
1986	504,300	249,264	504,300	249,164	228,400
1987	506,478	357,265	506,478	357,265	210,000
1988	498,513	503,106	498,513	503,106	195,069

For additional analytical, marketing, investment and business opportunities
information, please contact
Global Investment & Business Center, USA
(202) 546-2103. Fax: (202) 546-3275. E-mail: rusric@erols.com

1989	521,702	393,499	521,702	393,499	84,753
1990	500,286	454,777	500,286	454,777	149,963
1991	479,996	549,381	479,996	549,381	160,041
1992	477,904	711,405	477,904	711,405	95,610
1993	6,275,524*	817,953	6,274,904*	817,571	346,026
1994	360,891	845,267	360,891	845,116	261,869
1995	208,003	1,352,657*	208,003	1,352,657*	27,760
1996	459,865	852,576	459,865	852,576	20,392
1997	353,737	5,696,155*	353,737	5,696,155*	261,136

* F-16 costs

**For additional analytical, marketing, investment and business opportunities information, please contact
Global Investment & Business Center, USA
(202) 546-2103. Fax: (202) 546-3275. E-mail: rusric@erols.com**

IMPORTANT DOCUMENTS DEFINING US – TAIWAN RELATIONS

U.S.-TAIWAN RELATIONS

Randall Schriver, Deputy Assistant Secretary of State for East Asian and Pacific Affairs
Remarks to U.S.-Taiwan Business Council Defense Industry Conference
San Antonio, Texas
February 14, 2003

Secretary Cohen, Vice Minister Chen, distinguished guests, I am honored to speak to you today. I want to thank the U.S.-Taiwan Business Council for giving me this opportunity to address you and comment on issues that are of great interest to both the U.S. and Taiwan.

When this council met last year, we were in the early stages of our campaign against global terrorism. From then to now, we remain united in the fight against terrorism. We have had support from friends around the world. And I say with sincere gratitude, that includes our friends in Taiwan. Taiwan President Chen Shui-bian was among the first world leaders to express his support for the United States after September 11. On behalf of A/S Kelly, I would like to express once again our thanks to President Chen and his representatives here, Vice Minister Chen and Representative C.J. Chen, for Taiwan's continuing and steadfast support to our country in these challenging times.

Taiwan has taken important steps in its commitment to the global war against terrorism. Terrorism is a worldwide problem which will continue to require a response from nations on every continent. There are many dangers still facing us. Last week, Secretary of State Powell laid out our case against Iraq's ongoing efforts to develop weapons of mass destruction and continued violations of United Nations Security Council Resolution 1441. On the Korean Peninsula, we continue to work with our allies and regional neighbors for a diplomatic solution to North Korea's nuclear weapons development. We appreciate Taiwan's support on these issues and its acknowledgement that weapons of mass destruction are a grave threat to the peace and stability of the world as well as Taiwan's commitment to support the U.S.-led global war on terrorism operations.

Taiwan is also, as our colleagues in private industry know well, a key economic power in the region and the world. It is the U.S.' eighth-largest trading partner. As of November 2002, the U.S. exported $16.9 billion worth of goods to Taiwan, and imported $29.4 billion. Taiwan is a world leader in several key IT areas such as notebook computers, LCD displays, and associated technologies. Taiwan is also positioning itself to be a player in emerging fields like biotechnology.

While there are many variables in the global environment as we work to bring together cooperative efforts to achieve our common purpose, a constant in this environment continues to be the mutual friendship between the people of the United States and Taiwan. Our policy toward Taiwan and the P.R.C. has not changed. Our policy has been consistent for more than 20 years. It is articulated in the Taiwan Relations Act, the Three U.S.-China joint communiques, and the Six Assurances. It has not changed. It will not change.

America's best interests and those of people on both sides of the Taiwan Strait are advanced by a candid, constructive, and cooperative relationship between the United States and the P.R.C. We have some continuing differences with the P.R.C. Our interaction with the P.R.C. on these matters serves global interests. We believe that it also strengthens mutual understanding between our two countries and supports U.S. and Taiwan interests in security, stability, and prosperity.

But let me reiterate what A/S Kelly has said many times: we will not improve our relations with China at Taiwan's expense. We seek the reduction of cross-Strait tensions. We have called on the P.R.C. to renounce the use of force and reduce military deployments targeted against Taiwan. We encourage the P.R.C. to show more transparency in this area to build trust and reduce tensions across the Taiwan Strait. We are convinced we can do this as we pursue with the P.R.C. a broad range of U.S. strategic interests ranging from human rights, counterterrorism, and non-proliferation to regional stability and trade.

The U.S. has an abiding interest, above all else, in the peaceful resolution of cross-Strait differences. It is our fundamental objective in our relations with Taiwan and the P.R.C. To that end, we are very encouraged by the expansion of peaceful, mutually beneficial cross-Strait interactions in the areas of trade, investment, culture, and education.

Our position continues to be embodied in the so-called "six assurances" offered to Taiwan by President Reagan. We will neither seek to mediate between the P.R.C. and Taiwan, nor will we exert pressure on Taiwan to come to the bargaining table. Of course, the United States is also committed to make available defensive arms and defensive services to Taiwan in order to help Taiwan meet its self-defense needs. A secure and self-confident Taiwan is a Taiwan that is more capable of engaging in political interaction and dialogue with the P.R.C.

The United States has provided Taiwan with a significant quantity of defensive weapons over the last 20 years, and during that period has been Taiwan's most reliable supplier of weapons. We continue to fulfill our commitment under the Taiwan Relations Act to provide for Taiwan's legitimate defensive needs. We have assisted Taiwan's military modernization program. In doing so, the United States is careful to provide weapons that are defensive in nature and which would not destabilize the cross-Strait situation.

The U.S. Government remains committed to maintaining our dialogue with Taiwan about its national security. The process through which we review Taiwan's defensive requirements has evolved from the annual Arms Sales Talks to a more normal process.

This new framework for dialogue more effectively meets our respective practical requirements. We continue to work with Taiwan on determining the defensive capabilities it will need in the medium- to long-term.

The U.S.-Taiwan relationship, although not formal, has succeeded in enhancing Taiwan's security and regional stability. Our military cooperation is healthy and robust. We both have a fundamental interest in the stability of the Taiwan Strait and the peaceful resolution of differences. Taiwan's ability to defend itself is essential to create the conditions that are conducive to peaceful dialogue, which contributes to regional stability as a whole. President Bush has stated U.S. intent with regard to the P.R.C.'s use of force against Taiwan. At the same time, we expect that there will be no surprises and no attempt to unilaterally change the status quo in the Taiwan Strait.

Taiwan's leaders have made it clear that it is committed to a strong defense, but that Taiwan's security in the long term requires reaching out to the other side to begin moving toward a peaceful resolution of cross-Strait differences. The United States supports you in both efforts.

Taiwan's implementation of the National Defense Law and the revised Ministry of National Defense Organization Law has brought Taiwan's military command and administrative structures more clearly under civilian control. As Taiwan's political and military leaders have recognized, Taiwan's military needs to reform. There are several elements of this reform program that are underway and we realize you are still adjusting to this reorganization as your military carries out ongoing transitions. But much still needs to be done.

Today's military challenges require coordination across military service lines and a joint perspective of military operations. This perspective must be tied into the realities of deterring and defending Taiwan against modern air and sea forces. The P.R.C. is engaged in an accelerated force modernization program. Taiwan is vulnerable to air and missile threats from the P.R.C. Taiwan's lack of an integrated Anti-Submarine Warfare (ASW) capability is another vulnerability.

We urge Taiwan to take the steps needed to acquire defensive weapons and systems sufficient to address the ever increasing threat posed by the P.R.C. Modernization of Taiwan's command and control architecture continues to be a key priority to achieve this capability. Additionally, acquiring modern systems for air and missile defense, and integrated ASW are essential for Taiwan's self-defense as well as to provide an effective deterrence to potential adversaries. They also fill critical gaps in your self-defense that would make the difference in giving you time and preserving your options.

Taiwan's efforts to offset the PLA's increasing capabilities will depend on the vision and leadership of its civilian and military leaders. Decisions to ensure Taiwan's deterrent capability will require an effective national security structure of professional civilians and military officers prepared to make the right acquisition choices and implement them.

In the area of acquisition and armaments, Taiwan's Ministry of National Defense is in the process of developing the expertise and organization, including a cadre of civilian leaders, that will help to prioritize weapons acquisitions in an atmosphere of declining budgets. In support of these efforts we are engaged in a range of interactions with MND. We want to see Taiwan build a self-defense capability that is flexible, joint, and responsive to civilian control. Through our dialogue, our two sides are coming to understand better each other's way of thinking about security issues.

We are greatly interested in the progress of Taiwan's current defense reforms. This reform program is essential for Taiwan's military to achieve greater efficiency in joint operations, ensure a modernized force structure, and strengthen civilian control. The challenge is to continue to make progress along this path. Taiwan's military doctrine should enable its forces to be able to respond effectively to the new and emerging challenges facing Taiwan's security. It must demonstrate that its armed services can work jointly to counter threats such as integrated precision air strikes, ballistic and cruise missile attacks, blockade, information warfare, special operations forces actions, and electronic warfare. As Taiwan implements reorganization and reform, we must remember that the full benefits are still years away. We encourage our friends to implement the actions in the near term that you need to improve your joint operations capabilities and readiness.

The differences between the P.R.C and Taiwan are fundamentally political, not social, economic, or military. However, Taiwan must be prepared for military contingencies as a last resort. The United States has a long term interest in the peaceful resolution of cross-strait relationships. We are committed to help create the conditions for security that are conducive to political freedom and economic growth. We hope for renewal of cross-Strait dialogue so that Taiwan and the P.R.C. move closer to their ultimate peaceful resolution of the differences that separate them.

**For additional analytical, marketing, investment and business opportunities information, please contact
Global Investment & Business Center, USA
(202) 546-2103. Fax: (202) 546-3275. E-mail: rusric@erols.com**

It is the responsibility of people on both sides of the Taiwan Strait to make that happen. Taiwan's military can help create and ensure the conditions for security and stability that foster cooperation and dialogue over coercion and conflict.

To the leaders of Taiwan's defense community gathered here today, your participation in this conference is an important sign of your commitment to achieve this goal. Once again, I am honored to have this opportunity to address you and look forward to the rest of the sessions today.

TAIWAN RELATIONS ACT PUBLIC LAW 96-8 96TH CONGRESS

An Act

To help maintain peace, security, and stability in the Western Pacific and to promote the foreign policy of the United States by authorizing the continuation of commercial, cultural, and other relations between the people of the United States and the people on Taiwan, and for other purposes.

Be it enacted by the Senate and House of Representatives of the United States of America in Congress assembled,

SHORT TITLE

SECTION 1. This Act may be cited as the "Taiwan Relations Act".

FINDINGS AND DECLARATION OF POLICY

- SEC. 2. (a) The President- having terminated governmental relations between the United States and the governing authorities on Taiwan recognized by the United States as the Republic of China prior to January 1, 1979, the Congress finds that the enactment of this Act is necessary--
  - (1) to help maintain peace, security, and stability in the Western Pacific; and
  - (2) to promote the foreign policy of the United States by authorizing the continuation of commercial, cultural, and other relations between the people of the United States and the people on Taiwan.
- (b) It is the policy of the United States--
  - (1) to preserve and promote extensive, close, and friendly commercial, cultural, and other relations between the people of the United States and the people on Taiwan, as well as the people on the China mainland and all other peoples of the Western Pacific area;
  - (2) to declare that peace and stability in the area are in the political, security, and economic interests of the United States, and are matters of international concern;
  - (3) to make clear that the United States decision to establish diplomatic relations with the People's Republic of China rests upon the expectation that the future of Taiwan will be determined by peaceful means;

- (4) to consider any effort to determine the future of Taiwan by other than peaceful means, including by boycotts or embargoes, a threat to the peace and security of the Western Pacific area and of grave concern to the United States;
- (5) to provide Taiwan with arms of a defensive character; and
- (6) to maintain the capacity of the United States to resist any resort to force or other forms of coercion that would jeopardize the security, or the social or economic system, of the people on Taiwan.
- (c) Nothing contained in this Act shall contravene the interest of the United States in human rights, especially with respect to the human rights of all the approximately eighteen million inhabitants of Taiwan. The preservation and enhancement of the human rights of all the people on Taiwan are hereby reaffirmed as objectives of the United States.

IMPLEMENTATION OF UNITED STATES POLICY WITH REGARD TO TAIWAN

- SEC. 3. (a) In furtherance of the policy set forth in section 2 of this Act, the United States will make available to Taiwan such defense articles and defense services in such quantity as may be necessary to enable Taiwan to maintain a sufficient self-defense capability.
- (b) The President and the Congress shall determine the nature and quantity of such defense articles and services based solely upon their judgment of the needs of Taiwan, in accordance with procedures established by law. Such determination of Taiwan's defense needs shall include review by United States military authorities in connection with recommendations to the President and the Congress.
- (c) The President is directed to inform the Congress promptly of any threat to the security or the social or economic system of the people on Taiwan and any danger to the interests of the United States arising therefrom. The President and the Congress shall determine, in accordance with constitutional processes, appropriate action by the United States in response to any such danger.

APPLICATION OF LAWS; INTERNATIONAL AGREEMENTS

- SEC. 4. (a) The absence of diplomatic relations or recognition shall not affect the application of the laws of the United States with respect to Taiwan, and the laws of the United States shall apply with respect to Taiwan in the manner that the laws of the United States applied with respect to Taiwan prior to January 1, 1979.
- (b)The application of subsection (a) of this section shall include, but shall not be limited to, the following:
  - (1) Whenever the laws of the United States refer or relate to foreign countries, nations, states, governments, or similar entities, such terms shall include and such laws shall apply with such respect to Taiwan.
  - (2) Whenever authorized by or pursuant to the laws of the United States to conduct or carry out programs, transactions, or other relations with respect to foreign countries, nations, states, governments, or similar entities, the President or any agency of the United States Government is authorized to conduct and carry out, in accordance with section 6 of this Act, such programs, transactions, and other relations with respect to Taiwan (including, but not limited to, the performance of services for the United States through contracts with commercial entities on Taiwan), in accordance with the applicable laws of the United States.
  - (3)(A) The absence of diplomatic relations and recognition with respect to Taiwan shall not abrogate, infringe, modify, deny, or otherwise affect in any way any rights or obligations (including but not limited to those involving contracts, debts, or property interests of any kind) under the laws of the United States heretofore or hereafter acquired by or with respect to Taiwan.
  - (B) For all purposes under the laws of the United States, including actions in any court in the United States, recognition of the People's Republic of China shall not affect in any way the ownership of or other rights or interests in properties, tangible and intangible, and other things of value, owned or held on or prior to December 31, 1978, or thereafter acquired or earned by the governing authorities on Taiwan.

- (4) Whenever the application of the laws of the United States depends upon the law that is or was applicable on Taiwan or compliance therewith, the law applied by the people on Taiwan shall be considered the applicable law for that purpose.
- (5) Nothing in this Act, nor the facts of the President's action in extending diplomatic recognition to the People's Republic of China, the absence of diplomatic relations between the people on Taiwan and the United States, or the lack of recognition by the United States, and attendant circumstances thereto, shall be construed in any administrative or judicial proceeding as a basis for any United States Government agency, commission, or department to make a finding of fact or determination of law, under the Atomic Energy Act of 1954 and the Nuclear Non-Proliferation Act of 1978, to deny an export license application or to revoke an existing export license for nuclear exports to Taiwan.
- (6) For purposes of the Immigration and Nationality Act, Taiwan may be treated in the manner specified in the first sentence of section 202(b) of that Act.
- (7) The capacity of Taiwan to sue and be sued in courts in the United States, in accordance with the laws of the United States, shall not be abrogated, infringed, modified, denied, or otherwise affected in any way by the absence of diplomatic relations or recognition.
- (8) No requirement, whether expressed or implied, under the laws of the United States with respect to maintenance of diplomatic relations or recognition shall be applicable with respect to Taiwan.
- (c) For all purposes, including actions in any court in the United States, the Congress approves the continuation in force of all treaties and other international agreements, including multilateral conventions, entered into by the United States and the governing authorities on Taiwan recognized by the United States as the Republic of China prior to January 1, 1979, and in force between them on December 31, 1978, unless and until terminated in accordance with law.
- (d) Nothing in this Act may be construed as a basis for supporting the exclusion or expulsion of Taiwan from continued membership in any international financial institution or any other international organization.

OVERSEAS PRIVATE INVESTMENT CORPORATION

- SEC. 5. (a) During the three-year period beginning on the date of enactment of this Act, the $1,000 per capita income restriction in insurance, clause (2) of the second undesignated paragraph of section 231 of the reinsurance, Foreign Assistance Act of 1961 shall not restrict the activities of the Overseas Private Investment Corporation in determining whether to provide any insurance, reinsurance, loans, or guaranties with respect to investment projects on Taiwan.
- (b) Except as provided in subsection (a) of this section, in issuing insurance, reinsurance, loans, or guaranties with respect to investment projects on Taiwan, the Overseas Private Insurance Corporation shall apply the same criteria as those applicable in other parts of the world.

THE AMERICAN INSTITUTE OF TAIWAN

- SEC. 6. (a) Programs, transactions, and other relations conducted or carried out by the President or any agency of the United States Government with respect to Taiwan shall, in the manner and to the extent directed by the President, be conducted and carried out by or through--
  - (1) The American Institute in Taiwan, a nonprofit corporation incorporated under the laws of the District of Columbia, or
  - (2) such comparable successor nongovermental entity as the President may designate, (hereafter in this Act referred to as the "Institute").
- (b) Whenever the President or any agency of the United States Government is authorized or required by or pursuant to the laws of the United States to enter into, perform, enforce, or have in force an agreement or transaction relative to Taiwan, such agreement or transaction

shall be entered into, performed, and enforced, in the manner and to the extent directed by the President, by or through the Institute.

- (c) To the extent that any law, rule, regulation, or ordinance of the District of Columbia, or of any State or political subdivision thereof in which the Institute is incorporated or doing business, impedes or otherwise interferes with the performance of the functions of the Institute pursuant to this Act; such law, rule, regulation, or ordinance shall be deemed to be preempted by this Act.

SERVICES BY THE INSTITUTE TO UNITED STATES CITIZENS ON TAIWAN

- SEC. 7. (a) The Institute may authorize any of its employees on Taiwan--
  - (1) to administer to or take from any person an oath, affirmation, affidavit, or deposition, and to perform any notarial act which any notary public is required or authorized by law to perform within the United States;
  - (2) To act as provisional conservator of the personal estates of deceased United States citizens; and
  - (3) to assist and protect the interests of United States persons by performing other acts such as are authorized to be performed outside the United States for consular purposes by such laws of the United States as the President may specify.
- (b) Acts performed by authorized employees of the Institute under this section shall be valid, and of like force and effect within the United States, as if performed by any other person authorized under the laws of the United States to perform such acts.

TAX EXEMPT STATUS OF THE INSTITUTE

- SEC. 8. (a) The Institute, its property, and its income are exempt from all taxation now or hereafter imposed by the United States (except to the extent that section 11(a)(3) of this Act requires the imposition of taxes imposed under chapter 21 of the Internal Revenue Code of 1954, relating to the Federal Insurance Contributions Act) or by State or local taxing authority of the United States.
- (b) For purposes of the Internal Revenue Code of 1954, the Institute shall be treated as an organization described in sections 170(b)(1)(A), 170(c), 2055(a), 2106(a)(2)(A),, 2522(a), and 2522(b).

FURNISHING PROPERTY AND SERVICES TO AND OBTAINING SERVICES FROM THE INSTITUTE

- SEC. 9. (a) Any agency of the United States Government is authorized to sell, loan, or lease property (including interests therein) to, and to perform administrative and technical support functions and services for the operations of, the Institute upon such terms and conditions as the President may direct. Reimbursements to agencies under this subsection shall be credited to the current applicable appropriation of the agency concerned.
- (b) Any agency of the United States Government is authorized to acquire and accept services from the Institute upon such terms and conditions as the President may direct. Whenever the President determines it to be in furtherance of the purposes of this Act, the procurement of services by such agencies from the Institute may be effected without regard to such laws of the United States normally applicable to the acquisition of services by such agencies as the President may specify by Executive order.
- (c) Any agency of the United States Government making funds available to the Institute in accordance with this Act shall make arrangements with the Institute for the Comptroller General of the United States to have access to the; books and records of the Institute and the opportunity to audit the operations of the Institute.

TAIWAN INSTRUMENTALITY

- SEC. 10. (a) Whenever the President or any agency of the United States Government is authorized or required by or pursuant to the laws of the United States to render or provide to or to receive or accept from Taiwan, any performance, communication, assurance, undertaking, or other action, such action shall, in the manner and to the. extent directed by the President, be rendered or Provided to, or received or accepted from, an instrumentality established by Taiwan which the President determines has the necessary authority under the laws applied by the people on Taiwan to provide assurances and take other actions on behalf of Taiwan in accordance with this Act.

- (b) The President is requested to extend to the instrumentality established by Taiwan the same number of offices and complement of personnel as were previously operated in the United States by the governing authorities on Taiwan recognized as the Republic of China prior to January 1, 1979.
- (c) Upon the granting by Taiwan of comparable privileges and immunities with respect to the Institute and its appropriate personnel, the President is authorized to extend with respect to the Taiwan instrumentality and its appropriate; personnel, such privileges and immunities (subject to appropriate conditions and obligations) as may be necessary for the effective performance of their functions.

SEPARATION OF GOVERNMENT PERSONNEL FOR EMPLOYMENT WITH THE INSTITUTE

- SEC. 11. (a)(1) Under such terms and conditions as the President may direct, any agency of the United States Government may separate from Government service for a specified period any officer or employee of that agency who accepts employment with the Institute.
- (2) An officer or employee separated by an agency under paragraph (1) of this subsection for employment with the Institute shall be entitled upon termination of such employment to reemployment or reinstatement with such agency(or a successor agency) in an appropriate position with the attendant rights, privileges, and benefits with the officer or employee would have had or acquired had he or she not been so separated, subject to such time period and other conditions as the President may prescribe.
- (3) An officer or employee entitled to reemployment or reinstatement rights under paragraph (2) of this subsection shall, while continuously employed by the Institute with no break in continuity of service, continue to participate in any benefit program in which such officer or employee was participating prior to employment by the Institute, including programs for compensation for job-related death, injury, or illness; programs for health and life insurance; programs for annual, sick, and other statutory leave; and programs for retirement under any system established by the laws of the United States; except that employment with the Institute shall be the basis for participation in such programs only to the extent that employee deductions and employer contributions, as required, in payment for such participation for the period of employment with the Institute, are currently deposited in the program's or system's fund or depository. Death or retirement of any such officer or employee during approved service with the Institute and prior to reemployment or reinstatement shall be considered a death in or retirement from Government service for purposes of any employee or survivor benefits acquired by reason of service with an agency of the United States Government.
- (4) Any officer or employee of an agency of the United States Government who entered into service with the Institute on approved leave of absence without pay prior to the enactment of this Act shall receive the benefits of this section for the period of such service.
- (b) Any agency of the United States Government employing alien personnel on Taiwan may transfer such personnel, with accrued allowances, benefits, and rights, to the Institute without a break in service for purposes of retirement and other benefits, including continued participation in any system established by the laws of the United States for the retirement of employees in which the alien was participating prior to the transfer to the Institute, except that employment with the Institute shall be creditable for retirement purposes only to the extent that employee deductions and employer contributions.. as required, in payment for such participation for the period of employment with the Institute, are currently deposited in the system' s fund or depository.
- (c) Employees of the Institute shall not be employees of the United States and, in representing the Institute, shall be exempt from section 207 of title 18, United States Code.
- (d)(1) For purposes of sections 911 and 913 of the Internal Revenue Code of 1954, amounts paid by the Institute to its employees shall not be treated as earned income.

Amounts received by employees of the Institute shall not be included in gross income, and shall be exempt from taxation, to the extent that they are equivalent to amounts received by civilian officers and employees of the Government of the United States as allowances and benefits which are exempt from taxation under section 912 of such Code.

- (2) Except to the extent required by subsection (a)(3) of this section, service performed in the employ of the Institute shall not constitute employment for purposes of chapter 21 of such Code and title II of the Social Security Act.

REPORTING REQUIREMENT

- SEC. 12. (a) The Secretary of State shall transmit to the Congress the text of any agreement to which the Institute is a party. However, any such agreement the immediate public disclosure of which would, in the opinion of the President, be prejudicial to the national security of the United States shall not be so transmitted to the Congress but shall be transmitted to the Committee on Foreign Relations of the Senate and the Committee on Foreign Affairs of the House of Representatives under an appropriate injunction of secrecy to be removed only upon due notice from the President.
- (b) For purposes of subsection (a), the term "agreement" includes-
  - (1) any agreement entered into between the Institute and the governing authorities on Taiwan or the instrumentality established by Taiwan; and
  - (2) any agreement entered into between the Institute and an agency of the United States Government.
- (c) Agreements and transactions made or to be made by or through the Institute shall be subject to the same congressional notification, review, and approval requirements and procedures as if such agreements and transactions were made by or through the agency of the United States Government on behalf of which the Institute is acting.
- (d) During the two-year period beginning on the effective date of this Act, the Secretary of State shall transmit to the Speaker of the House and Senate House of Representatives and the Committee on Foreign Relations of Foreign Relations the Senate, every six months, a report describing and reviewing economic relations between the United States and Taiwan, noting any interference with normal commercial relations.

RULES AND REGULATIONS

- SEC. 13. The President is authorized to prescribe such rules and regulations as he may deem appropriate to carry out the purposes of this Act. During the three-year period beginning on the effective date speaker of this Act, such rules and regulations shall be transmitted promptly to the Speaker of the House of Representatives and to the Committee on Foreign Relations of the Senate. Such action shall not, however, relieve the Institute of the responsibilities placed upon it by this Act.'

CONGRESSIONAL OVERSIGHT

- SEC. 14. (a) The Committee on Foreign Affairs of the House of Representatives, the Committee on Foreign Relations of the Senate, and other appropriate committees of the Congress shall monitor-
  - (1) the implementation of the provisions of this Act;
  - (2) the operation and procedures of the Institute;
  - (3) the legal and technical aspects of the continuing relationship between the United States and Taiwan; and
  - (4) the implementation of the policies of the United States concerning security and cooperation in East Asia.
- (b) Such committees shall report, as appropriate, to their respective Houses on the results of their monitoring.

DEFINITIONS

- SEC. 15. For purposes of this Act-
  - (1) the term "laws of the United States" includes any statute, rule, regulation, ordinance, order, or judicial rule of decision of the United States or any political subdivision thereof; and

- (2) the term "Taiwan" includes, as the context may require, the islands of Taiwan and the Pescadores, the people on those islands, corporations and other entities and associations created or organized under the laws applied on those islands, and the governing authorities on Taiwan recognized by the United States as the Republic of China prior to January 1, 1979, and any successor governing authorities (including political subdivisions, agencies, and instrumentalities thereof).

AUTHORIZATION OF APPROPRIATIONS

- SEC. 16. In addition to funds otherwise available to carry out the provisions of this Act, there are authorized to be appropriated to the Secretary of State for the fiscal year 1980 such funds as may be necessary to carry out such provisions. Such funds are authorized to remain available until expended.

SEVERABILITY OF PROVISIONS

- SEC. 17. If any provision of this Act or the application thereof to any person or circumstance is held invalid, the remainder of the Act and the application of such provision to any other person or circumstance shall not be affected thereby.

EFFECTIVE DATE

- SEC. 18. This Act shall be effective as of January 1, 1979. Approved April 10, 1979.

THE JOINT U.S.-CHINA COMMUNIQUE, SHANGHAI, FEBRUARY 27, 1972

President Richard Nixon of the United States of America visited the People's Republic of China at the invitation of Premier Chou En-lai of the People's Republic of China from February 21 to February 28, 1972. Accompanying the President were Mrs. Nixon, U.S. Secretary of State William Rogers, Assistant to the President Dr. Henry Kissinger, and other American officials.

President Nixon met with Chairman Mao Tse-tung of the Communist Party of China on February 21. The two leaders had a serious and frank exchange of views on Sino-U.S. relations and world affairs.

During the visit, extensive, earnest and frank discussions were held between President Nixon and Premier Chou En-lai on the normalization of relations between the United States of America and the People's Republic of China, as well as on other matters of interest to both sides. In addition, Secretary of State William Rogers and Foreign Minister Chi Peng-fei held talks in the same spirit.

President Nixon and his party visited Peking and viewed cultural, industrial and agricultural sites, and they also toured Hangchow and Shanghai where, continuing discussions with Chinese leaders, they viewed similar places of interest.

The leaders of the People's Republic of China and the United States of America found it beneficial to have this opportunity, after so many years without contact, to present candidly to one another their views on a variety of issues. They reviewed the international situation in which important changes and great upheavals are taking place and expounded their respective positions and attitudes.

The U.S. side stated: Peace in Asia and peace in the world requires efforts both to reduce immediate tensions and to eliminate the basic causes of conflict. The United States will work for a just and secure peace: just, because it fulfills the aspirations of peoples and nations for freedom and progress; secure, because it removes the danger of foreign aggression. The United States supports individual freedom and social progress for all the peoples of the world, free of outside pressure or intervention. The United States believes that the effort to reduce tensions is served by improving communication between countries that through accident, miscalculation or misunderstanding. Countries should treat each other with mutual respect and be willing to compete peacefully, letting performance be the ultimate judge. No country should claim infallibility and each country should be prepared to re-examine its own attitudes for the common good. The United States stressed that. the peoples of Indochina should be allowed to determine their destiny without outside intervention; its constant primary objective has been a negotiated solution; the eight-point proposal put forward by the Republic of Vietnam and the United States on January 27, 1972 represents a basis for the attainment of that objective; in the absence of a negotiated settlement the United States envisages the ultimate withdrawal of all U.S. forces from the region consistent with the aim of selfdetermination for each country of Indochina. The United States will maintain its close ties with and support for the Republic of Korea; the United States will support efforts of the Republic of Korea to seek a relaxation of tension and increased communication in the Korean peninsula. The United States places the highest value on its friendly relations with Japan; it will continue to develop the existing close bonds. Consistent with the United Nations Security Council Resolution of December 21, 1971, the United States favors the continuation of the ceasefire between India and Pakistan and the withdrawal of all military forces to within their own territories and to their own sides of the ceasefire line in Jammu and Kashmir; the United States supports the right of the peoples of South Asia to shape their own future in peace, free of military threat, and without having the area become the subject of great power rivalry.

The Chinese side stated: Wherever there is oppression, there is resistance. Countries want independence, nations want liberation and the people want revolution--this has become the irresistible trend of history. All nations, big or small, should be equal; big nations should not bully the small and strong nations should not bully the weak. China will never be a superpower and it opposes hegemony and power politics of any kind. The Chinese side stated that it firmly supports the struggles of all the oppressed people and nations for freedom and liberation and that the people of all countries have the right to choose their social systems according to their own wishes and the right to safeguard the independence, sovereignty and territorial integrity of their own countries and oppose foreign aggression, interference, control and subversion. All foreign troops should be withdrawn to their own countries.

The Chinese side expressed its firm support to the peoples of Vietnam, Laos and Cambodia in their efforts for the attainment of their goal and its firm support to the seven-point proposal of the Provisional Revolutionary Government of the Republic of South Vietnam and the elaboration of February this year on the two key problems in the proposal, and to the Joint Declaration of the Summit Conference of the Indochinese Peoples. It firmly supports the eight-point program for the peaceful unification of Korea put forward by the Government of the Democratic People's Republic of Korea on April 12, 1971, and the stand for the abolition of the "U.N. Commission for the Unification and Rehabilitation of Korea." It firmly opposes the revival and outward expansion of Japanese militarism and firmly supports the Japanese people's desire to build an independent, democratic, peaceful and neutral Japan. It firmly maintains that India and Pakistan should, in accordance with the United Nations resolutions on the India-Pakistan question, immediately withdraw all their forces to their respective territories and to their own sides of the ceasefire line in Jammu and Kashmir and firmly supports the Pakistan Government and people in their struggle to preserve their independence and sovereignty and the people of Jammu and Kashmir in their struggle for the right of selfdetermination.

There are essential differences between China and the United States in their social systems and foreign policies. However, the two sides agreed that countries, regardless of their social systems, should conduct their relations on the principles of respect for the sovereignty and territorial integrity of all states, non-aggression against other states, non-interference in the internal affairs of other states, equality and mutual benefit, and peaceful coexistence. International disputes should be settled on this basis, without resorting to the use or threat of force. The United States and the People's Republic of China are prepared to apply these principles to their mutual relations.

With these principles of international relations in mind the two sides stated that:

- progress toward the normalization of relations between China and the United States is in the interests of all countries:

- both wish to reduce the danger of international military conflict;

- neither should seek hegemony in the Asia-Pacific region and each is opposed to efforts by any other country or group of countries to establish such hegemony; and

- neither is prepared to negotiate on behalf of any third party or to enter into agreements or understandings with the other directed at other states.

Both sides are of the view that it would be against the interests of the peoples of the world for any major country to collude with another against other countries, or for major countries to divide up the world into spheres of interest.

The two sides reviewed the long-standing serious disputes between China and the United States. The Chinese reaffirmed its position: The Taiwan question is the crucial question obstructing the normalization of relations between China and the United States; the Government of the People's Republic of China is the sole legal government of China; Taiwan is a province of China which has long been returned to the motherland; the liberation of Taiwan is China's internal affair in which no other country has the right to interfere; and all U.S. forces and military installations must be withdrawn from Taiwan. The Chinese Government firmly opposes any activities which aim at the creation of "one China, one Taiwan," "one China, two governments," "two Chinas," and "independent Taiwan" or advocate that "the status of Taiwan remains to be determined."

The U.S. side declared: The United States acknowledges that all Chinese on either side of the Taiwan Strait maintain there is but one China and that Taiwan is a part of China. The United States Government does not challenge that position. It reaffirms its interest in a peaceful settlement of the Taiwan question by the Chinese them-selves. With this prospect in mind, it affirms the ultimate objective of the withdrawal of all U.S. forces and military installations from Taiwan. In the meantime, it will progressively reduce its forces and military installations on Taiwan as the tension in the area diminishes.

The two sides agreed that it is desirable to broaden the understanding between the two peoples. To this end, they discussed specific areas in such fields as science, technology, culture, sports and journalism, in which people-to-people contacts and exchanges would be mutually beneficial. Each side undertakes to facilitate the further development of such contacts and exchanges.

Both sides view bilateral trade as another area from which mutual benefit can be derived, and agreed that economic relations based on equality and mutual benefit are in the interest of the peoples of the two countries. They agree to facilitate the progressive development of trade between their two countries.

The two sides agreed that they will stay in contact through various channels, including the sending of a senior U.S. representative to Peking from time to time for concrete consultations to further the normalization of relations between the two countries and continue to exchange views on issues of common interest.

The two sides expressed the hope that the gains achieved during this visit would open up new prospects for the relations between the two countries. They believe that the normalization of relations between the two countries is not only in the interest of the Chinese and American peoples but also contributes to the relaxation of tension in Asia and the world.

President Nixon, Mrs. Nixon and the American party expressed their appreciation for the gracious hospitality shown them by the Govern-ment and people of the People's Republic of China.

JOINT COMMUNIQUE ON THE ESTABLISHMENT OF DIPLOMATIC RELATIONS BETWEEN THE UNITED STATES OF AMERICA AND THE PEOPLE'S REPUBLIC OF CHINA JANUARY 1, 1979

(The communique was released on December 15, 1978, in Washington and Peking.)

The United States of America and the People's Republic of China have agreed to recognize each other and to establish diplomatic relations as of January 1, 1979.

The United States of America recognizes the Government of the People's Republic of China as the sole legal Government of China. Within this context, the people of the United States will maintain cultural, commercial, and other unofficial relations with the people of Taiwan.

The United States of America and the People's Republic of China reaffirm the principles agreed on by the two sides in the Shanghai Communique and emphasize once again that:

¡ÎBoth wish to reduce the danger of international military conflict.

¡ÎNeither should seek hegemony in the Asia-Pacific region or in any other region of the world and each is opposed to efforts by any other country or group of countries to establish such hegemony.

¡ÎNeither is prepared to negotiate on behalf of any third party or to enter into agreements or understandings with the other directed at other states.

¡ÎThe Government of the United States of America acknowledges the Chinese position that there is but one China and Taiwan is part of China.

¡ÎBoth believe that normalization of Sino-American relations is not only in the interest of the Chinese and American peoples but also contributes to the cause of peace in Asia and the world.

The United States of America and the People's Republic of China will exchange Ambassadors and establish Embassies on March 1, 1979.

U.S.-PRC JOINT COMMUNIQUE, AUGUST 17, 1982

1. In the Joint Communique on the Establishment of Diplomatic Relations on January 1, 1979, issued by the Government of the United States of America and the Government of the People's Republic of China, the United States of America recognized the Government of the People's Republic of China as the sole legal government of China, and it acknowledged the Chinese position that there is but one China and Taiwan is part of China. Within that context, the two sides agreed that the people of the United States would continue to maintain cultural, commercial, and other unofficial relations with the people of Taiwan. On this basis, relations between the United States and China were normalized.

2. The question of United States arms sales to Taiwan was not settled in the course of negotiations between the two countries on establishing diplomatic relations. The two sides held differing positions, and the Chinese side stated that it would raise the issue again following normalization. Recognizing that this issue would seriously hamper the development of United States-China relations, they have held further discussions on it, during and since the meetings between President Ronald Reagan and Premier Zhao Ziyang and between Secretary of State Alexander M. Haig, Jr., and Vice Premier and Foreign Minister Huang Hua in October 1981.

3. Respect for each other's sovereignty and territorial integrity and non-interference each other's internal affairs constitute the fundamental principles guiding United States-China relations. These principles were confirmed in the Shanghai Communique of February 28, 1972 and reaffirmed in the Joint Communique on the Establishment of Diplomatic Relations which came into effect on January 1, 1973. Both sides emphatically state that these principles continue to govern all aspects of their relations.

4. The Chinese government reiterates that the question of Taiwan is China's internal affair. The Message to the Compatriots in Taiwan issued by China on January 1, 1979, promulgated a fundamental policy of striving for Peaceful reunification of the Motherland. The Nine-Point Proposal put forward by China on September 30, 1981 represented a Further major effort under this fundamental policy to strive for a peaceful solution to the Taiwan question.

5. The United States Government attaches great importance to its relations with China, and reiterates that it has no intention of infringing on Chinese sovereignty and territorial integrity, or interfering in China's internal affairs, or pursuing a policy of "two Chinas" or "one China, one Taiwan." The United States Government understands and appreciates the Chinese policy of striving for a peaceful resolution of the Taiwan question as indicated in China's Message to Compatriots in Taiwan issued on January 1, 1979 and the Nine-Point Proposal put forward by China on September 30, 1981. The new situation which has emerged with regard to the Taiwan question also provides favorable conditions for the settlement of United States-China differences over the question of United States arms sales to Taiwan.

6. Having in mind the foregoing statements of both sides, the United States Government states that it does not seek to carry out a long-term policy of arms sales to Taiwan, that its arms sales to Taiwan will not exceed, either in qualitative or in quantitative terms, the level of those supplied in recent years since the establishment of diplomatic relations between the United States and China, and that it intends to reduce gradually its sales of arms to Taiwan, leading over a period of time to a final resolution. In so stating, the United States acknowledges China's consistent position regarding the thorough settlement of this issue.

7. In order to bring about, over a period of time, a final settlement of the question of United States arms sales to Taiwan, which is an issue rooted in history, the two governments will make every effort to adopt measures and create conditions conducive to the thorough settlement of this issue.

8. The development of United States-China relations is not only in the interest of the two peoples but also conducive to peace and stability in the world. The two sides are determined, on the principle of equality and mutual benefit, to strengthen their- ties to the economic, cultural, educational, scientific, technological and other fields and make strong. joint efforts for the continued development of relations between the governments and peoples of the United States and China.

9. In order to bring about the healthy development of United States China relations, maintain world peace and oppose aggression and expansion, the two governments reaffirm the principles agreed on by the two sides in the Shanghai Communique and the Joint Communique on the Establishment of Diplomatic Relations. The two sides will maintain contact and hold appropriate consultations on bilateral and international issues of common interest.

CONGRESSIONAL TESTIMONIES AND STATEMENTS ON US-TAIWAN RELATIONS

DAS SUSAN SHIRK TESTIMONY ON TAIWAN RELATIONS ACT AT 20

(U.S. as contributor to peaceful resolution, not mediator)

Washington -- The U.S. should not play the role of a mediator between Taiwan and the People's Republic of China (PRC), but instead should be a contributor to an environment in which the two sides can take good ideas and build on them, according to Deputy Assistant Secretary of State Susan Shirk.

In testimony before the House International Relations Subcommittee on Asia and the Pacific April 14, Shirk said that such a role has three elements:

- having sound relationships with Taiwan and the People's Republic of China (PRC);
- maintaining stable, consistent, and predictable policies in the region so that both Taiwan and the PRC focus energies on engaging one another directly rather than trying to make the United States take sides; and
- adhering to the overall China policy framework that has served U.S. interests well during this Administration and the five that preceded it.

"There is no shortage of good ideas to resolve differences, and there is no unique solution. There are many ways that the two sides can enhance trust and reduce tension. They have made a start, and the channel of communication is open," Shirk said.

Shirk's testimony also served as a speech to an April 14 conference on Taiwan sponsored by the American Enterprise Institute and the Heritage Foundation.

Both the testimony and speech marked the 20th anniversary of the Taiwan Relations Act (TRA) which, Shirk said, has preserved U.S. substantive ties with Taiwan and contributed to a stable regional environment in which Taiwan has prospered and cross-Strait ties have grown.

Following is the text of Shirk's testimony, as prepared for delivery:

(begin text)

TESTIMONY OF

SUSAN L. SHIRK
DEPUTY ASSISTANT SECRETARY
EAST ASIAN AND PACIFIC BUREAU
U.S. DEPARTMENT OF STATE

BEFORE THE HOUSE INTERNATIONAL RELATIONS COMMITTEE, SUBCOMMITTEE ON ASIA AND THE PACIFIC

"THE TAIWAN RELATIONS ACT AT TWENTY"

APRIL 14, 1999

Introduction

Mr. Chairman, good afternoon.

Thank you for the invitation to speak today as we mark the twentieth anniversary of the Taiwan Relations Act. I welcome this opportunity to discuss this innovative legislation and our relationship with Taiwan.

Today, I would like first to review how the Taiwan Relations Act (TRA) has preserved our substantive ties with Taiwan and contributed to a stable regional environment in which Taiwan has prospered and cross-Strait ties have grown. Then I would like to give you some thoughts about the future challenges and how the TRA will help us address them. The TRA -- A Resounding Success

Twenty years ago, our government faced the challenge of preserving the long-standing friendship and common interests between the U.S. and Taiwan in the absence of diplomatic relations. Bipartisan efforts as well as cooperation across agencies and branches of government produced the Taiwan Relations Act to ensure that normalization of our relations with the People's Republic of China did not result in the abandonment of Taiwan. Those of you in the audience who participated in crafting the TRA know that this was not an easy task.

The TRA that emerged from this process set forth two fundamental goals:

"...(1) to help maintain peace, security, and stability in the Western Pacific; and

(2) to promote the foreign policy of the United States by authorizing the continuation of commercial, cultural, and other relations between the people of the United States and the people on Taiwan."

I am sure you would agree that the TRA has met these goals, and indeed has succeeded far beyond the hopes and expectations of its framers. This resounding success is a tribute to the careful, comprehensive design of the legislation, the strong commitment on each side to make sure that the new arrangements worked, and the strength of the affinity between the two peoples.

Taiwan's Progress

One measure of the TRA's success is the remarkable democratic transformation and economic prosperity achieved by Taiwan. Twenty years ago, Taiwan was under martial law, and human rights violations occurred with regularity. Today, Taiwan has a vibrant democracy characterized by free elections, a free press, and dynamic political campaigns. Taiwan's economic development on free market principles has been no less impressive, as seen in its ranking as the 14th largest trading economy in the world and in its success in weathering the Asian Financial Crisis. Taiwan's experience is a powerful example in the region and beyond.

Of course, Taiwan's people deserve the full credit for their achievements. But the TRA helped both to ensure that the unofficial status of our relations did not harm Taiwan's interests and to create a stable environment favorable to Taiwan's transformation.

Consistency of U.S. Commitment

One way the U.S. government has fostered this stable environment is by upholding the security provisions of the TRA. In close consultation with Congress, successive administrations have implemented our obligation under the TRA to provide articles and services necessary to Taiwan to maintain a sufficient self-defense capability. We have provided Taiwan with F-16s, Knox class frigates, helicopters, and tanks as well as a variety of air-to-air, surface-to-air, and anti-ship defensive missiles. We continually reevaluate Taiwan's posture to ensure we provide Taiwan with sufficient self-defense capability while complying with the terms of the 1982 U.S.-PRC Communique.

The Department of Defense's recent assessment of the security situation in the Taiwan Strait concludes that, except in a few areas, despite improvements in the military forces of both sides, the dynamic equilibrium of those forces in the Taiwan Strait has not changed dramatically over the last two decades. This assessment reflects the effectiveness of the TRA.

As you know, the U.S. also maintains a significant forward-deployed presence in East Asia in connection with our alliances with Japan, the Republic of Korea, and other allies. This presence contributes importantly to regional stability, including the area around Taiwan.

Growth of U.S.-Taiwan Ties

That the TRA has succeeded in nurturing U.S.-Taiwan ties can be seen clearly in a number of areas. On the economic front, we have a vibrant, mutually beneficial trade relationship, with total annual trade of over $50 million. Taiwan is the seventh largest market for U.S. exports and our fifth largest foreign agricultural market. For our part, the U.S. absorbs one fourth of all Taiwan exports. Taiwan and the U.S. passed a milestone in their economic relationship last year with the completion of the bilateral market access agreement in conjunction with Taiwan's application to the World Trade Organization. Last year, we also signed a bilateral "Open Skies" agreement to expand civil aviation links.

We also have extensive cooperation in science and technology, environment, public health, and other fields. AIT and TECRO, for example, have concluded over 100 agreements -- another indication of the richness of the ties with Taiwan.

Clinton Administration Policy

Like its predecessors, the Clinton Administration is fully committed to faithful implementation of the TRA. Indeed, the Administration in 1994 conducted an extensive interagency review of U.S.-Taiwan policy -- the first such review since 1979 -- to make sure that all that could be done was being done. On the basis of that review, the Administration has undertaken a number of specific steps: authorized high-level U.S. officials from economic and technical agencies to travel to Taiwan when appropriate; expanded economic dialogue through the Trade and Investment Framework Agreement (TIFA) talks and the Subcabinet-Level Economic Dialogue (SLED); and supported Taiwan's participation in international organizations where statehood is not an issue. Let me emphasize one aspect of the Administration's policy that is firm and unchanging. The Administration continues to insist that cross-Strait differences be resolved peacefully, as demonstrated in March 1996, when President Clinton ordered U.S. carriers to the waters near Taiwan.

Not A Zero Sum Game

The U.S. policy framework, of which the TRA is part, allows us to retain substantive, but unofficial relations with Taiwan, while pursuing improved ties with the PRC. Six U.S. administrations of both parties have engaged Beijing in order to promote U.S. interests and to encourage a responsible PRC role in the world. The U.S.-PRC relationship that followed the normalization decision -- for all of its ups and downs -- has contributed enormously to stability and peace in Asia -- an environment which is very much in Taiwan's interest.

In reviewing the past twenty years of the three intertwined relationships -- U.S.-PRC, U.S.-Taiwan, Taiwan-PRC -- what becomes absolutely apparent is that gains in one relationship do not dictate a loss in either of the other two. In fact, the reverse is true: gains in one have contributed to gains in the others. To illustrate my point about this positive dynamic, I would like to note that the resumption of cross-Strait discussions after a hiatus of three years occurred simultaneously with the improvement of our relations with the PRC.

Cross-Strait Relations

Arguably, while the gains in the U.S.-PRC and U.S.-Taiwan relations have been formidable, the Beijing-Taipei relationship has actually experienced the most dramatic improvement. The trade, personal contacts, and dialogue now taking place across the strait were unimaginable twenty years ago.

Economic figures demonstrate how much things have changed. Trade between Taiwan and the PRC totaled nearly $23 billion at the end of 1998. The PRC is Taiwan's third largest overall trade partner surpassed only by the U.S. and

Japan. Commitments of Taiwan investment in the PRC now exceed $30 billion. With 30,000 individual Taiwan firms having invested in the PRC, over three million mainland Chinese are now employed with firms benefiting from that commitment of funds. Economic ties have led to increasing personal ties. Up to 200,000 Taiwan business people now live and work in the PRC. Last year, there were 1.7 million visits by Taiwan residents to the mainland.

This greater economic interaction is not just positive -- it is the basis for a sense of confidence that common interests across the Strait will motivate the two sides toward productive dialogue. Taiwan's security over the long term depends more on the two sides coming to terms with each other than on the particular military balance. The economic and social ties across the Strait are a force for stability and a basis for improved cross-Strait relations in the political realm.

One of the most salutary developments in East Asia during the early 1990s was the emergence of a dialogue between Taiwan's Straits Exchange Foundation, or SEF, responsible for Taiwan's unofficial relations with the mainland, and the Mainland's Association for Relations Across the Taiwan Strait, or ARATS. The two sides moved to restore the formal dialogue, suspended in 1995, with the October 1998 visit to the mainland by SEF Chairman Koo Chen-fu. Koo and his ARATS counterpart, Wang Daohan, reached a four-point consensus, which included a return visit to Taiwan by Wang, now scheduled for Fall. Koo's meeting with President Jiang Zemin was the highest level contact between Beijing and Taipei since 1949. As such, it substantially improved the climate for cross-Strait exchanges. The consensus that was forged provides an excellent basis for developing the approaches necessary to resolve the difficult issues between the two sides.

The TRA in the Future

The Taiwan Relations Act has guided us successfully through the last twenty years. Looking forward, I believe the TRA provides the comprehensive framework for dealing with future challenges. We should be extremely cautious about any adjustments to this Act which has worked so well.

As I have said, insisting on peaceful resolution of differences between the PRC and Taiwan will remain U.S. policy. Our belief is that dialogue between the PRC and Taiwan fosters an atmosphere in which tensions are reduced, misperceptions can be clarified, and common ground can be explored. The exchange of visits under the SEF/ARATS framework, currently rich in symbolism but still nascent in substance, has the potential to contribute to the peaceful resolution of difficult substantive differences. Clearly, this will not be easy, but this Administration has great confidence in the creativity of the people on Taiwan and the people on the mainland to give the dialogue real meaning. Imaginative thinking within this dialogue might result in new understandings or confidence building measures on any number of difficult topics. But, only the participants on both sides of the strait can craft the specific solutions that balance their interests while addressing their most pressing concerns.

Neither the PRC nor Taiwan would be served by over-emphasis on military hardware while neglecting the art of statesmanship. From the PRC's perspective, it should think twice about whether development or upgrade of any one type of weapons system will contribute to the PRC's security, or, conversely, whether it might actually detract from that security by fostering tension, anxiety, political instability, or an arms build up in the region. At the heart of this calculation is the reality that the PRC cannot expect to pursue its defense policy in a vacuum. Its decisions on military modernization will generate responses from other actors.

Or, as Secretary Albright recently said in Beijing:

"Nothing would better serve China's interest than using its developing dialogue with Taiwan to build mutual confidence and reduce the perceived need for missiles or missile defense."

From Taiwan's perspective, the TRA's continuing guarantee that Taiwan will not suffer for lack of defensive capability enhances Taiwan's confidence and counterbalances anxieties over PRC military capabilities. There has been a lot of attention focused on potential U.S. provision of theater missile defense to Taiwan. This is premature. High-altitude TMD is still in development and is therefore not going to be provided to anyone in the immediate future. Down the road, as with our consideration of sale of other defensive capabilities, our decisions on provision of any sort of missile defense will be based on an assessment of Taiwan's legitimate defense needs. As we consider these needs, we will certainly take into account the security situation in the Strait, including PRC deployments, the pace and scope of dialogue between the PRC and Taiwan, and the overall regional security picture.

In this age of highly sophisticated weaponry, I think we are all sometimes prone to equating security with military capability. But a durable peace will rest less on arms than success in addressing differences through dialogue on a mutually acceptable basis. Thus, whereas missiles and missile defense systems ultimately cannot in themselves secure peace and prosperity, dialogue and creative compromise can do so.

Dialogue and compromise cannot be wedded to an imposed timetable. Good faith is required of, and in the interest of, both sides. The provisions of the TRA and general U.S. policy in the region will continue to contribute to an environment conducive to dialogue and therefore to finding a lasting resolution to differences across the Taiwan strait.

Conclusion

U.S. relations with the PRC and the people on Taiwan are likely to be one of our most complex and important foreign policy challenges for many years to come. This Administration, like the five Republican and Democratic Administrations before it, firmly believes that the future of cross-Strait relations is a matter for Beijing and Taipei to resolve peacefully.

There is no shortage of good ideas to resolve differences, and there is no unique solution. There are many ways that the two sides can enhance trust and reduce tension. They have made a start, and the channel of communication is open.

Our role should not be as a mediator but instead as a contributor to an environment in which the two sides can take good ideas and build on them. This role has three elements: having sound relationships with Taiwan and the PRC; maintaining stable, consistent, and predictable policies in the region so that both Taiwan and the PRC focus energies on engaging one another directly rather than trying to pull us over to their side; and adhering to the overall China policy framework that has served our interests well.

For the U.S. to play this role effectively and instill confidence, agreement between the legislative and executive branches on policy in the region is essential. And we must have a policy that will be supported by the American people. The experience of the TRA over the past twenty years provides a useful model for us to follow.

ON THE 20TH ANNIVERSARY OF THE TAIWAN RELATIONS ACT: U.S. ANCHOR INTERESTS ACROSS THE TAIWAN STRAIT

Testimony of Dr. Gerrit W. Gong
Freeman Chair and Director Asian Studies Program
Center for Strategic & International Studies

before the Subcommittee on Asia and the Pacific
House Committee on International Relations

April 14, 1999

Introduction

Mr. Chairman, it is always a pleasure to testify before you and this distinguished committee on U.S. Asia policy.

The U.S. has six anchor interests in cross-strait relations, including our interpretation and application of the Taiwan Relations Act (TRA), the 20th anniversary of which we observed last Saturday, April 10.

Six U.S. Anchor Interests in Cross-Strait Relations

First, to help preserve an equilibrium of confidence so those on both sides of the Taiwan Strait can determine the pace and scope of their mutual interaction peacefully.

An equilibrium of confidence means both Beijing and Taipei have the defensive articles and services and thereby the minimal sense of security necessary to engage in cross-strait dialogue free of intimidation or coercion; both sides feel the U.S. is taking an even-handed approach toward the other; neither side feels the U.S. is pressuring it into negotiations and that any arrangements concluded are mutually acceptable to both sides.

Some say the U.S. interest in Beijing-Taipei relations is founded on power - that China and the U.S. are natural competitors in Asia and maintenance of the Taiwan Strait status quo is therefore a U.S. strategic interest. Others say the U.S. interest in Beijing-Taipei relations is founded on principle - either in the free democratic expression of the 21 million people in Taiwan or in the eventual unification of "one China."

Defining the U.S. interest in maintaining an equilibrium of confidence recognizes both power and principle. It does not commit the U.S. simply to support a status quo peace and stability, nor necessarily even simply a dynamic status quo.

The U.S. interest is that both sides peacefully determine what is mutually acceptable to them, free from coercive pressure one to the other or from the U.S. The U.S. should thus reject any challenge to the status quo by force, and discourage Taiwan independence, while leaving it to Beijing and Taipei to create the positive conditions necessary to entice peaceful unification. In this regard, the U.S. can welcome expanding Beijing-Taipei meaningful and constructive dialogue in areas such as confidence building measures, international space, and cross-strait contact including deepening cross-strait economic involvement.

Second, to maintain the responsibility of Taipei and Beijing for their continuing dynamic balancing of cooperation and competition, not shifting responsibility for cross-strait peace and communication to Washington for restraint or adjudication.

In this regard, major strains in Sino-U.S. relations, particularly should Taiwan reemerge as an issue in Sino-U.S. and in domestic U.S. politics, could raise U.S. expectations for cross-strait dialogue, perhaps to unreasonable levels. Efforts to establish interim arrangements or especially interim agreements must be careful to avoid unintended, potentially destabilizing consequences of their otherwise clearly well-intentioned efforts.

For example, some current confidence building measures include proposals for Beijing-Taipei arms control talks. Arms control initiatives which establish hot-lines or appropriate military-to-military contacts between Beijing and Taipei could be helpful. But arms control discussions involving Beijing, Taipei, and Washington must be careful to avoid, for example, complicating de facto consultations or prior notification regarding Taiwan arms requests.

The U.S. interest is to minimize the tendency a) by some in Beijing to underestimate U.S. resolve or to assume that Washington could simply "deliver" Taiwan and b) by some in Taipei alternatively to overestimate the nature or scope of U.S. support or to assume that Washington could "sell" Taiwan out. The U.S. gives neither side a veto or a blank check. As demonstrated by the U.S. deployment of two aircraft carrier battle groups on one occasion and by the President's enunciation of three no's on another, the U.S. will indicate a limit to those who might engage in provocative or threatening behavior on either side of the strait.

Though Beijing-Taipei competition will continue, the U.S. interest is to build margins of safety, not simply limits of tension.

Third, to see constructive and authorized direct dialogue between Taipei and Beijing deal directly with differences between them, with multiple levels and channels as the best way for Taipei and Beijing to engage each other directly.

There is an important role for Track 2 dialogue convened and facilitated by institutions such as mine. But there is also a need for consistent, confirmed, authoritative messages between the two sides of the Taiwan Strait if cross-strait trust and confidence are to be built on a solid foundation.

In this regard, both Beijing and Taipei must each be sufficiently confident to enter into constructive and meaningful dialogue. Intentionally undermining the confidence of Beijing or Taipei as a means to promoting cross-strait dialogue is likely to be counter-productive. At the same time, there is a practical linkage between the pace and scope for improved U.S.-PRC

**For additional analytical, marketing, investment and business opportunities information, please contact
Global Investment & Business Center, USA
(202) 546-2103. Fax: (202) 546-3275. E-mail: rusric@erols.com**

relations and U.S.-Taiwan relations and the pace and scope for improved Beijing-Taiwan cross-strait dialogue.

Fourth, to encourage other Asia-Pacific countries publicly to state their interest in regional peace, security, and stability.

All countries in Northeast and Southeast Asia have a stake in maintaining the principle and practice that change in the region occur peacefully, and in publicly expressing that interest.

This does not mean other countries should take sides in what they may see as a Chinese political issue. But there is a danger to all the region if non-peaceful means are employed to resolve questioned borders, territorial lines, or other disputes. While formal collective security agreements have yet to be developed in the Asia-Pacific, emerging regional institutions should perceive a collective interest in peaceful dispute resolution, including issues touching sovereign concerns.

Fifth, in the domestic sphere, it is in the U.S. interest to maintain a working Executive and Congressional working consensus on U.S.-China-Taiwan relations. Particularly in the last two years of a second presidential term, the importance of maintaining a working consensus on U.S.-China-Taiwan relations may be directly proportional to the difficulty of its achievement.

This consensus should be built around four points:

 a. reestablish executive branch leadership and bipartisan congressional support regarding the direction and priorities of U.S.-China-Taiwan relations;
 b. establish a long-term positive framework for U.S.-China-Taiwan relations that encompasses specific concerns within more overarching frameworks;
 c. accommodate the demands of both pragmatism and idealism; and,
 d. acknowledge that both sides of the Taiwan Strait maintain there is one China, as reflected in the three U.S.-PRC joint communiqués and Taiwan Relations Act.

Healthy discussion of the alternative merits of different policy approaches is a hallmark of U.S. democracy, but it is not in the U.S. interest for domestic politics in Washington to become the dispute resolution mechanism for issues better resolved directly by involved parties.

Sixth, to consider in advance the application of the Taiwan Relations Act in circumstances changed by evolving strategic developments.

Important to maintaining an equilibrium of confidence are accurate mutual assessments of intent and capability by Beijing, Taipei, and Washington as part of the process of ongoing adjustment to the mutual understanding of what and how the TRA applies in circumstances changed by ongoing strategic developments. For example, new developments in information warfare and aspects of the revolution in military affairs require ongoing efforts to fulfill U.S. obligations under the TRA. In particular, as air, land, sea, space, and electromagnetic spectrum are brought together in new strategic combinations, situations could well arise in which vital centers of national security gravity for Taiwan could come under attack without visibly triggering the TRA.

Indeed, new combinations of familiar and emerging strategies (such as a PRC air-borne blockade of Taiwan by missile-carrying planes) must be analyzed within the parameters of the three communiqués and TRA so as to forestall any misunderstandings about where and how the TRA might apply within the context of new technologies, strategies, or their applications.

**For additional analytical, marketing, investment and business opportunities information, please contact
Global Investment & Business Center, USA
(202) 546-2103. Fax: (202) 546-3275. E-mail: rusric@erols.com**

New patterns of cooperative engagement capability; of dealing with classic time, distance, and weight issues in new definitions of theater, front lines, "reach back," etc.; questions regarding effective political presence - these and many other emerging issues will shape the nature of competition and conflict in ways which will require constantly updated discussion of the U.S. interest in cross-strait applications of the TRA so as to minimize misunderstanding or miscalculation.

Mr. Chairman, I have reviewed and defined six U.S. anchor interests in the Taiwan Strait:

- preserve an equilibrium of confidence;
- maintain Taipei and Beijing's responsibility to balance their cooperation and competition;
- see Beijing and Taipei engage each other directly;
- encourage other Asia-Pacific countries publicly to state their interest in peaceful dispute resolution;
- not allow U.S. domestic politics to become the dispute resolution mechanism for Beijing-Taipei issues; and
- consider in advance U.S. obligations under the Taiwan Relations Act to changing strategic and technological circumstances.

It now remains, Mr. Chairman, to thank you and the committee again for convening us to examine this important topic at this timely juncture, and to thank you as well for your kind attention.

STRENGTHENING U.S.-TAIWAN RELATIONS: CONFIDENCE-BUILDING AND BUILDING CONFIDENCE

Dr. Hung-mao Tien, Minister of Foreign Affairs
ROC Government Information Office
20 March 2001
Good morning
Ambassador Koo,
Dr. Brown,
Ambassador Fairbanks,
Kurt
Gerrit,

Ladies and gentlemen,

It's my pleasure to address this annual CSIS Taipei roundtable meeting, now in its eighth round. Let me first thank Ambassador Koo and his stag for their efforts to maintain this important Track Two forum. As most of you know, I am a firm believer in the importance of Track Two, especially for the ROC, with our special situation.

I would also like to take this opportunity to congratulate our guests from the CSIS on the appointment of your colleagues, Bob Zoelick, Jim Kelley and Torkel Patterson to important posts in the Bush administration. I am sure they will do an excellent job, and their solid understandings of Taiwan will be of great benefit to both our countries.

Introduction

As we all know, relations between the ROC and the US are based on our many common interests, including peace and security, economic well-being, and democratic values. The question is, how can we work together to achieve these goals?

I would like to focus on the peace and security aspect, because I think we can all agree that this is the bottom line for maintaining prosperity and democracy.

Obviously, the main threat to peace and security is the possibility of the use of force across the Taiwan Strait. The US, including many of you here today, have worked hard to try to stabilize this situation, and we very much appreciate those efforts. I can

tell you very firmly that no one is more interested in maintaining peace than we are, since we will suffer the most in any conflict. But the US and other regional partners also recognize that they cannot simply stand by, since their vital interests would also be affected.

The people of Taiwan strongly desire stability. Indeed, 70 to 80 percent of the public supports steady maintenance of the status quo. This is the basic foundation for our cross-Strait policy, which President Chen made explicit by enunciating the so-called "five no's " in his inauguration speech.

Lack of mutual trust and confidence

Since then, the government has not only pledged not to destabilize the situation, but also offered many gestures of goodwill to Beijing, including the so-called "small three links" and allowing mainland reporters to come to Taiwan. However, rather like Kim Dae-jung's "sunshine policy" we aren't getting much in return. In fact, we have gotten nothing in return so far. Although President Chen has repeatedly offered to talk with

Beijing without preconditions, the PRC is still blocking any meaningful dialogue. Instead, it has launched a"united front" campaign of wooing opposition politicians and business leaders, while ignoring the goodwill of the government. Not to mention that it continues to rule out the use of force against Taiwan. This behavior has made people in Taiwan understandably nervous and suspicious.

There is, then, a potential crisis of confidence brewing in the Strait. This has two aspects. First, the most likely cause of a conflict in the shod or medium term is misperception or misunderstanding. Second, the main obstacle to a genuine peace process, moving towards a lasting settlement is the lack of trust between the two

sides. Both of these problems require greater efforts to expand communication and dialogue, well as to ensure that the two sides can approach each other on a level playing field.

The role Of the US

Here is where the United States can play a key role. First, the US should continue its arms sales to us in accordance with the Taiwan Relations Act. Also, perhaps even more importantly, it should upgrade cooperation and exchanges between the two militaries that will allow us to make the best use of the equipment we already have.

The Bush Administration will make its first decision On weapons sales to Taiwan next month. Although there is a lot of media hype about some kind of "special signal " that this decision might send, we hope that our requests will be handled according to their merits, based on our concrete defense needs, rather than unduly influenced by political factors. In this context, Secretary Powell's recent reaffirmation of the Six Assurances, that US arms sales to Taiwan will not be subject to prior consultation with Beijing, was very reassuringn.

**For additional analytical, marketing, investment and business opportunities information, please contact
Global Investment & Business Center, USA
(202) 546-2103. Fax: (202) 546-3275. E-mail: rusric@erols.com**

Second, the US can facilitate the establishment of confidence-building measures across the Strait. Some of these might be traditional military CBMs, such as transparency in defense budgeting and doctrine. Others would include promoting mutual interaction through "Track Two" venues such as CSCAP and other regional security mechanisms.

Third, the US can boost our psychological confidence, which would help lay the groundwork for future cross-Strait political talks and increase the likelihood of their success. One way in which to do this is to fulfil the pledge made in the 1994 Taiwan Policy Review to promote our substantive participation in international organizations and activities.

The continued US support for our WTO entry and clear rejection of Beijing's attempt to set new conditions on our membership is very much appreciated. In addition, assisting us to gain at least observer status at the WHO is a case in point.

Such organizations could be useful venues for officials for both sides to meet on an equal footing. I believe this would have spill-over effects into the political arena, promoting stability by creating an atmosphere of cooperation. In addition, the WTO

framework should help reduce concerns about the steady growth in trade and investment across the Strait. while Taiwanese businessmen are eagerly seeking opportunities in the mainland market, the fact that there are no clear game rules for economic exchanges means that we need to be cautious about the security implications. Finally, we should continue to work to strengthen the bilateral ties between our two countries, for example by adjusting the current restrictions on the mutual visits of senior government officials. Our Cabinet officials should be able to meet their American counterparts from the US here and in the States, as well as at other venues such as APEC. This is not a merely symbolic issue for us -- in fact, we would like such exchanges to be more routine and less politicized, so that we can engage in high-level discussions of substantive policy issues.

Conclusion

I hope this Roundtable will help promote these goals, and I look forward to your suggestions. Even better, I look forward to the day I can join this kind of forum again in Washington, as a"track one" participant! Until then, I wish you an enjoyable stay in Taipei, and all the best success for this conference.

Thank you.

SEN. TORRECELLI INTRODUCES RESOLUTION SUPPORTING PEACEFUL AND DEMOCRATIC FUTURE FOR TAIWAN

S. Con. Res. 123
25 June 2002
U.S. Senator Robert Torrecelli (D-N.J.) introduced this Senate resolution to express support for the peaceful and democratic solution on the future of Taiwan. It was referred to the Senate Foreign Relations Committee.

SENATE CONCURRENT RESOLUTION 123--EXPRESSING THE SENSE OF CONGRESS THAT THE FUTURE OF TAIWAN SHOULD BE RESOLVED PEACEFULLY, THROUGH A DEMOCRATIC MECHANISM, WITH THE EXPRESS CONSENT OF THE PEOPLE OF TAIWAN AND FREE FROM OUTSIDE THREATS, INTIMIDATION, OR INTERFERENCE -- (Senate - June 25, 2002)

Whereas in the San Francisco Peace Treaty signed on September 8, 1951 (3 U. S. T. 3169) (in this resolution referred to as the ``treaty''), Japan renounced all right, title, and claim to Taiwan;

Whereas the signatories of the treaty left the status of Taiwan undetermined;

Whereas the universally accepted principle of self-determination is enshrined in Article 1 of the United Nations Charter;

Whereas the United States is a signatory of the United Nations Charter;

Whereas the United States recognizes and supports that the right to self-determination exists as a fundamental right of all peoples, as set forth in numerous United Nations instruments;

Whereas the people of Taiwan are committed to the principles of freedom, justice, and democracy as evidenced by the March 18, 2000, election of Mr. Chen Shui-bian as Taiwan's President;

Whereas the 1993 Montevideo Convention on Rights and Duties of States defines the qualifications of a nation-state as a defined territory, a permanent population, and a government capable of entering into relations with other states;

Whereas on February 24, 2000, and March 8, 2000, President Clinton stated: ``We will . . . continue to make absolutely clear that the issues between Beijing and Taiwan must be resolved peacefully and with the assent of the people of Taiwan'';

Whereas both the 2000 Republican party platform and the Democratic party platform emphasized and made clear the belief that the future of Taiwan should be determined with the consent of the people of Taiwan; and

Whereas Deputy Secretary of State Richard Armitage said in a Senate Foreign Relations Committee hearing on March 16, 2001, that ``what has changed is that any eventual agreement that is arrived at has to be acceptable to the majority of the people on Taiwan'': Now, therefore, be it

Resolved by the Senate (the House of Representatives concurring), That it is the sense of Congress that--

(1) the future of Taiwan should be resolved peacefully, through a democratic mechanism such as a plebiscite and with the express consent of the people of Taiwan; and

(2) the future of Taiwan must be decided by the people of Taiwan without outside threats, intimidation, or interference.

UNOFFICIAL TIES WITH FREE TAIWAN

Saturday State Times/Morning Advocate (Baton Rouge, LA)
15 June 2002

The Republican Party in the United States is a member in good standing of the international association of center-right political parties, although the definition of what is "conservative" varies widely from nation to nation. Nevertheless, President Bush and Vice President Dick Cheney went out of their way to host about 50 leaders of the International Democrat Union, the association of conservatives, at the White House recently.

The American hosts used their talks to help rally international support for the need to continue and increase action against transnational terrorism.

The meeting also struck one small blow for democracy and freedom in Asia, with the inclusion of the former vice president of Taiwan at the White House dinner. Lien Chang attended as chairman of the Kuomintang Party. It is believed to be the first time that a leader from Taiwan has been invited to an official White House event since the United States normalized relations with China in 1979.

The communist leadership of mainland China did not like the symbolism. Part of the totalitarian nation's foreign policy is the incorporation of free Taiwan into the People's Republic of China, by force if necessary.

We, however, are delighted at this event. The men and women at the White House dinner were invited because of their membership in an international organization, but it is no accident that mainland China - a one-party dictatorship, without free elections and the rule of law - had no eligible representatives. Taiwan's leadership, once authoritarian under the Kuomintang Party of the 1940s and 1950s, has evolved into a vibrant multiparty democracy.

There has been a small, slow, but nevertheless welcome warming of relations between the United States and Taiwan in the Bush administration. We hope that this trend continues and grows broader and stronger with time.

U.S. LAWMAKERS SAY TAIWAN DESERVES UNWAVERING SUPPORT

Nelson Chung
Central News Agency
13 June 2002
Washington, June 12 (CNA): Four co-chairmen of the U.S. Congressional Taiwan Caucus have written Secretary of State Colin Powell and Deputy Defense Secretary Paul Wolfowitz, stressing that Taiwan, as a model democracy, "deserves the unwavering support of the American people and government."

In their June 7 letters, Reps. Robert Wexler (D-Fla.), Steve Chabot (R-Ohio), Sherrod Brown (R-Ohio) and Dana Rohrabacher (R-Calif.) welcomed Wolfowitz's clarification of his earlier statement concerning U.S. policy toward Taiwan. He said in an interview with the Taipei-based Central News Agency that "The president said from the beginning we have a one-China policy. It basically rests on two propositions. One is that we do not support Taiwan independence, but just as strongly and, I believe, central to the whole notion, we oppose the use of force."

"While we understand and support President Bush's efforts to seek a 'peaceful environment' in the Taiwan Straits, we believe that U.S. policies in the region must take into account the rights and well-being of the Taiwanese people who look to America for moral and political support," wrote the congressmen.
Taiwan, they pointed out, "as a model democracy that upholds the highest standards of political freedom and respect for human rights, deserves the unwavering support of the American people and government."

The congressmen urged both Powell and Wolfowitz to "re-affirm our nation's iron-clad commitment to Taiwan as agreed to under the Taiwan Relations Act and take steps to ensure that the Taiwan Straits issue be resolved peacefully and with the express consent of the people of Taiwan."

While addressing the Asia Society in New York Monday, Powell stressed that "On the subject of Taiwan, America's position is clear and it will not change. We will uphold our 'one China' policy and we continue to insist that the mainland solve its differences with Taiwan peacefully. Indeed a peaceful resolution is the foundation on which the breakthrough Sino-American communiques were built, and the United States takes our responsibilities under the Taiwan Relations Act very, very seriously."

SEC. OF STATE POWELL PRAISES TAIWAN

Colin L. Powell
U.S. Department of State
10 June 2002

U.S. Secretary of State Colin Powell praises Taiwan as a "become a resilient economy, a vibrant democracy and a generous contributor to the international community," in these remarks before the Asia Society.

An excerpt from Secretary Powell's speech on U.S. relations with China and Taiwan and peace and stability in the Taiwan strait.

Remarks at Asia Society Annual Dinner

Secretary Colin L. Powell
New York City
June 10, 2002

EXCERPT ON CHINA, TAIWAN AND CROSS-STRAIT RELATIONS

We remain deeply concerned about continued Chinese involvement in the proliferation of missile technology and equipment. And there is a gap between China's promises and its fulfillment of those promises. President Bush made clear at the Beijing summit that China's fulfillment of its nonproliferation commitments would be crucial to determining the quality of the United States-China relationship.

An arms build-up, like those new missiles opposite Taiwan, only deepen tensions, deepen suspicion. Whether China chooses peace or coercion to resolve its differences with Taiwan will tell us a great deal about the kind of relationship China seeks not only with its neighbors, but with us.

The differences between China and Taiwan are fundamentally political. They cannot be solved by military means.

On the subject of Taiwan, America's position is clear and it will not change. We will uphold our "One China" policy and we continue to insist that the mainland solve its differences with Taiwan peacefully. Indeed a peaceful resolution is the foundation on which the breakthrough Sino-American communiques were built, and the United States takes our responsibilities under the Taiwan Relations Act very, very seriously.

People tend to refer to Taiwan as "The Taiwan Problem". I call Taiwan not a problem, but a success story. Taiwan has become a resilient economy, a vibrant democracy and a generous contributor to the international community.

The People's Republic of China and Taiwan are both evolving rapidly. The constant in their cross-strait relationship is a common, long-term interest in the bloodless resolution of their differences. We wish them well as they work directly with one another to narrow those differences. They're doing pretty well. Taiwan has invested $80-100 billion in the mainland. Several hundred thousand Taiwanese businesspeople and their families live and work in the greater Shanghai area. Over 500,000 telephone calls cross the Strait every day. The two sides are building a foundation for a peaceful, shared future, and we applaud that.

Ultimately, how China uses its increasing wealth at home and growing influence abroad are matters for China to decide.

The United States wants to work with China to make decisions and take actions befitting a global leader. We ask China to collaborate with us and with our allies and friends to promote stability and well-being worldwide. To pressure governments that sponsor or harbor terrorists. To bring peace to regions in crisis. To become a global partner against poverty and disease, environmental degradation and proliferation.

The experience of many other Asian countries suggests that as China continues to prosper and integrate itself into the international community, its citizens will demand ever-increasing personal and political freedom.

Some think China is different -- that its culture, history and size mean that ordinary Chinese people do not care about human rights and that democracy cannot develop there. I disagree.

The desire for freedom is hard-wired into human beings. Freedom is not an optional piece of software, compatible with some cultures but not with others. No "Great Firewall of China" can separate the Chinese people from their God-given rights or keep them from joining an ever-growing community of democracies. The Chinese people want what all people want: respect for their fundamental human rights. A better life for themselves and their children. A real say in the future of their country.

Again and again in Asia, the development of large middle classes has generated growing demands for more accountability, pluralistic governance. This pattern has been repeated in places with very different cultural and religious make-ups -- Confucian, Christian and Muslim.

Again and again we have seen authoritarian regimes give way to tides of democratic reform: the Philippines in 1986, Taiwan in 1987, South Korea in 1988, Thailand in 1990, Mongolia in 1992. In 1998, Indonesia embarked on a democratic path. And just this month, as Dick Holbrooke noted, East Timor celebrated its independence and swore in its first democratically-elected government.

What we have seen in East Asia and the Pacific over the past half century, then, is a region undergoing historic transformations, all of them interrelated.

A vast and varied region engulfed in hot and cold wars and rife with internecine conflict being transformed into one of new and unprecedented stability.

To be sure, peace has not come to the Korean peninsula. Many other disputes within the region have yet to find political settlement. And how China will choose to exercise its growing power remains an open question. Still and yet, the East Asia-Pacific is more pacific now than ever.

The change on the economic front has been just as dramatic. Some Asian economies got their start earlier, some later. But in just a few generations, Asian countries that have embraced the market have gone from near universal poverty to unprecedented new levels of prosperity. Indeed, Asia's economic transformation from dominoes to dynamos has become cliché.

However, the transformation is not complete. Asian countries must undertake the reforms needed to spur their recovery from the 1997 crisis and to ensure their sustained success.

Asia's transformation toward greater political freedom can be traced from Thailand to Taiwan, from Indonesia to South Korea.

This transformation, too, is incomplete. We see new cause for hope in Burma as Aung San Suu Kyi re-enters the political process. Cambodia is strengthening a fragile democracy through more free and fair elections and the consolidation of democratic institutions. China, Laos and Vietnam have opened their economies but have yet to open their political systems. North Korea remains the chronic outlier.

But I have no doubt, no doubt whatsoever, that Asia's great transformation from dominoes to dynamos, and from dynamos to democracies will only accelerate in this new century. There will be setbacks and dangers ahead for sure. I am equally sure that they will be surmounted by the determination and ingenuity of the peoples of Asia.

TAIPEI-WASHINGTON TIES BETTER THAN EVER: PRESIDENT

CNA
23 May 2002

Taipei, May 23 (CNA) The present bilateral relations between Taipei and Washington are better since U.S. President George W. Bush came to power in 2000 than they have been for the last 30 years, President Chen Shui-bian said Thursday.

Chen made the remarks while giving a speech to welcome a 30-member delegation of the United States-based National Newspaper Association.

Describing Taipei-Washington ties as in their best shape ever, Chen said the two countries are "inseparable democratic allies" and he thanked the United States for its long-term support for Taiwan.

Based on common aspirations jointly shared by the two countries, such as democracy, freedom and human rights, Chen said the United States is willing to help Taiwan safeguard its democracy, while
Taiwan will do its best to help maintain international order in the Asia-Pacific region and the rest of the world.

"Both countries hope for stability and prosperity in the Taiwan Strait and increased trade and economic exchanges are mutually beneficial," the president noted.

Stressing that he has been pursuing a normalized and peaceful relationship between Taiwan and mainland China since his inauguration two years ago, he said that building Taiwan into an advanced and vigorous "green silicon island" and a progressive democracy has been high on the government's agenda.

Now, he noted, with Taiwan's entry into the World Trade Organization after a 12-year-long effort, the country is keen to be a constructive member of the international community and has cooperated in the U.S.-led war against terrorism, as well as extending humanitarian assistance to Afghan refugees.

However, the president also lamented the unfair treatment Taiwan receives in international society due to the strong pressure from Beijing. As the world's 14th-largest exporter and the seventh-largest trade partner of the United States, Taiwan does not enjoy the rightful dignity and international status due to a sovereign state, he added.

Although Taiwan has recently suffered a fresh defeat -- the sixth in a row -- in its bid to observe this year's World Health Assembly, Chen said Taiwan still thanks Washington and the American people for their firm backing for Taiwan.

"As a sovereign and independent state, Taiwan will continue seeking to participate in major international organizations such as the United Nations," he said.

Turning to relations between the two sides of the Taiwan Strait, Chen said Taiwan is willing to conduct negotiations with mainland China without any set preconditions, as long as "Taiwan is not downgraded or marginalized to the status of a local government by the mainland."

He also said setting up direct transport, trade and postal links across the strait is an unavoidable issue and that Taiwan should sign free trade agreements with the United States, Japan and Singapore to fend off the pull of the vast mainland Chinese market.

"Taiwan and the mainland should increase contacts, dialogue and understanding to reduce misunderstanding and miscalculation," Chen urged, voicing his hope that mainland President Jiang Zemin will visit Taiwan and that he himself can embark on a trip to Fujian Province to trace his ancestral roots as soon as possible.
(By Flor Wang)

TAIWAN RELATIONS ACT -- HON. JOHN B. LARSON (EXTENSIONS OF REMARKS - APRIL 10, 2002)

[Page: E484]

HON. JOHN B. LARSON

OF CONNECTICUT

IN THE HOUSE OF REPRESENTATIVES

Wednesday, April 10, 2002

Mr. LARSON of Connecticut. Mr. Speaker, I rise today on the twenty-third anniversary of the Taiwan Relations Act (P.L. 96-8) to reaffirm our commitment to the security of Taiwan.

First, I believe it is important to remember that this law was enacted ``to preserve and promote extensive, close, and friendly commercial, cultural, and other relations between the people of the United States and the people on Taiwan, ... to declare that peace and stability in the area are in the political, security, and economic interests of the United States, and are matters of international concern; ..... to make clear that the United States decision to establish diplomatic relations with the People's Republic of China rests upon the expectation that the future of Taiwan will be determined by peaceful means; ..... to provide Taiwan with arms of a defensive character, ... and to maintain the capacity of the United States to resist any resort to force or other forms of coercion that would jeopardize the security, or the social or economic system, of the people of Taiwan."

Even though we do not have official diplomatic relations with Taiwan, we have many "unofficial" contacts. Taiwan and the United States share common interests in many areas, such as trade and investment, science and technology, education, culture and security. The recent legislative elections in Taiwan shows that it shares our commitment to true democratic values and serve as a model for other nations in the region. We also share a respect for the freedom of the press, which I hope continues.

On the twenty-third anniversary of the enactment of the Taiwan Relations Act, I hope we will continue our cooperation with the democratically elected government of Taiwan by taking a number of steps; such as allowing Taiwan officials and our officials to meet freely in Washington and Taipei, improving Taiwan's access to our government agencies, and helping Taiwan become a member of appropriate international organizations such as the World Health Organization. The officials of Taiwan were chosen by the twenty-two million people of Taiwan to represent them and we should respect their choice. Taiwan is our seventh largest trading partner, and there are many critical economic, trade, health, security, and other issues which its officials need to discuss with our government officials as well as officials of international organizations.

Mr. Speaker, I believe that the recent formation of the Congressional Taiwan Caucus shows our support for the Taiwan Relations Act and our commitment to maintaining the military balance across the Taiwan Strait to counter the buildup on the Mainland. Therefore, I rise today to commemorate the twenty-third anniversary of the Act, to restate our commitment to the security of Taiwan, and to show our support for cooperation between Taiwan and the United States. Thank you.

NEW TRENDS IN TAIWAN DIPLOMACY

NGOS GIVE TAIWANESE A VOICE TO THE WORLD

Nongovernmental organizations have become increasingly important locally and internationally

By Diana Freundl
CONTRIBUTING REPORTER
Sunday, Jul 25, 2004, Page 18

"It's unbelievable how many people still ask me, `How do you make enough money to live?' Most people don't want to get involved in NGOs as their life career, because they worry about making a lot of money," said Klaus Ding (丁元亨), the executive director of Vision Youth Action.

After attending an international conference on youth leadership in the US, Ding, 30, and colleague Antonio Chen (陳建銘), 24, were so inspired by the participation of so many youngsters in NGOs they decided to create their own organization.

In March 2002 they formed Vision Youth Action (VYA), a youth-run and youth-serving NGO. It organizes seminars taught by senior members of international NGOs, as well as sponsoring volunteer exchange programs with NGOs in the US.

Founders of the youth-run and youth-serving NGO, Vision Youth Action, executive director Klaus Ding, left, and Antonio Chen stand with intern Eva Wu, in their new office in Taipei.
PHOTO: DIANA FREUNDL, TAIPEI TIMES

NGOs are nonprofit organizations that typically promote local or global social justice and environmental issues. Also referred to as the "third sector" (the first and second being public and private), or civil society sector, NGOs have grown to become a vital part of the international community.

At the International Volunteers Exchange Program, in Tianmu, mothers share stories on community building.
PHOTO: DIANA FREUNDL, TAIPEI TIMES

While the number of NGOs in Taiwan is increasing, as is the number of young people interested in short term work experience, society's attitudes regarding NGOs as a viable career path have yet to catch up.

A study by the Ministry of Interior showed there was a total of 30,699 NGOs registered in Taiwan last year, which accounts for 2.2 percent of the world total (placing Taiwan second behind the US).

Despite strong global business ties Taiwan's international diplomacy is officially limited to a short list of allies. Since 1971 when Taiwan lost its seat in the UN, the island's diplomacy has been under the watchful eye of China, making it difficult for Taiwan to participate in international government organizations.

The formation of NGOs after the lifting of martial law in 1987, however, has become an important channel for Taiwan to participate in the international community, said the director of the third sector of the National Youth Commission (NYC) under the Executive Yuan, Li Chen-chang (林辰璋).

The future development of Taiwan's civil society, he said, depends on the participation of the next generation. "There are four distinct characteristics of young people: energetic, creative, passionate, idealistic. These are the exact qualities NGOs need. NGOs provide an important stage for young people to show those characteristics and at the same time those people further develop this sector," Li said.

Recruiting young persons to work in NGOs is easy, said Wu Yi-ming (吳英明), a political economics professor at Sun Yat-sen University, who witnessed an increase in interest among university students over the past five years.

"I see the young generation take more responsibility in terms of volunteering in, and organization of civil society," Wu said. A staunch supporter of Taiwan's third sector, he feels NGOs not only strengthen Taiwan's diplomatic position, but also provide a vehicle for youths to gain valuable work experience.

"Nowadays students need more involvement in extra curricular activities to get into university, it's not only about entrance exams anymore. Volunteering for NGOs is a useful tool for these students to get valuable life and work experience," he said.

Curiosity and the prospect of building up their resumes might attract interns and short term employees, but the stability of NGOs depends on long-term commitment, said Lu Huang Li-juan (劉黃麗娟) of the Taiwan branch of International Medical Alliance.

"The international aspect is attractive and yes it's a precious experience, but what about the long term? This is a serious issue for future NGO development. We will need younger generations to replace people as they retire, but are they [young people] interested in working in NGOs as their career?" she said.

Part of the problem, Lu said has to do with the stigma attached to NGOs as an unstable career choice. "People are very concerned with economic stability and job promotion and there is a view that NGO work is unstable."

This is a view that needs to change before the third sector can prosper in Taiwan, she said. "It's not flourishing, but it's growing. We are seeing more opportunities, but it's going to take time to mature."

Dedicated to creating a stronger civil society sector the NYC has begun to offer a number of training programs to improve the skills of those already employed in NGOs, as well as offering information seminars aimed at university students who might not know anything about the opportunities open to them.

"Students in Taiwan don't have much exposure to the third sector, therefore we hope to build up their awareness of NGOs as a career choice. A group might start as volunteers, but eventually they may consider working for a NGO as a full-time employee," Lin said.

He didn't have figures for the number of full-time NGO employees between the ages of 18 to 35, but said the number of young people working in the sector has increased dramatically in the last few years.

With five interns currently placed as NGOs in the US, Ding is optimistic his NGO will offer many young people in Taiwan the opportunity to intern at NGOs around the world in the future. For now, however, he is realistic about just how much impact he has on the youth of Taiwan.

**For additional analytical, marketing, investment and business opportunities information, please contact
Global Investment & Business Center, USA
(202) 546-2103. Fax: (202) 546-3275. E-mail: rusric@erols.com**

"Even if it is just the international affairs aspect that first attracts them, I think as long as there is an interest, it can be cultivated," he said.

Serena Lin (林辰㛃) is one of five Taiwanese graduates on the VYA internship at the Woodrow Wilson Center in Washington. The idea of working and living abroad is what initially attracted her to working for an NGO, but she said young people like her will play an essential part in the future development of Taiwan's civil society.

"A framework of democracy was built by the last generation, but the actual content still needs to be filled. Our role as the next generation is to build up the civil service sector."

**For additional analytical, marketing, investment and business opportunities information, please contact
Global Investment & Business Center, USA
(202) 546-2103. Fax: (202) 546-3275. E-mail: rusric@erols.com**

POLITICAL AND GOVERNMENT SYSTEM

CHEN SHUI-BIAN, TENTH-TERM PRESIDENT OF THE REPUBLIC OF CHINA

Chen Shui-bian was born to a tenant farming family in Kuantien Township of Tainan County in the ninth month of the lunar calendar in 1950. Because he was very weak as an infant, the family did not register his birth with the local census bureau until 1951. Thus, his identification certificate shows his date of birth as February 18, 1951.

The Chen family's poverty did not diminish his aspirations for a better future. The family borrowed money to put him through school, and he graduated at the top of his class from Lungtien Elementary School, the junior department of Tsengwen High School, and the Tainan First High School.

In 1969, he passed the Joint College and University Entrance Examinations and was admitted to the business administration division of the commerce department of National Taiwan University (NTU), his first choice. However, he soon found that this course of study did not interest him. Coincidentally, the first supplementary and additional by-elections for the Legislative Yuan were held around that time. Huang Hsin-chieh, who later became the chairman of the Democratic Progressive Party, was running in the election, and Mr. Chen was deeply moved by his campaign speech. He decided to study law instead.

The following year, Mr. Chen again participated in the Joint College and University Entrance Examinations. This time, he ranked first among all students admitted into the NTU's department of law. During his junior year, he took the national bar examination and passed with the highest grade, becoming the nation's youngest lawyer at the time. Before he graduated from the university, Mr. Chen worked at a law office on international legal cases.

Later, he realized that the island of Taiwan had always maintained maritime contact with the outside world and relied on sea transportation to develop international trade and increase its strength. Therefore, Mr. Chen decided to become a specialist in maritime law. In 1975, Mr. Chen married Miss Wu Shu-chen, and he became a full-time lawyer. They have one daughter and one son.

In 1980, the "Kaohsiung Incident" resulted in the arrest of many activists, after a mass demonstration turned violent, with hundreds injured. The defendants were sent for trial under martial law. In effect, the arrests and trials consolidated the opposition's demands for changes in the government and focused world attention on the political situation in Taiwan. With the support of his wife, Mr. Chen became a member of the team of defense attorneys, acting as lawyer for Huang Hsin-chieh. Thus, Mr. Chen began to dedicate himself to politics.

Along with the other leaders of the opposition, Mr. Chen continued the work of the older generation in seeking freedom, human rights, and democracy for the people on Taiwan. He spread his opinions and theories on the parliamentary checks and balances, thus presenting the best defense in the "court of people's conscience" that freedom and human rights should be of the utmost importance, and democracy should be irreproachable.

In 1979, Mr. Chen ran for public office for the first time. He was elected as a member of the Fourth Taipei City Council with the highest number of votes. Adhering to his good conscience and viewing good and evil in terms of black and white, Mr. Chen became well-known for exposing injustice and incisively criticizing government administration.

In 1984, the libel case referred to as the "Formosa magazine incident" occurred. Since Mr. Chen was the director of the magazine, he was accused of libel. In 1985, after the court's decision in the first trial, Mr. Chen left his post as Taipei city councilman and returned to his hometown in Tainan County to run for county magistrate. He was defeated by a narrow margin, as a result of the KMT's concerted efforts.

On November 18, 1985, while Mr. Chen was thanking voters for their support, his wife was hit by an improvised tractor-truck. Although Mrs. Chen's life was saved, the lower part of her body became paralyzed even after several operations. The pain of the accident has since all the more strengthened his determination to support and assist the weak.

In 1986, Mr. Chen was sentenced to eight months in prison for criminal libel. On June 10, he began serving his sentence in the Tucheng Penitentiary along with Huang Tien-fu and Lee Yi-yang, two other defendants in the same case. This was the most difficult time for the Chen family. Fortunately, Mr. and Mrs. Chen shared a very strong affection toward each other and continuously supported and encouraged each other.

At the end of 1986, Mrs. Chen was elected to the Legislative Yuan. After Mr. Chen was released from prison in 1987, he joined the Democratic Progressive Party and served as assistant to Mrs. Chen, while continuing to practice law.

In December 1989, Mr. Chen was elected to the Legislative Yuan under the call for justice, progress, and security, and he took the post as the first executive director of the DPP caucus. In December 1992, he was re-elected. During his term as a legislator, Mr. Chen urged replacing political struggle with policy debate, greatly changing the opposition party's attitude and opening additional opportunities for political participation.

Mr. Chen was the first to set up a legislator's office and concentrated his efforts on professionalism. He was also the first legislator from an opposition party to become the convener of the National Defense Committee of the Legislative Yuan.

Mr. Chen proposed placing the command of the armed forces directly under the nation, laying a legal foundation for intelligence units, unifying military administration and military command, and making military procurements public. Mr. Chen also dedicated his efforts to protecting the rights of servicemen and consequently received praise as the best legislator by many professional groups and journalists reporting on legislative affairs.

In the party, Mr. Chen moderated DPP statements on Taiwan independence. In 1988, the DPP released its policy statements on "Taiwan Independent Sovereignty" and "Self-determination by the People of Taiwan." Mr. Chen coordinated with party factions and advocated the "four if's," as the premise for DPP's advocacy of Taiwan independence in order to demonstrate the fundamental spirit of communication and dialogue among the entire citizenry.

The "four if's" were: If the KMT and the Chinese communists unilaterally carry out peace talks; if the KMT sells out the interests of the Taiwan people; if the Chinese communists annex Taiwan; and if the KMT does not truly implement constitutional democracy.

**For additional analytical, marketing, investment and business opportunities information, please contact
Global Investment & Business Center, USA
(202) 546-2103. Fax: (202) 546-3275. E-mail: rusric@erols.com**

In 1991, based on the principle that sovereignty belongs to the people, the DPP was prepared to establish a Taiwan nation as its goal. Mr. Chen suggested adding in the procedures: "Based on the principle that sovereignty belongs to the people, the issue should be decided by the entire populace on Taiwan through a referendum."

Thus, the DPP independence platform was revised to include a plebiscite, which would accommodate dialogue among different ideological groups. This represents Mr. Chen's well-considered, rational, and pragmatic approach to cross-strait relations to open opportunities for historic dialogue and progress.

Mr. Chen has always abided by his motto "Do your best for whatever the job requires." This fully demonstrates his attitude that preparedness ensures success. In August 1993, in order to prepare for the first-term popularly elected provincial governor and city mayors scheduled for 1994, he set up the Chen Shui-bian Municipal Administration Center to host lectures and seminars to get acquainted with city administration and planning.

When he was nominated by the DPP, Mr. Chen proposed the idea of "Happy Citizenry and City of Hope," emphasizing citizenship and the cooperation and coexistence of the four ethnic groups. He was elected and became the first popularly elected Taipei mayor, after the city was elevated to the status of a special municipality in 1967.

This was the first time the position of Taipei mayor was held by an opposition political party. Talent and ability, rather than ethnic origins or party affiliation, were the basic requirements of Mr. Chen's city administration. He transformed the Taipei City Government into a new team by realizing the conceptual revolution of administering city government with entrepreneurship, professionalism, resolve, and task orientation.

In his inaugural speech as Taipei mayor, he outlined three points as the focus of his administration: establishing a clean government, promoting efficiency, and conveniently serving the public. His administration also consistently emphasized the principles of citizenry, strengthening social welfare and cultural leisure activities, and reforming transportation and communications, education, and urban development.

During Mr. Chen's term of office as Taipei mayor, Taipei citizens generally praised his achievements and efforts. Significant progress was made in such areas as supervising the schedules of large-scale construction works, improving Taipei's traffic and opening the Taipei Rapid Transit Systems (TRTS), expanding the city's sewage system, promoting the Taipei Art Festival and Lantern Festival, and eliminating electronic game arcades and other specially licensed businesses.

The improvement of Taipei's civil administration and the quality services provided by the Mucha line of the TRTS were awarded the ISO 9002 certificate. Taipei City was ranked as the fifth-best city in Asia for quality of life in 1998 by Asian Week magazine (formerly ranked below ten). Mr. Chen was selected as one of the one hundred top world leaders of the new century by Time magazine and one of the top fifty future Asian leaders by Asian Week magazine.

Mr. Chen advocates "letting Taipei go out and the world come in," as a part of his concept of promoting city-state diplomacy and enhancing national consciousness to prevent Taiwan from vanishing from the international scene. During his term of office as mayor, Taipei established 14 sister-city relationships and one partner-city relationship. In 1998, Taipei hosted the first World Capitals Forum, with 58 countries and 67 cities participating, thus expanding Taiwan's diplomacy and increasing its international visibility.

For additional analytical, marketing, investment and business opportunities information, please contact
Global Investment & Business Center, USA
(202) 546-2103. Fax: (202) 546-3275. E-mail: rusric@erols.com

In December 1998, Mr. Chen stated, after losing his re-election bid for the mayor's office, "Indifference to a progressive team is a phenomenon of a great city." The people urged him to run for the presidency instead. Although defeated, he did not give up. On the contrary, he clearly realizes that politicians need to make continuous progress in order to fulfill the high expectations of the people and win their confidence.

After his departure from the mayor's office, Mr. Chen has engaged in quiet study and sought advice from many sectors of society. In 1999, he began a fact-finding journey throughout the island, listening to what people say and considering the country's future. He also visited Japan, South Korea, and Mongolia to discuss the establishment of a collective security system in the Asia-Pacific region.

He also traveled to the United States and held talks with outstanding research institutes and leading policy-makers, claiming that the security of Taiwan was essential to international stability. Even as a private citizen when out of office, Mr. Chen showed his concern for Taiwan's development and security under the impact of globalization.

In view of Taiwan's many differences in ethnic identity and ideology, Mr. Chen advocated a "New Middle Road," focusing on national security during his campaign for the second direct presidential election of the Republic of China. He supported the ideals of forgiving wrongs, transcending differences, and elevating political thought. While emphasizing clear and firm concepts, he insisted on tolerant and pragmatic approaches to policy implementation.

In July 1999, Mr. Chen accepted the nomination of the Democratic Progressive Party as its candidate for the 2000 presidential election. In his speech "New Politics is the Good Foundation for Taiwan's Next Century," he urged the people to cooperate in terminating the "black gold system" (money politics) and to implement a change of ruling parties. Subsequently, he advocated establishing a "Young Taiwan and Energetic Government" to sustain Taiwan's vitality.

During the campaign, Mr. Chen asserted that both sides of the Taiwan Strait should uphold the principles of "Goodwill Reconciliation, Active Cooperation, and Permanent Peace," thereby initiating the normalization of their bilateral relationship. Since permanent peace is not only the most rational and highest goal, but is also the ethical duty of a head-of-state, Mr. Chen has continuously expressed his goodwill to the Chinese mainland and opened the possibility of holding dialogue and conducting cooperation, under the premise of maintaining sovereignty, dignity, and security.

On March 18, 2000, Mr. Chen Shui-bian and Ms. Hsiu-lien Annette Lu were elected as the tenth-term president and vice president of the Republic of China. With their inauguration on May 20, 2000, the peaceful transfer of presidential power to another political party is an constant reminder that the democratic process is rapidly maturing in Taiwan and is an outstanding example for developing democracies around the world, as well as the Chinese mainland.

Shortly after he was elected, Mr. Chen invited the Minister of National Defense Mr. Tang Fei, a member of the KMT, to form a "Government for all People," with a balanced representation of both men and women. Mr. Chen considers honesty and professionalism in the new government as essential for the overall benefit of the economy, politics, and cross-strait relations. Developing Taiwan into a high-tech "Green Silicon Island," promoting permanent peace in the Taiwan Strait through a consensus on the island, and dedicating the national spirit and achievements to the world are the major themes of the Chen administration.

Mr. Chen is the author of The Son of Taiwan and other books. He was awarded an Honorary Doctorate of Laws and an Honorary Doctorate in Political Science by Kyungnam University and Yong-In University, respectively, in Korea, and an Honorary Doctorate in Economics by Plekhanov Academy of Economics in Russia.

In December 1999, at the invitation of Professor Anthony Giddens, the Director of the London School of Economics and Political Science, he delivered a speech titled "The New Middle Road for Taiwan: A New Political Perspective" and explained his political philosophy.

STRUCTURE OF THE GOVERNMENT

The ROC government is divided into three main levels: central, provincial, municipal, and county/city, each of which has well-defined powers. The central government consists of the Office of the President , the National Assembly , and five governing branches (called "yuan"), namely the Executive Yuan , the Legislative Yuan , the Judicial Yuan , the Examination Yuan , and the Control Yuan .

At the provincial level, the provincial governments exercise administrative responsibility. Since the ROC government administers only Taiwan Province and two counties in Fukien Province, only two provincial governments are currently operational--the Taiwan Provincial Government and the Fukien Provincial Government . The Fukien Provincial Government oversees the regional affairs of Kinmen County and Lienchiang County . Likewise, the Taiwan Provincial Government exercises full jurisdiction over Taiwan's 16 counties and all the cities except for Taipei and Kaohsiung, which are special municipalities directly under the jurisdiction of the central government instead of the Taiwan Provincial Government.

At the local level and under the Taiwan Provincial Government, there are five cities--Keelung, Hsinchu, Taichung, Chiayi, and Tainan--and 16 counties, and under each county there are county municipalities .

EXECUTIVE

The president of the Republic of China is the highest representative of the nation and is granted specific constitutional powers to conduct national affairs. Scores of agencies and advisors assist the president in reaching decisions on state affairs. They include senior advisors, national policy advisors, military advisors, and organizations and institutions such as the Academia Sinica, Academia Historica, National Security Council, and National Unification Council.

The May 20, 1996 inauguration of President Lee Teng-hui as the ninth-term president of the ROC ushered in a new period of development for the then 84-year-old republic. Lee served in the presidency as the first popularly elected head-of-state in Chinese history. Taiwan has undergone dramatic changes since Lee became the head-of-state in 1988 upon the death of President Chiang Ching-kuo. After accomplishing astounding economic development over the decades, the ROC achieved an equivalent political miracle--the much acclaimed "quiet revolutions."

The tenth term presidential election was held in March 2000. Nominees for president were Lien Chan for KMT, Chen Shui-bian for DPP, and Li Ao for the New Party, and two independents--James Soong and Hsu Hsin-liang. Chen Shui-bian was the winner with 39.3 percent of the votes, followed closely by James Soong with 36.84 percent. Lien Chan, the KMT candidate was a distant third with 23.1 percent.

FUNCTIONS

As chief of state, the president represents the country in its foreign relations and at state functions. All acts of state are conducted in his name, including command of the land, sea, and air forces; promulgation of laws and decrees; declaration of martial law with the approval of the Legislature; conclusion of treaties; declaration of war and cease-fire; convening of the National Assembly; granting of amnesty and commutations; appointment and removal of civil service officials and military officers; and conferring of honors and decorations. All these powers are exercised in accordance with the provisions of the Constitution and the law.

SPECIAL POWERS

NOMINATING OFFICIALS

The President is entitled to appoint the president of the Executive Yuan. With the consent of the Legislature, he also appoints the auditor-general of the Control Yuan, the president, vice president, and the grand justices of the Judicial Yuan (Judiciary); the president, vice president, and members of the Examination Yuan; and the president, vice president, and members of the Control Yuan.

RESOLVING INTER-BRANCH DISPUTES

In the event of a dispute among the various branches, such as a controversy between the Executive Yuan and the Legislature, the president may intervene to seek a solution. Article 44 of the Constitution states: "In case of disputes between two or more branches other than those for which there are relevant provisions in the Constitution, the president may call a meeting of the presidents of the branches concerned for consultation with a view to reaching a solution."

EXERCISING EMERGENCY POWERS

According to Article 2 of the *Additional Articles of the Constitution of the Republic of China* revised in July 1997, the president may, by resolution of the Executive Yuan council, issue emergency orders and take all necessary measures to avert an imminent threat to the security of the state or the people, or to cope with any serious financial or economic crisis, without being subject to the restrictions prescribed in Article 43 of the Constitution. However, such orders must, within 10 days of issuance, be presented to the Legislature for confirmation. Should the Legislature withhold confirmation, the said emergency orders immediately cease to be valid.

DISSOLVING THE LEGISLATIVE YUAN

The president may, within ten days following passage by the Legislative Yuan of a no-confidence vote against the president of the Executive Yuan, declare the dissolution of the Legislative Yuan after consulting with its president. However, the president may not dissolve the Legislative Yuan while martial law or an emergency order is in effect. Following the dissolution of the Legislative Yuan, an election for legislators will be held within 60 days. The new Legislative Yuan is to convene of its own accord within ten days after the results of the said election have been confirmed, and the term of the said Legislative Yuan will be figured from that date.

**For additional analytical, marketing, investment and business opportunities information, please contact
Global Investment & Business Center, USA
(202) 546-2103. Fax: (202) 546-3275. E-mail: rusric@erols.com**

Following the dissolution of the Legislative Yuan by the president and prior to the inauguration of its newly elected members, the Legislative Yuan will be regarded as in recess.

THE OFFICE OF THE PRESIDENT

ADMINISTRATION

The secretary-general to the president takes general charge of the affairs of the Office of the President and directs and supervises staff members. The president is assisted by two deputy secretaries-general.

The bureaus and offices under the Office of the President perform the following functions: The First Bureau is in charge of promulgation of laws and decrees, drafting and safekeeping of confidential documents, and other general political affairs, while the bureau director also serves as chancellor of the national seal; the Second Bureau is in charge of information systems and transmission of documents; the Third Bureau is in charge of protocol and awarding honors, making and distributing official seals, publications, and other administrative and technical affairs; the Code Office is in charge of telegraphic correspondence and national archives; the Office of the Guards is in charge of security. The Department of Public Affairs, set up in January 1996, is in charge of public relations.

SUBORDINATE OFFICES

There are four institutions under the direct administrative supervision of the Office of the President: Academia Sinica, Academia Historica, the National Unification Council, and the National Security Council.

The Academia Sinica, the leading research institution in the ROC, was established in Nanking on June 9, 1928. Its two basic missions are to conduct scientific research and to direct, coordinate, and promote scientific research throughout the ROC. Although it is a unit of the government, the Academia Sinica enjoys virtually independent status. The most important body within the Academia Sinica is the Assembly of Members. The members, commonly known as "academicians," are elected for life from among Chinese scholars of distinction. On July 9, 1998, 23 new members--ten from outside the ROC and 13 based in Taiwan--were elected, marking the first time that Taiwan-based scholars outnumbered those from overseas. The 23 new members brought the total number of academicians to 197. Their duties include formulating national research policy and pursuing specific research at the request of the government. As of mid-1998, the Academia Sinica had 24 institutes, six of them still preparatory offices, including the two newly established Institute of Bioagriculture and Institute of Linguistics. The Academia Sinica is staffed by approximately 800 full-time research fellows.

The Academia Historica is responsible for preserving documents and conducting research in modern Chinese history, particularly that of the republican period. The academy has a collection of 7.5 million publications and national records, mainly from the Office of the President, the Executive Yuan, provincial and local governments, plus some personal and other archives. Most of the records are open to the staff of Academia Historica and researchers.

Founded in 1990, the National Unification Council now consists of 32 leaders in various fields, from both the government and the private sector, organized into task groups. The NUC recommends national unification policies to the president, helps the government to devise a national unification framework, and builds consensus at all levels of society and in all political parties concerning the issue of national unification. The NUC has already approved the

Guidelines for National Unification, which are the highest directives governing ROC mainland policy.

The National Security Council, established in 1967 and chaired by the president, is an advisory body to the president. The main functions of the National Security.Council and its subsidiary organ, the National Security Bureau, are to determine the ROC's national security policies and to assist in planning the ROC's security strategy.

THE NATIONAL ASSEMBLY

The National Assembly is more limited in scope than the parliament or congress of a Western democracy. In the Republic of China, the role of "parliament" is jointly filled by the National Assembly and the Legislative Yuan.

Six functions of the National Assembly were as follows: (1) to elect the vice president when the said office becomes vacant; (2) to recall the president and the vice president; (3) to pass a resolution on the impeachment of the president or vice president instituted by the Legislative Yuan; (4) to amend the Constitution; (5) to vote in the exercise of its rights of referendum on proposed constitutional amendments submitted by the Legislative Yuan; (6) to exercise the power of consent to confirm the appointment of personnel nominated by the president of the ROC.

The president may issue a notice of convocation when the National Assembly is to exercise its powers prescribed in items (4) and (5), or when requested by no less than two-fifths of its members. The Speaker of the National Assembly may convoke a session to institute the recall or impeachment of the president or vice-president. The National Assembly is required to implement initiatives and referendums decided by the people of the Republic of China in accordance with Article 17 of the Constitution.

Another unique power of the National Assembly is spelled out in Article 4 of the Constitution: "The territory of the Republic of China within its existing national boundaries shall not be altered except by resolution of the National Assembly."

The assembly is led by a Speaker and Deputy Speaker, both of whom are chosen by the Assembly from among its delegates.

DELEGATES

Delegates to the National Assembly are elected according to Article 1 of the Additional Articles of the Constitution without being subject to the restrictions in Articles 26, 28 and 135 of the Constitution. In 1996, an election for the Third National Assembly was held in accordance with the old version of the Additional Articles of the Constitution of the Republic of China. Of the 334 members elected, 234 delegates were from the Taiwan area, with an additional 80 members representing a nationwide constituency and 20 representing overseas Chinese.

The four-year tenure for the Third National Assembly began on May 20, 1996. Former Assembly Speaker Fredrick Chien was nominated by President Lee Teng-hui on December 3, 1998, as the new president of the Control Yuan, and Shieh Lung-sheng, former Deputy Speaker of the Assembly, was called upon to accept a new post. Su Nan-cheng was elected Speaker of the National Assembly in a by-election on January 13, 1999 and Chen Ching-jang was elected Deputy Speaker. On September 4, 1999, the Third National Assembly passed constitutional amendments which significantly changed the election and composition of the Fourth and Fifth

National Assemblies. As a result of the controversy surrounding the tenure extension for members of the ROC's Third National Assembly, Su resigned in late September and Chen became the acting speaker.

The amendments on election procedures and composition were intended to make the National Assembly further reflect popular opinion. However, the Council of Grand Justices ruled the amendments invalid, because the deputies cast secret ballots. Claiming that the grand justices have no right to make this decision, the DPP wanted to dissolve the National Assembly immediately and establish a unicameral legislative system. With the support of the KMT and the New Party, the deputies passed yet another series of Constitution amendments on April 24, 2000. The Third National Assembly will be terminated on May 19, 2000, and a 300-member non-standing body will be elected on a proportional-representation system, according to laws to be passed by the Legislative Yuan. The National Assemblys functions will be limited to vote on Constitution amendments, presidential impeachment, or alternation of the national boundaries, as proposed by the Legislative Yuan. Other powers, such as hearing the presidents State of Nation Report and approving presidential appointments to the Judicial, Examination, and Control Yuans, will be transferred to the Legislative Yuan.

FIVE GOVERNMENT BRANCHES

The ROC Constitution provides for a central government with five "yuan" (branches)--the Executive Yuan, the Legislative Yuan (Legislature), the Judicial Yuan (Judiciary), the Examination Yuan, and the Control Yuan.

EXECUTIVE YUAN

The Executive Yuan has a president, usually referred to as the premier of the ROC; a vice president; a number of ministers and chairmen of commissions; and five to seven ministers-without-portfolio. The president of the Executive Yuan is appointed by the president of the Republic. If the president of the Executive Yuan resigns or if his office becomes vacant, his functions are temporarily exercised by the vice president of the Executive Yuan.

The vice president of the Executive Yuan, ministers, and chairmen are appointed by the president of the Republic on the recommendation of the president of the Executive Yuan. In addition to supervising the operations of the various subordinate agencies of the Executive Yuan, the president of the Executive Yuan is also responsible for the following: performing the duties of the president of the Republic in the event of vacancies in both the presidency and the vice presidency (this caretaker duty is limited to three months); presenting administrative policies and reports to the Legislature and responding, either orally or in writing, to the interpellations of legislators; countersigning laws and decrees proclaimed by the president of the Republic; and requesting, with the approval of the president, the Legislative Yuan to reconsider its resolutions.

Tang Fei was appointed to serve as the president of the ROC's Executive Yuan beginning May 20, 2000.

There are three levels of subordinate organizations under the Executive Yuan: the Executive Yuan Council; executive organizations, i.e., the eight ministries, the Mongolian and Tibetan Affairs Commission and the Overseas Chinese Affairs Commission; and subordinate departments, including the Directorate General of Budget, Accounting, and Statistics, the Government Information Office, and other special commissions and ad hoc committees.

EXECUTIVE YUAN COUNCIL

The Executive Yuan Council is a policy-making organization that comprises the president of the Executive Yuan, who presides over its meetings, the vice president of the Executive Yuan, ministers-without-portfolio, the heads of the ROC's eight ministries, and the heads of the Mongolian and Tibetan Affairs Commission as well as the Overseas Chinese Affairs Commission. According to Article 58 of the Constitution, the Council discusses and decides on statutory and budgetary bills and bills concerning martial law, amnesty, declarations of war, conclusion of peace or treaties, and other important affairs, which are to be submitted to the Legislature, as well as matters of common concern to the various ministries and commissions. The Council may invite heads of other organizations under the Executive Yuan to attend council meetings and answer any questions that may arise pertaining to affairs under their jurisdiction. The secretary-general and the deputy secretary-general also attend the meetings; however, they have no vote.

MINISTRIES AND OTHER ORGANIZATIONS

There are eight ministries under the Executive Yuan. They are the ministries of the Interior, Foreign Affairs, National Defense, Finance, Education, Justice, Economic Affairs, and Transportation and Communications.

In addition to the Mongolian and Tibetan Affairs Commission and the Overseas Chinese Affairs Commission, a number of commissions and subordinate organizations have been formed with the resolution of the Executive Yuan Council and the Legislature to meet new demands and handle new affairs. Examples include the Environmental Protection Administration, which was set up in 1987 as public awareness of pollution control rose; the Mainland Affairs Council, which was established in 1990 to handle the thawing of relations between Taiwan and the Chinese mainland; the Fair Trade Commission, which was established in 1992 to promote a fair trade system; and the Consumer Protection Commission, which was set up in July 1994 to study and review basic policies on consumer protection.

Since 1995, even more commissions have been set up to provide a wider scope of services: the Public Construction Commission was set up in July 1995, the Council of Aboriginal Affairs in December 1996, and the National Council on Physical Fitness and Sports in July 1997.

RELATIONSHIP WITH THE LEGISLATIVE YUAN

The Executive Yuan has to present the Legislative Yuan with an annual policy statement and a report on administration. When the Legislative Yuan is in session, its members have the right to interpellate the premier, ministers, and chairmen of commissions of the Executive Yuan.

If the Legislative Yuan disagrees with an important policy of the Executive Yuan, it may, by resolution, request the Executive Yuan to alter it. Confronted with the Legislative Yuan's resolution, the Executive Yuan may, with the approval of the president of the Republic, request the Legislature's reconsideration. If after reconsideration one-half of the attending members of the Legislature uphold the original resolution, the premier must either abide by the same or tender his resignation. Similar procedures apply, if the Executive Yuan deems a resolution on a statutory, budgetary, or treaty bill passed by the Legislative Yuan difficult to execute. The Executive Yuan shall, three months prior to the end of each fiscal year, present to the Legislative Yuan the budgetary bill for the following fiscal year.

With the signatures of more than one-third of the total number of Legislative Yuan members, the Legislative Yuan may propose a no-confidence vote against the president of the Executive Yuan. Seventy-two hours after the no-confidence motion is made, an open-ballot vote is to be taken within 48 hours. Should more than one-half of the total number of Legislative Yuan members approve the motion, the president of the Executive Yuan must tender his resignation within ten days and at the same time may request that the president dissolve the Legislative Yuan. Should the no-confidence motion fail, the Legislative Yuan may not initiate another no-confidence motion against the same president of the Executive Yuan for one year.

RELATIONSHIP WITH THE JUDICIAL YUAN

If problems arise in the enforcement of provincial self-governance regulations, the president of the Executive Yuan organizes a committee with the presidents of the Legislative Yuan, Judicial Yuan, Examination Yuan, and Control Yuan in a joint effort to solve them.

Meanwhile, after the constitutional amendment completed in July 1997, the proposed budget submitted by the Judicial Yuan may not be eliminated or reduced by the Executive Yuan, which is noteworthy and significant. The Executive Yuan may instead indicate its opinions on the budget and include it in the central government's proposed budgetary bill for submission to the Legislative Yuan for deliberation.

RELATIONSHIP WITH THE EXAMINATION YUAN

Public functionaries to be appointed by the Executive Yuan must be qualified by examinations held by the Examination Yuan.

RELATIONSHIP WITH THE CONTROL YUAN

The Control Yuan has the authority to request the Executive Yuan and its ministries and subordinate organizations to submit original orders issued for perusal.

The Control Yuan may set up a number of committees to investigate the activities of the Executive Yuan and its ministries and subordinate organizations to determine whether they are guilty of violation of the law or dereliction of duty. It may propose corrective measures and forward them to the Executive Yuan and the agencies concerned.

The Executive Yuan shall, within four months after the end of each fiscal year, present final accounts of revenues and expenditures to the Control Yuan for auditing.

PROSECUTORIAL ARM

The Ministry of Justice handles legal affairs for the Executive Yuan, including prosecution procedures, investigation of crimes, and management of prisons and rehabilitation programs. It consists of departments of Prosecutorial Affairs, Corrections, Rehabilitation and Social Protection, and Legal Affairs. The Investigation Bureau is also under its jurisdiction.

For additional analytical, marketing, investment and business opportunities information, please contact
Global Investment & Business Center, USA
(202) 546-2103. Fax: (202) 546-3275. E-mail: rusric@erols.com

LEGISLATIVE YUAN

The Legislative Yuan (Legislature) is the highest legislative organ of the state, comprising popularly elected representatives who serve for three years and are eligible for re-election. Elections for the Fourth Legislative Yuan were held in December 1998. Amendments made in 1999 will extend terms to four years beginning with the Fifth Legislative Yuan.

FUNCTIONS AND POWERS

In accordance with the Constitution, the Legislature has the following functions and powers:

General legislative power: The Legislature exercises legislative power on behalf of the people. The term "law" as used in the Constitution denotes any legislative bill passed by the Legislature and promulgated by the president of the Republic.

Confirmation of emergency orders: Emergency orders and measures proclaimed by the president in the case of an imminent threat to national security or a serious financial or economic crisis during the recess of the Legislature are presented to the Legislature for confirmation within ten days of issuance. Should the president issue an emergency order after dissolving the Legislative Yuan, the Legislative Yuan is to convene of its own accord within three days and has seven days to decide whether to ratify the order.

Hearing reports on administration and revision of government policy: The Executive Yuan presents to the Legislative Yuan a statement of its administrative policies and a report on its administration. If the Legislative Yuan does not concur in any important policy of the Executive Yuan, it may, by resolution, request the Executive Yuan to alter such a policy.

Examination of budgetary bills and audit reports: The Legislative Yuan has the power to decide by resolution upon budgetary bills, which the Executive Yuan is required to present to the Legislative Yuan three months before the beginning of each fiscal year. The auditor-general, within three months after presentation by the Executive Yuan of the final accounts of revenues and expenditures, completes the auditing thereof in accordance with the law and submits an auditing report to the Legislative Yuan.

Right of consent: The presidents of the Control, Examination and Judical Yuan are nominated and, with the consent of the Legislative Yuan, appointed by the president of the Republic.

Amendment of the Constitution: Upon the proposal of one-fourth of the members of the Legislative Yuan, and also by a resolution of three-fourths of the members present at a meeting having a quorum of three-fourths of the members of the Yuan, a bill to amend the Constitution may be drawn up and submitted to the National Assembly for deliberation.

Settlement of disputes concerning self-governance: The Legislature settles any disputes over items and matters of self-governance in provinces, special municipalities, counties/cities, or other administrative units.

Meanwhile, in accordance with the Additional Articles of the Constitution of the Republic of China, the Legislature has been given the additional power to institute impeachment proceedings against the president or vice president of the Republic. Impeachment of the president or vice president for treason or rebellion will be initiated upon the agreement of more than two-thirds of all members of the Legislative Yuan after being proposed by more than one-half of the legislators, whereupon the resolution will be submitted to the National Assembly. Should such a motion of impeachment be passed by a two-thirds majority of all delegates to the National Assembly, the party impeached will forthwith be dismissed from office.

JUDICIAL YUAN

The Judicial Yuan (Judiciary) is the highest judicial organ of the state. According to Article 5 of the Additional Articles, the Judicial Yuan is to have 15 grand justices. The 15 grand justices, including the president and the vice president of the Judicial Yuan to be selected from among them, will be nominated and, with the consent of the Legislative Yuan. appointed by the president of the Republic. This will take effect from the year 2003 and the provisions of Article 79 of the Constitution will no longer apply. The subordinate organs of the Judicial Yuan are the Supreme Court, the high courts, the district courts, the Administrative Court, and the Commission on the Disciplinary Sanctions of Public Functionaries. The Judiciary exercises administrative supervision of the ROC court system while enforcing compliance by ROC court personnel with constitutionally mandated structures for juridical independence from the other branches of government.

EXAMINATION YUAN

The Examination Yuan is responsible for the examination, employment, and management of all civil service personnel in the Republic of China. Specifically, the Examination Yuan oversees all examination-related matters; all matters relating to qualification screening, security of tenure, pecuniary aid in case of death, and the retirement of civil servants; and all legal matters relating to the employment, discharge, performance evaluation, scale of salaries, promotion, transfer, commendation, and award of civil servants.

The examination system is applicable to all Chinese civil servants, high- or low-ranking, appointed or elected. The system is also applicable to Chinese and foreign specialized professionals and technicians. The examination function, being exercised solely by the Examination Yuan at the level of the central government, is separated from the executive power and thereby free from partisan influence.

CIVIL SERVICE

There were 602,396 civil servants in the ROC at the end of 1998. As a group, ROC civil servants are well-educated, with 65.8 percent holding college degrees or higher. As for gender, the majority--59.84 percent--were male, a 0.24 percent growth over the previous year. However, the ratio of males to females passing the civil service examinations over the last six years is 35:65.

Unlike the political appointees under whom they serve, civil servants are classified into senior (grades 10-14), intermediate (grades 6-9), or junior (grades 1-5) levels. The 14-grade scheme for administrative officials is designed to reflect an employee's abilities, experience, and seniority. One's salary increases with grade and civil servants at grade 14 can earn up to five times that of those at grade 1. Every year civil servants are reviewed by their superiors. In general, those servants who receive good reviews increase in grade annually. However, one must either pass a difficult civil service exam or be specially recommended by one's superior to enter grades six and ten.

CONTROL YUAN

The Control Yuan is the highest control body of the state, exercising the powers of impeachment, censure, and audit. The Control Yuan was formerly a parliamentary body, with its members elected by provincial and municipal councils. However, constitutional amendments in May 1992 transformed it into a quasi-judicial organization. The new Control Yuan started operations on February 1, 1993. From July 1997 onwards, its power to institute the impeachment against the president and vice president of the Republic expired after the constitutional amendment, and the Legislative Yuan has been empowered to take over the duty. It now has 29 members, including a president and a vice president, all of whom were nominated and, with the consent of the National Assembly, appointed by the president of the ROC, as stipulated in the Additional Articles of the Constitution. The term of office for all members is six years. The president of the Yuan takes overall charge of its affairs and serves as chairman at meetings.

PROVINCIAL GOVERNMENT

A provincial government is the highest administrative organ of local self-governance prescribed by the Constitution of the Republic of China. Altogether, the ROC Constitution designates 35 provinces, but there is only one complete province, Taiwan, under the effective control of the ROC. The Fukien Provincial Government, headquartered in Kinmen County, enjoys fewer powers than its Taiwan counterpart as some of its powers have been relegated to the Kinmen and Lienchiang county governments.

SPECIAL MUNICIPALITY GOVERNMENT

The passage of the Municipal Self-governance Law in 1994 provides a clear demarcation of the powers to be exercised by the central and local governments. One distinct move towards local autonomy has been the popular election of Taipei and Kaohsiung city mayors, who, prior to 1994, were nominated by the premier and appointed by the president of the Republic. The mayors serve a four-year term and may be re-elected to a second term in office. They may appoint two deputies, one in charge of political affairs and the other in charge of administrative affairs. The political deputy mayor must resign if the mayor who appointed him is no longer in office.

TAIPEI CITY GOVERNMENT

The Taipei City Government is headed by Ma Ying-jeou, a member of the Kuomintang. It has 21 departments, a secretariat, nine subordinate agencies, the Bank of Taipei, and an administrative office for each distric.

In March 1990, the 16 districts of Taipei City were reorganized into 12 districts: Chungcheng, Nankang, Neihu, Shihlin, Peitou, Hsinyi, Taan, Sungshan, Chungshan, Wenshan, Tatung, and Wanhua. These districts encompass a total of 435 boroughs.

CITY COUNCILS

According to Article 15 of the Municipal Self-governance Law, the main functions of the Taipei and Kaohsiung city councils are:

to adopt municipal statutes and regulations;

to approve the municipal budget;

to approve the levying of special taxes, temporary taxes and surtaxes in the special municipality;

to approve the disposal of municipal properties;

to approve the organic laws of the municipal government and municipally owned businesses;

to approve proposals made by the city government;

to screen the auditor's reports on municipal accounts;

to approve proposals made by the council members;

to hear petitions from citizens; and

to carry out other functions as prescribed by law or endowed by laws promulgated by the central government.

The term of office for a city councilor is four years. Councils meet for 60 days every six months. A session may be extended by ten days at the request of the mayor, council speaker, or one-third of the council members. In each session, various committees are formed to scrutinize proposals. A councilor may join only one committee.

REINVENTION OF GOVERNMENT

The ROC has placed the reinvention of government at the top of its administrative agenda. The goal is the transformation of the entire government into a streamlined, flexible, innovative, and resilient organization that functions like a well-managed private enterprise. To achieve this goal, efforts will be taken in a number of areas: specifically, government agencies will be streamlined and the organization and functions of the central government will be modified to suit present needs. The government also plans to promote a more flexible hierarchy and personnel structure within government organizations as well as overhaul the government budgetary system. By computerizing operations and using information technology and networked systems, the ROC is seeking to establish "electronic" government, including an information service network to increase administrative efficiency and enhance public services. Finally, government ethics are being heavily emphasized.

Harmony and cooperation between the central and local governments are vital to the smooth implementation of any government policy. As part of streamlining efforts, the administrative and financial responsibilities of the Taiwan Provincial Government will be delegated to other local and central government offices.

In January 1998, the Executive Yuan passed the Government Reinvention Guidelines as well as established a committee to formulate policy and draw up plans for the reinvention of government and review implementation. The committee is convened by the premier, while other members are drawn equally from three groups: heads of government agencies, mid-level civil servants, and grassroots-level civil servants. In addition, a government reinvention advisory committee was established to provide advice and arrange consultations among relevant agencies. The 15 to 21 committee members are scholars, experts, and entrepreneurs experienced in successfully reinventing private enterprises. Under this committee are three task forces, one charged with reinventing organization, one with personnel, and one with legal affairs. These task forces are staffed by personnel from the Executive Yuan's Research, Development and Evaluation Commission; Central Personnel Administration; and Council for Economic Planning and Development. Plans formulated by these task forces were sent to various government agencies for implementation after being approved by the Executive Yuan Council in June 1998.

FOREIGN RELATIONS

The Republic of China has been an independent and sovereign state since its founding as the first Asian republic in 1912. After the Chinese Civil War, the People's Republic of China was established on the Chinese mainland in 1949, while the Republic of China, retained its sovereign state status, and exercised full authority over the remaining territory, including Taiwan, Penghu, Kinmen, and Matsu. Both states across the strait have since then functioned separately, with neither subject to the other's rule.

The international community fully understands the fact that the ROC is an established state which rules a defined territory, has its own constitution, national flag, legal system, and armed forces. All members of the United Nations also know that the ROC conducts it own foreign relations with other countries, and that the ROC government represents the 22 million people living on Taiwan, over whom no other government in the world has any legitimate authority. Hence, the recognition of the international and legal status of the ROC within the ever-changing world order is entirely in accord with the principles, obligations, and values professed in the UN Charter.

Continued exclusion of the ROC from formal diplomacy is detrimental to world peace. Foreign relations in the post-Cold War era have been characterized by multilateralism and the development of regional organizations dedicated to promoting both economic and security issues. Exclusion of any single state in the Asia-Pacific region severely compromises the integrity and effectiveness of multilateralism. Unable in many cases to join international bodies, to participate in multilateral forums, or to join international conventions, the ROC finds itself forced to resort to an indirect form of bilateralism. The ROC could deal much more effectively with issues ranging from international aid to the conservation of endangered species, if it were a signatory to relevant international conventions and allowed to attend the multilateral forums within the United Nations framework.

OBSTRUCTION

For many years, the PRC has sought to obstruct the ROC's relations with the world community, by asserting that China is ruled by the Marxist-Leninist Chinese Communist party in Beijing. The Chinese Communists have even attempted to denigrate the ROC government as a "renegade province." The objective is to compel the people in the Taiwan area to accept the rule of a communist dictatorship and to deny them the right to pursue their own foreign policy. Peking continuously threatens to sever or downgrade relations with any country establishing or strengthening relations with the ROC. In an attempt to exclude the ROC from international organizations, the Chinese communists have relentlessly incited discord in political, economic business, scientific, and cultural forums over issues such as the ROC's right of representation and membership nomenclature in international organizations and activities.

The ROC acknowledges the fact that Taiwan is currently separated from the Chinese mainland and that the ROC government and the Chinese communists must coexist peacefully. Worldwide diplomatic recognition of the two states on both sides of the Taiwan Strait would be a fundamental step toward true reconciliation and, eventually, peaceful unification. It would also contribute to regional peace in the Asia-Pacific region.

MULTILATERALISM

Over the past year, the ROC's efforts to participate in international organizations have produced significant results. The ROC enjoys membership in a number of inter-governmental organizations such as the Asian Development Bank (ADB), the International Cotton Advisory Committee (ICAC), the Asian Productivity Organization (APO), the Afro-Asian Rural Reconstruction Organization (AARRO), and the Central American Bank for Economic Integration (CABEI). The ROC also holds membership in 953 international non-governmental organizations.

THE UN ISSUE

The Republic of China was one of the founding members of the United Nations, as delegates from the ROC signed the UN Charter in San Francisco on 26 June 1945. For over 20 years, the ROC served as a permanent member of the Security Council. From 1950 to 1971, the UN attempted to resolve the dispute over the seat for China, which had been divided into two antagonistic political entities since 1949, each with its own territory, people, and government. The passing of Resolution 2758 by the 26th session of the UN General Assembly in October 1971, which substituted the People's Republic of China for the Republic of China in the UN, did not result in the disappearance of the ROC. On the contrary, the ROC continued to be an active member of the international community and now maintains close and friendly relations with more than 150 nations. The government and people of the Republic of China are seeking to participate in the United Nations, so that they can more constructively contribute to the international community.

Since the Republic of China's departure from the United Nations in 1971, the issue of its participation in the UN has remained highly sensitive. The ROC started its UN campaign in 1993, in order to help the international community more clearly understand the implications of the ROC's exclusion from the UN.

From 1993 to 1996, the ROC's allies requested that the United Nations establish an ad hoc committee to study the issue of the right of the ROC's citizens to participate in the UN, thus allowing member states more time to discuss and exchange views on this issue and help create a friendlier atmosphere for the ROC in the UN.

In 1997 and 1998, the ROC continued its UN campaign and focused on drawing the attention of the UN members to the injustice imposed upon the people of the Republic of China resulting from Resolution 2758. In 1998, fifteen countries sponsored a proposal requesting that the UN General Assembly reexamine General Assembly Resolution 2758, with the view of restoring the right to participate in the activities of the UN to the people on Taiwan. The proposal was extensively debated in the General Committee and drew considerable attention from the members of the United Nations.

During the 53rd session of the UN General Assembly, twenty-five countries voiced their encouragement and support for the ROC's UN bid. They were Belize, Burkina Faso, Chad, Costa Rica, the Czech Republic, Dominica, the Dominican Republic, El Salvador, Fiji, The Gambia, Grenada, Guatemala, Haiti, Honduras, Latvia, Liberia, Malawi, Nicaragua, Paraguay, Saint Christopher and Nevis, Saint Vincent and the Grenadines, Senegal, the Solomon Islands, Sao Tome and Principe, and Swaziland.

In 1997, the ROC government began to seek observer status in the World Health Organization (WHO), one of the specialized agencies of the United Nations. Since then, a proposal titled "Inviting the Republic of China (Taiwan) to Participate in the World Health Organization (WHO) as an Observer" has been put forward to each annual World Health Assembly (WHA) for consideration.

Regrettably, the proposal was not considered by the WHA. However, the ROC believes that, as a global health organization, the WHO should not exclude any state. The Republic of China is determined to continue its efforts to secure participation in the WHO.

ECONOMIC ORGANIZATIONS

The Republic of China is an active member of many international economic organizations. To fulfill its commitment to the world community, the ROC is expanding its role in many international economic forums. One such example is the World Trade Organization (WTO). Although the ROC was one of the founding members of the WTO's predecessor, the General Agreement on Tariffs and Trade (GATT), it lost its membership following the communist takeover of the Chinese mainland. The ROC returned to GATT as an observer in 1965, but was forced out again in 1972, shortly after the Chinese mainland replaced the ROC in the United Nations.

In 1987, the ROC sought re-entry to GATT, and in 1990 filed a formal application for membership under the name of the "Separate Customs Territory of Taiwan, Penghu, Kinmen and Matsu." On September 29, 1992, GATT established a working party to examine the ROC's Foreign Trade Memorandum and to draft a protocol of accession. Meanwhile, GATT offered the ROC observer status, which allowed the ROC to participate in related meetings before becoming a full member. On January 1, 1995, the WTO replaced GATT, and the ROC was granted observer status on January 31, 1995. On December 1, 1995, the ROC, switched its membership application from GATT to the WTO.

Conducting bilateral consultations with WTO member states has been a prerequisite for any applicant's entry to the WTO. By the end of July 1999, the Republic of China had reached bilateral agreements with all 26 WTO members who had registered to negotiate with the ROC.

The ROC has also played a significant role in various other multilateral economic activities. It is an active member of the Pacific Economic Cooperation Council (PECC) and the Pacific Basin Economic Council (PBEC). As a full member of the Asia Pacific Economic Cooperation (APEC) forum--as "Chinese Taipei" the ROC also wholeheartedly participated in various APEC forums and conferences. Currently, the ROC holds the position of Lead Shepherd in three APEC Working Groups: Trade Promotion (WGTP), Agricultural Technical Cooperation (ATC), and Marine Resource Conservation (MRC). Also, the ROC co-chairs with New Zealand APEC's Food System Steering Group. Over the past years, the ROC has made significant contributions to and has thus won widespread recognition in APEC.

HUMANITARIAN AID

The Republic of China, as a responsible member of the international community, never hesitates to help others in need. For example, after Hurricane Mitch ravaged Central America in late October 1998, the ROC donated US$52 million in cash and US$3 million worth of medical supplies, food, and clothing to Honduras, Nicaragua, El Salvador, and Guatemala.

In 1999, when Macedonia's economy suffered the influx of more than 140,000 refugees from the war in Kosovo, the ROC sent medical groups to help improve health conditions in refuge camps. Morever, in a June 7 announcement, ROC president Lee Teng-hui announced a US$300 million humanitarian aid package to help the Kosovo refugees, including emergency relief and rehabilitation assistance.

BILATERAL RELATIONS

The Republic of China has full diplomatic relations with 29 countries, in which its 29 embassies and three consulates general promote bilateral cooperation. On the basis of pragmatic diplomacy, the ROC is continuing its endeavors to establish or substantially enhance relations with countries which do not maintain full diplomatic ties with the ROC. In order to strengthen its relations with those countries, the ROC now maintains 98 representative offices. Among these offices, 62 are located in the host countries' capitals, and 13 carry the official name of the "Republic of China."

Representative offices can offer some but not all, of the services usually provided by embassies and consulates general. At present, most of the ROC representative offices in Europe and North America use either the name "Taipei Economic and Cultural Office" or "Taipei Representative Office."

Reciprocally, 47 countries that do not have diplomatic relations with the ROC have set up 53 representative offices, or visa-issuing centers in Taiwan.

US TAIWAN RELATIONS

The relationship between the Republic of China and the United States of America has continued to progress in a wide variety of fields. The Taiwan Relations Act of 1979, the "Six Assurances" of 1982 and the policy review of 1994 form the basis of the bilateral relations. In the policy review of 1994, the US made some adjustments in the way ROC-USA relations were conducted. Accordingly, sub-cabinet economic dialogues at the under-secretary (minister) level were held regularly, and the US government was authorized to send cabinet-level officials to visit the ROC. The US is also committed to more actively supporting the ROC membership in international organizations in which statehood is not required, and identifying ways for the ROC's voice to be heard in other international organizations.

In US-PRC summits held in October 1997 and June 1998, President Clinton and ranking US officials reiterated that US policy and commitments toward the ROC remain unchanged; that any improvement in US-PRC relations would not be made at the expense of the ROC; and that US arms sales to the ROC would not be affected. In response, the ROC government urged the US to take more positive measures to further enhance US-ROC bilateral relations.

In spite of the changes in the US-PRC relationship, the US Congress continued to show its firm support of the ROC by holding public hearings, making floor statements, sending letters to the administration, and passing relevant resolutions. In the 106th Congress, both the Senate and the House of Representatives had adopted several resolutions favorable to the ROC.

During 1999, many US dignitaries visited the ROC. In addition to the former President Jimmy Carter and former Secretary of Defense William Perry, Director of the Office of Personnel Management Janice R. Lachance, Chairman of the Merit Systems Protection Board Ben L. Erdreich, Managing Director of the American Institute in Taiwan Richard Bush, Senator Jay Rockefeller, and Chairman of East Asian and Pacific Affairs of the Senate Committee on Foreign Relations Craig Thomas also visited Taipei.

As of the end of June 1998, 80 state legislative bodies in 44 US states and 16 American cities and counties had passed resolutions supporting the ROC's participation in the United Nations.

The ROC and the US have signed more than 100 agreements, covering education, customs duties, postal service, air transportation, and technological cooperation.

Trade between the two countries reached US$49 billion in 1998, a significant rise compared to 1978, when the US switched its diplomatic recognition from Taipei to Peking. The ROC ranked 7th largest among all US trading partners, while the US was the ROC's largest trading partner in 1998. As of the end of 1998, there were 1,683 approved ROC investment projects with an approximate value of US$4.1 billion in the US. In terms of 1998 US agricultural exports, the ROC market ranked 5th, showing the importance of the ROC market for US goods. In 1998, the ROC market was 1.25 times that of mainland China. In each of the last five years, Taiwan imported from the US an average of 1.09 times as much as the Netherlands and 1.23 times as much as France did.

OVERSEAS CHINESE

Aside from pragmatic diplomatic endeavors and attempts to participate in international organizations, the ROC government has in recent years stepped up contacts with overseas Chinese around the world and strengthened efforts to serve their interests. By tradition, any person of Chinese descent living outside the borders of the Republic of China is considered a *hua chiao*, or an overseas Chinese. Earlier overseas Chinese consisted mainly of emigrants who left China to make their fortunes or pursue higher studies abroad during the 19th and early 20th centuries. In the past few decades, emigrants from Taiwan have increased, initially for academic reasons and more recently for business as the ROC has continued to experience rapid economic growth and growing prosperity. These relatively new overseas Chinese, comprising mainly of intellectuals and businessmen, face different challenges in their new environment compared with those encountered by the old overseas Chinese.

OVERSEAS CHINESE AFFAIRS COMMISSION

Therefore, while equal attention will still be given to both old and new emigrants, the ROC government has adjusted its overseas Chinese policy to meet new demands arising from this demographic change in the overseas Chinese population. Previously, the emphasis was on preserving ethnic ties with the overseas Chinese by maintaining contact, providing education to new generations born overseas, offering economic assistance to overseas Chinese businessmen, and encouraging investment in the ROC. Recent trends have led to a policy shift toward planned and guided emigration by Taiwan residents, as well as the integration of the business interests of the established overseas Chinese with those of recent emigrants who are completely unfamiliar with their new adopted cultures. Meanwhile, the earlier focus on keeping overseas Chinese informed of domestic developments has been replaced by an effort to increase domestic understanding of Chinese residing overseas.

MAJOR DESTINATIONS FOR ROC EMIGRANTS

Among the 9,328 overseas Chinese associations which were registered with the OCAC as of December 1998, about 28 percent maintain close contact with the commission. Approximately 55 percent of the associations were formed by old immigrants, while the rest have been established by new immigrants from Taiwan. Interestingly, the number of associations formed by emigrants from Taiwan has increased rapidly over the past 20 years.

**For additional analytical, marketing, investment and business opportunities information, please contact
Global Investment & Business Center, USA
(202) 546-2103. Fax: (202) 546-3275. E-mail: rusric@erols.com**

These developments have prompted the ROC government to make adjustments in the selection of the 180 delegates to the OCAC who are chosen from among overseas Chinese to serve as a bridge between the ROC government and Chinese residing abroad. Younger and more educated delegates have been chosen, and Taiwanese and women are better represented. Guidance is provided to potential emigrants to help them make plans for their settlement overseas. Overseas Chinese and emigration lawyers have been invited to OCAC-sponsored seminars dealing with emigration to a number of countries to address issues such as living environments, education, business opportunities, investment markets, and emigration laws.

Since the 1989 Tienanmen Incident erupted in Peking, the number of democracy activists, scholars and students from the Chinese mainland seeking political asylum overseas has increased dramatically. According to statistics compiled by the US Immigration and Naturalization Service, at least 80,000 people in this category were granted permanent resident status between 1995 and July 1, 1997. Other statistics show that more than 600,000 people from the Chinese mainland have emigrated to the US either legally or illegally within the last ten years, most of them from Fujian Province. The growth in the number of new emigrants from the Chinese mainland is particularly significant in North America, such emigrants now account for 70 percent of the local Chinese population. These new immigrants are very capable of adapting to the new environment and language and have thus become increasingly influential in overseas Chinese associations. Given the changing makeup of overseas Chinese associations over recent years, the OCAC is poised to extend its services to these new immigrants from the mainland.

THE STATUS OF A DIVIDED CHINA

The Republic of China was founded in 1912, and it has since maintained sovereignty over the territories that have been administered by a succession of Chinese governments down through the ages. The international community referred to these territories as "China."

Ten years after the founding of the Republic of China, the Chinese Communist Party was established under the aegis of international communist activists. In 1949, the Chinese communists gained control of the Chinese mainland through military force, and on October 1, 1949, they proclaimed the establishment of the People's Republic of China. The ROC government was compelled to move to the island of Taiwan, and China was thus divided. Since that time, two distinct societies, with different ideologies and contrasting political, economic, and social systems, have existed simultaneously on opposite sides of the Taiwan Strait.

For many years after gaining control of the Chinese mainland, the Chinese communists sought to "liberate" Taiwan by force. Beginning in the early 1950s, they launched a series of military attacks against areas controlled by the ROC government in an effort to achieve reunification by force: the artillery bombardment of Kinmen (Quemoy) in 1958 is one of the most well-known of these incidents. Beijing changed its policy toward Taiwan, after establishing diplomatic relations with the United States in 1979, and began pursuing a course of peaceful confrontation. Although references to "liberation" in propaganda concerning Taiwan were dropped in favor of the term "peaceful reunification," Beijing has, to this day, refused to renounce the use of military force to solve the "Taiwan problem." In Taiwan, the pace of economic liberalization, social pluralization, and political democratization accelerated throughout the 1980s, and, with the lifting of martial law in July 1987, the government adopted a more open policy toward the Chinese mainland. In November 1987, the ROC government, for humanitarian considerations, began to allow people residing in the Taiwan area to visit relatives on the Chinese mainland. This decision moved cross-strait relations away from a state of complete estrangement and opened the door for private-level exchanges.

The people-to-people exchanges, the indirect trade and investment, and the cultural exchanges between the two sides of the Taiwan Strait, which blossomed in the wake of this thaw, have engendered a range of issues that necessitated a more systematic approach to bilateral contacts. The ROC government thus established a legal and organizational foundation through which the development of relations between Taiwan and the Chinese mainland could be pursued.

UNIFICATION GUIDELINES

The ROC government and the majority of the people of Taiwan earnestly hope for the peaceful unification of China. The termination of the Period of National Mobilization for the Suppression of the Communist Rebellion by President Lee Teng-hui on May 1, 1991, signifies the ROC government's determination not to use force to achieve national unification. Beijing, however, has pointedly refused to respond in kind to this friendly gesture.

To articulate its position as clearly as possible, the ROC government has devised a blueprint for this process, the *Guidelines for National Unification*, which outline the principles and positive steps that both sides can take to expedite China's unification. According to this gradual, sequential plan, China's unification is imperative not only for the sake of territorial unity, but also for the political freedom and equitable distribution of wealth for all Chinese.

The guidelines state that China's unification should be achieved in three phases: a short-term phase of exchanges and reciprocity, a mid-term phase of mutual trust and cooperation, and a long-term phase of consultations and unification. The phased approach was chosen with the full realization that the unification of China will be a long and arduous process. China's unification will not be achieved overnight, because the two sides have divergent social, political, and economic systems, not to mention vast differences in lifestyles. However, there is no fixed time frame for each stage. Progress may be slow or fast, depending on the pace with which the mainland authorities respond to the ideas outlined in the guidelines.

In the short-term phase, neither side should deny the other's existence as a political entity, and both sides should expand unofficial people-to-people contacts. In addition, the guidelines call for Beijing to renounce the use of force against Taiwan and respect Taiwan's position in the international community.

The first task in the medium-term phase is to set up channels for official communication between the two sides on the basis of parity. The goals of the second-term phase also include the establishment of direct postal, commercial, and transportation links across the Taiwan Strait, as well as exchange of visits by high-ranking officials from both sides. Only after the goals of this phase have been achieved can the process of national unification be brought into active consideration.

In the long-term phase, a bilateral consultative body should be established to jointly discuss the overall political and economic structure of a unified China, in accordance with the wishes of the people on both sides of the Taiwan Strait. A China that realizes peaceful, democratic unification, and prosperous growth will have a significant stabilizing effect on the Asia-Pacific region, in particular, and on world peace, in general.

Currently, relations between the two sides are in the short-term phase, although exchanges in many areas have already moved into the second stage.

STATUTE GOVERNING RELATIONS

The ROC is a constitutional democracy, and all major governmental policies are formulated in accordance with due process of law. The evolving policy toward the Chinese mainland and the mainland authorities is no exception. At present, the most significant piece of legislation in this regard is the *Statute Governing the Relations Between the People of the Taiwan Area and the Mainland Area*. The statute, which was promulgated in September 1992, covers administrative, civil, and criminal affairs and recognizes the rights of the people living under the control of the authorities in the mainland. Thus, with certain exceptions necessary to maintain the economic and social stability of Taiwan, the people living on the Chinese mainland are basically the same as those living in Taiwan, in the eyes of the law.

ORGANIZATIONAL STRUCTURES

In addition to a clear set of principles and laws to guide the development of relations, appropriate channels of communication are also an obvious necessity. This has led to the establishment of specific institutions which are authorized to handle relations with the Chinese mainland. In 1990 and 1991, the ROC government set up a three-tier network of government and private-sector institutions. The first, the National Unification Council (NUC), was established in September 1990. Then, in January 1991, the Executive Yuan's Mainland Affairs Council (MAC) was formed. In February 1991, the MAC approved the formation of a private non-profit organization, the Straits Exchange Foundation (SEF).

NATIONAL UNIFICATION COUNCIL

The National Unification Council functions as an advisory board and provides the president with research findings and ideas. The NUC is currently headed by the president himself, with the vice president and two opposition party members as deputies. The president has also invited respected civic leaders in Taiwan to sit on the NUC. The tenure for NUC members is one year, renewable at the president's discretion. As a non-partisan board, the NUC forges a consensus among various interest groups regarding the reunification of China.

MAINLAND AFFAIRS COUNCIL

The Mainland Affairs Council , a formal administrative agency under the supervision of the ROC premier, is responsible for the overall planning, coordination, evaluation, and partial implementation of the ROC government's policy toward the Chinese mainland. As a decision-making body, it also oversees rules and measures proposed by various ministries concerning cross-strait relations. The MAC is headed by a chairman and three vice chairmen and is organized into seven departments and three divisions. Its members include most of the ROC cabinet ministers and related commissioners or council chairmen.

STRAITS EXCHANGE FOUNDATION

The Straits Exchange Foundation , headed by a chairman and draws its funds from both the private sector and the government, is the only private organization empowered by the government to handle relations with the mainland. Nevertheless, the SEF currently deals only with matters of a technical or business nature that might involve the government's public authority, but would be inappropriate for the ROC government to handle under its policy of no official contacts with the mainland authorities. Accordingly, the SEF is not authorized to deal with political issues. "policy dialogue," as exemplified by talks concerning the establishment of direct postal, commercial, and transportation links, is however an area of relations that the MAC may commission the SEF to conduct on its behalf.

CROSS-STRAIT CONSULTATIONS

On December 16, 1991, a little over ten months after the establishment of the SEF, the Beijing government set up its Association for Relations Across the Taiwan Straits (ARATS) , with Wang Daohan as its chairman. In April 1993, SEF chairman Koo Chen-fu and the ARATS chairman met in Singapore and held the first discussions between Taipei and Beijing since 1949. This first round of Koo-Wang talks resulted in several agreements dealing with document authentication, the handling of mail, and future meetings. Provisions were made for regular and non-periodic meetings between SEF and ARATS officials.

Following the meeting in Singapore, Taiwan and the Chinese mainland held seven rounds of functional talks and three rounds of secretary-general-level talks through the SEF and the ARATS. These meetings focused largely on practical issues and led to a number of agreements in areas such as the repatriation of hijackers, illegal entrants, and fishing disputes. Dates for future talks were also settled. At a preparatory meeting held in May 1995, it was decided that a second round of Koo-Wang talks would be held in Beijing on July 20, 1995. Both sides agreed

---

For additional analytical, marketing, investment and business opportunities information, please contact
Global Investment & Business Center, USA
(202) 546-2103. Fax: (202) 546-3275. E-mail: rusric@erols.com

that the talks would cover such issues as the implementation of accords signed during the first round of Koo-Wang talks, Taiwan investment rights on the Chinese mainland, and a wide range of unofficial exchanges.

Unfortunately, the mainland authorities postponed indefinitely this second round of Koo-Wang talks in June 1995, and began test-firing missiles near the Taiwan Strait the following month. Predictably, relations between Taiwan and the Chinese mainland at the semi-official level suffered.

But the ROC's consistent stance has remained unchanged. Since then, ROC government leaders have made 114 public appeals calling on the mainland authorities to resume communications and consultations as soon as possible.

In February 1998, the Beijing authorities finally expressed their consent to resume communications and consultations in an official letter to Taipei. In the latter half of April 1998, one of the deputy secretaries-general of Taipei's Straits Exchange Foundation led a delegation to Beijing to visit their mainland counterparts from the Association for Relations Across the Taiwan Straits and resume cross-strait consultations that had been suspended for nearly three years. On the eve of US President Bill Clinton's visit to the Chinese mainland to meet with PRC President Jiang Zemin at the end of June, the issue of Taiwan and mainland relations has once again emerged as the focus of world attention. The SEF and the ARATS finally agreed that SEF Chairman Koo Chen-fu would visit the Chinese mainland during October 14-19, the same year.

It was Chairman Koo Chen-fu's first visit to the mainland since the foundation's establishment in 1991. Also, the trip made Koo the highest-level negotiator from Taiwan to visit the mainland since the Chinese civil war divided the two sides 50 years ago.

Koo's 12-member delegation visited Shanghai and Beijing during the trip. In Shanghai, Koo met with his mainland counterpart, ARATS chairman Wang Daohan. During the stop in Beijing, he held discussions with mainland Chinese President Jiang Zemin, Vice Premier Qian Qichen , and Chen Yunlin , director of the Taiwan Affairs Office of the State Council.

During their meetings in Shanghai, Koo and Wang agreed on four points conducive to bringing about closer cross-strait ties. Their consensus calls for Wang to visit Taiwan at an appropriate time and for the two intermediary bodies to resume contacts and negotiations. It was also agreed that the SEF and the ARATS should help reinforce Taiwan-mainland exchanges at various levels. The fourth point was that the two organizations should provide more assistance on matters concerning protection of the property and personal safety of visitors from both sides.

Despite this Koo-Wang consensus, no significant breakthroughs were achieved on the thorniest issues during the meetings on the mainland. The two sides continue to present different definitions of the "one China" principle. Also, the mainland authorities still refuse to acknowledge that the two sides of the strait are ruled separately. Moreover, Beijing has kept intact its threat of military force against Taiwan, as a possible means of unification.

DEFINING CROSS-STRAIT RELATIONS

In an interview with a German radio station in July 1999, President Lee Teng-hui stated that relations between the two sides of the Taiwan Strait should be characterized as a "special state-to-state relationship."

President Lee's declaration carries a three-fold significance. First, it is pragmatic. Although the Chinese communists established the People's Republic of China in 1949, its jurisdiction has never extended over Taiwan, Penghu, Kinmen, and Matsu, the area ruled by the government of the Republic of China. It is an indisputable political and historical fact that the ROC and the PRC are separate governments ruling, respectively, the Taiwan area and the mainland area. Second, President Lee's declaration is primarily a clarification of the current state of cross-strait relations. There has been no significant change or revision in our mainland China policy. Third, it is innovative. In the Guidelines for National Unification published in 1991, the ROC declared that the two sides of the Taiwan Strait are two equal political entities. This definition was established to temporarily set aside disputes over sovereignty, and create extended opportunities for interactions between the two sides. Subsequently, the ROC adopted a series of policy adjustments, including terminating the Period of National Mobilization for Suppression of the Communist Rebellion, promoting consultations, and expanding exchanges.

The cross-strait relationship is "special" because it involves the national sentiment and cultural factors, which are present in no other relationships. Thus, an equal and normalized cross-strait relationship should be better and closer than other country-to-country relationships. President Lee's redefination of cross-strait relationship will provide an important basis for the cross-strait relations in the next century.

Some people have oversimplified President Lee's remarks as a "two states theory," which not only distorts his original meaning but also leads to misunderstandings and speculations. President Lee's remark of the "special relationship" at this juncture is primarily meant to lay a foundation of parity between the two sides across the Taiwan Straits to elevate the level of dialogue and to help build a mechanism for democracy and peace. Therefore, government leaders at various levels have reiterated that there is no change in the government policy on promoting cross-strait dialogue, implementing bilateral agreements (including those reached at the Koo-Wang talks) and pursuing the ROC's stated goal of a new China unified under democracy, freedom, and prosperity in the future.

UNOFFICIAL EXCHANGES

Public opinion in the ROC has always welcomed Taiwan-mainland exchanges. Polls commissioned by the MAC in August 1996 indicated that 55.2 percent of respondents felt that the pace for the relaxation of cross-strait exchanges was just right, while 21.6 percent felt it was too fast, and 14.9 percent felt it was too slow. In a similar poll in August 1997, the figures changed slightly to 51.4, 22.2, and 12.5, respectively. However, by September 1998, figures in a similar poll had substantial changes: 35.5 percent felt it was just right, while 25.9 percent felt it was too fast, and 14.6 percent felt it was too slow.

The rapid expansion of exchanges between the two sides since 1987 seems to have imparted a certain momentum to their continued development. For the entire year of 1998, exchanges in almost all areas were up over 1997 levels. Social exchanges continue to grow steadily. According to China Travel Service in Hong Kong, 1.8 million Taiwan visitors went to the mainland during the year 1997. The number during the same period in 1998 dropped 22.22 percent to 1.4 million. On the other hand, 67,731 mainlanders (not including visitors for cultural and educational exchanges) came to Taiwan in 1997 and 83,435, in 1998, registering a 23 percent growth.

The number of mainland visitors for cultural and educational exchanges grew from 7,232 in 1997 to 10,660 in 1998, registering an all time high. The most rapid growth was in the number of those who attended athletic activities, technological researches, and religious activities.

**For additional analytical, marketing, investment and business opportunities information, please contact
Global Investment & Business Center, USA
(202) 546-2103. Fax: (202) 546-3275. E-mail: rusric@erols.com**

Investment and trade continued active growth. According to the statistics provided by the Ministry of Economic Affairs, Taiwan investment on the Chinese mainland in 1998 registered US$2.04 billion in direct investment that year. And Taiwan-mainland trade amounted to US$23.97 billion in 1998.

INDIRECT TRADE

Indirect shipments between the two sides of the Taiwan Strait find their main entrepot in Hong Kong. In 1998, Taiwan-mainland transshipment trade through Hong Kong dropped 12.6 percent to US$10.01 billion. In 1998, exports to the mainland through Hong Kong were stagnant at US$8.36 million. Imports from the mainland through Hong Kong dropped slightly to US$1.65 billion. The Hong Kong Customs statistics showed that Taiwan still enjoyed a US$6.71 billion trade surplus with the mainland.

POLICY TOWARD HONG KONG AND MACAU

The ROC maintains very close ties with both Hong Kong and Macau. In terms of the flow of people alone, Taiwan residents made 1.74 million trips to Hong Kong in 1998, while residents of Hong Kong made 194,116 trips to Taiwan. Economic ties are also strong. According to statistics published by the Ministry of Finance, the volume of trade between Taiwan and Hong Kong was US$ 26.79 billion in 1998; while Taiwan-Macau trade grew to US$360.8 million. In the same year, there were 48 Taiwan-to-Hong Kong investment cases, totaling US$68.64 million; and 67 Hong Kong-to-Taiwan investment projects, totaling US$257.62 million. In addition to Hong Kong's importance as a site for direct investment, the territory also serves as a transshipment point for cross-strait trade. Hong Kong customs officials estimated that in 1998, US$10.01 billion in Taiwan-mainland trade passed through Hong Kong. Capital goods and funds for investment on the Chinese mainland are also typically transferred through the territory.

In light of such close and comprehensive links, it should come as no surprise that policy concerning Hong Kong and Macau is a high priority of the ROC government. The ROC responded to the negotiations between Britain and the mainland authorities by forming a special Hong Kong Affairs Task Force in August 1983. After London and Beijing signed the Joint Declaration, the Task Force was upgraded to a Coordination Panel, under the direct supervision of the vice premier of the ROC government. Following the signing of the Sino-Portuguese Joint Declaration in July 1987, the name of the Hong Kong Affairs Task Force was changed to the Hong Kong and Macau Affairs Task Force . At the end of January 1991 when the ROC government set up the MAC, the Task Force was incorporated into the new organization as its Department of Hong Kong and Macau Affairs to coordinate ROC government policies toward the two areas. The ROC government has stated that it will retain its agencies in Hong Kong and Macau, and the MAC has formulated plans regarding the post-handover names, status, structures, and functions of these agencies. The number and types of services provided by these agencies have largely gone unchanged, and responsibility for Hong Kong and Macau affairs has been redistributed to reflect the change in Hong Kong's legal and political status. The MAC will take charge of the overall planning and administration of Hong Kong and Macau affairs, after responsibilities currently handled by the Ministry of Foreign Affairs are transferred.

In order to establish a legal basis for the ROC's relations with Hong Kong and Macau after Beijing assumes control, the MAC has drafted the *Statute Governing Relations with Hong Kong and Macau*, which was passed by the Legislative Yuan on March 18, 1997, and promulgated by the president on April 2 of the same year. The operative principle behind the statute is that, as long as the two territories retain a high degree of autonomy, the ROC government will regard them as special regions separate from the rest of the Chinese mainland. The statute addresses a number of issues, including travel, finance, trade, and transportation. According to the statute, people from Taiwan entering Hong Kong and Macau will follow normal regulations and will not be subject to special restrictions, while residents of Hong Kong and Macau may enter Taiwan after receiving approval. Calling for "free transportation links in principle, and restriction or prohibition in exceptional cases," the statute aims to preserve direct transportation and trade links. As for business and finance, the statute permits direct investment in Hong Kong and Macau by individuals and corporations from the ROC, and provides for such investment to be handled according to existing foreign investment and technical cooperation measures. The statute also indicates that investment in Taiwan by individuals and corporations from Hong Kong and Macau is to be handled according to existing laws on investment and technical cooperation by overseas Chinese.

NATIONAL DEFENSE

The primary objective of the ROC's de-fense policy is to defend the area cur-rently under ROC control, which includes Taiwan, Penghu, Kinmen, and Matsu. This entails establishing a fighting force of sufficient readiness to guard the nation and protect its people. The direct and most serious threat to the ROC's national security remains the unwillingness of Peking to renounce the use of military force against Taiwan. Thus, while ROC national defense strategy calls for balanced development of the three armed forces, naval and air supremacy receive first priority. In addition to current defensive preparations, a long-term policy of developing an elite fighting force and self-sufficiency in defense technology is also being strictly followed. This calls for restructuring the armed forces, streamlining command levels, renovating logistical systems, merging or reassigning military schools and upper-ranking staff units, and reducing the total number of men in uniform.

BUDGETARY REDUCTION TREND

The defense budget for the ROC military has generally been trimmed each year over the past decade, and an increasing percentage has become open to public scrutiny. The defense budget for July 1, 1999 to Dec. 31, 2000 amounted to US$12.6 billion (NT$402.9 billion), or 18 percent of the total national budget during the same period, maintaining an overall downward trend (Please note that the beginning of the fiscal year has been changed from July 1 to January 1, thus the above figures cover an 18-month period).

DOING MORE WITH LESS

The thinking behind changes to the ROC's Armed Forces over the past few years reflects a shift from equally stressing offense and defense to simply assuring defense. This strategic principle, as implemented under the Ten-Year Troop Reduction Plan , has led to a targeted force of less than 400,000 troops by the year 2003 and an increase in the ratio of combat troops to overall military manpower.

Facing the threat of high-tech warfare from the Chinese mainland, the ROC's Armed Forces have not only streamlined their organization and introduced cost effectiveness measures by de-centralizing organizational levels, shortening the chain of command, accelerating reaction times, and promoting increased efficiency, but they have also reformed management and the processing mechanism, thus shortening process flow times, fostering the creativity of grassroots units and individuals, and eliminating outdated approaches, in order to establish a new military organization.

The allocation of resources among the three services will give priority to air superiority and control of the seas in defensive operations, as well as to coastal defense. Accordingly, a ten-year program to develop a practicable table of organization for the three services is being implemented in three phases. This program will facilitate training and carry out peacetime missions, eliminate the overlapping of staff units in the three major services, consolidate the General Staff Headquarters of the Ministry of National Defense (MND) and the general headquarters of the three services, and transfer nonmilitary tasks to organizations outside the MND.

Second-generation weapon systems used by the three armed services are also being actively updated. These include E-2T air defense warning systems, the Ching-kuo indigenous defense fighter (IDF) squadron, the commissioning of the Taiwan-built Cheng-kung class missile frigates, French-built Lafayette (Kang-ting) class missile frigates, and US-rented Knox class missile frigates. Other new equipment includes F-16 and Mirage 2000-5 fighter planes, a second batch of AH-1W attack helicopters and OH-58D reconnaissance helicopters.

COMMAND STRUCTURE

Article 36 of the *ROC Constitution* stipulates that the president of the republic "shall have supreme command of the land, sea and air forces of the whole country," and Article 3 of the *Organic Law of the Executive Yuan* states that "the Executive Yuan shall establish (among others) a Ministry of National Defense." According to the *Organization Law of the MND*, the ministry shall be in charge of the defense affairs of the whole country.

Within the Ministry of National Defense is the General Staff Headquarters (GSH), under which are the various services, including the Army, Navy, Air Force, Combined Services Forces, Armed Forces Reserve Command, Coast Guard Command, and Military Police Command. The GSH is headed by a chief of the general staff who is in charge of military affairs; in the military command system, he acts as the chief of staff to the president for operational matters, while in the administrative system, he serves as chief of staff to the minister of national defense.

MINISTRY OF NATIONAL DEFENSE

The Ministry of National Defense is responsible for formulating military strategy, setting military personnel policies, devising draft and mobilization plans, delineating supply distribution policies, arranging the research and development of military technology, compiling the national defense budget, setting military regulations, conducting court martial proceedings, and administering military law. The ministry itself has a Minister's Office; Departments of Manpower, Materials, and Law; a Bureau of the Comptroller, and the Judge Advocates Bureau.

GENERAL STAFF HEADQUARTERS, MND

**For additional analytical, marketing, investment and business opportunities information, please contact
Global Investment & Business Center, USA
(202) 546-2103. Fax: (202) 546-3275. E-mail: rusric@erols.com**

The General Staff Headquarters, MND is in charge of the planning and supervision of joint war activities, political warfare, personnel, military intelligence, operations, education and training, logistics, organization and equipment calibration, communications, military archives management, and medical services. It contains the Office of the Chief of the General Staff; the Department of Supervision and Inspection; the General Political Warfare Department; Offices of the Deputy Chiefs of the General Staff for Personnel, Intelligence, Operations, Logistics, and Planning; the Bureau of Communications and Electronics; the Military History and Translation Bureau; the Military Medical Bureau; and the General Affairs Bureau.

On July 1, 1995, various military purchasing units were integrated into the Procurement Bureau, MND, which became responsible for the overall planning and purchasing of major weapon systems and equipment required by the ROC Armed Forces. The Bureau consists of five departments, two offices, and one overseas procurement section.

STUDYING COUNTRY THROUGH THE CONSTITUTION

CONSTITUTIONAL DEVELOPMENT

ENACTMENT AND FUNDAMENTAL FEATURES

The ROC Constitution was adopted on December 25, 1946, by the National Assembly convened in Nanking. It was promulgated by the National Government on January 1, 1947, and put into effect on December 25 of the same year. In addition to the preamble, the Constitution comprises 175 articles in 14 chapters. In essence the Constitution embodies the ideal of "sovereignty of the people," guarantees human rights and freedoms, provides for a central government with five branches and a local self-government system, ensures a balanced division of powers between the central and local governments, and stipulates fundamental national policies.

CONSTITUTION[3]

*T*he National Assembly of the Republic of China, by virtue of the mandate received from the whole body of citizens, in accordance with the teachings bequeathed by Dr. Sun Yat-sen in founding the Republic of China, and in order to consolidate the authority of the State, safeguard the rights of the people, ensure social tranquility, and promote the welfare of the people, do hereby establish this Constitution, to be promulgated throughout the country for faithful and perpetual observance by all.

CHAPTER I. GENERAL PROVISIONS

Article 1 The Republic of China, founded on the Three Principles of the People, shall be a democratic republic of the people, to be governed by the people and for the people.
Article 2 The sovereignty of the Republic of China shall reside in the whole body of citizens.
Article 3 Persons possessing the nationality of the Republic of China shall be citizens of the Republic of China.
Article 4 The territory of the Republic of China according to its existing national boundaries shall not be altered except by resolution of the National Assembly.
Article 5 There shall be equality among the various racial groups in the Republic of China.
Article 6 The national flag of the Republic of China shall be of red ground with a blue sky and a white sun in the upper left corner.

CHAPTER II. RIGHTS AND DUTIES OF THE PEOPLE

Article 7 All citizens of the Republic of China, irrespective of sex, religion, race, class, or party affiliation, shall be equal before the law.
Article 8 Personal freedom shall be guaranteed to the people. Except in case of flagrante delicto as provided by law, no person shall be arrested or detained otherwise than by a judicial or a police organ in accordance with the procedure prescribed by law. No person shall be tried or punished otherwise than by a law court in accordance with the procedure prescribed by law. Any arrest, detention, trial, or punishment which is not in accordance with the procedure prescribed by law may be resisted.

---

[3] *Adopted by the National Assembly on December 25, 1946, promulgated by the National Government on January 1, 1947, and effective from December 25, 1947.*

For additional analytical, marketing, investment and business opportunities information, please contact
Global Investment & Business Center, USA
(202) 546-2103. Fax: (202) 546-3275. E-mail: rusric@erols.com

When a person is arrested or detained on suspicion of having committed a crime, the organ making the arrest or detention shall in writing inform the said person, and his designated relative or friend, of the grounds for his arrest or detention, and shall, within 24 hours, turn him over to a competent court for trial. The said person, or any other person, may petition the competent court that a writ be served within 24 hours on the organ making the arrest for the surrender of the said person for trial.

The court shall not reject the petition mentioned in the preceding paragraph, nor shall it order the organ concerned to make an investigation and report first. The organ concerned shall not refuse to execute, or delay in executing, the writ of the court for the surrender of the said person for trial.

When a person is unlawfully arrested or detained by any organ, he or any other person may petition the court for an investigation. The court shall not reject such a petition, and shall, within 24 hours, investigate the action of the organ concerned and deal with the matter in accordance with law.

Article 9 Except those in active military service, no person shall be subject to trial by a military tribunal.

Article 10 The people shall have freedom of residence and of change of residence.

Article 11 The people shall have freedom of speech, teaching, writing and publication.

Article 12 The people shall have freedom of privacy of correspondence.

Article 13 The people shall have freedom of religious belief.

Article 14 The people shall have freedom of assembly and association.

Article 15 The right of existence, the right to work and the right of property shall be guaranteed to the people.

Article 16 The people shall have the right of presenting petitions, lodging complaints, or instituting legal proceedings.

Article 17 The people shall have the right of election, recall, initiative and referendum.

Article 18 The people shall have the right of taking public examinations and of holding public offices.

Article 19 The people shall have the duty of paying taxes in accordance with law.

Article 20 The people shall have the duty of performing military service in accordance with law.

Article 21 The people shall have the right and the duty of receiving citizens' education.

Article 22 All other freedoms and rights of the people that are not detrimental to social order or public welfare shall be guaranteed under the Constitution.

Article 23 All the freedoms and rights enumerated in the preceding Articles shall not be restricted by law except such as may be necessary to prevent infringement upon the freedoms of other persons, to avert an imminent crisis, to maintain social order or to advance public welfare.

Article 24 Any public functionary who, in violation of law, infringes upon the freedom or right of any person shall, in addition to being subject to disciplinary measures in accordance with law, be held responsible under criminal and civil laws. The injured person may, in accordance with law, claim compensation from the State for damage sustained.

CHAPTER III. THE NATIONAL ASSEMBLY

Article 25 The National Assembly shall, in accordance with the provisions of this Constitution, exercise political powers on behalf of the whole body of citizens.

Article 26 The National Assembly shall be composed of the following delegates:
1. One delegate shall be elected from each hsien, municipality, or area of equivalent status. In case its population exceeds 500,000, one additional delegate shall be elected for each additional 500,000. Areas equivalent to hsien or municipalities shall be prescribed by law;

2. Delegates to represent Mongolia shall be elected on the basis of four for each league and one for each Special banner;
3. The number of delegates to be elected from Tibet shall be prescribed by law;
4. The number of delegates to be elected by various racial groups in frontier regions shall be prescribed by law;
5. The number of delegates to be elected by Chinese citizens residing abroad shall be prescribed by law;
6. The number of delegates to be elected by occupational groups shall be prescribed by law;
7. The number of delegates to be elected by women's organizations shall be prescribed by law.

Article 27 The function of the National Assembly shall be as follows:
1. To elect the President and the Vice President;
2. To recall the President and the Vice President;
3. To amend the Constitution; and
4. To vote on proposed Constitutional amendments submitted by the Legislative Yuan by way of referendum.

With respect to the rights of initiative and referendum, except as is provided in Items 3 and 4 of the preceding paragraph, the National Assembly shall make regulations pertaining thereto and put them into effect after the above-mentioned two political rights shall have been exercised in one half of the hsien and municipalities of the whole country.

Article 28 Delegates to the National Assembly shall be elected every six years.

The term of office of the delegates to each National Assembly shall terminate on the day on which the next National Assembly convenes.

No incumbent government official shall, in the electoral area where he holds office, be elected delegate to the National Assembly.

Article 29 The National Assembly shall be convoked by the President to meet 90 days prior to the date of expiration of each presidential term.

Article 30 An extraordinary session of the National Assembly shall be convoked in any one of the following circumstances:
1. When, in accordance with the provisions of Article 49 of this Constitution, a new President and a new Vice President are to be elected;
2. When, by resolution of the Control Yuan, an impeachment of the President or the Vice President is instituted;
3. When, by resolution of the Legislative Yuan, an amendment to the Constitution is proposed; and
4. When a meeting is requested by not less than two-fifths of the delegates to the National Assembly.

When an extraordinary session is to be convoked in accordance with Item 1 or Item 2 of the preceding paragraph, the President of the Legislative Yuan shall issue the notice of convocation; when it is to be convoked in accordance with Item 3 or Item 4, it shall be convoked by the President of the Republic.

Article 31 The National Assembly shall meet at the seat of the Central Government.
Article 32 No delegate to the National Assembly shall be held responsible outside the Assembly for opinions expressed or votes cast at meetings of the Assembly.

Article 33 While the Assembly is in session, no delegate to the National Assembly shall, except in case of flagrante delicto, be arrested or detained without the permission of the National Assembly.

Article 34 The organization of the National Assembly, the election and recall of delegates to the National Assembly, and the procedure whereby the National Assembly is to carry out its functions, shall be prescribed by law.

CHAPTER IV. THE PRESIDENT

Article 35 The President shall be the head of the State and shall represent the Republic of China in foreign relations.

Article 36 The President shall have supreme command of the land, sea and air forces of the whole country.

Article 37 The President shall, in accordance with law, promulgate laws and issue mandates with the counter-signature of the President of the Executive Yuan or with the counter-signatures of both the President of Executive Yuan and the Ministers or Chairmen of Commissions concerned.

Article 38 The President shall, in accordance with the provisions of this Constitution, exercise the powers of concluding treaties, declaring war and making peace.

Article 39 The President may, in accordance with law, declare martial law with the approval of, or subject to confirmation by, the Legislative Yuan. When the Legislative Yuan deems it necessary, it may by resolution request the President to terminate martial law.

Article 40 The President shall, in accordance with law, exercise the power of granting amnesties, pardons, remission of sentences and restitution of civil rights.

Article 41 The President shall, in accordance with law, appoint and remove civil and military officials.

Article 42 The President may, in accordance with law, confer honors and decorations.

Article 43 In case of a natural calamity, an epidemic, or a national financial or economic crisis that calls for emergency measures, the President, during the recess of the Legislative Yuan, may, by resolution of the Executive Yuan Council, and in accordance with the Law on Emergency Decree, issue emergency orders, proclaiming such measures as may be necessary to cope with the situation. Such orders shall, within one month after issuance, be presented to the Legislative Yuan for confirmation; in case the Legislative Yuan withholds confirmation, the said orders shall forthwith cease to be valid.

Article 44 In case of disputes between two or more Yuan other than those concerning which there are relevant provisions in this Constitution, the President may call a meeting of the Presidents of the Yuan concerned for consultation with a view to reaching a solution.

Article 45 Any citizen of the Republic of China who has attained the age of 40 years may be elected President or Vice President.

Article 46 The election of the President and the Vice President shall be prescribed by law.

Article 47 The President and the Vice President shall serve a term of six years. They may be re-elected for a second term.

Article 48 The President shall, at the time of assuming office, take the following oath:

"I do solemnly and sincerely swear before the people of the whole country that I will observe the Constitution, faithfully perform my duties, promote the welfare of the people, safeguard the security of the State, and will in no way betray the people's trust. Should I break my oath, I shall be willing to submit myself to severe punishment by the State. This is my solemn oath."

Article 49 In case the office of the President should become vacant, the Vice President shall succeed until the expiration of the original presidential term. In case the office of both the

President and the Vice President should become vacant, the President of the Executive Yuan shall act for the President; and, in accordance with the provisions of Article 30 of this Constitution, an extraordinary session of the National Assembly shall be convoked for the election of a new President and a new Vice President, who shall hold office until the completion of the term left unfinished by the preceding President. In case the President should be unable to attend to office due to any cause, the Vice President shall act for the President. In case both the President and the Vice President should be unable to attend to office, the President of the Executive Yuan shall act for the President.

Article 50 The President shall be relieved of his functions on the day on which his term of office expires. If by that time, the succeeding President has not yet been elected, or if the President-elect and the Vice-President-elect have not yet assumed office, the President of the Executive Yuan shall act for the President.

Article 51 The period during which the President of the Executive Yuan may act for the President shall not exceed three months.

Article 52 The President shall not, without having been recalled, or having been relieved of his functions, be liable to criminal prosecution unless he is charged with having committed an act of rebellion or treason.

CHAPTER V. ADMINISTRATION

Article 53 The Executive Yuan shall be the highest administrative organ of the state.

Article 54 The Executive Yuan shall have a President, a Vice President, a certain number of Ministers and Chairmen of Commissions, and a certain number of Ministers without Portfolio.

Article 55 The President of the Executive Yuan shall be nominated and, with the consent of the Legislative Yuan, appointed by the President of the Republic.

If, during the recess of the Legislative Yuan, the President of the Executive Yuan should resign or if his office should become vacant, his functions shall be exercised by the Vice President of the Yuan, acting on his behalf, but the President of the Republic shall, within 40 days, request a meeting of the Legislative Yuan to confirm his nominee for the vacancy.

Pending such confirmation, the Vice President of the Executive Yuan shall temporarily exercise the functions of the President of the said Yuan.

Article 56 The Vice President of the Executive Yuan, Ministers and Chairmen of Commissions, and Ministers without Portfolio shall be appointed by the President of the Republic upon the recommendation of the President of the Executive Yuan.

Article 57 The Executive Yuan shall be responsible to the Legislative Yuan in accordance with the following provisions:

1. The Executive Yuan has the duty to present to the Legislative Yuan a statement of its administrative policies and a report on its administration. While the Legislative Yuan is in session, Members of the Legislative Yuan shall have the right to question the President and the Ministers and Chairmen of Commissions of the Executive Yuan;
2. If the Legislative Yuan does not concur in any important policy of the Executive Yuan, it may, by resolution, request the Executive Yuan to alter such a policy. With respect to such resolution, the Executive Yuan may, with the approval of the President of the Republic, request the Legislative Yuan for reconsideration. If, after reconsideration, two-thirds of the Members of the Legislative Yuan present at the meeting uphold the original resolution, the President of the Executive Yuan shall either abide by the same or resign from office;
3. If the Executive Yuan deems a resolution on a statutory, budgetary, or treaty bill passed by the

Legislative Yuan difficult of execution, it may, with the approval of the President of the Republic and within ten days after its transmission to the Executive Yuan, request the Legislative Yuan to reconsider the said resolution. If after reconsideration, two-thirds of the Members of the Legislative Yuan present at the meeting uphold the original resolution, the President of the Executive Yuan shall either abide by the same or resign from office.

Article 58 The Executive Yuan shall have an Executive Yuan Council, to be composed of its President, Vice President, various Ministers and Chairmen of Commissions, and Ministers without Portfolio, with its President as Chairman.

Statutory or budgetary bills or bills concerning martial law, amnesty, declaration of war, conclusion of peace, treaties, and other important affairs, all of which are to be submitted to the Legislative Yuan, as well as matters that are of common concern to the various Ministries and Commissions, shall be presented by the President and various Ministers and Chairmen of Commissions of the Executive Yuan to the Executive Yuan Council for decision.

Article 59 The Executive Yuan shall, three months before the beginning of each fiscal year, present to the Legislative Yuan the budgetary bill for the following fiscal year.

Article 60 The Executive Yuan shall, within four months after the end of each fiscal year, present final accounts of revenues and expenditures to the Control Yuan.

Article 61 The organization of the Executive Yuan shall be prescribed by law.

CHAPTER VI. LEGISLATION

Article 62 The Legislative Yuan shall be the highest legislative organ of the State, to be constituted of members elected by the people. It shall exercise legislative power on behalf of the people.

Article 63 The Legislative Yuan shall have the power to decide by resolution upon statutory or budgetary bills or bills concerning material law, amnesty, declaration of war, conclusion of peace or treaties, and other important affairs of the State.

Article 64 Members of the Legislative Yuan shall be elected in accordance with the following provisions:

1. Those to be elected from the provinces and by the municipalities under the direct jurisdiction of the Executive Yuan shall be five for each province or municipality with a population of not more than 3,000,000, one additional member shall be elected for each additional 1,000,000 in a province or municipality whose population is over 3,000,000;
2. Those to be elected from Mongolian Leagues and Banners;
3. Those to be elected from Tibet;
4. Those to be elected by various racial groups in frontier regions;
5. Those to be elected by Chinese citizens residing abroad; and
6. Those to be elected by occupational groups.

The election of Members of the Legislative Yuan and the number of those to be elected in accordance with Items 2 to 6 of the preceding paragraph shall be prescribed by law. The number of women to be elected under the various items enumerated in the first paragraph shall be prescribed by law.

Article 65 Members of the Legislative Yuan shall serve a term of three years, and shall be re-eligible. The election of Members of the Legislative Yuan shall be completed within three months prior to the expiration of each term.

Article 66 The Legislative Yuan shall have a President and a Vice President, who shall be elected by and from among its Members.

Article 67 The Legislative Yuan may set up various committees.

Such committees may invite government officials and private persons concerned to be present at their meetings to answer questions.

Article 68 The Legislative Yuan shall hold two sessions each year, and shall convene of its own accord. The first session shall last from February to the end of May, and the second session from September to the end of December. Whenever necessary a session may be prolonged.

Article 69 In any of the following circumstances, the Legislative Yuan may hold an extraordinary session:
1. At the request of the President of the Republic;
2. Upon the request of not less than one-fourth of its members.

Article 70 The Legislative Yuan shall not make proposals for an increase in the expenditures in the budgetary bill presented by the Executive Yuan.

Article 71 At the meetings of the Legislative Yuan, the Presidents of the various Yuan concerned and the various Ministers and Chairmen of Commissions concerned may be present to give their views.

Article 72 Statutory bills passed by the Legislative Yuan shall be transmitted to the President of the Republic and to the Executive Yuan. The President shall, within ten days after receipt thereof, promulgate them; or he may deal with them in accordance with the provisions of Article 57 of this Constitution.

Article 73 No Member of the Legislative Yuan shall be held responsible outside the Yuan for opinions expressed or votes cast in the Yuan.

Article 74 No Member of the Legislative Yuan shall, except in case of flagrante delicto, be arrested or detained without the permission of the Legislative Yuan.

Article 75 No Member of the Legislative Yuan shall concurrently hold a government post.

Article 76 The organization of the Legislative Yuan shall be prescribed by law.

CHAPTER VII. JUDICIARY

Article 77 The Judicial Yuan shall be the highest judicial organ of the State and shall have charge of civil, criminal, and administrative cases, and over cases concerning disciplinary measures against public functionaries.

Article 78 The Judicial Yuan shall interpret the Constitution and shall have the power to unify the interpretation of laws and orders.

Article 79 The Judicial Yuan shall have a President and a Vice President, who shall be nominated and, with the consent of the Control Yuan, appointed by the President of the Republic.

The Judicial Yuan shall have a number of Grand Justices to take charge of matters specified in Article 78 of this Constitution, who shall be nominated and, with the consent of the Control Yuan, appointed by the President of the Republic.

Article 80 Judges shall be above partisanship and shall, in accordance with law, hold trials independently, free from any interference.

Article 81 Judges shall hold office for life. No judge shall be removed from office unless he has been guilty of a criminal offense or subjected to disciplinary measure, or declared to be under interdiction. No judge shall, except in accordance with law, be suspended or transferred or have his salary reduced.

Article 82 The organization of the Judicial Yuan and of law courts of various grades shall be prescribed by law.

CHAPTER VIII. EXAMINATION

Article 83 The Examination Yuan shall be the highest examination organ of the State and shall have charge of matters relating to examination, employment, registration, service rating, scales of salary, promotion and transfer, security of tenure, commendation, pecuniary aid in case of death, retirement and old age pension.

Article 84 The Examination Yuan shall have a President and a Vice President and a certain number of Members, all of whom shall be nominated and, with the consent the Control Yuan, appointed by the President of the Republic.

Article 85 In the selection of public functionaries, a system of open competitive examination shall be put into operation, and examination shall be held in different areas, with prescribed numbers of persons to be selected according to various provinces and areas. No person shall be appointed to a public office unless he is qualified through examination.

Article 86 The following qualifications shall be determined and registered through examination by the Examination Yuan in accordance with law:
1. Qualification for appointment as public functionaries; and
2. Qualification for practice in specialized professions or as technicians.

Article 87 The Examination Yuan may, with respect to matters under its charge, present statutory bills to the Legislative Yuan.

Article 88 Members of the Examination Yuan shall be above partisanship and shall independently exercise their functions in accordance with law.

Article 89 The organization of the Examination Yuan shall be prescribed by law.

CHAPTER IX. CONTROL

Article 90 The Control Yuan shall be the highest control organ of the State and shall exercise the powers of consent, impeachment, censure, and auditing.

Article 91 The Control Yuan shall be composed of Members who shall be elected by Provincial and Municipal Councils, the local Councils of Mongolia and Tibet, and Chinese citizens residing abroad. Their numbers shall be determined in accordance with the following provisions:
1. Five Members for each Province;
2. Two Members for each municipality under the direct jurisdiction of the Executive Yuan;
3. Eight Members for the Mongolian Leagues and Banners;
4. Eight Members for Tibet; and
5. Eight Members for Chinese citizens residing abroad.

Article 92 The Control Yuan shall have a President and a Vice President, who shall be elected by and from among its Members.

Article 93 Members of the Control Yuan shall serve a term of six years and shall be re-eligible.

Article 94 When the Control Yual exercises the power of consent in accordance with this Constitution, it shall do so by resolution of a majority of the Members present at the meeting.

Article 95 The Control Yuan may, in the exercise of its power of control, request the Executive Yuan and its Ministries and Commissions to submit to it for perusal the original orders issued by them and all other relevant documents.

Article 96 The control Yuan may, taking into account the work of the Executive Yuan and its various Ministries and Commissions, set up a certain number of committees to investigate their activities with a view to ascertaining whether or not they are guilty of violation of law or neglect of duty.

Article 97 The Control Yuan may, on the basis of the investigations and resolutions of its committees, propose corrective measures and forward them to the Executive Yuan and the Ministries and Commissions concerned, directing their attention to effecting improvements.

When the Control Yuan deems a public functionary in the Central Government or in a local government guilty of neglect of duty or violation of law, it may propose corrective measures or institute an impeachment. If it involves a criminal offense, the case shall be turned over to a law court.

Article 98 Impeachment by the Control Yuan of a public functionary in the Central Government or in a local government shall be instituted upon the proposal of one or more than one Member of the Control Yuan and the decision, after due consideration, by a committee composed of not less nine Members.

Article 99 In case of impeachment by the Control Yuan of the personnel of the Judicial Yuan or of the Examination Yuan for neglect of duty or violation of law, the provisions of Articles 95, 97, and 98 of this Constitution shall be applicable.

Article 100 Impeachment by the Control Yuan of the President or the Vice President shall be instituted upon the proposal of not less than one fourth of the whole body of Members of the Control Yuan and the resolution, after due consideration, by the majority of the whole body of members of the Control Yuan, and the same shall be presented to the National Assembly.

Article 101 No Member of the Control Yuan shall be held responsible outside the Yuan for opinions expressed or votes cast in the Yuan.

Article 102 No Member of the Control Yuan shall, except in case of flagrante delicto, be arrested or detained without the permission of the Control Yuan.

Article 103 No member of the Control Yuan shall concurrently hold a public office or engage in any profession.

Article 104 In the Control Yuan, there shall have an Auditor General who shall be nominated and, with the consent of the Legislative Yuan, appointed by the President of the Republic.

Article 105 The Auditor General shall, within three months after presentation by the Executive Yuan of the final accounts of revenues and expenditures, complete the auditing thereof in accordance with law and submit an auditing report to the Legislative Yuan.

Article 106 The organization of the Control Yuan shall be prescribed by law.

CHAPTER X. POWERS OF THE CENTRAL AND LOCAL GOVERNMENTS

Article 107 In the following matters, the Central Government shall have the power of legislation and administration:
1. Foreign affairs;
2. National defense and military affairs concerning national defense;
3. Nationality law and criminal, civil, and commercial law;
4. Judiciary system;
5. Aviation, national highways, state-owned railways, navigation, postal and telecommunication services;
6. Central Government finance and national revenues;
7. Demarcation of national, provincial, and hsien revenues;
8. State-operated economic enterprises;
9. Currency system and state banks;
10. Weights and measures;
11. Foreign trade policies;
12. Financial and economic matters affecting foreigners or foreign countries; and
13. Other matters relating to the Central Government as provided by this Constitution.

Article 108 In the following matters, the Central Government shall have the power of legislation and administration, but the Central Government may delegate the power of Administration to the provincial and hsien governments:
1. General principles of provincial and hsien self-government;
2. Division of administrative areas;
3. Foresty, industry, mining, and commerce;

4. Educational system;
5. Banking and exchange system;
6. Shipping and deep-sea fishery;
7. Public utilities;
8. Cooperative enterprises;
9. Water and land commnunication and transportation covering two or more provinces;
10. Water conservancy, waterways, agriculture and pastoral enterprises covering two or more provinces;
11. Registration, employment, supervision, and security of tenure of officials in Central and local governments;
12. Land legislation;
13. Labor legislation and other special legislation;
14. Eminent domain;
15. Census-taking and compilation of population statistics for the whole country;
16. Immigration and land reclamation;
17. Police system;
18. Public health;
19. Relief, pencuniary aid in case of death and aid in case of unemplyment; and
20. Preservation of ancient books and articles and sites of cultural value.

With respect to the various items enumerted in the preceding paragraph, the provinces may enact separate rules and regulations, provided they are not in conflict with national laws.

Article 109 In the following matters, the provinces shall have the power of legislation and administration, but the provinces may delegate the power of administration to the hsien:
1. Provincial education, public health, industries, and communications;
2. Management and disposal of provincial property;
3. Administration of municipalities under provincial jurisdiction;
4. Province-operated enterprises;
5. Provincial cooperative enterprises;
6. Provincial agriculture, forestry, water conservancy, fishery, animal husbandry, and public works;
7. Provincial finance and revenues;
8. Provincial debts;
9. Provincial banks;
10. Provincial police administration;
11. Provincial charitible and public welfare works; and
12. Other matters delegated to the provinces in accordance with national laws.

Except as otherwise provided by law, any of the matters enumerated in the various items of the preceding paragraph, in so far as it covers two or more provinces, may be undertaken jointly by the provinces concerned.

When any province, in undertaking matters listed in any of the items of the first paragraph, finds its funds insufficient, it may, by resolution of the Legislative Yuan, obtain subsidies from the National Treasury.

Article 110 In the following matters, the hsien shall have the power of legislation and adminstration:
1. Hsien education, public health, industries and communications;
2. Management and disposal of hsien property;
3. Hsien-operated enterprises;

4. Hsien cooperative enterprises;
5. Hsien agriculture and forestry, water conservancy, fishery, animal husbandry and public works;
6. Hsien finance and revenues;
7. Hsien debts;
8. Hsien banks;
9. Admistration of hsien police and defense;
10. Hsien charitable and public welfare works; and
11. Other matters delegated to the hsien in accordance with national laws and provincial Self-Government Regulations.

Except as otherwise provided by law, any of the matters enumerated in the various items of the proceding paragraph, in so far as it covers two or more hsien, may be undertaken jointly by the hsien concerned.

Article 111 Any matter not enumerated in Articles 107, 108, 109, and 110 shall fall within the jurisdiction of the Central Government, if it is national in nature; of the province, if it is provincial in nature; and of the hsien, if it concerns the hsien. In case of dispute, it shall be settled by the Legislative Yuan.

CHAPTER XI. SYSTEM OF LOCAL GOVERNMENT

SECTION 1. THE PROVINCE

Article 112 A Province may convoke a Provincial Assembly to enact, in accordance with the General Principles of Provincial and Hsien Self-Government, regulations, provided the said regulations are not in conflict with the Constitution.

The organization of the provincial assembly and the election of the delegates shall be prescribed by law.

Article 113 The Provincial Self-Government Regulations shall include the following provisions:
1. In the province, there shall be a provincial council. Members of the Provincial council shall be elected by the people of the province.
2. In the province, there shall be a provincial government with a Provincial Governor who be elected by the people of the Province.
3. Relationship between the province and the hsien.

The legislative power of the province shall be exercised by the Provincial Council.

Article 114 The Provincial Self-Government Regulations shall, after enactment, be forthwith submitted to the Judicial Yuan. The Judicial Yuan, if it deems any part thereof unconstitutional, shall declare null and void the articles repugnant to the Constitution.

Article 115 If, during the enforcement of Provincial Self-Goverment Regulations, there should arise any serious obstacle in the application of any of the articles contained therein, the Judical Yuan shall first summon the various parties concerned to present their views; and thereupon the Presidents of the Executive Yuan, Legislative Yuan, Judicial Yuan, Examination Yuan and Control Yuan shall form a Committee, with the President of Judicial Yuan as Chairman, to propose a formula for solution.

Article 116 Provincial rules and regulations that are in conflict with national laws shall be null and void.

Article 117 When doubt arises as to whether or not there is a conflict between provincial rules or regulations and national laws, interpretation thereon shall be made by the Judicial Yuan.

Article 118 The self-government of municipalities under the direct jurisdiction of the Executive Yuan shall be prescribed by law.

Article 119 The local self-government of Mongolian Leagues and Banners shall be prescribed by law.

Article 120 The self-government system of Tibet shall be safeguarded.

SECTION 2. THE HSIEN

Article 121 The hsien shall enforce hsien self-government.

Article 122 A hsien may convoke a hsien assembly to enact, in accordance with the General Principles of Provincial and Hsien Self-Government, hsien self-government regulations, provide the said regulations are not in conflict with the Constitution or with provincial self-government regulations.

Article 123 The people of the hsien shall, in accordance with law, exercise the rights of initiative and referendum in matters within the sphere of hsien self-government and shall, in accordance with law, exercise the rights of election and recall of the magistrate and other hsien self-government officials.

Article 124 In the hsien, there shall be a hsien council. Members of the hsien council shall be elected by the people of the hsien.

The legislative power of the hsien shall be exercised by the hsien council.

Article 125 Hsien rules and regulations that are in conflict with national laws, or with provincial rules and regulations, shall be null and void.

Article 126 In the hsien, there shall be a hsien government with hsien magistrate who shall be elected by the people of the hsin.

Article 127 The hsien magistrate shall have charge of hsien self-government and shall administer matters delegated to hsien by the central or provincial government.

Article 128 The provisions governing the hsien shall apply mutatis mutandis to the municipality.

CHAPTER XII. ELECTION, RECALL, INITIATIVE AND REFERENDUM

Article 129 The various kinds of elections prescribed in this Constitution, except as otherwise provided by this Constitution, shall be by universal, equal, and direct suffrage and by secret ballot.

Article 130 Any citizen of the Republic of China who has attained the age of 20 years shall have the right of election in accordance with law. Except as otherwise provided by this Constitution or by law, any citizen who has attained the age of 23 years shall have the right of being elected in accordance with law.

Article 131 All candidates in the various kinds of election prescribed in this Constitution shall openly campaign for their election.

Article 132 Intimidation or inducements shall be strictly forbidden in elections. Suits arising in connection with elections shall be tried by courts.

Article 133 A person elected may, in accordance with law, be recalled by his constituency.

Article 134 In the various kinds of election, quotas of successful candidates shall be assigned to women; methods of implementation shall be prescribed by law.

For additional analytical, marketing, investment and business opportunities information, please contact
Global Investment & Business Center, USA
(202) 546-2103. Fax: (202) 546-3275. E-mail: rusric@erols.com

Article 135 The number of delegates to the National Assembly and the manner of their election from people in interior areas, who have their own conditions of living and habits, shall be prescribed by law.

Article 136 The exercise of the rights of initiative and referendum shall be prescribed by law.

CHAPTER XIII. FUNDAMENTAL NATIONAL POLICIES

SECTION 1. NATIONAL DEFENSE

Article 137 The national defense of the Republic of China shall have as its objective the safeguarding of national security and the preservation of world peace.

The organization of national defense shall be prescribed by law.

Article 138 The land, sea, and air forces of the whole country shall be above personal, regional, and party affiliations, shall be loyal to the state and shall protect the people.

Article 139 No political party and no individual shall make use of armed forces as an instrument in the struggle for political powers.

Article 140 No military man in active service may concurrently hold a civil office.

SECTION 2. FOREIGN POLICY

Article 141 The foreign policy of the Republic of China shall, in a spirit of independence and initiative and on the basis of the principles of equality and reciprocity, cultivate good-neighborliness with other nations, and respect treaties and the interests of Chinese citizens residing abroad, promote international cooperation, advance international justice and ensure world peace.

SECTION 3. NATIONAL ECONOMY

Article 142 National economy shall be based on the Principle of People's Livelihood and shall seek to effect equalization of land ownership and restriction of private capital in order to attain a well-balanced sufficiency in national wealth and people's livelihood.

Article 143 All land within the territory of the Republic of China shall belong to the whole body of citizens. Private ownership of land, acquired by the people in accordance with law, shall be protected and restricted by law. Privately-owned land shall be liable to taxation according to its value, and the Government may buy such land according to its value.

Mineral deposits which are embedded in the land, and natural power which may, for economic purpose, be utilized for public benefit shall belong to the State, regardless of the fact that private individuals many have acquired ownership over such land.

If the value of a picec of land has increased, not through the exertion of labor or the employment of capital, the State shall levy thereon an increment tax, the proceeds of which shall be enjoyed by the people in common.

In the distribution and readjustment of land, the State shall in principle assist self-farming land-owners and persons who make use of the land by themselves, and shall also regulate their appropriate areas of operation.

Article 144 Public utilities and other enterprises of a monopolistic nature shall, in principle, be under public operation. In cases permitted by law, they may be operated by private citizens.

Article 145 With respect to private wealth and privately operated enterprises, the State shall restrict them by law if they are deemed detrimental to a balanced development of national wealth and people's livelihood.

Cooperative enterprises shall receive encouragement and assistance from the State.

Private citizens' productive enterprises and foreign trade shall receive encouragement, guidance and protection from the State.

Article 146 The State shall, by the use of scientific techniques, develop water conservancy, increase the productivity of land, improve agricultural conditions, develop agricultural resources and hasten the industrialization of agriculture.

Article 147 The Central Government, in order to attain a balanced economic development among the provinces, shall give appropriate aid to poor or unproductive provinces.

The provinces, in order to attain a balanced economic development among the hsien, shall give appropriate aid to poor or unproductive hsien.

Article 148 Within the territory of the Republic of China, all goods shall be permitted to move freely from place to place.

Article 149 Financial institutions shall, in accordance with law, be subject to State control.

Article 150 The State shall extensively establish financial institutions for the common people, with a view to relieving unemployment.

Article 151 With respect to Chinese citizens residing abroad, the State shall foster and protect development of their economic enterprises.

SECTION 4. SOCIAL SECURITY

Article 152 The State shall provide suitable opportunities for work to people who are able to work.

Article 153 The State, in order to improve the livelihood of laborers and farmers and to improve their productive skills, shall enact laws and carry out policies for their protection.

Women and children engaged in labor shall, according to their age and physical condition, be accorded special protection.

Article 154 Captial and labor shall, in accordance with the principles of harmony and cooperation, promote productive enterprises. Conciliation and arbitration of disputes between capital and labor shall be prescribed by law.

Article 155 The State, in order to promote social welfare, shall establish a social insurance system. To the aged and the infirm who are unable to earn a living, and to victims of unusual calamities, the State shall give appropriate assistance and relief.

Article 156 The State, in order to consolidate the foundation of national existence and development, shall protect motherhood and carry out a policy for the promoting of the welfare of women and children.

Article 157 The State, in order to improve national health, shall establish extensive services for sanitation and health protection, and a system of public medical service.

SECTION 5. EDUCATION AND CULTURE

Article 158 Education and culture shall aim at the development among the citizens of the national spirit, the spirit of self-government, national morality, good physique, scientific knowledge and ability to earn a living.
Article 159 All citizens shall have an equal opportunity to receive an education.
Article 160 All children of school age from 6 to 12 years shall receive free primary education. Those from poor families shall be supplied with book by the Government.

All citizens above school age who have not received primary education shall receive supplementary education free of charge and shall also be supplied with books by the Government.

Article 161 The national, provincial, and local government shall extensively establish scholarships to assist students of good scholastic standing and exemplary conduct who lack the means to continue their school education.
Article 162 All public and private educational and cultural institutions in the country shall, in accordance with law, be subject to State supervision.
Article 163 The State shall pay due attention to the balanced development of education in different regions, and shall promote social education in order to raise the cultural standards of the citizens in general. Grants from the National Treasury shall be made to frontier regions and economically poor areas to help them meet their education and cultural expanse. The Central Government may either itself undertake the more important educational and cultural enterprises in such regions or give them financial assistance.
Article 164 Expenditures of educational programs, scientific studies and cultural service shall not be, in respect of the Central Government, not less than 15 per cent of the total national budget; in respect of each province, not less than 25 percent of the total provincial budget; and in respect of each municipality or hsien, less than 35 percent of the total municipal or hsien budget. Educational and cultural foundations established in accordance with law shall, together with their property, be protected.
Article 165 The State shall safeguard the livelihood of those who work in the field of education, sciences and arts, and shall, in accordance with the development of national economy, increase their remuneration from time to time.
Article 166 The State shall encourage scientific discoveries and inventions, and shall protect ancient sites and articles of historical, cultural or artistic value.
Article 167 The State shall give encouragement or subsidies to the following enterprises or individuals:
1. Educational enterprises in the country which have been operated with good record by private individuals;
2. Educational enterprises which have been operated with good record by Chinese citizens residing abroad;
3. Persons who have made discoveries or inventions in the field of learning and technology; and
4. Persons who have rendered long and meritorious services in the field of education.

SECTION 6. FRONTIER REGIONS

Article 168 The State shall accord to various racial groups in the frontier regions legal protection of their status and shall give special assistance to their local self-government undertakings.
Article 169 The State shall, in a positive manner, undertake and foster the develop of education, culture, communications, water conservancy, public health and other economic and social enterprises of the various racial group in the frontier regions. With respect to the utilization of land, the State shall, after taking into account the climatic conditions, the nature of the soil, and

the life and habits of the people, adopt measures to protect the land and to assist in its development.

CHAPTER XIV. ENFORCEMENT AND AMENDMENT OF THE CONSTITUTION

Article 170 The term "law" as used in this Constitution, shall denote any legislative bill that have been passed by the Legislative Yuan and promulgated by the President of the Republic.

Article 171 Laws that are in conflict with the Constitution shall be null and void. When doubt arises as to whether or not a law is in conflict with the Constitution, interpretation thereon shall be made by the Judicial Yuan.

Article 172 Ordinance that are in conflict with the Constitution or with laws shall be null and void.

Article 173 The Constitution shall be interpreted by the Judicial Yuan.

Article 174 Amendments to the Constitution shall be made in accordance with one of the following procedures:

1. Upon the propsal of one-fifth of the total number of delegates to the National Assembly and by a resolution of three-fourths of the delegates present at a meeting having a quorum of two-thirds of the entire Assembly, the Constitution may be amended.

2. Upon the propsal of one-fourth of the members of the Legislative Yuan and by a resolution of three-fourths of the members present at a meeting having a quorum three-fourths of the members of the Yuan, an amendment may be drawn up and submitted to the National Assembly by way of referendum. Such a proposed amendment to the Constitution shall be publicly announced half a year before the National Assembly convenes.

Article 175. Whenever necessary, enforcement procedures in regard to any matter prescribed in this Constitution shall be separately provided by law.

The preparatory procedures for the enforcement of this Constitution shall be decided upon by the same National Assembly which shall have adopted this Constitution.

TRAVELING

US STATE DEPARTMENT SUGGESTIONS

COUNTRY DESCRIPTION: Taiwan is a stable democracy and has a strong and well-developed economy. Tourist facilities are widely available.

ENTRY REQUIREMENTS: Passport required. Taiwan previously required that U.S. visitors to Taiwan hold passports valid for at least six months. This is no longer the case: Taiwan now considers U.S. passports valid for return to the United States for six months beyond the expiration date of the passport. For specific information about entry requirements, travelers may contact the Taipei Economic and Cultural Representative Office (TECRO), 4201 Wisconsin Avenue, N.W., Washington, D.C. 20016-2137, via either its main telephone number,(202) 895-1800, or its visa section telephone number,(202) 895-1814. The main fax number at TECRO is (202) 363-0999, and the visa section fax number is (202) 895-0017. There is also an Internet address: http://www.taipei.org/teco.htm. The Taipei Economic and Cultural Office (TECO) also has offices in Atlanta, Boston, Chicago, Guam, Honolulu, Houston, Kansas City, Los Angeles, Miami, New York, San Francisco and Seattle.

For additional analytical, marketing, investment and business opportunities information, please contact
Global Investment & Business Center, USA
(202) 546-2103. Fax: (202) 546-3275. E-mail: rusric@erols.com

INFORMATION ON CRIME AND SAFETY: Although there has been an increase in the crime rate over the last year, due in part to local enforcement reporting methods, the overall crime rate in Taiwan remains relatively low. Nonetheless, there has been intense public concern in Taipei resulting from several violent crime cases in 1996-97. Residential burglaries and thefts are the predominant crimes affecting foreigners in Taiwan, but other more serious crimes do occasionally occur. Generally, U.S. citizen visitors to Taiwan should follow the basic security precautions that would apply in any large city.

Women should exercise caution when traveling alone in taxis, especially at night, as there have been incidents reported involving violence directed towards unaccompanied female taxi passengers; calling for a radio-dispatched taxi is an option. Local police departments have foreign affairs sections which are normally staffed by English-speaking officers. Police contact numbers for the major cities in Taiwan are as follows: Taipei (02)2556-6007, Kaohsiung (07) 215-4342, Tainan (06) 222-9704, Taichung (04) 327-3875, Taitung (089) 334-756, Pingtung (08) 733-6283. The loss or theft abroad of a U.S. passport should be reported immediately to the local police, and to the American Institute in Taiwan, at Taipei or Kaohsiung. Useful information on guarding valuables and protecting personal security while traveling abroad is provided in the Department of State pamphlet, *A Safe Trip Abroad*. It is available by mail from the Superintendent of Documents, U.S. Government Printing Office, Washington, D.C. 20402, via the Internet at http://www.access.gpo.gov/su_docs, or via the Bureau of Consular Affairs home page at http://travel.state.gov.

CRIMINAL PENALTIES: When outside the U.S., a U.S. citizen is subject to local laws and regulations, which sometimes differ significantly from those in the United States and do not afford the protections available to the individual under U.S. law. Penalties for breaking the law can be more severe than in the United States for similar offenses. Persons violating the law, even unknowingly, may be expelled, arrested or imprisoned. Criminal penalties for possession, use, or trafficking of illegal drugs are strict, and convicted offenders can expect severe jail sentences and fines. Taiwan law provides for the death penalty for some narcotics offenses.

COMPULSORY MILITARY SERVICE: Taiwan law provides for compulsory military service. Men between the ages of 18 and 45 who were born in Taiwan or who have ever held a Taiwan passport should be aware that they may be subject to compulsory military service in Taiwan, even if they are also U.S. citizens, and even if they have entered Taiwan on U.S. passports. Affected individuals are urged to consult with the nearest office of the Taipei Economic and Cultural Office (TECO) in the United States before visiting Taiwan to determine whether they are subject to the military service requirement.

MEDICAL FACILITIES: Health facilities in Taiwan are fully adequate for routine medical treatment. Doctors and hospitals may expect immediate cash payment for health services, and U.S. medical insurance is not always valid outside the United States. The Medicare/Medicaid program does not provide for payment of medical services outside the United States.

MEDICAL INSURANCE: Serious medical problems requiring hospitalization and/or medical evacuation to the United States can cost from $10,000 to $100,000. Supplemental overseas medical insurance, including coverage for medical evacuation, may prove useful. Check with your own insurance company to confirm whether your policy applies overseas, and whether it includes a provision for medical evacuation. Ascertain whether payment will be made to the overseas hospital or doctor, or whether you will be reimbursed later for expenses you incur. Some insurance policies also include coverage for psychiatric treatment and for disposition of remains in the event of death. Useful information on medical emergencies abroad, including overseas insurance programs, is provided in the Department of State, Bureau of Consular Affairs' brochure

Medical Information for Americans Traveling Abroad, available via the Bureau's home page and autofax service.

For additional health information, travelers may call the toll-free numbers of the Centers for Disease Control and Prevention's international travelers hotline 1-877-FYI-TRIP (1-877-394-8747), may use the CDC autofax service, 1-888-CDC-FAXX (1-888-232-3299), or may access the CDC home page on the Internet: http://www.cdc.gov.

AVIATION SAFETY OVERSIGHT: The U.S. Federal Aviation Administration (FAA) has assessed the Civil Aviation Authority of Taiwan as Category 1 -- in compliance with international aviation safety standards for oversight of Taiwan's air carrier operations. For further information, travelers may contact the Department of Transportation within the U.S. at 1-800-322-7873, or visit the FAA Internet home page at http://www.faa.gov/avr/iasa/index.htm. The U.S. Department of Defense (DOD) separately assesses some foreign air carriers for suitability as official providers of air services. For information regarding the DOD policy on specific carriers, travelers may contact DOD at 618-256-4801.

TRAFFIC SAFETY AND ROAD CONDITIONS: Roads in Taiwan's major cities are generally congested, and driving conditions are made worse by large numbers of scooters and motorcycles that weave in and out of traffic. Special caution should be taken when driving on mountain roads, which are typically narrow, winding, and poorly banked, and which may be made impassable by mudslides after heavy rains.

REGISTRATION AND PASSPORTS: U.S. citizens are encouraged to register at the American Institute in Taiwan, and to obtain updated information on travel and security. The American Institute in Taiwan does not issue U.S. passports but accepts passport applications and forwards them to the Passport Agency in Honolulu for processing. Processing time takes three to four weeks. In an emergency, the American Institute in Taiwan can issue a travel letter to permit a U.S. citizen who has lost a passport to return to the United States.

CHILDREN'S ISSUES: For information on international adoption of children, international parental child abduction, and international child support enforcement issues, please refer to our Internet site at http://travel.state.gov/children's_issues.html or telephone (202) 736-7000.

AMERICAN INSTITUTE IN TAIWAN: Unofficial relations with the people of Taiwan are conducted through the American Institute in Taiwan, whose offices are authorized by law to perform American citizen services. For assistance, U.S. citizen travelers may contact the American Institute in Taiwan at No. 7 Lane 134, Hsin Yi Road Section 3, Taipei, Taiwan; telephone (886-2) 2709-2000; fax: (886-2) 2709-0908; or the American Institute in Taiwan branch office at No. 2 Chung Cheng 3rd Road, 5th Floor, Kaohsiung, Taiwan, telephone: (886-7) 224-0154; fax: (886-7) 223-8237. In case of emergencies after working hours, the duty officer at the American Institute in Taiwan at Taipei may be contacted at (886-2) 2709-2013.

GETTING THERE

Air

The national airline is *China Airlines (CI)*. *EVA Air* offers flights to destinations throughout Asia, Europe, North America, Australia and New Zealand. Other airlines serving Taiwan include *British Asia Airways, Continental Airlines, Singapore Airlines* and *Thai Airways*.

**For additional analytical, marketing, investment and business opportunities information, please contact
Global Investment & Business Center, USA
(202) 546-2103. Fax: (202) 546-3275. E-mail: rusric@erols.com**

Approximate flight time: From Taipei to Los Angeles is 14 hours.

International airports

Chiang Kai-shek–Taipei (TPE) is 40km (25 miles) southwest of the city (travel time – 30 minutes). Airport facilities include an outgoing duty-free shop (0800-2100), post office, car hire, bank/bureau de change (0900-1700), bar/restaurant (0900-2100) and tourist information. Buses depart every 15 minutes for both *Sung Shan* (domestic) airport and the main railway station. Taxis and buses are available to the city centre.

Kaohsiung International (KHH) is 9km (4 miles) from the town centre. Airport facilities include an outgoing duty-free shop (0800-1900), car hire (0900-1900), bank/bureau de change (0900-1900) and bar/restaurant (0900-1900). A regular bus service is available (travel time – 30 minutes). There is a taxi service to the town.

Sea

There are sea links with Macau, Hong Kong and Japan.

GETTING AROUND

Air

China Airlines, Eva Air, Far Eastern Air Transport, Formosa Airlines and five other domestic airlines run services to local destinations from *Sung Shan* airport, Taipei.

Sea

There are reasonable connections from local ports. For details contact port authorities.

Train

Services are provided to destinations all over the island by the *Taiwan Railway Administration*. The main tourist routes are Taipei–Taichung–Chiayi–Tainan–Kaohsiung (a top-class service), Taipei–Taichung–Sun Moon Lake (with the last leg of the journey by bus), Chiayi–Alishan (with spectacular mountain scenery) and Taipei–New Hualian–Taitung (scenic coastal route). Air-conditioned electric trains run at least hourly from Taipei to Kaohsiung; some trains have restaurant cars. Children under three travel free; children aged 3-13 pay half fare. Train tickets can be purchased at many major hotels in Taipei, as well as at the main railway station.

Road

Traffic drives on the right. There is an adequate road system joining all major cities. A highway links Taipei and Kaohsiung. Some main streets have English signs.

Bus

There are both local and long-distance bus and coach services.

For additional analytical, marketing, investment and business opportunities information, please contact
Global Investment & Business Center, USA
(202) 546-2103. Fax: (202) 546-3275. E-mail: rusric@erols.com

Taxi

These are plentiful and inexpensive (metered). The destination must be written in Chinese for the driver.

Car rental

This is available in major towns.

Documentation: An International Driving Permit is required.

Urban

A number of private bus companies provide extensive services in Taipei. Two lines of a Mass Rapid Transit (MRT) system, a monorail train system serving Taipei and its suburbs, opened in 1996. Metered taxis are available in Taipei; tipping is not expected, but it is starting to come into practice.

Travel Times

The following chart gives approximate journey times (in hours and minutes) from Taipei to other major cities/towns.

	Air	Road	Train
Kaohsiung	0.40	5.30	4.40
Tainan	0.40	4.30	4.10
Taichung	0.30	2.30	2.30
Hualien	0.30	7.00	3.00
Taitung	0.50	10.00	5.30
Sun Moon L.	-	4.30	-
Alishan	-	6.00	-
Kenting	-	6.30	-
Makung	0.40	-	-

ACCOMMODATION

Hotels

There are over 398 tourist hotels in the country offering a broad range of accommodation and services. Prices range from US$30-50 a day for smaller hotels with US$90-150 a day being average. For details, contact the Press Division of the Taipei Representative Office in the UK or the Taiwan Visitors Bureau. Many hotels belong to the International Tourist Hotel Association of Taipei, 8th Floor-1, 369 Fu Shing N Road. Tel: (2) 27 17 21 55. Fax: (2) 27 17 24 53.

Grading: Hotels are rated on a scale of 1 to 5 'Plum Blossoms' using a system equivalent to the more familiar 5-star system, with three Plum Blossoms being about average:

4 to 5 Plum Blossoms: 50 hotels (half of which are in Taipei) are in these categories. The hotels are luxury class with a range of services and facilities, eg tennis courts, swimming pools and beauty salons.

2 and 3 Plum Blossoms: The 80 hotels in these categories are clean, comfortable and functional.

Camping

Campsites are available.

Youth Dorms

Dormitory and non-dormitory rooms are available in major cities and in scenic areas.

MONEY

Currency

New Taiwan Dollar (NT$) = 100 cents. Notes are in denominations of NT$1000, 500, 100 and 50. Coins are in denominations of NT$50, 10, 5 and 1, and 50 cents.

Currency exchange

All travelers are required to make a currency declaration in writing together with the baggage declaration. Unused currency can be reconverted on departure, on production of exchange receipts.

Credit cards

Accepted in most hotels, restaurants and shops.

Travelers' checks

Accepted in most hotels, restaurants and shops. To avoid additional exchange rate charges, travelers are advised to take travelers' checks in US Dollars.

Exchange rate indicators against the US Dollar

The following figures are included as a guide to the movements of the New Taiwan Dollar against Sterling and the US Dollar:

Date	Aug'99	Nov'99	May'00	Aug'00
$1.00=	32.17	31.73	30.74	31.10

Currency restrictions

The import and export of local currency is limited to NT$40,000. Free import of foreign currency is allowed, subject to declaration. The export of foreign currency is limited to the equivalent of US$5000 or up to the amount imported and declared. All exchange receipts must be retained.

Banking hours: 9AM-3.30PM Monday to Friday; 9AM-12PM Saturday.

SUPPLEMENTS

TAIWAN SECURITY ENHANCEMENT ACT (S. 693)

S. 693 was introduced on 24 March 1999 in the 1st Session of the 106th Congress by Senator Jesse Helms (R-N.C.) for himself and Senator Robert Torricelli (D-N.J.).

S 693 IS

106th CONGRESS
1st Session
S. 693

To assist in the enhancement of the security of Taiwan, and for other purposes.

IN THE SENATE OF THE UNITED STATES

March 24, 1999

Mr. HELMS (for himself and Mr. TORRICELLI) introduced the following bill; which was read twice and referred to the Committee on Foreign Relations

---

A BILL

To assist in the enhancement of the security of Taiwan, and for other purposes.

> *Be it enacted by the Senate and House of Representatives of the United States of America in Congress assembled,*

SEC. 1. SHORT TITLE.

This Act may be cited as the "Taiwan Security Enhancement Act."

SEC. 2. FINDINGS.

Congress makes the following findings: --

(1) Since 1949, the close relationship between the United States and Taiwan has been of enormous benefit to both societies.

(2) In recent years, Taiwan has undergone a major political transformation, and Taiwan is today a true multiparty democracy with a political system separate from and totally unlike that of the People's Republic of China.

(3) The economy of Taiwan is based upon free market principles and is separate and distinct from the People's Republic of China.

(4) Although on January 1, 1979, the United States Government withdrew diplomatic recognition of the government on Taiwan as the legitimate government of China, neither at that time nor since has the United States Government adopted a formal position as to the ultimate status of Taiwan other than to state that status must be decided by peaceful means. Any determination of the ultimate status of Taiwan must have the express consent of the people on Taiwan.

(5) The government on Taiwan no longer claims to be the sole legitimate government of all of China.

(6) The Taiwan Relations Act (Public Law 96-8) states that --

>(A) peace and stability in the Taiwan Strait area are in the political, security, and economic interests of the United States and are of international concern;

>(B) the decision of the United States to establish diplomatic relations with the People's Republic of China rests upon the expectation that the future of Taiwan will be determined by peaceful means;

>(C) the United States would consider any effort to determine the future of Taiwan by other than peaceful means, including boycotts or embargoes, a threat to the peace and security of the Western Pacific region and of grave concern to the United States;

>(D) the United States will maintain the capacity to resist any form of coercion that jeopardizes the security, or the social or the economic system, of the people on Taiwan; and

>(E) the preservation and enhancement of the human rights of all the people on Taiwan are objectives of the United States.

(7) On the basis of these provisions, the Taiwan Relations Act establishes on the part of the United States a continuing connection with and concern for Taiwan, its people, and their ability to maintain themselves free of coercion and free of the use of force against them. The maintenance by Taiwan of forces adequate for defense and deterrence is in the interest of the United States in that it helps to maintain peace in the Taiwan Strait area.

(8) Since 1954, when the United States and Taiwan signed the Mutual Defense Treaty, the United States and Taiwan have maintained a defense and security relationship that has contributed greatly to freedom, peace, and stability in Taiwan and the East Asia and Pacific regions.

(9) The United States and Taiwan no longer conduct joint training missions, have no direct military lines of communication, and have only limited military-to-military contacts. This lack of communication and interoperation between the United States and Taiwan hinders planning for the defense of Taiwan and could prove detrimental in the event of future aggression against Taiwan.

(10) Since 1979, the United States has continued to sell defensive weapons to Taiwan in accordance with the Taiwan Relations Act, and such sales have helped Taiwan maintain its autonomy and freedom in the face of persistent hostility from the People's Republic of China. However, pressures to delay, deny, and reduce arms sales to Taiwan have been prevalent since the signing of the August 17, 1982, communiqué with the People's Republic of China. Over time, such delays, denials, and reductions could prevent Taiwan from maintaining a sufficient capability for self-defense.

(11) As has been affirmed on several occasions by the executive branch of Government, the provisions of the Taiwan Relations Act take legal precedence over any communiqué with the People's Republic of China.

(12) The People's Republic of China has consistently refused to renounce the use of force against Taiwan and has repeatedly threatened force against Taiwan, including implied threats by unnamed People's Republic of China officials on January 10, 1999, who warned Taiwan not to participate in the development of theater missile defense capabilities with the United States.

(13) The missile firings by the People's Republic of China near Taiwan in August 1995 and March 1996 clearly demonstrate the willingness of the People's Republic of China to use forceful tactics to limit the freedom of the people on Taiwan.

(14) As most nations in East Asia reduce military spending, the People's Republic of China continues a major and comprehensive military buildup.

(15) This military buildup includes the development of advanced ballistic and cruise missiles that will incorporate precision guidance capability and the construction of new imaging, radar, navigation, and electronic intelligence satellites that will help target and guide ballistic and cruise missiles. According to the Department of Defense report entitled "The Security Situation in the Taiwan Strait," submitted to Congress in February 1999, the size of the missile force of the People's Republic of China is expected to grow substantially and, by 2005, the People's Republic of China will possess an "overwhelming advantage" in offensive missiles vis-a-vis Taiwan. The Department of Defense has also noted that the People's Republic of China may already possess the capability to damage satellite optical sensors with lasers, is researching advanced anti-satellite lasers that could blind United States intelligence satellites, and is procuring radio frequency weapons that disable electronic equipment. These missile and anti-satellite capabilities pose a grave threat to Taiwan.

(16) This military buildup also includes the construction or procurement from abroad of advanced naval systems, including Russian Kilo submarines that are difficult to detect, Russian technology to assist the development of new nuclear-powered attack submarines, Russian Sovremenny class destroyers armed with supersonic SS-N-22 Sunburn anti-ship missiles, a new long-range, all-weather naval attack aircraft called the JH-7, and new indigenous land-attack cruise missiles that could be launched from submarines, ships, and naval attack aircraft. These naval capabilities pose a grave threat of blockade to Taiwan.

(17) This military buildup also includes the improvement of air combat capabilities by procuring and co-producing hundreds of Russian Sukhoi Su-27 fighters,

seeking to purchase Russian Su-30 all-weather attack aircraft, arming these aircraft with advanced air-to-air missiles such as the Russian R-77 missile and other precision guided munitions, constructing the indigenously designed J-10 fighter, and seeking advanced airborne warning and control systems from abroad. These capabilities pose a grave airborne threat to Taiwan.

(18) Because of the introduction of advanced submarines into the Taiwan Strait area by the People's Republic of China and the increasing capability of the People's Republic of China to blockade Taiwan, Taiwan needs to acquire diesel-powered submarines in order to maintain a capability to counter a blockade, to conduct antisubmarine warfare training, and for other purposes.

(19) Because of the democratic form of government on Taiwan and the historically nonaggressive foreign policy of Taiwan, it is highly unlikely that Taiwan would use submarines in an offensive manner.

(20) The current defense relationship between the United States and Taiwan is deficient in terms of its capacity over the long term to counter and deter potential aggression against Taiwan by the People's Republic of China.

SEC. 3. SENSE OF CONGRESS.

It is the sense of Congress that--

(1) the Secretary of Defense and the Secretaries of the military departments should make every effort to reserve additional positions for Taiwan officers at the National Defense University, the senior war colleges, and the military academies; and

(2) the Secretary of State should, when considering foreign military sales to Taiwan--

(A) take into account the special status of Taiwan; and

(B) make every effort to ensure that Taiwan has full and timely access to price and availability data for defense articles and defense services.

SEC. 4. DETERMINATIONS OF DEFENSE NEEDS OF TAIWAN.

(a) INCREASE IN TECHNICAL STAFF OF THE AMERICAN INSTITUTE IN TAIWAN- Upon the request of the Defense Security Cooperation Agency, the President shall use funds available to the Department of Defense under the Arms Export Control Act for the assignment or detail of additional technical staff to the American Institute in Taiwan.

(b) ANNUAL REPORTS- Beginning 60 days after the next round of arms talks between the United States and Taiwan, and annually thereafter, the President shall submit a report to Congress--

(1) detailing each of Taiwan's requests for purchase of defense articles and defense services during the one-year period ending on the date of the report;

(2) describing the defense needs asserted by Taiwan as justification for those requests; and

(3) describing any decision to reject, postpone, or modify any such request that was made during the one-year period ending on the date of the report, the level at which the final decision was made, and a justification for the decision.

SEC. 5. STRENGTHENING THE DEFENSE OF TAIWAN.

(a) MAINTENANCE OF SUFFICIENT SELF-DEFENSE CAPABILITIES OF TAIWAN- Congress finds that any determination of the nature or quantity of defense articles or defense services to be made available to Taiwan that is made on any basis other than the defense needs of Taiwan, whether pursuant to the August 17, 1982, Communiqué signed with the People's Republic of China, or any similar executive agreement, order, or policy would violate the intent of Congress in the enactment of section 3(b) of the Taiwan Relations Act (22 U.S.C. 3302(b)).

(b) PLAN-

(1) IN GENERAL - The Secretary of Defense, in consultation with the Secretary of State, shall develop a plan for the enhancement of programs and arrangements for operational training and exchanges of personnel between the armed forces of the United States and Taiwan for work in threat analysis, doctrine, force planning, operational methods, and other areas. The plan shall provide for exchanges of officers up to and including general and flag officers in the grade of O-10.

(2) REPORT- Not later than 180 days after the date of enactment of this Act, the Secretary of Defense shall submit a report to Congress, in classified or unclassified form, containing the plan required under paragraph (1).

(3) IMPLEMENTATION- Not later than 30 days after the date on which the report described in paragraph (2) is submitted or required to be submitted, the Secretary of Defense shall implement the plan contained in the report.

(c) COMMUNICATIONS BETWEEN UNITED STATES AND TAIWAN MILITARY COMMANDS - Not later than 180 days after the date of enactment of this Act, the Secretary of Defense shall establish secure direct communications between the United States Pacific military command and the Taiwan military command.

(d) MISSILE DEFENSE EQUIPMENT- Subject to subsection (h), the President is authorized to make available for sale to Taiwan, at reasonable cost, theater missile defense equipment and related items, including--

(1) ground-based and naval-based missile defense systems; and

(2) reconnaissance and communications systems, as may be necessary to target and cue missile defense systems sold to Taiwan.

(e) SATELLITE EARLY WARNING DATA - Subject to subsection (h), the President is authorized to make available for sale to Taiwan, at reasonable cost, satellite early warning data.

(f) AIR DEFENSE EQUIPMENT - Subject to subsection (h), the President is authorized to make available for sale to Taiwan, at reasonable cost, modern air-defense equipment, including the following:

(1) AIM-120 AMRAAM air-to-air missiles.

(2) Additional advanced fighters and airborne warning and control systems (AWACS).

(3) Equipment to better defend airfields from air and missile attack.

(4) Communications infrastructure that enables coordinated joint-force air defense of Taiwan.

(g) NAVAL DEFENSE SYSTEMS - Subject to subsection (h), the President is authorized to make available for sale to Taiwan, at reasonable cost, defensive systems that counter the development by the People's Republic of China of new naval capabilities, including defense systems such as--

(1) diesel-powered submarines;

(2) anti-submarine systems, including airborne systems, capable of detecting new Kilo and advanced Chinese nuclear submarines;

(3) naval anti-missile systems, including Aegis destroyers, capable of defeating Russian supersonic anti-ship missiles; and

(4) communications systems that better enable Taiwan to conduct joint-force naval defense operations.

(h) RELATION TO ARMS EXPORT CONTROL ACT - Nothing in this section supersedes or modifies the application of section 36 of the Arms Export Control Act to the sale of any defense article or defense service under this section.

STRATEGIC GOVERNMENT AND BUSINESS CONTACTS

TAIWAN INFORMATION OFFICES NI NORTH AMERICA

INFORMATION DIVISION
TAIPEI ECONOMIC AND CULTURAL REPRESENTATIVE OFFICE
IN THE UNITED STATES

4201 Wisconsin Ave., N.W.
Washington, DC 20016
U.S.A.
Phone: (202) 895-1850
 VISA: (202) 895-1800
Fax:(202) 362-6144, 364-0416
E-mail: tecroinfodc@tecro-info.org

駐洛杉磯台北經濟文化辦事處新聞組
INFORMATION DIVISION
TAIPEI ECONOMIC AND CULTURAL OFFICE IN LOS ANGELES

6300 Wilshire Blvd., Suite #1510
Los Angeles, CA 90048
U. S. A.
Phone: (323) 782-8765
Fax: (323) 782-8761
E-mail: teco-la@roc-taiwan.org

駐休士頓臺北經濟文化辦事處新聞組
INFORMATION DIVISION
TAIPEI ECONOMIC AND CULTURAL OFFICE
IN HOUSTON

5 Greenway Plaza, Suite 270
Houston, TX 77046
U. S. A.
(Mailing address):
5 Greenway Plaza, Suite 270
Houston, TX 77046
Phone: (713) 961-9465
Fax: (713) 961-1365
E-mail: teco-houston@roc-taiwan.org

駐邁阿密台北經濟文化辦事處新聞組
INFORMATION DIVISION
TAIPEI ECONOMIC AND CULTURAL OFFICE
IN MIAMI

2333, Ponce de Leon Blvd., Suite 610
Coral Cables, FL 33134
U. S. A.
Phone: (305) 461-3420

For additional analytical, marketing, investment and business opportunities information, please contact
Global Investment & Business Center, USA
(202) 546-2103. Fax: (202) 546-3275. E-mail: rusric@erols.com

Fax: (305) 461-3221
E-mail: teipai@bellsouth.net

駐紐約臺北經濟文化辦事處新聞組
INFORMATION DIVISION
TAIPEI ECONOMIC AND CULTURAL OFFICE
IN NEW YORK

90 Park Avenue, 31st Floor
New York, NY 10016
U.S.A.
Phone: (212) 557-5122
Fax: (212) 557-3043;557-3044
E-mail: roctaiwan@taipei.org

駐舊金山台北經濟文化辦事處新聞組
INFORMATION DIVISION
TAIPEI ECONOMIC AND CULTURAL OFFICE
IN SAN FRANCISCO

555 Montgomery Street, Suite 504
San Francisco, CA 94111
U. S. A.
Phone: (415) 362-5303
Fax: (415) 362-5304
E-mail: teco-sf@roc-taiwan.org

駐亞特蘭大台北經濟文化辦事處新聞組
INFORMATION DIVISION
TAIPEI ECONOMIC AND CULTURAL OFFICE
IN ATLANTA

1180 West Peachtree Street, NW
Suite 820
Atlanta, GA 30309
U.S.A.
Phone: (404) 532-1940
Fax: (404) 532-7438
E-mail: teco-atlanta@roc-taiwan.org

駐芝加哥台北經濟文化辦事處新聞組
INFORMATION DIVISION
TAIPEI ECONOMIC AND CULTURAL OFFICE
IN CHICAGO

180 N. Stetson Ave., Suite 5702
Chicago, IL60601
U.S.A.
Phone: (312) 616-6716
Fax: (312) 616-1497
E-mail: teco-chicago@roc-taiwan.org

**For additional analytical, marketing, investment and business opportunities information, please contact
Global Investment & Business Center, USA
(202) 546-2103. Fax: (202) 546-3275. E-mail: rusric@erols.com**

駐波士頓臺北經濟文化辦事處新聞組
**INFORMATION DIVISION
TAIPEI ECONOMIC AND CULTURAL OFFICE
IN BOSTON**

99 SUMMER STREET, SUITE 801
BOSTON, MA 02110
U.S.A.
Phone: (617) 737-2057
(617) 737-2058
Fax: (617) 737-2061
E-mail: infob@broadviewnet.net

駐加拿大台北經濟文化代表處新聞組
**INFORMATION DIVISION
TAIPEI ECONOMIC AND CULTURAL OFFICE, CANADA**

45 O'Connor St., Suite 1960
Ottawa, Ontario K1P 1A4
Canada
Phone: (613) 231-4203, 231-4636
Fax: (613) 231-7727
E-mail: infoteco@ca.inter.net

駐溫哥華台北經濟文化辦事處新聞組
**INFORMATION DIVISION
TAIPEI ECONONMIC AND CULTURAL OFFICE, VANCOUVER**

Suite 2010, Cathedral Place
925 West Georgia Street
Vancouver, B.C. Canada V6C 3L2
Phone: (604) 689-7147
Fax: (604) 689-7149
E-mail: infotecovan@telus.net

駐多倫多台北經濟文化辦事處新聞組
**INFORMATION DIVISION
TAIPEI ECONOMIC AND CULTURAL OFFICE, TORONTO**

151 Yonge Street, Suite 1212
Toronto, Ontario M5C 2W7
Canada
Phone: (416) 360-8778
Fax: (416) 360-8765
E-mail: rocinfo@bellnet.ca or torgio@bellnet.ca

1. U.S. TRADE RELATED CONTACTS

American Institute in Taiwan (AIT)
Commercial Section
Chief: William Brekke
Deputy Chief: Rosemary Gallant

**For additional analytical, marketing, investment and business opportunities
information, please contact
Global Investment & Business Center, USA
(202) 546-2103. Fax: (202) 546-3275. E-mail: rusric@erols.com**

Suite 3207, 333 Keelung Rd., Sec. 1, Taipei, Taiwan
Tel: 886-2-2720-1550, Fax: 886-2-2757-7162

Agriculture Section
Chief: Debra Henke
Trade Officer: Daniel Martinez
7, Lane 134, Hsin Yi Rd., Sec. 3, Taipei, Taiwan
Tel: 886-2-2709-2000, 886-2-2332-7981
Fax: 886-2-2709-2054, 886-2-2305-2120

Economic Section
Chief: Marc Wall
Deputy Chief: Matthew Matthews
7, Lane 134, Hsin Yi Rd., Sec. 3, Taipei, Taiwan
Tel: 886-2-2709-2000, Fax: 886-2-2706-3023

WASHINGTON-BASED COUNTRY CONTACTS

AIT/Washington
Trade and Commercial Programs
Director: Ray Sander
Suite 1700, 1700 N. Moore Stret
Arlington, VA 22209
Tel: 703-525-8474, Fax: 703-841-1385

U.S. Department of Commerce
Taiwan Desk Officers
Laurette Newsom
Room 2327, 14th and Constitution Ave. NW
Washington, D.C. 20230
Tel: 202-482-4681, Fax: 202-482-4098

U.S. Department of Commerce
US&FCS East Asia Pacific
Director: Alice Davenport
Room 1229, 14th and Constitution Ave. NW
Washington, D.C. 20230
Tel: 202-482-2429, Fax: 202-482-5179

U.S. Department of Commerce
Trade Information Center
Room 7424, 14th and Constitution Ave. NW
Washington, D.C. 20230
Tel: 1-800-USA-TRADE

U.S. Department of Agriculture
Foreign Agricultural Service
Trade Assistance and Promotion Office
South Building, 14th and Independent Ave. SW

For additional analytical, marketing, investment and business opportunities information, please contact
Global Investment & Business Center, USA
(202) 546-2103. Fax: (202) 546-3275. E-mail: rusric@erols.com

Washington, D.C. 20250
Tel: 202-720-7420

2. AMCHAM AND/OR BILATERAL BUSINESS COUNCILS

American Chamber of Commerce
President: Jeffrey Williams
Rm. 1012, 96 Chungshan N. Rd., Sec. 2, Taipei, Taiwan
Tel: 886-2-2581-7089, Fax: 886-2-2542-3376

China External Trade Development Council
Secretary-General: Ricky Y.S. Kao
3-8F, 333 Keelung Rd., Sec. 1, Taipei, Taiwan
Tel: 886-2-2725-5200, Fax: 886-2-2757-6653

3. TRADE OR INDUSTRY ASSOCIATIONS

Chinese National Asociation of Industry & Commerce
Chairman: Jeffrey Koo
13F, 390 Fuhsing S. Rd., Sec. 1, Taipei, Taiwan
Tel: 886-2-2707-0111, Fax: 886-2-2701-7601

Chinese National Federation of Industries
Chairman: Kao Chin-yen
12F, 390 Fuhsing S. Rd., Sec. 1, Taipei, Taiwan
Tel: 886-2-2703-3500, Fax: 886-2-2703-3982

4. PUBLIC AGENCIES

Ministry of Economic Affairs (MOEA)
Minister: Wang Chih-Kang
15 Foochow St., Taipei, Taiwan
Tel: 886-2-2321-8124, Fax: 886-2-2391-9398

Ministry of Finance (MOF)
Minister: Paul C. H. Chiu
2 Aikuo W. Rd., Taipei, Taiwan
Tel: 886-2-2322-8006, Fax: 886-2-2321-1205

Board of Foreign Trade (BOFT), MOEA
Director General: Chen Ruey-long
1 Hukou St., Taipei, Taiwan
Tel: 886-2-2321-0717, Fax: 886-2-2351-3603

Ministry of Transportation and Communications (MOTC)
Minister: Fong-Cheng Lin
2 Changsha St., Sec. 1, Taipei, Taiwan
Tel: 886-2-2349-2000, Fax: 886-2-2389-6009

Directorate General of Telecommunications, MOTC
Director General: Chien Jen-Ter

**For additional analytical, marketing, investment and business opportunities information, please contact
Global Investment & Business Center, USA
(202) 546-2103. Fax: (202) 546-3275. E-mail: rusric@erols.com**

16 Chi-Nan Rd., Taipei, Taiwan
Tel: 886-2-2343-3953, Fax: 886-2-2343-3772

Council of Agriculture (COA), Executive Yuan
Chairman: Peng Tso-Kwei
37 Nanhai Rd., Taipei, Taiwan
Tel: 886-2-2311-9175, Fax: 886-2-2361-4397

Council for Economic Planning and Development (CEPD)
Chairman: Chiang Pin-kung
3, Paoching Rd., Taipei, Taiwan
Tel: 886-2-2316-5306, Fax: 886-2-2370-0403

Department of Health (DOH), Executive Yuan
Director-General: Chan Chi-Shean M.D.
100 Aikuo E. Rd., Taipei, Taiwan
Tel: 886-2-2396-7166, Fax: 886-2-2341-8994

Environmental Protection Administration (EPA), Executive Yuan
Administrator: Hsung-hsiung Tsai
41 Chunghwa Rd., Sec. 1, Taipei, Taiwan
Tel: 886-2-2321-7888, Fax: 886-2-2371-9759

5. MARKET RESEARCH FIRMS (PARTIAL LISTING)

Dun & Bradstreet International Ltd., Taiwan Branch
General Manager: James B. Barnett
12F, 188 Nanking E. Rd., Sec. 5, Taipei, Taiwan
Tel: 886-2-2756-2922, Fax: 886-2-2749-1936

AC Nielsen
Managing Director: Titan Wang
12F, 188 Nanking E. Rd., Sec. 5, Taipei, Taiwan
Tel: 886-2-2756-8668, Fax: 886-2-2754-8883

Investec-Coopers Lybrand Consulting Ltd.
Managing Director: Michael McNabb
3/F, 367 Fu Hsing N. Rd., Taipei, Taiwan
Tel: 886-2-2715-2822, Fax: 886-2-2545-1185

6. COMMERCIAL BANKS (PARTIAL LISTING)

American Express Bank, Ltd.
Senior Director & Gen. Mgr: Howard Law
3rd & 4th Fl, 214 Tunhwa N. Rd., Taipei, Taiwan
Tel: 886-2-2715-1581, Fax: 886-2-2713-0263

Citibank, N.A.
Corporate Officer: Peper Baumann

52 Minsheng E. Rd., Sec. 4, Taipei, Taiwan
Tel: 886-2-2715-5931, Fax: 886-2-2712-7388

Bank Boston, N.A. Taipei Branch
VP Corporate Banking: Francis Wu
5F, 137 Nanking E. Rd., Sec. 2, Taipei, Taiwan
Tel: 886-2-2506-3443, Fax: 886-2-2517-1653

Bank of Taiwan
Chairman: James C.T. Lo
120, Chungking S. Rd., Sec. 1, Taipei, Taiwan
Tel: 886-2-2349-3456, Fax: 886-2-2331-5840

International Commercial Bank of China
Chairman: James T.T. Yuan
100 Chilin Rd., Taipei, Taiwan
Tel: 886-2-2563-3156, Fax: 886-2-2561-1216

The Multilateral Development Bank
Office Director: Janet Thomas
14th and Constitution, NW
Washington, D.C. 20007
Tel: 202-482-3399, Fax: 202-482-5179

KEY ECONOMIC INDICATORS

(Millions of U.S. Dollars unless otherwise indicated)

	1997	1998	1999 1/
Income, Production and Employment:			
GDP (at current prices)	283.3	260.6	282.9
Real GDP Growth (percent)	6.8	4.7	5.3
GDP by Sector:			
Agriculture	7.7	7.1	7.6
Manufacturing	78.4	70.6	74.9
Services	155.8	146.0	166.0
Government	29.5	26.8	29.8
Per Capita GDP (US$)	13,130	11,967	12,866
Labor Force (000s)	9,432	9,546	9,690
Unemployment Rate (percent)	2.7	2.7	2.9
Money and Prices (annual percentage growth):			

For additional analytical, marketing, investment and business opportunities information, please contact
Global Investment & Business Center, USA
(202) 546-2103. Fax: (202) 546-3275. E-mail: rusric@erols.com

Money Supply (M2)	8.0	8.6	9.5
Consumer Price Inflation	0.9	1.7	0.9
Exchange Rate (NT$/US$) 2/			
Official	28.95	33.44	32.24
Balance of Payments and Trade: 3/			
Total Exports FOB 4/	122.1	110.6	119.5
Exports to U.S. CV 5/	32.6	33.1	34.9
Total Imports CIF 4/	114.4	104.7	112.1
Imports from U.S. FAS 5/	20.4	18.2	18.8
Trade Balance 4/	7.7	5.9	7.4
Trade Balance with U.S. 5/	12.2	14.9	16.1
External Public Debt	0.1	.05	0.02
Fiscal Deficit/GDP (pct)	3.9	3.3	5.3
Current Account Surplus/GDP (pct)	2.5	1.3	2.1
Debt Service Payments/GDP (pct)	0.8	1.1	0.7
Gold and Foreign Exchange Reserves	88.2	95.1	110.0
Aid from U.S. 6/	0	0	0
Aid from Other Countries	0	0	0

TAIWAN: RECENT DEVELOPMENTS AND U.S. POLICY CHOICES[4]

SUMMARY

U.S. policy concerns over Taiwan in recent years have centered on easing tensions and striking a balance between the People's Republic of China (PRC) and Taiwan. Despite extensive Taiwanese trade with, and investment in, the Chinese mainland, the two sides remain politically far apart and compete strongly for international influence. U.S. policy in this triangular U.S.-PRC-Taiwan relationship is complicated because:

-- Taiwan is moving away from past advocacy of "one China" to positions favoring an official status for Taipei - as in a remark by Taiwan's former President, Lee Teng-hui, that Taiwan-China ties should be conducted on a "state-to-state" basis. Such statements have complicated the U.S. "one China" policy and appear to challenge Beijing's claim to sovereignty over the island;

-- Beijing is strongly nationalistic and remains adamant about its claim to Taiwan. Also, Beijing continues to claim that it has the right to use force against Taiwan - a claim repeated again in a white paper on Taiwan which the PRC issued on February 21, 2000;

---

[4] **Kerry B. Dumbaugh** Foreign Affairs, Defense, and Trade Division **May 4, 2001**

**For additional analytical, marketing, investment and business opportunities information, please contact
Global Investment & Business Center, USA
(202) 546-2103. Fax: (202) 546-3275. E-mail: rusric@erols.com**

-- Many in Congress favor formal efforts, including legislation, that go beyond administration policy to strengthen U.S.-Taiwan relations in ways sure to antagonize the PRC.

Meanwhile, U.S. officials in Congress and elsewhere want to enhance investment opportunities for U.S. companies and ease trade issues, notably Taiwan's large trade surplus. They also encourage political democratization, even though it may foster separatist tendencies among ethnic groups that Beijing regards as threatening to state security.

Amid considerable congressional criticism of President Clinton's treatment of the Taiwan issue during a trip to China in late June 1998, the Senate that year passed resolutions (S.Con.Res. 107, S.Con.Res. 30) in support of Taiwan on July 10; a resolution in support of Taiwan (H.Con.Res. 301) passed the House on July 20. Proposed legislation in the 106th Congress, (S. 693, the Taiwan Security Enhancement Act) focused on representational and defense issues.

Taiwan's security and potential vulnerability to the Chinese military is of special concern. The U.S. Defense Department issued a congressionally mandated report on rising military strengths on both sides of the Taiwan Strait in 1999. The report intensified arguments on whether the United States should provide ballistic missile defense systems to Taiwan despite strenuous objections from Beijing. In late April, 1999, the Clinton Administration sold to Taiwan advanced early warning radars useful against missile attacks. Taiwan continues to seek Aegis destroyers and other advanced weapons systems from the United States which could enhance its defense capabilities.

In hotly contested presidential elections on March 18, 2000, Taiwan voters elected Chen Shui-bian, a member of the pro-independence Democratic Progressive Party (DPP). Chen's victory was Beijing's most feared outcome in the elections, and raises concerns that Taiwan-PRC tensions will increase still further. U.S. options include attempting to negotiate a new arrangement to manage U.S. relations with Beijing and Taipei, or remaining flexible given competing pressures from the two capitals, while deferring a solution of the Taiwan issue.

MOST RECENT DEVELOPMENTS

On April 24, 2001, the Bush Administration announced its willingness to sell Taiwan a new assortment of defense articles, to include diesel submarines, P-3C anti-submarine aircraft, and Kidd-class destroyers.

On February 14, 2001, Premier Chang Chun-hsiung announced that Taiwan would immediately resume construction of its 4th nuclear power plant. Construction had been halted on October 27, 2000, by Taiwan's new President, Chen Shui-bian, in a decision that engendered much controversy and an effort to oust Chen from office. The 4th nuclear power plant project had been championed by the former ruling Nationalist Party.

BACKGROUND AND ANALYSIS

Background to U.S. Interests in Taiwan

U.S. involvement with the government of Taiwan (known as the Republic of China or ROC) has its roots in the World War II U.S. alliance with the Nationalist Chinese government of Chiang Kai-shek, then on mainland China. In October 1949, upon its defeat by the Chinese communist forces of Mao Zedong, Chiang's government fled to Taiwan, an island off the south China coast. While on the mainland the Chinese Communist Party established the People's Republic of China

(PRC), Chiang's ROC government on Taiwan insisted that the communist government was not credible, and that Chiang's ROC administration was the only legitimate government of all China. For the next 30 years, the United States supported this claim with U.S. military protection and over $5 billion in military and economic aid, allowing Chiang and his one- party government (the Kuomintang Party, or KMT) to consolidate their position on Taiwan.

In the 1950s and 1960s, U.S. forces used Taiwan as a forward base against Sino-Soviet communism in Asia. After President Nixon's opening to Beijing in 1971-72, and the major pullback of U.S. forces in Asia under the guidelines of the "Nixon doctrine," U.S. officials viewed the mainland government more as a strategic asset against the U.S.S.R. than an adversary to be confronted in the Taiwan Strait. In 1979, the United States broke defense and other official ties with Taiwan to establish formal diplomatic relations with the PRC. The United States subsequently affirmed its security and other interests in Taiwan through the Taiwan Relations Act (TRA) and the continued supply of U.S. arms to Taiwan. But this reflected a moral commitment to a former ally rather than U.S. interest in using Taiwan's strategic position for broader policy ends.

With the thaw in the Cold War in the late 1980s and subsequent collapse of the Soviet Union, U.S. interest in the PRC as a "strategic asset" in global politics declined. China's burgeoning economy and sometimes assertive foreign policy in the 1990s revived U.S. interest in finding pragmatic ways to deal with rising Chinese power. Concurrently, the United States deepened a broad array of economic, military, social, and other contacts with Taiwan's rapidly developing economy and society, and its newly democratic political system.

Today, the United States is an important investor and trading partner for Taiwan. U.S. markets receive about 25% of Taiwan's exports, while the United States supplies a much smaller percentage of Taiwan's imports, leading to a $14.9 billion U.S. trade deficit with Taiwan in 1998. Taiwan continues to enjoy Export-Import Bank financing, Overseas Private Investment Corporation (OPIC) guarantees, most-favored-nation status, and ready access to U.S. markets. Meanwhile, many U.S. leaders want to encourage Taiwanese enterprises to invest in the United States.

U.S.-PRC-Taiwan Relations Since 1979

On January 1, 1979, the United States switched its diplomatic recognition from Taipei to Beijing. In the U.S.-PRC joint communique announcing the change, the United States recognized the government of the PRC as the sole legal government of China and acknowledged the Chinese position that there is but one China, and Taiwan is part of China. [1] As part of de-recognition, the United States also notified Taiwan authorities of intent to terminate, effective January 1, 1980, the 1954 U.S.-ROC Mutual Defense Treaty. In a unilateral statement released on December 16, 1978, the United States declared that it "continues to have an interest in the peaceful resolution of the Taiwan issue and expects that the Taiwan issue will be settled peacefully by the Chinese themselves."

Arms Sales to Taiwan. Since de-recognition, U.S. policy toward Taiwan has been one of studied ambiguity. On the one hand, U.S. policymakers have adhered to a "one-China" policy framework - acknowledging the PRC as China's only legitimate political entity, while promising not to recognize Taiwan as an independent entity with a separate identity. On the other hand, the United States continues to sell defense weapons and equipment to Taiwan and to have other, extensive contacts with Taiwan under the auspices of the Taiwan Relations Act (TRA) [2] which created the domestic legal authority for conducting unofficial relations with Taiwan. The TRA is essentially a congressional construct, enacted by a Congress unhappy with the Carter Administration's minimal plans for how U.S. relations were to be conducted with Taiwan after official relations were severed. Of particular importance in the current environment is Section 3 of the TRA, dealing with U.S. defense commitments to Taiwan. Section 3 is non-specific about the defense articles and services the United States will provide. It merely calls for "such defense articles and services...as may be necessary," and gives Congress a role in determining what needs Taiwan may have.

Some in Congress believe that the TRA is outdated, and that Taiwan's self-defense capabilities have eroded while China has grown militarily more capable and more hostile. The conclusions of a congressionally mandated report issued by the U.S. Department of Defense (DoD) in February 1999 appear to bolster this view. The report assesses the military balance between Taiwan and China, and concludes that in light of improvements in offensive military capabilities, by the year 2005 China will have acquired the ability "to attack Taiwan with air and missile strikes which would degrade key military facilities and damage the island's economic infrastructure." Congressional proponents of enhanced security for Taiwan suggest that U.S. policy should be adjusted accordingly. Policymakers are also disturbed that China continues to insist publicly on its right to use force against Taiwan.

U.S. arms sales to Taiwan have often prompted strong objections from the PRC. On August 17, 1982, a U.S.- PRC joint communique addressed this point. In that communique, the PRC cited a "fundamental policy" of striving for a peaceful solution to the Taiwan question. The United States stated in the communique that it did not

> seek to carry out a long-term policy of arms sales to Taiwan, that its arms sales to Taiwan will not exceed, either in qualitative or quantitative terms, the level of those supplied in recent years since the establishment of diplomatic relations between the United States and China, and that it intends to reduce gradually its sales of arms to Taiwan.

U.S. government arms sales levels have slowly declined, but have remained over $600 million a year. Taiwan's 1992 purchase of 150 F-16 aircraft (worth $5.9 billion) represented an exception to this trend. U.S. transfers of military-related technology have allowed Taiwan to develop advanced fighter aircraft and other military equipment to defend the island. (See CRS Report RS20483, *Taiwan; Major U.S. Arms Sales Since 1990.*) On August 1, 1999, the Pentagon announced it would sell two E-2 electronic warfare aircraft to Taiwan, along with radar detection equipment, and along with $150 million in aircraft spare parts. On April 17, 2000, the Clinton Administration decided to sell Taiwan an assortment of air defense weapons, including PAVE PAWS radar (designed to monitor ballistic missiles); an upgraded model of the Maverick air-to-ground missile; and the advanced medium range air-to-air missile (or AMRAAM), with the latter to be stored in the United States unless China acquires a similar missile capability. The Administration followed a Pentagon recommendation not to sell more sophisticated and controversial weapons that Taiwan had requested, such as the Aegis battle management system, submarines, and P-3 Orion anti-submarine aircraft.

The Taiwan Security Enhancement Act. On February 17, 1999, the U.S. Defense Department issued a congressionally mandated report on rising military strengths on both sides of the Taiwan Strait. The report intensified arguments on whether the United States should provide ballistic missile defense systems to Taiwan despite strenuous objections from Beijing, and it reinforced the concerns of some Members that China poses more of a threat now to Taiwan than in the past, and that Taiwan's ability to defend itself has eroded over time. Consequently, in the 106th Congress, Members of both Houses introduced the Taiwan Security Enhancement Act: S. 693 (Helms, introduced on March 24, 1999), and H.R. 1838 (DeLay, introduced on May 18, 1999; H.Rept. 106-423). These similar bills provided for enhanced U.S.-Taiwan military communication and cooperation, and the strengthening of Taiwan's security. While maintaining that it shared the desire to bolster Taiwan, the Clinton Administration saw the legislation as unnecessarily provocative and potentially harmful to U.S. security interests. Although the House passed its version of the legislation on February 1, 2000, by a vote of 341-70, the Senate never took up the bill.

"One-China" Policy. In addition to arms sales, Beijing criticizes other aspects of continued U.S. support for Taiwan, saying that such gestures reduce Taipei's interest in negotiations on reunification of Taiwan with the mainland. One of the most notable examples of this occurred on May 22, 1995, when President Clinton, bowing to substantial congressional pressure, changed Administration policy, and decided to allow Taiwan President Lee Teng-hui to make a private visit to the United States. Beijing reacted with strong military and rhetorical pressure on Taiwan. Prior to Taiwan's March 23, 1996 elections, the United States sent two carrier battle groups in response to PRC military exercises in the Taiwan Strait. The PRC exercises, which ended on March 25, 1996, were a vain effort to discredit Lee, who won 54% of the vote in a field of four candidates in presidential elections.

Tensions began to ease after the election. During 1997 and 1998, Taiwan officials and supporters of Taiwan in the United States were concerned with the Clinton Administration's willingness to respond to PRC pressure in strongly reaffirming the U.S. "one China" policy in ways that appeared to curb support for Taiwan's greater role in world affairs and its possible independence in the future. Some also suspected that the U.S. government was behind suggestions from delegations of prestigious Americans visiting Taiwan and the mainland in early 1998 that Taiwan should be more flexible in seeking political talks with mainland China. The Clinton Administration said the suspicions were wrong and that it had not changed its longstanding "One China" policy in ways that would negatively affect Taiwan.

The 105th and 106th Congresses were inclined to support Taiwan despite objections from Beijing or concerns by the Clinton Administration. H.R. 2386 urging consideration of U.S. support for a ballistic missile defense of Taiwan passed the House in the week after Chinese President Jiang Zemin's visit to Washington in October 1997. H.R. 1757, a foreign affairs authorization bill, passed the House and Senate in 1998 with a provision urging Taiwan's early entry into the WTO. The Taiwan provision was included in H.R. 4328 (P.L. 105-277) signed October 21, 1998. H.Con.Res. 270 urging U.S. support for Taiwan's security unanimously passed the House two weeks before President Clinton's departure for a summit in Beijing in late June 1998. H.R. 4103, the FY1999 Defense Appropriations bill, passed Congress on September 29, 1998 with a provision calling for a Department of Defense study of cross Strait military capabilities. H.Con.Res. 334 urging Taiwan's participation in the World Health Organization passed the House on October 10, 1998.

Taiwan-Mainland Relations

President Lee's "State-to-State" relations comment. Relations between the PRC and Taiwan became noticeably more tense at the end of the 1990s. Heightened tensions began on July 9, 1999, when President Lee Teng-hui said that ties between Taiwan and China should be considered on a "special state-to-state" basis. Taiwan officials had been moving incrementally in this direction for some time; in 1995, for instance, President Lee emphasized that China and Taiwan were governed by "two governments," and proposed that each side enter international organizations "on an equal footing." Nevertheless, Lee's July 1999 remark was seen by many as the most direct challenge to date concerning Beijing's claim to sovereignty over Taiwan. Beijing objected strenuously to the statement, saying it proved that Lee had fundamentally changed previous policy in which Taiwan had claimed that there was only "one China," of which Taiwan was a part. China adheres to the "one-China" policy, and claims Taiwan as a "break-away" province that belongs to China. Taiwan officials insisted that Lee's statement was not a policy change, but a "statement of fact" meant to reflect that the island government's 85-year existence entitled it to a status equal with China's in cross-strait dialogue. The Lee remark also complicated U.S. policy toward China and Taiwan, since the "one-China" premise has been used in various formulations by American officials to describe U.S. policy concerning Taiwan.

PRC "white papers". On February 21, 2000, the PRC issued its second "white paper" about Taiwan, the first having been issued in August 1993. In the most recent statement, "The One-China Principle and the Taiwan Issue," PRC officials offered a mix of apparent conciliatory gestures and a new ominous-sounding assertion that if Taiwan authorities tried to indefinitely delay cross-Strait talks about Taiwan's future, then the PRC would be "forced to adopt all drastic measures possible, including the use of force." Previously, the PRC had reserved the right to use force in only two instances: if Taiwan declared independence; and if Taiwan were invaded and occupied by a foreign country. A *Washington Post* article of February 23, 2000, cited a top Pentagon official as responding to the new statement by warning the PRC of "incalculable consequences" if the PRC resorted to force against Taiwan.

On October 16, 2000, China published its third national security white paper, entitled "China's National Defense in 2000." The document listed China's national defense expenditures for 2000 at 121.29 billion renminbi - roughly U.S. $14.65 billion. In describing its view of the current international security situation, the white paper declared that there are "new negative developments in the security situation" in the region. The paper cited U.S. weapons sales to Taiwan and consideration of the Taiwan Security Enhancement Act by the 106th Congress as some of these negative developments. The paper also stated that if Taiwan were invaded or continues to refuse to negotiate on reunification with China, the Chinese government "will have no choice but to adopt all drastic measures possible, including the use of force, to safeguard China's sovereignty..."

China's harsh rhetoric on Taiwan has raised concerns in some policy circles about the prospects for military conflict in the area. The danger of military conflict first became evident during the PRC military exercises held at the time of Taiwan's presidential elections in March 1996. Following Taiwan President Lee Teng-hui's personal visit to Cornell University in the United States in June 1995, Beijing broke off high-level talks on cross-Strait relations, stridently excoriated Lee for allegedly attempting to split China and lead Taiwan toward independence, and conducted series of military exercises designed to intimidate the Taiwan people.

Following the U.S. show of force in the Taiwan area and Lee's impressive victory in the March 1996 presidential election, Beijing once again moderated its criticism of the Taiwanese leader. The PRC returned to reiterating its adherence to an ostensibly flexible stance to cross-Strait relations, and advised that a renewed PRC use of force would only come as a last resort in the face of egregious actions by Taipei and/or foreign powers designed to split Taiwan from the mainland. Chinese officials nonetheless remained suspicious and critical of Lee, stressing that resumed dialogue in cross-Strait relations and improvement in the current tense atmosphere depended on Taiwan's adherence to the "principle of one China."

Beijing has also given top priority to checking Taiwan's efforts to broaden its international standing through so-called pragmatic diplomacy. Thus, it has countered Taiwan's efforts to establish formal relations with states already maintaining official ties with Beijing, and it has pressed foreign governments to refuse to receive Taiwan leaders traveling to their countries on an ostensibly private basis. Partly as a result of PRC efforts, Taiwan now maintains official relations with less than 30 countries, mostly small states in Central America and the Caribbean,

Africa, and the South Pacific. It is unable to host senior-level meetings of the Asian Pacific Economic Cooperation (APEC) forum, even though Taiwan is a member in good standing of the group, and it has been unsuccessful in gaining even observer status in such U.N. affiliated groups as the World Health Organization. Both China and Taiwan have so far dealt reasonably well with the economic consequences of the 1997-1998 Asian economic crisis. Politically, Taipei quickly used the crisis as an opportunity to broaden high-level official contacts with most Southeast Asian governments seeking outside assistance, and Beijing was unsuccessful is dissuading cash-starved Southeast Asian leaders from seeking economic advantage through talks with senior Taiwan political leaders.

Despite PRC-Taiwan sparring on political issues, cross-Strait talks were held in April 1998, and high-level discussions took place in Shanghai and Beijing during October 14-19, 1998. These talks improved the atmosphere but did little to bridge the wide gap between the negotiating positions of Beijing and Taipei. Both sides were anxious to show U.S. and world opinion that they were not being obstructionist over cross-Strait issues. Meanwhile, economic, cultural and other exchanges between Taiwan and mainland China have grown. By 1999, Taiwanese investment in the mainland had reached a reported $30 billion. Bilateral trade, heavily in Taiwan's favor, amounts to about $30 billion a year.

Over 13 million visits have taken place from Taiwan to the mainland. Over 250,000 mainland Chinese experts, entrepreneurs and others have traveled to Taiwan for consultations and exchanges. Exchanges of PRC-Taiwan scholars and experts for consultations on cross-Strait and other issues provide, in the view of some Taiwanese officials, an active "second track" for PRC-Taiwan dialogue. Recent events in cross-Strait relations have included the decision by oil companies in the PRC and Taiwan to explore jointly offshore areas for oil; the start of flights from Taiwan to the mainland with only a short stopover in Macao or Hong Kong; and Taiwan's opening to third-country ships, and selected mainland and Taiwanese ships, to carry cargo to and from designated ports in Taiwan and on the mainland. Cross-Strait economic relations are now so important for Taiwan that Taiwan government and business leaders have been among the strongest, albeit largely silent, supporters of continued U.S. most-favored-nation (MFN--now called "normal trade relations," or NTR) tariff treatment for China. Withdrawal of MFN would have a serious negative impact on many Taiwan businesses.

U.S. Policy Choices. The United States remains the foreign power most closely involved in PRC-Taiwan relations. It seeks closer relations with both the PRC and Taiwan and favors the peaceful exchanges across the Taiwan Strait. Cross-Strait tensions since mid-1995 challenge U.S. interest in stability in the region and raise the possibility of U.S. involvement in a potential conflict there.

U.S. policy faces major challenges in attempting to strike a proper balance in the U.S.- PRC-Taiwan triangular relationship:

- China's growing economic, political and military power. Increased Chinese military capabilities are coupled with a reluctance to defer to the United States, Taiwan, or others. Strong nationalistic emphasis in Chinese domestic politics and leadership uncertainty sometimes prompt PRC decision makers to avoid other than politically safe nationalistic positions on key issues like Taiwan.

- Taiwan's assertiveness. Economic growth, rapidly changing social conditions and recent democratization reinforce efforts to increase Taiwan's stature in international affairs despite the objections of the PRC, and ongoing efforts inside Taiwan to move away from a "one China" policy to one seen by Beijing as a fundamental challenge.

These competing forces sometimes combine with U.S. domestic interests. For instance, many in the 104th and 105th Congresses pushed for greater U.S. support for Taiwan while Clinton administration officials warned against the effects of such initiatives on U.S.-PRC relations.

Judging that the U.S. "one China" policy framework no longer works, some American experts favor U.S. negotiations with Beijing and Taipei to strike a new "strategic bargain." The alternative, in their view, is continued conflicting pressure from Beijing and Taipei and related U.S. domestic interests, leading to a passive U.S. policy that would increase confrontation and possibly military conflict.

Others judge that such negotiations would cause more trouble than they are worth, especially for what they see as a relatively weak U.S. Administration. Rather, the administration can continue to adjust its "one China" policy to accommodate pressures from Taipei and Beijing and their U.S. domestic supporters. From this perspective, not all trends in Taiwan and Beijing argue for increased confrontation; Beijing and Taipei have moderated their respective political positions recently, while economic, social, cultural and other non-governmental interchange grows markedly. If both Taipei and Beijing can be persuaded that continuation of current trends is acceptable, then U.S. policy can continue deferring a solution of the Taiwan issue into the future.

U.S. policymakers also are called on to respond to recent prominent calls from both sides of the Strait for the United States to "facilitate" or "mediate" a reduction in tensions. The governments in Beijing, Taipei, and Washington maintain that the issue of Taiwan's reunification is to be handled by people on both sides of the Strait. The United States is not to mediate cross-Strait differences. Nevertheless, officials and nongovernment opinion leaders in both Beijing and Taipei are now forthright in urging the United States to take actions to ease cross-Strait tensions.

PRC officials want the United States to press Taiwan to avoid egregious efforts to achieve greater international recognition, and to limit arms sales to Taiwan so that Taiwanese leaders will not be able to use such U.S. support to resist PRC efforts to achieve reunification. Officials and observers in Taipei ask the United States to press Beijing to avoid intimidation, and to solidify U.S. ties with Taiwan so that Taipei can deal with the PRC on a more equitable basis.

Predictably, officials in Beijing and Taipei favor U.S. intervention that benefits their respective sides. There is little support for true mediation -- that is, efforts by a neutral party to get both sides to give up some significant parts of their respective negotiating positions in order to reach a compromise solution. Any U.S. efforts to press for such a compromise could be portrayed as outside interference and redound negatively for U.S. relations with both capitals.

ECONOMIC AND POLITICAL ISSUES

Economic Prospects and Concerns

Prospects for continued economic growth in Taiwan are reasonably good. The economy grew rapidly (around 10% a year) in the 1970s and 1980s. Growth declined to around 5-6% a year in the 1990s as the economy matured.

Taiwan's economy remains vulnerable to rises in oil prices, decline in the U.S. economy, and international protectionism, especially in the United States. The 1997-1998 Asian financial crisis prompted a 20% decline in the value of Taiwan's currency relative to the U.S. dollar and an increase in inflationary pressures, but on balance Taiwan's large foreign exchange reserves, little foreign debt, and continued vigorous (5-6%) growth made it attractive to investors and trading partners. Taiwan's GNP growth depends heavily on exports, and about 25% of these exports go

For additional analytical, marketing, investment and business opportunities information, please contact
Global Investment & Business Center, USA
(202) 546-2103. Fax: (202) 546-3275. E-mail: rusric@erols.com

to the United States. (Leading exports to the United States include clothing and footwear, toys, and various electronic products.)

In recent years, Taiwanese government officials have attempted to accommodate increased U.S. pressure on trade issues. They met many U.S. demands for greater market access for U.S. goods and services and responded to U.S. complaints by taking stronger measures to protect U.S. copyrights and other intellectual property rights. Taiwan in recent years has worked hard to meet U.S. and other nations' requirements for entry into the World Trade Organization (WTO); it negotiated a market access agreement with the United States in February 1998 as a prelude to WTO entry.

A different set of economic issues flows from Taiwan's large foreign exchange reserves and growing international economic power. On the one hand, this trend prompts United States and other foreign officials and business representatives to seek investment or financial support from Taiwan. On the other hand, it prompts some Americans to worry that Taipei enterprises may use acquisitions of distressed U.S. companies to gain quick entry into important markets heretofore dominated by the United States.

U.S. Policy Choices. Many Americans concerned with the large U.S. trade deficit call for strong action (possibly including limitations on foreign access to U.S. markets) to improve the U.S. trade balance. Others call for strict protection of U.S. Intellectual Property Rights against infringement from Taiwan and elsewhere. They recognize that such action could negatively affect the economic prosperity and related political stability of a number of important U.S. trading partners, including Taiwan. But they judge that the United States has little choice but to take firm measures to protect its own markets and economic advancement.

Concern with American industrial competitiveness also motivates Americans who question the sale of sophisticated U.S. industries and equipment to wealthy Taiwan enterprises. They favor strict review of such sales to insure that Taiwanese investors do not reap a large competitive advantage through investment in technologically advanced U.S. companies.

An opposing view comes from U.S. supporters of the Nationalist government, U.S. supporters of the political opposition, Americans concerned with promoting greater political democracy and continued economic prosperity in Taiwan, and free trade advocates who tend to oppose measures designed to restrict foreign exporters' access to U.S. markets. They emphasize the potentially negative results in terms of hampering U.S. investment in Taiwan, Taiwanese investment in the United States, and U.S. interest in the political and social stability long associated with economic prosperity in Taiwan. They also emphasize the negative results for U.S. interests in a free international trading system that they believe would come from restrictive trade legislation or administrative actions aimed at Taiwan or others.

U.S. opinion also divides on Taiwan's entry into the WTO. Advocates in Congress and elsewhere emphasize that Taiwan has satisfied almost all economic requirements for entry, and charge that its entry is actually being held hostage to that of Beijing, which is not as far along. (Beijing insists that Taiwan cannot enter the WTO until after China has gained entry.) The contrary U.S. view holds that to push for Taiwan's entry before China's would surely anger the mainland leadership and perhaps jeopardize the current U.S. policy of engagement with China; and it would have little chance of success as other WTO members would likely bow to PRC pressure if the United States did not.

POLITICAL LIBERALIZATION

Under the leadership of Chiang Kai-shek (who ruled the Republic of China from 1945-1975), the Nationalist Party-dominated government ruled in a sometimes harsh authoritarian fashion. It pursued policies of a strong national defense against the Communist mainland and export-oriented economic growth. It tolerated little open political dissent.

In the 1970s, the United States and most developed countries recognized the PRC and broke official ties with Taipei. Under international pressure, Taiwan lost the China seat in the U.N. and most official international bodies. These international setbacks challenged a major source of the political legitimacy of the Nationalist regime. It was harder to argue that people on Taiwan should accept and pay for an elaborate central government administration that included a majority of representatives who were elected on mainland China prior to the Communist victory there in 1949 and the subsequent Nationalist retreat to Taiwan. Nationalist leaders, especially Chiang Kai-shek's son, Chiang Ching-kuo, emphasized other elements in support of the Nationalists' rule, noting in particular the leadership's successful supervision of Taiwan's dramatic economic progress. Chiang and his associates also were at pains to introduce to power more "Taiwanese" -- 85% of the island's population whose roots go back to Taiwan prior to the influx of two million "mainlanders" associated with the Nationalist regime at the time of the Communist victory on the mainland. The vast majority of the Nationalist Party's rank and file were Taiwanese, and important Taiwanese dignitaries, including the current President, Lee Teng-hui, were raised to high positions.

A combination of international and domestic pressures accelerated the pace of political reform in the middle and late 1980s. In September 1986, a formal opposition party, the Democratic Progressive Party (DPP), was formed. President Chiang Ching-kuo ended martial law in July 1987. Following Chiang Ching-kuo's death in January 1988, the new President, Lee Teng-hui, reaffirmed a commitment to reform that would legalize opposition parties and restructure parliamentary bodies. In 1991, President Lee ended the state of civil war with the PRC and the associated "temporary provisions" that had given Nationalist leaders "emergency" powers to deal with dissent. Members of legislative bodies elected in the mainland over 40 years earlier retired. An election was held to fill all seats in a new National Assembly, and in 1992 a new legislature was elected.

In annual island-wide elections since then, the Nationalist Party incrementally lost ground to the DPP and the New China Party, founded in 1993. In the March 23, 1996 presidential elections, Lee Teng-hui won 53.9% of the vote, the DPP candidate, 21.1%, and two conservative independents, 14.9%, and 9.9%, respectively. In concurrent elections for the National Assembly's 334 seats, the Nationalists got 183 seats with 49.7% of the vote; the DPP got 99 seats with 29.9%; and the New China Party got 46 seats with 13.7%. A December 23-28, 1996, multiparty National Development Conference in Taiwan saw continued strong Taiwanese opposition to Beijing's "one country-two systems" reunification formula and agreement on government reforms, notably the downgrading of Taiwan provincial government functions. The reforms were legally passed on July 18, 1997. In Beijing, officials voiced concern that the decision to diminish the Taiwanese provincial government suggested that Taiwan was determined to highlight its status as an international actor separate from China.

Island-wide elections for 23 mayors and magistrates on November 29, 1997, registered a big defeat for the Nationalist Party and big gains for the opposition Democratic Progressive Party (DPP). The DPP won 12 positions, up from 6 in the last election in 1993. The Nationalists won 8, down from 16 four years earlier. The rest went to independents. The DPP for the first time ever out-polled the Nationalists in the popular vote, 43.4% to 42%. The results left DPP leaders in charge of local government for 72% of Taiwan's people, while the Nationalist leaders were in charge of only 22%.

**For additional analytical, marketing, investment and business opportunities information, please contact
Global Investment & Business Center, USA
(202) 546-2103. Fax: (202) 546-3275. E-mail: rusric@erols.com**

Taiwan's legislative and municipal elections of December 5, 1998 were an important victory for the ruling Nationalist Party and calmed for a time concerns in the United States, mainland China, and Taiwan that voters might favor the opposition DPP, which in the past has fielded a party platform favoring Taiwan self-determination -- anathema for Beijing. The Nationalists won a comfortable majority in the legislature, 123 out of 225 seats, with 46.4% of the vote. The DPP won 70 seats with 29.5% of the vote. In the closely watched race for mayor of Taipei municipality, the Nationalist candidate defeated the DPP incumbent, Chen Shui-bian, and slowed Chen's perceived drive to run as the party's standard bearer in the March 2000 presidential election.

Taiwan's Presidential Elections, March 18, 2000. On March 18, 2000, Taiwan voters went to the polls for only the second time to elect a new president in a hotly contested election that was judged too close to call in the final days. (The first direct election for president was held in March 1996 when President Lee Teng-hui was elected over the strong objections of Beijing.) The winning candidate in the election of 2000, Chen Shui-bian, is a member of the opposition DPP, the party that had been illegal until 1986. The vote handed a stunning defeat to Chiang Kai-shek's Nationalist Party, the Kuomintang (KMT), which had had an unbroken tenure in power for 50 years. With three leading presidential candidates, Chen won with 39% of the popular vote, while an independent challenger, James Soong, ran a close second with 36.5% of the vote. The KMT candidate, sitting vice-president Lien Chan, ran a distant third with only 23% of the vote. President Chen took office on May 20, 2000.

U.S. officials have generally praised Chen for his careful political maneuvering in the first year of his administration. His political appointments of KMT members to high office suggest that he wants to emphasize continuity as much as possible during the difficult transition in the political landscape. He has tried to maintain a balance between the more radical, pro-independence advocates in his party while trying to avoid antagonizing Beijing on the cross-strait issue. On the latter point, he has made a pledge (conditioned upon Beijing's not using force against Taiwan) to 5 principles designed to appeal to Beijing: no declaration of independence; no change in Taiwan's formal name (Republic of China); no amendment of Taiwan's constitution with the "state-to-state" formula; no public referendum on independence; and no repeal of Taiwan's Guidelines on National Unification (with China).

LEGISLATION

H.R. 428 (Brown, S.)
Taiwan Participation in the World Health Organization (WHO). Requires the Secretary of State to initiate a U.S. plan to endorse and obtain observer status for Taiwan at the annual week-long summit of the World Health Assembly in May 2001 in Geneva, Switzerland; and requires the Secretary of State to submit the plan to Congress in a written, unclassified report. Introduced on February 6, 2001, and referred to the House International Relations Committee. A non-binding resolution on Taiwan's participation in the WHO passed the Senate on April 12, 1999.

S. 693 (Helms)/H.R. 1838 (DeLay) (106th Congress)
Taiwan Security Enhancement Act. Both Senate and House measures authorize the President to sell certain and specified weapons systems, such as diesel submarines and theater missile defense equipment, to Taiwan. S. 693 introduced March 24, 1999; referred to Committee on Foreign Relations. Senate held hearings August 4, 1999. H.R. 1838 introduced May 18, 1999, and referred to Committee on International Relations. Committee held markup October 26, 1999, and by a vote of 32-6, ordered bill to be reported, amended. Reported October 28, 1999 [H.Rept. 106-423]. House passed H.R. 1838 February 2, 2000, by a vote of 341-70.

CHRONOLOGY

For additional analytical, marketing, investment and business opportunities information, please contact
Global Investment & Business Center, USA
(202) 546-2103. Fax: (202) 546-3275. E-mail: rusric@erols.com

02/14/01 -- Premier Chang Chun-hsiung announced that Taiwan would immediately resume construction of its 4th nuclear power plant. Construction had been halted on October 27, 2000, by Taiwan's new President, Chen Shui-bian.
02/08/01 -- Two Xinhua News Agency correspondents from the People's Republic of China (PRC) became the first PRC reporters ever to be posted in Taiwan.
01/22/01 -- Vincent Siew, Vice-Chairman of Taiwan's former ruling party, the Kuomintang (KMT), proposed establishing a "cross-strait common market" between Taiwan and China.
01/02/01 -- Taiwan established the first direct shipping link with China in more than 5 decades when 3 Taiwan ships embarked from Quemoy and Matsu and later docked in the Chinese ports of Xiamen and Fuzhou. China's reaction to the direct visit was cautious.
10/16/00 -- China issued a white paper, "China's National Defense 2000," reinforcing its claim that it would use force against Taiwan if Taiwan continued to refuse to negotiate for reunification with China.
08/17/00 -- Taiwan's President, Chen Shui-bian, made a brief transit stop in Los Angeles. Originally invited to attend a private dinner with several U.S. Members of Congress, President Chen declined to attend, reportedly under pressure from U.S. government officials to avoid inflaming China.
05/20/00 -- Chen Shui-bian was inaugurated as Taiwan's newly elected president. His inauguration speech was viewed generally as a moderate attempt to lower tensions with Beijing.
04/14/00 -- According to the *Washington Post*, Taiwan is seeking to buy from the United States 4 Aegis destroyers, which would enhance Taiwan's air defense capability.
03/24/00 -- President Lee Teng-hui resigned as head of the ruling Nationalist Party because of his party's unprecedented defeat in the presidential election.
03/18/00 -- In presidential elections in Taipei, DPP candidate Chen Shui-bian won with approximately 39% of the vote.
02/21/00 -- The PRC issued a White Paper, "The One-China Principle and the Taiwan Issue," with a mix of conciliatory gestures and a new threat that Taiwan's indefinite deLay in cross-Strait talks may prompt use of force by the PRC.
02/01/00 -- The House passed H.R. 1838, the Taiwan Security Enhancement Act, by a vote of 341-70.
11/17/99 -- The ruling Kuomintang (KMT) Party expelled presidential candidate James Soong and six of his key staff.
09/21/99 -- An earthquake measuring 7.6 on the Richter scale hit central Taiwan, killing more than 2,000 people and leaving 100,000 homeless.
07/09/99 -- Taiwan's President, Lee Teng-hui, said that ties between Taiwan and the PRC should be conducted on a "state-to-state" basis.
04/19/99 -- Taiwan DPP leader Chen Shui-bian began several days of seminars and meetings in Washington, DC.
02/17/99 -- The U.S. Defense Department issued a congressionally mandated report on rising military strengths on both sides of the Taiwan Strait. The report intensified arguments on whether the United States should provide ballistic missile defense systems to Taiwan despite strenuous objections from Beijing.
01/12/99 -- A PRC foreign ministry spokesman warned the United States not to transfer Theater Missile Defense and relevant technology to Taiwan.
11/10/98 -- Secretary of Energy Bill Richardson met Lee Teng-hui and other leaders during a trip to Taiwan.
10/23/98 -- Secretary of Defense William Cohen had an unofficial meeting with Taiwan's armed forces chief of staff then visiting Washington.
10/19/98 -- Taiwan negotiator Koo Chen-fu left Beijing after talks with Chinese party leader Jiang Zemin and other senior officials.
01/24/98 -- Elections for mayors of smaller cities, county assemblies, and city councils showed the KMT's continued dominance at the grass-roots level of Taiwanese politics. The Kuomintang won over 60% of the contested seats; the DPP about 20%.

**For additional analytical, marketing, investment and business opportunities information, please contact
Global Investment & Business Center, USA
(202) 546-2103. Fax: (202) 546-3275. E-mail: rusric@erols.com**

01/01/98 -- South Africa, the most important country to maintain official ties with Taiwan, broke official relations and established formal ties with China.
03/30/97 -- According to the *New York Times,* Speaker Gingrich disclosed in Shanghai that he had told Chinese leaders that if the PRC attacked Taiwan, "We will defend Taiwan. Period."
03/10/96 -- The Pentagon disclosed that two U.S. carrier battle groups had been ordered to the Taiwan area.
03/08/96 -- PRC forces began holding ballistic missile exercises in two impact areas near Taiwan. The actions were condemned by Congress and the administration.
01/24/96 -- The *New York Times* reported on a series of explicit warnings from Chinese leaders to the United States over the likelihood of military action in the Taiwan Strait.
12/02/95 -- In elections for the 164-seat Legislative Yuan, the KMT received 85 seats with 45% of the vote; the DPP, 54 seats; and the New China Party, 21 seats.
05/22/95 -- Yielding to congressional pressure, President Clinton decided to allow Taiwan's president to visit the United States the following month.
04/08/95 -- President Lee Teng-hui responded to President Jiang Zemin's eight-point proposal on cross-Strait relations with his own proposal.
01/30/95 -- China's leader Jiang Zemin issued a positive sounding eight-point proposal on Taiwanese-mainland relations.
09/07/94 -- The Clinton Administration's Taiwan policy review called for modestly increased contacts with Taiwan.
01/29/94 -- In elections for numerous local councils and other posts, the Kuomintang dominated, winning over 60% of the vote, while the DPP won about 15%.
09/02/92 -- President Bush agreed to sell 150 F-16 jet fighters to Taiwan.
07/15/87 -- Martial law ended in Taiwan.
FOR ADDITIONAL READING
Tsang, Steve. "China and Taiwan: a proposal for peace," *Security dialogue,* v. 31, Sept. 2000: pp. 327-336.
Clough, Ralph N. *Cooperation or Conflict in the Taiwan Strait,* Rowman and Littlefield, 1999.
Freeman, Charles, "Preventing War in the Taiwan Strait," *Foreign Affairs,* July-August 1998.
Nye, Joseph. "A Taiwan Deal." *Washington Post,* March 8, 1998.
CRS Reports
CRS Report RS20370. *The Taiwan Security Enhancement Act and Underlying Issues in U.S. Policy,* by Kerry Dumbaugh.
CRS Report 96-498. *China-U.S.-Taiwan Economic Relations,* by Wayne Morrison and William Cooper.
CRS Report RS20483. *Taiwan: Major U.S. Arms Sales Since 1990,* by Shirley Kan.
CRS Report RS20187 (pdf). *Taiwan's Defense: Assessing the U.S. Department of Defense Report, "The Security Situation in the Taiwan Strait,"* by Robert Sutter.
CRS Report 96-246 (pdf). *Taiwan: Texts of the Taiwan Relations Act and the China Communiques,* by Kerry Dumbaugh.

Footnotes

1. [back]The texts of the Taiwan Relations Act and the 3 U.S.-China communiques that underpin bilateral U.S.-China relations can be found in CRS Report 96-246 (pdf).
2. [back]The TRA was signed on April 10, 1979, and enacted as P.L. 96-8.
Return to CONTENTS section of this Issue Brief.

**For additional analytical, marketing, investment and business opportunities information, please contact
Global Investment & Business Center, USA
(202) 546-2103. Fax: (202) 546-3275. E-mail: rusric@erols.com**

WASHINGTON-TAIPEI RELATIONS AND THE ROC'S PRAGMATIC DIPLOMACY

Question and Answers

Q.1. *Most of the world has adopted the principle of one China in recognizing the PRC as the sole government of China. Taiwan also espouses the one China principle. So why do you want to pursue a separate international identity for Taiwan?*

A.1. It is true that we espouse the one China principle, but to us that "one China" is the Republic of China on Taiwan. We are a sovereign state and have been since 1912. We are entitled to the rights of a sovereign state, which includes participating in all international organizations and maintaining normal diplomatic relations with all other sovereign states. Article I of the 1933 Montevideo Convention on Rights and Duties of States defines a state as possessing a permanent population, a defined territory, a government, and the capacity to enter into relations with other states. We meet all these criteria. We have a sovereign government exercising effective jurisdiction over well-defined territories with over 21 million permanent residents, and we are recognized by some 30 states. The PRC obstructionism is the only reason that other states have not recognized us. However, irritating this obstructionism may be, it is irrelevant to our status as a sovereign state. Article 3 of the same Montevideo Convention specifically says that "the political existence of the state is independent of recognition by other states. Our existence as a sovereign state is independent of whether the PRC recognizes us or not.

The PRC government says that we cannot maintain normal diplomatic relations because we are only a province of the PRC. This is absolutely untrue. The PRC government has never exercised effective jurisdiction over Taiwan, never collected a dime of tax, nor drafted our young men into its People's Liberation Army (PLA). In fact, their personnel, aircraft and vessels can only enter our territory with our permission. In short, we are a sovereign state and as such we are entitled to normal international standing and participation according to international law.

It should be stressed here that the pragmatic diplomacy conducted by the Republic of China on Taiwan is definitely not aiming at "Taiwan Independence, as so absurdly alleged by the PRC. As a matter of fact, only when the Republic of China's international status is ensured can it begin talks with mainland China on an equal footing over the issue of how to unify the two sides of the Taiwan Strait. Therefore, pragmatic diplomacy is, for the Republic of China, an indispensable part of the overall process of reunifying the entire Chinese nation.

Q.2. *Japan has established normal diplomatic relations with the PRC since 1972. The United States of America has recognized the PRC government as the sole government of China since 1979. Since then, Japan and the United States have terminated diplomatic relations with ROC, and have had unofficial relations with ROC. In view of this, why do you ask the US and other states to help you get into all sorts of international organizations, including the United Nations?*

A.2. The reality is not as simple as your statement implies. Neither Japan nor the United States has recognized PRC sovereignty over Taiwan.
Japan's position is outlined in the September 1972 Joint Tanaka-Chou Communique which states:

The government of the PRC reaffirms that Taiwan is an inalienable part of the territory of the PRC. The Government of Japan fully understands and respects this stand of the Government of China and adheres to its stand of complying with Article 8 of the Potsdam Declaration.

Article 8 of the Potsdam Declaration affirms the 1943 Cairo Declaration that Japan, which then claimed sovereignty over Taiwan, would have to return Taiwan to the Republic of China, and not to the PRC. In 1952, Japan gave up its claim of sovereignty over Taiwan by way of the San Francisco Peace Treaty without specifying to whom the sovereignty would be transferred. In short, the PRC has no legally valid claim of sovereignty over Taiwan whatsoever.
In the Shanghai Communique of 1972, the PRC and the US state their respective positions separately. The PRC states:

The Chinese [the PRC] side reaffirms its position: . . .Taiwan is a province of China which has long been returned to the motherland; the liberation of Taiwan is China's internal affairs.

The ambiguous term "motherland is intended to substitute for the Cairo Declaration that Taiwan be returned to the "Republic of China. I don't think I have to remind anyone that the Republic of China on Taiwan was still in existence in 1972, and is still going strong to this very day.

In the same Shanghai Communique the US declares:
The United States acknowledges that all Chinese on either side of the Taiwan Strait maintain there is but one China and that Taiwan is a part of China. The US government does not challenge that position. It reaffirms its interest in a peaceful settlement of the Taiwan question by the Chinese themselves.
We have no quarrel with this statement of the US. However, it is important to point out that, here the US only acknowledges, not recognizes, the position of all Chinese on either side. Taiwan is a part of China, just as the PRC on the Chinese mainland is also a part of China. Both the PRC and ROC are parts of a divided China. Further, we absolutely support the US interest in a peaceful settlement of the dispute between us and the PRC. We do not know any other way of settling the dispute.

Q.3. *Why doesn't Taiwan talk to Peking and get their acquiescence, if not agreement, to Taiwan's having the international participation and standing to which you aspire?*

A.3. As a sovereign state, we do not need the approval, nor the acquiescence, of any state for the international participation and status to which we are entitled. Did your government ask for Peking's approval when it decided to join the ASEAN Regional Forum or any other international forum? Peking's obstructionism is the only reason that we have been excluded from many international organizations and that many states have refrained from maintaining normal diplomatic relations with us. What makes you think they will change their stance if we talk to Peking?

Q.4. *Whenever relations between the United States and the PRC are good, relations between Taiwan and mainland China are good. Conversely, when Washington-Peking relations deteriorate, Peking's pressure on Taipei increases. Therefore, it is in Taipei's interest not to hinder Washingtion's relations with Peking.*

Taipei knows full well that Peking is dead set against its pursuit of pragmatic diplomacy. Peking regards this as violating the one China principle. The PRC also dislikes the ROC's lobbying our Congress to assist its admission to a host of multilateral international organizations. We would love to see Taiwan admitted to as many international organizations as possible. But every time we help you out, mostly in response to a demand by Congress, where Taiwan has considerable sympathy, Peking becomes furious and our relations with Peking suffer. When that happens, Taipei also suffers. Why does Taipei often do things that come back to hurt it?

A.4. First, US differences with the PRC are multi-dimensional and multi-faceted. Your disagreement with Peking over the Taiwan issue is just one of many issues. How about human rights, the market access issue, the intellectual property rights issue, and the issue of the proliferation of weapons of mass destruction i.e., missile technology and chemical, biological and nuclear weapons? Even if we in Taiwan were to vanish suddenly from this earth, your dispute with Peking over these issues would not go away or be solved overnight. If the so-called Taiwan issue didn't exist, Peking would invent some other dispute to resist your demands on the issues mentioned above. So please don't blame Taiwan every time your relations with Peking deteriorate.

Second, the ROC should not be held hostage to US-PRC relations.
There are three sets of parallel relationships, Washington-Taipei, Washington-Peking, and Taipei-Peking. When Washington-Peking relations deteriorated, as in the immediate aftermath of the 1989 Tienanmen massacre, Taipei-Peking relations remained the same, no better, no worse. In recent months Washington-Peking relations have improved. But Peking's hostility toward us remains the same. The linkage simply does not exist.

Third, it is true that we have lobbied your government including Congress on this or that issue. But we always do it in accordance with US law, just as Israel and Japan do.

Fourth, Peking's policy toward us will not change regardless of whether we do or do not ask for US help in admitting us to various international organizations or selling us weapons of a defensive nature. Short of our succumbing to the "one country, two systems formula, Peking will continue to blame us for attempting to derail Washington-Peking relations.

Q.5. *The Clinton administration has decided to pursue a policy of engagement in hopes of fundamentally improving the relations with the PRC. What does Taipei think of this initiative?*

A.5. We are all for the engagement policy and wish the initiative well. The hope is that if it succeeds, it will improve bilateral relations and foster stability and prosperity in the Asia-Pacific region. The Clinton administration will carry out the engagement policy via strategic dialogue (i.e., mutual visits of the highest-level personnel) on the premise of not regarding the PRC as an enemy. Accommodation will be the modus operandi. The goal is to integrate mainland China into the international system. A second goal is peaceful transformation of the PRC. This is to be implemented by disseminating Western, or modern values (e.g., human rights, democratic rule, and rule of law) via cultural, educational exchange, trade and investment. This is all for the good.

The critically important question is: Will the PRC leaders reciprocate and accommodate? They believe that they know full well why the US has adopted this strategy. In their view, the US is trying to induce them to accept international norms in order to prevent the PRC from gaining influence and eventually replacing the US as the dominant power in the region. They also realize the consequences of peaceful transformation in the long run: demise of the Chinese communist dictatorship and with it their own and their children's privilege as the ruling class. They have learned the lesson of the demise of the Soviet Union. They attribute the catastrophe to Gorbachev's reckless undermining of the Leninist party.

We have ample evidence that the Chinese Communist Party (CCP) or the PRC leaders have no appetite for the existing international norms. In their mind these are a set of rules of the game worked out by the US, and benefiting the US at the PRC's expense. We have a vivid Chinese expression: "To ask the tiger for its fur. To persuade the CCP leaders to peacefully transform the Party would amount to asking the tiger for its fur. They are not particularly wise in governing the country and extricating their people from poverty. But they are not so stupid as to willingly allow peaceful transformation to complete its course. We wish the Clinton administration well. And we certainly will do nothing to sabotage the initiative, contrary to the allegation of the PRC partisans in America.

Q.6. *The last several years have seen the rise of nationalism in the PRC. Among others this will make the PRC leaders assume a tough posture vis-a-vis Taiwan, and will make any meaningful compromise more difficult. What are the implications of this for the management of the trilateral relations?*

A.6. The CCP leaders used to justify their dictatorship in the name of Marxism, Leninism and Mao Tse-tung Thought. This no longer works. With the grand failure of the communist experiment, they have found a useful substitute in a crude form of nationalism. They have fomented ultra-nationalism in hopes of staving off the inevitable collapse of the communist dictatorship. For instance, they have used the Taiwan issue to incite anti-American sentiment. This may bode ill for Taiwan. If they had no Taiwan issue they would invent some other issue to stir up their xenophobic version of Chinese nationalism. But nationalism is a double-edged sword which can end up hurting them as well. They are keenly aware of this. For instance, they have restrained their own people who demand compensation from Japan for wartime atrocities. They exploit their brand of nationalism at great risk, indeed.

They have attempted to cloak in the mantle of nationalism their resistance to the existing international order promoted by the United States and the West. They have also exploited nationalism to exert pressure on Washington with respect to the Taiwan issue. They also use nationalism to reject rightful demands from, and to justify their unreasonable demands of, the international community. Their demand to get into the World Trade Organization on their own terms comes to mind. Their willful but secret sale of missiles and other weapons of mass destruction to Pakistan and the Middle East are recent instances. Let me ask: Should the US accommodate them regardless of their deeds? Is the US prepared to sacrifice the rules of the game and the existing international order in order to accommodate the PRC? And is the US prepared to do so in spite of the fact that the PRC is interested in nothing less than replacing the US as the dominant regional power and dictating a new set of rules of the game? There are Americans who believe that mutual accommodation is the only way to bring about peaceful coexistence. Some PLA leaders have thought otherwise. They have already concluded internally that fundamental improvement in Sino-American relations is impossible given the enormous and long-standing gap between the US and mainland China in ideologies, social systems, and foreign policies.

Q.7. *The PRC has proposed "one country, two systems as a way out of the current impasse. Some in the United States have argued that the PRC has been very reasonable and conciliatory. After all, Peking would allow Taiwan to enjoy a degree of autonomy far greater than Hong Kong. All they demand is that Taiwan cease using its present name (ROC) and national flag, cease maintaining the Office of the President and the Executive Yuan of the Premier, and that no university use "national in its title. It would even allow Taiwan to maintain armed services. But it insists that Taiwan terminate all such activities as "head of state diplomacy, "alma mater diplomacy and seeking membership in international organizations, especially the UN. Peking considers all such activities provocative and tantamount to preparation for a declaration of de jure independence. There are those in the United States who feel that Taipei is indeed provocative and should be satisfied with what Peking has to offer. They say that Taipei'a foot-dragging and obstructionism may provoke a war. As such, Taipei is playing with fire. In their view, Taipei's diplomatic adventurism in recent years has provoked Peking's military adventurism. This bodes ill for peace and stability of the Asia-Pacific region. In short, Taiwan is provocative, reckless, and may bring disaster upon itself. What do you think of this assessment?*

A.7. For eighty-six years, the Republic of China has been a full-fledged sovereign state. Why should we renounce that status in order to please leaders in Peking who retain an obsolete 19th century mind-set and who are elected by no one and therefore do not even represent the people on the Chinese mainland? It is inappropriate to place us on the same level as Hong Kong. Hong Kong remains a British colony until July 1, 1997. We are and have been a sovereign state longer than most UN member states.

To characterize our pragmatic diplomacy as "diplomatic adventurism is grossly unfair. To identify our pragmatic diplomacy as instigating PRC attempts to contain our foreign relations, and as the "cause of the PRC's brazen military intimidation during the ROC's first-ever direct popular election of a president is to blame the victim instead of the bully. We adopted pragmatic diplomacy in an effort to stave off PRC attempts to completely eliminate our already muted international presence. Failing that, Peking resorted to military intimidation (in the form of missile tests) and then blamed us for it. What an absurd argument in support of a barbaric violation of international law! We do not buy the argument that the "one country, two systems is a symbolic issue. At the beginning of the Cold War, did Greece for the sake of existence, give in to the USSR's demand that it change its name, national flag, and refrain from having a president, a Foreign Office, and acquiring new weapons even of a defensive nature? Of course not.

The PRC government has indicated that President Lee Teng-hui is welcome to visit mainland China, provided that he comes in a "proper capacity (e.g., as the chairman of his party, the KMT). At the same time, it is adamantly opposed to his going abroad to any countries in whatever capacity. What kind of communist logic is this, anyway?

Q.8. *Last year, Taipei's diplomatic adventurism provoked Peking into military adventurism. It took the US sending two aircraft carrier battle groups to stop a possible escalation. Charles Freeman has warned Taiwan against dragging the US into a military conflict, saying that Taiwan cannot expect to write a check of independence to be cashed on American blood. What do you think of this characterization of the situation?*

A.8. Peking conducted the military exercises and missile tests because it was hoping to disrupt our presidential election, the first ever in the long history of China. Why? Because government by consent of the people is the one Western value and practice that the PRC leaders fear the most. The very existence of democracy on Taiwan poses a threat to the PRC dictatorship. The presidential election had nothing to do with Taiwan independence, because the Republic of China has long been a sovereign state. The PRC's hope to sway the outcome of the election was futile. None of the four presidential candidates advocated immediate reunification.

We very much appreciate the dispatch of the two aircraft carrier battle groups. The US acted in accordance with the provisions of section 2 of the Taiwan Relations Act which reads:

It is the policy of the United States. . . to declare that peace and stability in the area are in the political, security, and economic interests of the United States, and are matters of international concern. . . [and] to consider any effort to determine the future of Taiwan by other than peaceful means, including by boycotts, or embargoes, a threat to the peace and security of the Western Pacific area and of grave concern to the United States.

The US also acted to uphold the credibility of its commitment to peace and security in the Asia-Pacific region. If the US had stood idly by while the PRC carried out brazen coercion via military exercises and missile tests, America's allies and friends would have lost faith in the US's degree of commitment. Further, it is vitally important that the US stand firm and send an unmistakable message to Peking, lest there be even the slightest chance of repeating anything like the Korean War.

To hesitate and to appear weak is to invite avoidable military conflict.

INTERNATIONAL CONFERENCE ON UNITED STATES -- TAIWAN RELATIONS: TWENTY YEARS AFTER THE TAIWAN RELATIONS ACT

BEIJING-TAIPEI-WASHINGTON RELATIONS: OPPORTUNITIES AND RISKS

INTRODUCTION

It is always a pleasure to gather with colleagues and friends in beautiful Taipei, and especially so to exchange views on important developments at a timely juncture. I hereby express special appreciation to Dr. Lin Cheng-yi, Dr. Joanne Jaw-Ling Chang, and the Academia Sinica for convening us today on the 20th anniversary of the Taiwan Relations Act (TRA).

From a Washington perspective, I will focus today on four main themes.

Theme #1: Sino-U.S. relations, already strained, are likely to become even more uncertain over the next 18 months, in part as three U.S. perceptions of mainland China change.

Theme #2: Moderate strains in Sino-U.S. relations offer opportunities to improve U.S.-Taiwan relations and Taipei-Beijing cross-strait relations. But major strains in Sino-U.S. relations, particularly if Taiwan reemerges as a major issue in Sino-U.S. and in domestic U.S. politics, will raise U.S. expectations for cross-strait dialogue, perhaps to unreasonable levels, creating at least four fundamental dilemmas for Taipei.

Theme #3: We should deal with current issues – WTO, TMD, and cross-strait relations – each on its own merits; for example, trade issues in terms of trade; security in terms of security; cross-strait relations on their own terms, for reasons I will elaborate later.

Theme #4: Even while dealing with current issues on their merits, we should consider them – whether WTO, TMD, or cross-strait relations – within a larger context as means toward achieving strategic objectives with China, such as helping a modernizing and democratizing China see itself as a fully vested and responsible member of the international community, belonging to the major regional and global institutions, behaving according to the rule of law, including by making and keeping binding commitments according to bilateral and global standards.

Let me expand each of these main themes briefly, beginning with changing U.S. perceptions of China as both a cause and effect of already strained, and likely worsening, Sino-U.S. relations.

A first U.S. perceptual change is from China as an emerging economic power to China as an economically vulnerable country.

I call this a change from China as a Goldilock's economy to China as a three bear's economy.

For twenty years, the U.S. has perceived China as having a Goldilocks economy. To be sure, China experienced three major boom-bust inflationary cycles from 1978-1992, and ongoing concern about center-region tensions, income inequality, etc. But especially by the mid-1990s, China appeared to engineer a Goldilocks not too fast, not too slow soft economic landing based on high but sustainable growth, deepening structural reform, and political and financial system stability.

Today, that is changing. Many in the U.S. see China's Goldilocks growth, reform, and stability giving way to a three bears economy where growth slows, important reforms stall or stop, and political and financial system instability rise.

China's growth is slowing.

It is closer to 4-5% than the 7.8% reported last year or the 7% projected this year. China's exports and FDI were flat last year and FDI in particular could decline this year. Interest rate cuts, domestic fiscal stimulus particularly in infrastructure construction, export and FDI promotion, and other competitive incentives may be insufficient to sustain economic growth weakened by over-capacity and weak consumer confidence worried by rising unemployment (over 9% in the cities and 130 million redundant rural laborers).

Zhu Rongji was confronted by an untimely juxtaposition. The regional demand for China's exports slowed due to Asian crisis at the same time as China's domestic demand slowed as unemployment rose, as consumer confidence declined, and as anticipatory consumer caution due to domestic reforms in education, housing, and medicare boosted the domestic savings rate.

Specifically, ordinary citizens who in the past depended on state subsidies in education, housing, and medicare found themselves reducing consumption and increasing savings to meet anticipated needs as a state compelled by rising governmental debt shifted the social contract by making individuals increasingly responsible for aspects of their own social welfare. No wonder mainland China's domestic savings rate went from already high averages of 40-50% to today's even higher 63%.

Important Chinese reforms have stalled or stopped.

In March 1998, Zhu made two bold guarantees (8% GDP growth and currency stability) and five reform targets (SOE, grain circulation, housing, government organization, medicare). Yet, reform in the joint stock system, housing, and small and mid-sized enterprise privatization and government debt write-downs to SOEs have been superseded by promises to continue subsidies to SOEs and laid-off workers .

In other words, China's need for immediate social stability has overtaken reform – and just when Beijing is being pressed to make significant WTO commitments in agriculture, goods, and services. Deferred reforms and continued massive subsidies only increase the burdens of an already insolvent banking system, especially vulnerabilities in China's stock markets and non-state banking financial institutions.

No wonder Zhu Rongji perceived he had no choice but to close the Guangdong International Trade and Investment Corporation (GITIC) and other ITICs to assert both central political and financial control.

If China's concerns were limited to the economic and financial spheres they would be serious enough. But with slowing growth and deferred reform, there is growing Washington concern that potential political and social instability in China are rising.

**For additional analytical, marketing, investment and business opportunities information, please contact
Global Investment & Business Center, USA
(202) 546-2103. Fax: (202) 546-3275. E-mail: rusric@erols.com**

This political and social discontent reflects two fundamental issues. First is the popular belief held by over 60% of China citizens that those who have gained wealth have done so illegally; this is the thrust of He Qinglian's Pitfalls of China's Modernization which questions the legitimacy of reform by seeing it as little more than the corrupt transfer of state assets to well-connected individuals.

The second issue is something Beijing's leaders know well from studying developments in Indonesia. They know a shift of governmental authority and legitimacy from ideology to rising living standards is sustainable only so long as those increased standards in living in fact meet public expectations. But, as in Indonesia, legitimacy based on living standards can be lost quickly if uncontrolled economic distress is combined with widespread public condemnation of graft and corruption.

During his April U.S. visit, Zhu Rongji subtly appeal for personal political support and support for China's reforms at a time of economic challenge. And he brings formidable assets: an appealingly direct, unscripted speaking style; a savvy willingness and ability to deal; a vision and brave personal commitment to China's economic reform future. (Remember his comment about the 100 coffins -- 99 for corrupt officials, and the last one for him?)

Zhu will also benefit from residual U.S. good-will and positive reception as many come forward to make the case that he personally, the reform approach he symbolizes, and China's opportunity to integrate with the global trade system all U.S. support at a difficult, potentially watershed, period.

But a second shifting Washington perception may limit Zhu's ability to do so successfully.

That second U.S. perceptual change is from China as a possible strategic partner to China as a potential strategic competitor.

To be sure, the U.S. debate about China as partner or competitor is longstanding. For this reason, both Presidents Clinton and Jiang portrayed the 1997 and 1998 Sino-U.S. summits as re-establishing contact at the highest official levels and thereby stabilizing Sino-U.S. relations, albeit within an ill-defined concept of constructive strategic partnership.

But both sides oversold the summits. By the end of 1998, whatever understanding Washington thought it achieved on human rights was lost with Beijing's crackdown on political dissidents. Whatever understanding Beijing thought it achieved regarding Taiwan was challenged by Secretary Bill Richardson's visit and talk of theater missile defense cooperation.

Current reports from the bipartisan Cox committee about PRC espionage have created a public sensation. In a recent CSIS discussion on China policy that my program regularly sponsors on Capitol Hill, both Republican and Democrats reported a flood of constituent calls and letters, reflecting public attention at the local newspaper and talk-radio grassroots level, focused on a general U.S. outrage that the PRC could and would potentially use U.S. technology, including satellite, missile, and nuclear weapons technology, against the U.S.

This U.S. public mood shift corresponds with increased political attention to foreign policy, including China, as the U.S. presidential campaigns take shape. It may also reflect a more fundamental recognition that U.S. and PRC regional security concepts may be divergent.

A third change in U.S. perceptions is that Taiwan is reemerging as a major issue in Sino-U.S. relations and thereby in U.S. domestic politics.

Jiang Zemin appears increasingly determined to define his legacy by making China strong, economically developed, and unified in the 21st century.

To give credence to the idea of a unified China including at least a framework or timetable (however distant) including Taiwan unification, Jiang's approach includes hard and soft versions of three elements.

First, China seeks to maintain minimal strategic deterrence with the U.S. This is not strategic parity, only the ability to deter U.S. strategic nuclear pressure. It is for the purpose of maintaining its minimal strategic deterrence with the U.S. that Beijing has such strong misgivings about the U.S. establishing a national missile defense capability. Such a capability could degrade Beijing's strategic deterrent and thereby require significant unplanned and unbudgeted strategic force modernization.

Second, China seeks to build regional military superiority in doctrine and deployments. The purpose of regional military superiority is in part to deter the U.S., Japan, or others from intervening should conflict arise with Taiwan. Particularly if the PRC can successfully deter external involvement, or if it can win decisive accommodations from Taiwan before external involvement can be mobilized, it can if necessary exploit what it then conceives as local superiority in high-intensity and high-technology conditions.

Third, China seeks to establish a diplomatic strategy based on comprehensive national strength to persuade Taiwan and any of Taiwan's friends and allies that a Taiwan unified with the PRC is inevitable and desirable. This effort to develop acceptance for a unification framework and timetable within Taiwan and among Taiwan's external supporters which is more in the spirit of Hsun Tzu than Clausewitz.

That is, Beijing strategy aims at Taiwan's most important centers of strategic gravity – which are psychological and, over time, financial. This strategy will use irregular or asymmetric tactics across all the levers of hard and soft power, employing military force only when such maximizes the chance for decisive psychological victory.

So, to summarize thus far, changing U.S. perceptions of China as economically vulnerable, of China as potential strategic competitor, and of the reemergence of Taiwan as a Sino-U.S. and U.S. domestic issue all underscore the possibility that already strained Sino-U.S. relations could become even more uncertain in the upcoming period, though even with heated U.S. election campaigns, I do not believe they will go into downward free fall.

This leads to my second main theme.

Moderate strains in Sino-U.S. relations offer opportunities to improve U.S.-Taiwan relations and cross-strait relations. But major strains in Sino-U.S. relations, particularly as Taiwan becomes a major Sino-U.S. and U.S. domestic political issue, will increase the responsibilities and expectations the U.S. assigns to cross-strait dialogue.

This creates at least four fundamental dilemmas for Taipei.

First dilemma: Beijing will seek to define constructive cross-strait dialogue as requiring purposeful direction on its terms. It will then define purposeful direction as political talks leading toward unification.

Such an approach plays on the feeling among some in Washington and elsewhere that Taipei seeks to engage in dialogue as an end in itself, focusing on specific, but not necessarily over-arching issues, in part because Taipei has not created consensus regarding its overall direction or end-purpose for cross-strait dialogue. In this manner, Beijing will seek to establish meaningful and constructive cross-strait dialogue as a choice for Taipei between peaceful unification by negotiation and unification by pressure if necessary should Beijing successfully convince others that cross-strait negotiations, as China defines their purpose, are otherwise unproductive.

Second dilemma: Some in Washington feel Taipei is too confident and needs to be shaken somewhat to encourage meaningful cross-strait dialogue. Taipei will not want its caution regarding cross-strait dialogue to create a negative feed-back cycle where its perceived over-confident reluctance to engage in meaningful and constructive (see Dilemma #1 above) cross-straits dialogue leads to increased Washington "encouragement" regarding such talks.

Third dilemma: over time the U.S. Congress and others may see that cross-straits dialogue are indeed successful at increasing cross-strait understanding and decreasing cross-strait tensions, and thereafter conclude U.S. arms sales to Taiwan are no longer necessary or helpful.

Beijing's and Taipei's ability to raise or lower cross-strait tensions on both a short- and mid-term basis complicates U.S. calculations of the interplay of intents and capabilities across the Taiwan Strait.

Fourth dilemma: unintended consequences could arise from efforts to establish new cross-strait initiatives.

For example, some current confidence building measures include proposals for arms control talks. Cross-strait arms control initiatives which establish hotlines or appropriate military- to- military confidence building measures (see Dilemma #3 above) between Beijing and Taipei could be helpful. But arms control discussions involving Beijing, Taipei, and Washington could unwittingly result in de facto consultations or prior notification potentially giving Beijing a say if not a veto over Taiwan arms requests.

This paper's third main theme is that we should deal with current issues such as WTO, TMD, or cross-strait relations each on its own merits. For example, this means trade issues should be dealt with in terms of trade; security in terms of security; cross-strait relations on their own terms.

For example, it is time for China and Taiwan to join the WTO. Because trade can be a positive sum game, it is possible for Chinese Premier Zhu Rongji to sign a principle framework agreement on China's WTO accession this April, dependent on two factors.

First is whether the U.S. and China can agree on practical, and enforceable commitments to both end points and timetables in commercially meaningful terms for agriculture, on goods, and on services. This is challenging because the WTO disciplines which offer market standards useful to guide the reforms Beijing needs come at a time when China's economic and political vulnerabilities diminish its ability to fulfill such commitments.

Second is whether or not the WTO package Beijing offers can win Congressional approval. U.S. business support for China's WTO accession is necessary but insufficient by itself to guarantee Congressional support for China permanent MFN or what is now called NRT (Normal Trading Rights) status.

Regarding missile defense, the recent overwhelming U.S. votes to move forward with national missile defense underscores the U.S. intent to protect itself from ballistic missile attack and to help allies and friends do so as well. Here we recognize three basic facts.

First, to the extent U.S. national missile defense undermines China's minimal strategic deterrent, U.S. and China should discuss how to maintain stable deterrence on both sides if the U.S. builds defensive capabilities.

Second, any anti-missile capability in Japan, South Korea, or Taiwan would be defensive, not threatening to China or any other country because none of them have nuclear offensive capability.

Third, the U.S. will pursue longstanding security Asia-Pacific commitments by deepening security ties with Japan, Korea, and others while promoting Sino-China security cooperation.

Regarding the U.S. role in cross-strait relations, Washington's anchor interest centers on maintaining an equilibrium of confidence so those on both sides of the Taiwan Strait can determine the pace and scope of their mutual interaction peacefully. Equilibrium of confidence includes:

- each side has the defensive capabilities and thereby the minimal sense of security necessary to enter cross-strait dialogue free of intimidation or coercion;
- both sides feel confident the U.S. is taking an even-handed approach toward the other;
- neither side feels the U.S. is pressuring it into negotiations; and
- any arrangements concluded are mutually acceptable to both sides.

The U.S. interest in this cross-strait equilibrium of confidence does not mean the U.S. simply supports a status quo peace and stability, or even simply a dynamic status quo. The U.S. position should be to reject any challenge to the status quo by force, and to discourage Taiwan independence, while leaving it to Beijing and Taipei to create the positive conditions necessary to entice peaceful unification

Beijing has already threatened non-compliance on proliferation matters if U.S. and Taiwan TMD cooperation advances. Given the juxtaposition of WTO, TMD, and cross-straits issues, Beijing could subtly offer future restraint on security matters (such as TMD and Taiwan) in exchange for Washington's commitment to China's WTO accession.

The hard sell on China's WTO accession would thus come from the security side; the soft sell would be an appeal to Washington to support the political position of Zhu Rongji and others championing China's economic reforms. The U.S. should resist the temptation to bargain trade (WTO) and security (missile) issues. The U.S. has equal interest in shaping the Asia-Pacific's overall political, economic, and security architectures as part of its vision for a peaceful, stable, and prosperous Asia-Pacific.

And from this U.S. interest to participate in shaping global and regional political, economic, and security architectures comes my fourth main theme.

Even while dealing with current issues on their merits, we should consider them -- whether WTO, TMD, or cross-strait relations -- within a larger context. Thus we should not deal with specific issues in simply an individual or disparate fashion, but as means toward achieving strategic objectives with China. As Mr. C.F. Koo recently reminded us, we should keep our eye on longer-term strategic goals with respect to mainland China. These include helping a modernizing and democratizing China make and keep binding commitments as a responsible member of the international community, a fully vested member of its main regional and global institutions, adhering to bilateral and global standards in trade, non-proliferation, and human rights.

This will not be easy for Taipei, in part because of the challenge of linking the specifics of Taiwan's immediate cross-strait objectives of peace and increased understanding and its long-term objectives of unification with a democratized China. As Mr. Sun Ya-fu noted in Washington recently, Beijing has broadening and deepening experiences with democratization according to its own circumstances; thus, Beijing considers Taipei's references to a democratic China as an excuse to postpone meaningful cross-strait discussions. Squaring immediate and long-term objectives for both Taipei and Beijing regarding cross-strait dialogue within the larger context of their respective strategic objectives will seemingly be easier for a more authoritarian than a more popularly democratic system. These tactical and strategic asymmetries across the Taiwan Strait will likewise make it important but difficult for Washington to help maintain the cross-strait equilibrium of confidence which defines its interests, as detailed above.

CONCLUSION

This paper considered four main themes.

First, it outlined underlying trends relating to three changing U.S. perceptions of China that reflect and are reflected by increasingly uncertain Sino-U.S. relations in which the Taiwan Strait issue reemerges as a major concern in Sino-U.S. relations and in U.S. domestic politics during the presidential campaign season.

Second, it considered the interplay of those changing perceptions in a forward-looking fashion, anticipating four fundamental cross-strait dilemmas for Taiwan these changing perceptions and circumstances might create for Taipei.

Third, it noted that the PRC in the form of Zhu Rongji's April U.S. visit would seek to use China's immediate security assets to leverage concessions necessary for its longer-term economic growth, arguing Washington should resist such linkages by dealing with current issues such as the WTO, TMD, and cross-strait relation concerns as much as possible each on its own merits.

And, finally, this paper underscored the challenge of relating individual issues to larger strategic objectives with respect to mainland China, namely the ongoing effort to facilitates the PRC's making and abiding binding commitments to bilateral and global standards as a fully responsible member of the international community.

It now simply remains to congratulate again the organizers of this conference for so ably convening such a distinguished group, and to thank you for your kind attention and encouragement.

THE TAIWAN RELATIONS ACT AND US-TAIWAN MILITARY RELATIONS[5]

---

[5] Dr. Michael Pillsbury Visiting Research Fellow National Defense University
Washington D.C. 20510 (202) 544- 9700 Disclaimer: Nothing in this paper should be construed to represent the views of the NDU, DOD, or the US Government.

**For additional analytical, marketing, investment and business opportunities information, please contact
Global Investment & Business Center, USA
(202) 546-2103. Fax: (202) 546-3275. E-mail: rusric@erols.com**

Scope

This paper describes US-Taiwan military relations as conducted under Presidents Jimmy Carter, Ronald Reagan, George Bush, and Bill Clinton on the American side and Presidents Chiang Chingkuo and Lee Tenghui on the Taiwan side. A fundamental stability in the military balance and a very low profile have been the key features of US-Taiwan military relations during the twenty years of the Taiwan Relations Act. Both these features are changing, however. The first decade [1979-1989] has been covered in a number of scholarly books. The second decade [1989-1999] has been less well understood, and requires an increase in scholarly attention, especially in light of recently declassified documents and personal recollections about the first decade. For reasons of space, this paper does not address the significant issue of Beijing's shifting perceptions of US-Taiwan military relations, which have been a function of Beijing's changing views not only of Taiwan, but also of the international security environment and US-China relations.<1> The paper describes little known aspects of military relations by examining carefully both a March 1999 US legislative proposal and the February 1999 US Defense Department report on the security situation in the Taiwan Strait for the background these two documents provide about an area of US-Taiwan relations usually kept from public view.

Recent Background

Nearly three years after the People's Republic of China (PRC) conducted provocative military exercises opposite Taiwan on the eve of that island's first popular presidential election, the security situation in the Taiwan Strait remains calm with no threat of imminent hostilities. There has been little change in the military balance; Beijing has limited its military activity in the region to routine training; Taipei has reduced the size and scope of its military exercises and played down other activities which Beijing might misconstrue as provocative and destabilizing. Within the political arena, senior negotiators from the two quasi-official organizations responsible for managing cross-Strait relations --Taiwan's Straits Exchange Foundation (SEF) and China's Association for Relations Across the Taiwan Strait (ARATS)--met in China in mid-October 1998 and resumed direct contacts--suspended since 1995--aimed at reducing tensions and improving bilateral relations. Although they agreed on future SEF-ARATS dialogue, cooperation, and visits, there was little movement on resolving the more substantive political issues which divide the two sides.

Part One: What Are US-Taiwan Military Relations?

No public document describes the purposes or the details of US-Taiwan military relations. The Taiwan Relations Act is extremely sparse about the matter. Indeed, the draft legislation sent to Congress by President Carter did not mention any security or military matters. The language about military matters was added at the initiative of Democratic Senators Frank Church and John Glenn, working with Republican Senators like Jacob Javits and others. The House of Representatives added parallel language.<2> Vice Premier Deng Xiaoping, then visiting the United States, met with members of the Senate Foreign Relations Committee and warned that if the Taiwan Relations Act went too far about security issues, China would not agree to normalization.

The TRA language agreed to and signed by the President was much stronger than any President ever was willing to implement in the twenty years. The TRA stated that defense articles and services would be provided by the US to Taiwan to maintain its capability for self defense. Congress would play a role in determining what weapons and services would be provided. Yet Congress never did this. Almost immediately, the Senators who had authored the TRA publicly complained that President Carter was not implementing the TRA in its military aspects. The

Congressional criticism was stronger of President Reagan in 1982, when he agreed to the August 1982 US-China Communique. However, in one of the strangest developments in US-Taiwan relations since 1979, the US Congress never took any action or passed any law that challenged Presidents Carter, Reagan, Bush or Clinton with regard to the military aspects of the Taiwan Relations Act. Until March 24, 1999. On that date, three Senators introduced what they called the Taiwan Security Enhancement Act. Its text is a remarkable document that may be interpreted as a long list of steps and measures that the US has never taken in US-Taiwan military relations.

If the three Senators are correct in the lengthy analysis contained in their legislation [to be discussed below], then US-Taiwan military relations may never have been conducted as the original framers of the Taiwan Relations Act intended. However, one may ask why it took the US Congress twenty years to reach this conclusion. Several Congressional staff interviewed for this paper explained that until a few months ago, the government of Taiwan including the President, Vice President and the military leadership have been unwilling to tell the US Congress the details of the US-Taiwan military relationship for various reasons, including their perceptions that the executive branch of the US government did not want them to do so. Apparently, according to these Congressional staff, some officials in the government of Taiwan believes they will be punished if they Abehave like Israel and lobby the US Congress to improve US-Taiwan military relations. Other Congressional staff interviewed stated that they believe some on Taiwan are Acomplacent about defense issues, and cannot imagine that China will under any conceivable circumstances use force against Taiwan as along as Taiwan avoids an open or legal declaration of independence. One staff said that Taiwan is not like Israel in lobbying for a stronger defense, but more like Panama or a small African nation that is not really interested in self defense, and does not perceive a serious military threat.

The Nature of US-Taiwan Military Relations

As noted, there is no public document that describes the details of US-Taiwan military relations. It has been clear that ever since 1980, when the US security treaty with the former Republic of China was terminated, the US maintains no armed forces on Taiwan and no active duty military personnel. Lists of arms sold to Taiwan by the US as "Foreign Military Sales" have been made public annually, as are all arms exports covered under the US arms export law. However, the US does not seem to have a normal "military relationship" with Taiwan. For example, even symbolically, the US Defense Department appears to keeps its distance. When US military aircraft transport US Congressional delegations to Taiwan, the aircraft fly to Okinawa or Hong Kong to remain overnight, according to some published accounts.

The Taiwan Security Enhancement Act of March 24, 1999 appears to fill in some of the missing details about the military relationship. For example, it states that:

(9) The United States and Taiwan no longer conduct joint training missions, have no direct military lines of communication, and have only limited military-to-military contacts. This lack of communication and interoperation between the United States and Taiwan hinders planning for the defense of Taiwan and could prove detrimental in the event of future aggression against Taiwan.

If correct, it would seem that the rather ordinary aspects of military ties [joint training, military communication lines, and interoperability of forces] have been missing from US-Taiwan relations for two decades. Surprisingly, both the US Congress and the Taiwan authorities have tolerated this situation.

The Taiwan Security Enhancement Act describes other problems in US-Taiwan military relations:

(10) Since 1979, the United States has continued to sell defensive weapons to Taiwan in accordance with the Taiwan Relations Act . . . .However, pressures to delay, deny, and reduce arms sales to Taiwan have been prevalent since the signing of the August 17, 1982, communique with the People's Republic of China. Over time, such delays, denials, and reductions could prevent Taiwan from maintaining a sufficient capability for self-defense.

(11) As has been affirmed on several occasions by the executive branch of Government, the provisions of the Taiwan Relations Act take legal precedence over any communique with the People's Republic of China.. . . .The current defense relationship between the United States and Taiwan is deficient in terms of its capacity over the long term to counter and deter potential aggression against Taiwan by the People's Republic of China.

The Senators who authored this new legislation appear to be drawing attention to "delays, denials and reductions" in US arms sales to Taiwan. What is especially interesting in the legislation is the impression that Taiwan and executive branch have not consulted Congress about this issue. For that reason, the Taiwan Security Enhancement Act proposes an unusual remedy. It states:

ANNUAL REPORTS- Beginning 60 days after the next round of arms talks between the United States and Taiwan, and annually thereafter, the President shall submit a report to Congress

(1) detailing each of Taiwan's requests for purchase of defense articles and defense services during the one-year period ending on the date of the report;

(2) describing the defense needs asserted by Taiwan as justification for those requests;

and

(3) describing any decision to reject, postpone, or modify any such request that was made during the one-year period ending on the date of the report, the level at which the final decision was made, and a justification for the decision.

This proposal would almost certainly invite the US Congress to become involved in the determination of Taiwan's self-defense needs, as the language of the Taiwan Relations Act provided in 1979. The legislation is silent on the question why the US Congress has not taken this step in the last twenty years. One possibility may be the fear of a Presidential veto of any effort to obtain this information. It is curious that Congress does not seem to believe it can obtain this information from the Taiwan authorities, but must pass a law to obtain it from the Defense Department. It may be true that Taiwan does not lobby like Israel and is unwilling to tell the US Congress about US decisions to "reject, postpone or modify" its arms requests.

We may learn more about the nature of US-Taiwan military relations since 1979 by examining several other provisions of the Taiwan Security Enhancement Act. It states:

(1) IN GENERAL - The Secretary of Defense, in consultation with the Secretary of State, shall develop a plan for the enhancement of programs and arrangements for operational training and exchanges of personnel between the armed forces of the United States and Taiwan for work in threat analysis, doctrine, force planning, operational methods, and other areas. The plan shall provide for exchanges of officers up to and including general and flag officers in the grade of O-10.

(2) REPORT- Not later than 180 days after the date of enactment of this Act, the Secretary of Defense shall submit a report to Congress, in classified or unclassified form, containing the plan required under paragraph (1).

(3) IMPLEMENTATION- Not later than 30 days after the date on which the report described in paragraph (2) is submitted or required to be submitted, the Secretary of Defense shall implement the plan contained in the report.

This provision seems to suggest that the US government does not today have a plan for or even conduct operational training with Taiwan military personnel. Strangely, these words imply that Taiwan and the US may not have been working together since 1979 on "threat analysis, doctrine, force planning" and other normal military matters. If this is correct, it is difficult to understand how the US has been assisting Taiwan to maintain the kind of self defense capability that is mandated in the Taiwan Relations Act. Of course, there have been newspaper accounts that Taiwan Air Force Pilots are taught to fly US F-16s before they are delivered to Taiwan. But if the Senators are correct, there appears to be little other military interaction of the kind this legislation describes.

Four other provisions of the new legislation are very suggestive about other gaps in US-Taiwan military relations since 1979. It would be normal to have as US staff of experts in the American Institute on Taiwan familiar with Taiwan's defense needs. Normally, Taiwan should be able to get prices and data about possible future weapons sales. Just as ordinary would be to have Taiwan military students in US military training institutions. Finally, it would be routine for the US military to have some kind of a communications link with Taiwan=s military, in the event of some kind of military emergency, from search and rescue to an attack by China. Yet the legislation states that none of the these measures exists. It calls for all of them. It states:

(1) the Secretary of Defense and the Secretaries of the military departments should make every effort to reserve additional positions for Taiwan officers at the National Defense University, the senior war colleges, and the military academies; and

(2) the Secretary of State should, when considering foreign military sales to Taiwan

(A) take into account the special status of Taiwan; and

(B) make every effort to ensure that Taiwan has full and timely access to price and availability data for defense articles and defense services.

(a) INCREASE IN TECHNICAL STAFF OF THE AMERICAN INSTITUTE IN TAIWAN- Upon the request of the Defense Security Cooperation Agency, the President shall use funds available to the Department of Defense under the Arms Export Control Act for the assignment or detail of additional technical staff to the American Institute in Taiwan.

(c) COMMUNICATIONS BETWEEN UNITED STATES AND TAIWAN MILITARY COMMANDS - Not later than 180 days after the date of enactment of this Act, the Secretary of Defense shall establish secure direct communications between the United States Pacific military command and the Taiwan military command.

Press accounts have been very detailed in the twenty years of the Taiwan Relations Act in describing what arms sales requests from Taiwan after they have been granted by the United States. It has been almost impossible, however to get an idea of what future requests Taiwan

---

For additional analytical, marketing, investment and business opportunities information, please contact
Global Investment & Business Center, USA
(202) 546-2103. Fax: (202) 546-3275. E-mail: rusric@erols.com

may have, or how the US may deal with these future requests. Here too the draft legislation is helpful in suggesting ideas that these Senators believe will be the coming issues in the 2000-2005 period. It states:

(d) MISSILE DEFENSE EQUIPMENT- Subject to subsection (h), the President is authorized to make available for sale to Taiwan, at reasonable cost, theater missile defense equipment and related items, including

(1) ground-based and naval-based missile defense systems; and
(2) reconnaissance and communications systems, as may be necessary to target and cue missile defense systems sold to Taiwan.

(e) SATELLITE EARLY WARNING DATA - Subject to subsection (h), the President is authorized to make available for sale to Taiwan, at reasonable cost, satellite early warning data.

(f) AIR DEFENSE EQUIPMENT - Subject to subsection (h), the President is authorized to make available for sale to Taiwan, at reasonable cost, modern air-defense equipment, including the following:

(1) AIM-120 AMRAAM air-to-air missiles.
(2) Additional advanced fighters and airborne warning and control systems (AWACS).
(3) Equipment to better defend airfields from air and missile attack.
(4) Communications infrastructure that enables coordinated joint-force air defense of Taiwan.

(g) NAVAL DEFENSE SYSTEMS - Subject to subsection (h), the President is authorized to make available for sale to Taiwan, at reasonable cost, defensive systems that counter the development by the People's Republic of China of new naval capabilities, including defense systems such as

(1) diesel-powered submarines;
(2) anti-submarine systems, including airborne systems, capable of detecting new Kilo and advanced Chinese nuclear submarines;
(3) naval anti-missile systems, including Aegis destroyers, capable of defeating Russian supersonic anti-ship missiles; and
(4) communications systems that better enable Taiwan to conduct joint-force naval defense operations.

Part Two: The DOD report on the Taiwan Strait Security Situation

Senators Frank Murkowski, Robert Torricelli and Jesse Helms refer in their new legislation to the US Defense Department report on the security situation in the Taiwan Straits. The contents of this DOD report seem to have suggested to the what Taiwan's future defense needs may be. The report is a helpful source of detail on how the military balance has changed and what such change may mean for US-Taiwan military relations. The contents of the report about mainland China's forces may not be relevant to this paper. However, the DOD has for the first time in public provided an extremely detailed assessment of Taiwan's armed forces. Press attention has focused on what the DOD report said about growing military power in mainland China. Here, we examine the extensive list of shortcomings and weaknesses that the US Defense Department believes Taiwan suffers. This list was released in mid-February, 1999 and may have influenced the proposed Taiwan Security Enhancement Act, which was made public March 24, 1999.

Taiwan's Ten Weaknesses

Despite anticipated improvements to Taiwan's missile and air defense systems, the by 2005, the US Defense Department reports forecasts that PLA will "possess the capability to attack Taiwan with air and missile strikes" which would "degrade key military facilities and damage the island's economic infrastructure." Similarly, the report judges that despite improvements in Taiwan's ability to conduct ASW operations, "China will retain the capability to interdict Taiwan's SLOCs and blockade the island's principal maritime ports." The Taiwan Relations Act specifically states that the US must be able to counter such a blockade.

The DOD report describes ten key weaknesses Taiwan has. These all suggest areas that the US Congressional proposal may address, since these matters seem to have accumulated over the twenty years since the TRA was enacted.

1. *Missile Defense.* Taiwan's most significant vulnerability is its limited capacity to defend against the growing arsenal of Chinese ballistic missiles. These missiles pose a serious threat to non-hardened military targets, C2 nodes, and Taiwan's military infrastructure. As an initial response to this emerging threat, Taiwan has purchased the Modified Air Defense System (MADS), an improved variant of the PATRIOT surface-to-air missile (SAM) system which was used during DESERT STORM. The MADS, which began arriving on Taiwan in 1997, is expected to be deployed around heavily populated Taipei. Exclusive reliance on active missile defenses and associated BM/C3I, however, will not sufficiently offset the overwhelming advantage in offensive missiles which Beijing is projected to possess in 2005.

2. **Submarines.** Taiwan has four submarines: two relatively modern Dutch-built ZVAARDVIS Design boats (*Hai Lung-class*) acquired in the late 1980s and two obsolete, World War II-era GUPPY II boats provided by the United States in 1973 for ASW training. The two Dutch submarines reportedly are armed with wire-guided torpedoes. The U.S. boats are used primarily as training platforms with a secondary mission to lay mines. Acquisition of additional submarines remains one of Taiwan's most important priorities.

3. *Information Warfare.* As one of the world's largest producers of computer components, Taiwan has all of the basic capabilities needed to carry out offensive and defensive IW related activities, particularly computer network attacks and the introduction of malicious code. While information on formally integrating IW into warfighting doctrine is not available, there are indications that formal doctrine development to guide future employment of these capabilities may be in progress.

4. *Computer Warfare.* Taiwan has demonstrated a significant knowledge of viruses. A virus known as "Bloody" or "6/4" protesting the Tiananmen Square crackdown was first discovered in Taiwan in 1990. In 1992, personnel from The Hague--with support from INTERPOL--investigated the dissemination of the "Michelangelo" virus by a Taiwan firm. In 1996, Taiwan virus writers developed and distributed a computer virus protesting Japanese claims to the Diaoyutai Islands. Trend Micro was the first company to develop a response to the "Michelangelo" virus; it currently dominates the anti-virus software market in Japan. Trend Micro also has led in the area of virus recognition technology. Taiwan's Academia Sinica also has made impacts in the area of anti-virus software development.

5. *Sensors for Detection and Targeting.* During the 1980s, Taiwan's reconnaissance capability and 1970s vintage photographic technology was adequate for the limited capabilities and low threat posture of the PLAAF. Taiwan's airborne reconnaissance capability, however, began to decline precipitously in the 1990s. Last year, the TAF retired the last of its RF-104G tactical reconnaissance aircraft and replaced them with reconnaissance-configured RF-5E aircraft. Taipei continues to seek a new imaging system capable of exploiting targets at greater distances from the coast, but without exposing its reconnaissance flights to China's increasingly more sophisticated air defenses.

6. *Psychological Operations.* Taiwan reportedly possesses a well-developed PSYOP capability, under the auspices of the General Political Warfare Department (GPWD). PLA troops also are not likely to be susceptible to Taiwan PSYOP.

7. *Military Leadership*. Balanced against these attributes, the officer corps functions within a culture that values caution over innovation and initiative. While Army officers continue to dominate the senior leadership positions within the defense hierarchy--the Army comprises more than 50 percent of the armed forces-- the emphasis on the Air Force and Navy may lead to a corresponding rise in the influence of air and naval officers over matters such as defense procurement priorities and employment doctrine. Taiwan President Lee Teng-hui strongly supports the promotion of native Taiwanese officers to senior military positions. Currently, the Chief of General Staff and commanders of the air force and marines are ethnic Taiwanese. This trend will continue and probably will have a positive effect on the morale and cohesion of the lower ranks of the armed forces, who themselves are overwhelmingly native Taiwanese.

8. *Training*. Taiwan's large-scale training normally takes place quarterly with the major training centers hosting limited maneuver and live-fire exercises. *HAN KUANG 14*, conducted in mid-May 1998, was one of Taipei's more typical joint exercises to date. Primarily a C4I exercise, the training was of very short duration and the scenario allowed for only limited exercise play.

9. *Morale*. Morale, especially among the enlisted ranks, is generally assessed as poor, amidst efforts to retain competent, educated service members in the face of stiff private sector competition. The military competes poorly with the civilian economy in attracting Taiwan's youth, especially those who are technically-oriented. Continued personnel shortages stemming from low retention rates-- especially among NCOs--will remain a serious problem affecting morale. The military also is hampered by systemic problems of poor, antiquated management and a traditional military culture with very rigid command structures which discourages lower-level risk-taking, decisionmaking, and innovation. .

10. *Logistics and Sustainability*. Taiwan's logistics capability will support some defensive operations on Taiwan, but its probability of success is highly dependent on the tempo of operations. The critical requirements are major equipment end items like engines and transmissions, ammunition, fuel and especially obsolete spare parts which no longer are being manufactured.

Conclusions

US-Taiwan military relations has been a neglected subject. On the Taiwan side, the 1998 National Defense Report of the Republic of China has very little to say about relations with the US. Indeed, many Taiwan observers believe that Taiwan is making great strides toward being able to produce all its defense needs domestically with little further need for aid from the US. This is wishful thinking. On the US side, the subject is not a convenient one. Raising it risks needlessly antagonizing China, where nationalistic authors continue to accuse the US of plotting to separate Taiwan from China, in part through arms sales to Taiwan. Journalistic accounts have focused on specific high profile arms sales, such as the sale of 150 F16 fighters, agreed to after a delay of 15 years from Taiwan >s first request in 1977. This paper has suggested that recent information casts a new light on US-Taiwan military relations. The long list [in the appendix to this paper] of weapons supplied by the US to Taiwan since the TRA was enacted in 1979 do not tell the whole story. Focusing on the list of arms transferred tends to show a glass half full. The observations found in the DOD Report of February 1999 about Taiwan's military weaknesses, and the suggestions in the proposed Taiwan Security Enhancement Act tend to suggest a different image of US-Taiwan military relations -- a glass half empty.

There is an important reason for the shift from half full to half empty. According to US government analysts like John Culver in the book *Strategic Trends in China*, published by National Defense University Press in 1998, China has begun since about 1995 to focus its military resources for the first time mainly on Taiwan. China's defense spending remains at a low level, and its defense industrial base remains backward, but there is no doubt that China's military focus has changed during the last few years. This is a sharp contrast to the first ten or fifteen years of the Taiwan Relations Act. During that period, Taiwan was relatively secure because of good US-China relations, China's preoccupation with its northern and western borders, China's focus on economic reform that included major defense cuts in manpower and spending, as well as Taiwan's own natural advantages B only a few beaches that can be attacked and a very small mainland amphibious landing force. The change in the military balance should not be overstated. China still deploys only one of its 24 or so group armies near Taiwan. It has not concentrated its forces, and would probably be detected if it did so. Chinese military authors admit frankly that they have many defects to remedy in their land, air and naval forces. They have but a few thousand marines, and have demonstrated a limited airborne or paratroop capability. But, as the DOD report in February 1999 on the Taiwan Strait makes clear, Beijing has begun to improve its capacity to attack Taiwan in significant ways. It is now up to the leaders of Taiwan and the US to decide if they will change their military approach as well, or seek a diplomatic solution of some kind, or both.

1. Three recent books contain significant new material about US-Taiwan military relations: *About Face* by James Mann, *Face Off* by John Garver, and *The Kissinger Transcripts* from the National Security Archive, Washington D.C. Earlier US studies were Harry Harding, *A Fragile Relationship* [Brookings, 1992] Rosemary Foot, *The Practice of Power* [Oxford, 1995], Robert S. Ross, *Negotiating Cooperation* [Stanford, 1995], Nancy B. Tucker, *Taiwan, Hong Kong, and the United States, 1945-1992* [Macmillan 1992].
2. The Taiwan Relations Act (Public Law 96-8) is recapitulated in the Taiwan Security Enhancement Bill of March 24, 1999 as follows

> (A) peace and stability in the Taiwan Strait area are in the political, security, and economic interests of the United States and are of international concern;
> (B) the decision of the United States to establish diplomatic relations with the People's Republic of China rests upon the expectation that the future of Taiwan will be determined by peaceful means;
> (C) the United States would consider any effort to determine the future of Taiwan by other than peaceful means, including boycotts or embargoes, a threat to the peace and security of the Western Pacific region and of grave concern to the United States;
> (D) the United States will maintain the capacity to resist any form of coercion that jeopardizes the security, or the social or the economic system, of the people on Taiwan; and
> (E) the preservation and enhancement of the human rights of all the people on Taiwan are objectives of the United States.

IMPROVING THE NATURE AND QUALITY OF BILATERAL TRADE RELATIONS BETWEEN TAIWAN AND THE UNITED STATES WITH THE TRA[6]

Introduction

The Taiwan Relations Act was enacted1 in an era that came to great change globally and regionally. Before the United States' diplomatic recognition on Mainland China, Taiwan (with its formal name of the "Republic of China" or "ROC") was considered as the only political regime representing the whole China by the economically and politically most powerful country in the

---

[6] Institute of European and American Studies Academia Sinica, Taipei, Taiwan Professor Changfa Lo* April 8, 1999

For additional analytical, marketing, investment and business opportunities information, please contact
Global Investment & Business Center, USA
(202) 546-2103. Fax: (202) 546-3275. E-mail: rusric@erols.com

world. Although United States' previous recognition of the government on Taiwan to represent the whole China did not fully reflect the fact that most part of China was effectively controlled by the Chinese Mainland government, since re-cognition provided Taiwan with an opportunity to play a significant role in international politics; it still represented the theme that Taiwan was an important player in international arena. The switch of recognition of the United States from Taiwan to the Chinese Mainland indicated that Taiwan had to face the situation that not only was it no longer a significant player in the international politics, but also has to struggle for the national identity, which is essential for its continuing survival.

On the Mainland China side, it came to commence its open door policy and started to establish normal relationship with the United States and the rest of the world in the late 1970s before it earned recognition from the United States. More and more so, it decided to play a role commensurate with its geographical, economic and political scale. Diplomatic recognition by the United States marked the milestone of its international political success. But the enactment of the Taiwan Relations Act also marked a development to reverse the political de-recognition and produced long-term significance.

Although the existence and development of Taiwan do not and should not depend on the recognition of one particular country, the recognition or de-recognition of an important state still provide a guiding indicator to show Taiwan's legal status. Likewise, the "re-recognition" by the Taiwan Relations Act on Taiwan's legal status in cultural, economic and other matters to a certain extent has influenced the policies of other countries toward Taiwan. Bilateral arrangement between Taiwan and the United States has been "learned" by many other countries which decided to carry on their economic relations with Taiwan, while maintaining diplomatic relations with the People's Republic of China. This has been one of the reasons why Taiwan is able to maintain and develop its full scale of economic relations with so many countries in the world. However, the Taiwan Relations Act could also have contributed to the situation that a number of countries decided to switch their diplomatic recognition from Taiwan to Chinese mainland believing that Taiwan could still be satisfied with the maintenance of economic relations.

With these backgrounds in mind, the enactment of the Taiwan Relations Act was with great significance not only in that, in the absence of diplomatic relations, it commits to ensure the security of Taiwan, but also it is meant to preserve the common interests and maintain the status of Taiwan in some aspects, in addition to the practical approaches taken by the Act which has been "learned" by other countries toward Taiwan.

The Act was put into being by the U.S. Congress in the time when Taiwan faced greatest difficulty in regard to its political and legal status. People on Taiwan never reserve expressing their gratitude to the people from the faraway land of the United States with the understanding that people in the United States still consider Taiwan as a close friend and intend to maintain meaningful relationship with Taiwan.

During last twenty years from the Taiwan Relations Act being brought into existence, Taiwan has been given by the Act a great opportunity to develop normal relationship with the United States and its people. Because of the Act, it can be claimed that the legal status of Taiwan was more a theoretical problem than a practical one. The Act stood as the cornerstone of securing Taiwan's stability and prosperity. Observers and government officials of both sides generally consider the Act as a success.2

As far as the United States is concerned, the Taiwan government is still the authority that the United States has to deal with. The bilateral arrangement under the Act is carried on, mainly as it should be, in a rather smooth way. But from the perspective of Taiwan, it is apparent that some room for further improvement of the bilateral relations does exist, especially in the trade areas. This is the background making the topic worthy for our discussion. Note that the topic of the paper does not imply that the existing bilateral trade relationship is in any way defective. Rather, we would argue that, although current bilateral relationship is managed and handled in an acceptable way, there is still room for improvement and the Taiwan Relations Act can provide a solid legal basis for such pursuit.

1. **Contours of Important Documents or Arrangements Governing Bilateral Trade Relations**

Before we enter into discussions on the nature and quality of bilateral trade relations let us briefly review the documents that having great significance in governing trade ties. There are a number of legal documents and frameworks of this kind, some of these are bilateral arrangements or regional or multilateral frameworks whereas others are domestic laws enacted by one side. They are complementary to each other for maintaining and shaping current trade relationship. Some of them will be briefly discussed herewith.

1. Bilateral Treaties and Agreements:

The Treaty of Friendship, Commerce and Navigation (the FCN Treaty)[3] was of great importance in the early days of ROC government's move to Taiwan when there had not been many specialized treaties dealing with different areas. Trade flow was guaranteed by this treaty which deals with treatment not only on traded goods, but also on other areas, such as investment, access to courts and other matters. It is worthy to note that today's treaties and agreements mostly address specialized issues. The FCN Treaty plays less and less of a significant role in trade relations when more trade arrangements are concluded.

Another important bilateral arrangement is the bilateral trade agreement of 1978, which was concluded before the termination of diplomatic recognition by the United States. The agreement was to allow the application of the outcomes of GATT Tokyo Round negotiations onto the bilateral trade between Taiwan and the United States. It was made through the exchange of letters. Since Taiwan was not a contracting party to the GATT 1947, the agreement provided a legal basis that guarantees Taiwan's exports to the United States to be granted the most favored nation treatment by the United States. This agreement contributed greatly to Taiwan's continuation on its export performance and the maintenance of its economic prosperity.

The Trade and Investment Framework Agreement (the "TIFA")[4] was initially proposed by the United States in December 1992 which was signed and entered into force in April 1994. This Agreement provides a formal channel for both parties to conduct their consultation on a more regular basis. Up until now, three consultations have been held based on the Agreement, in 1995, 1996 and 1998 respectively. Any trade or investment issue concerned by either party may be brought into the agenda for consultation. Take 1998 consultation as an example: the agenda covered a wide range of topics, including, among others, intellectual property protection, pricing practice on medical devices and pharmaceuticals, matters relating to Taiwan's WTO accession, telecommunication and EMC mutual recognition agreement, hazardous waste management arrangement. Because of this framework agreement, both sides have a reliable mutually confident channel to resolve their differences and to establish some form of cooperation in a more efficient way.

2. Multilateral and Regional Frameworks:

For additional analytical, marketing, investment and business opportunities information, please contact
Global Investment & Business Center, USA
(202) 546-2103. Fax: (202) 546-3275. E-mail: rusric@erols.com

The only relations established and maintained under multilateral frameworks between two sides are under the World Trade Organization. Taiwan has yet to finish its accession process at the working party level. Bilateral trade negotiations conducted under the WTO framework had been in progress since the predecessor of the WTO (the GATT) decided to establish a working party to review the accession application to the organization submitted by Taiwan. Taiwan has completed most of the bilateral negotiations with WTO Members that have requested to conduct such negotiations. With respect to the bilateral negotiations with the United States, most of the issues raised by the United States were settled and a formal deal was concluded. Taiwan made substantial commitments in opening up its markets based on this bilateral agreement. As a matter of course, this commitment will be multilateralized after Taiwan joins the WTO. Notwithstanding this is only a bilateral arrangement, it clearly demonstrates the existence of intensive bilateral interactions between the two sides under multilateral framework.

The so-called "Information Technology Agreement" (ITA) was initiated mainly by the United States. It was concluded and put into effect in March 1997, covering a wide range of information technology products for an in-depth liberalization on tariffs. Some 39 countries and economies signed the agreement to participate in the liberalization process. In February 1998, the second phase of ITA was proposed and negotiated, hopefully to cover more products and to have wider country coverage. Taiwan participated actively in the ITA negotiations and extensive dialogues were exchanged between the United States and Taiwan5. It could be considered as a mode of interaction between two sides in the ITA negotiations.

In terms of APEC, the United States also uses this forum as an important channel to carry out its foreign trade policy. In 1998, one of the most important works promoted by the United States is to accelerate the liberalization process for some products. Taiwan had been very cooperative in this promotion, although accelerated liberalization is not an easy task for Taiwan. There were also active interactions between the two sides during the period when the proposals were considered. Although the proposal was not put into effect due to some APEC members' refusal to accept this proposal, it did provide both sides with a lesson in cooperating on particular topics in an international arena.

3. Domestic Laws of the United States:

As a matter of international norm, domestic laws usually do not apply to matters beyond the national boundary. Prescriptive jurisdiction of a law enacted in one country normally could not have extra-territorial reach. But the fact is: the domestic laws enacted by a country with great political influence could have much effect on other countries through unilateral, bilateral, or even multilateral measures.

The Taiwan Relations Act provides a legal basis to govern bilateral relations between Taiwan and the United States after the de-recognition of Taiwan by the U.S. side during the Carter Administration. Although this Act does not have any power or legal basis to intervene the domestic affairs of Taiwan and although it is a domestic law governing practices and policies of the United States, it has become one of the most important legal documents governing the bilateral relations. The TRA "re-recognizes" the existence of Taiwan (although on a de facto basis); and the recognition had made the trade and economic relations possible to be carried on as usual. Also through this Act, previous economic treaties remained effective and conclusions of more treaties were made possible. All these are essential to the further development and growth of bilateral trade relations.

A number of United States trade legislation and practices also have great effects on the interactions between two sides. For instance, the so-called "special 301" under the Trade Act of

1974, as amended, is still a major topic in bilateral trade relations and has been an important contributing factor in the shaping of Taiwan's current intellectual property right laws. In May 1992, Taiwan was listed as a "priority country" facing the threat of retaliation. This decision served as a catalyst for Taiwan to improve the protection of intellectual property rights. As a result of extensive reform, the United States dropped the retaliation threat. In 1993, the United States Trade Representative (the USTR) again identified Taiwan as one of the country in the "priority watch list". In 1994 and 1995, Taiwan was included in the respective "watch list". With the continuous progress made to improve the protection of intellectual property rights, Taiwan was for the first time excluded from the list in 1996; this exclusion extended to 1997. However, from 1998, there were a number intellectual property protection issues, including exportation of pirated TV games and CDs and the Fair Trade Commission's approach on right holders' sending warning letters to potential infringers. Special 301 is one of the most important U.S. domestic legislation constantly having effects on Taiwan government's measures and practices.

The Uruguay Round Agreements Act (the URAA)6 was enacted in 1994 for the purpose of implementing the Agreements entered into by the United States at the Uruguay Round Negotiations. The law is of importance for the reasons that it had made the establishment of the WTO possible and that it carries out the commitments made by the United States at the Uruguay Round Negotiations and thus further liberalizes the United States markets, which is essential to the world economy. Although Taiwan is still not a member of the WTO, the United States still grants Taiwan similar treatments that it grants to WTO members under the URAA.

2. **Nature of Bilateral Trade Relations Envisaged by the TRA and the Possible Improvement**

4. Particular Provisions under the TRA Governing or Relating to Bilateral Trade Relations:

There is no clear cut between the provisions in the TRA governing trade relations and those governing diplomatic and others. Some of the provisions can be applied to deal with or are relevant to trade ties and other relations, while others are more diplomatic or cultural in nature7. Before we review the current trade relations, it would be useful for us to mention some of the important provisions that directly govern or have more direct effects on the trade relations.

   a. General Policy: the Continuation of Trade Relations

The Taiwan Relations Act lays down the purposes of the enactment of the law by stating that it is "to help maintain peace, security, and stability in the Western Pacific"; "to promote the foreign policy of the United States by authorizing the continuation of commercial, cultural, and other relations between the people of the United States and people on Taiwan"; and "to preserve and promote extensive, close, and friendly commercial, cultural, and other relations between the people of the United States and the people on Taiwan, as well as the people on the China mainland and all other peoples of the Western Pacific area". Most of the words used here are very neutral but constructive. The basic theme of the TRA in regard to the trade relations is the maintenance and continuation of trade relations. There are no words indicating that such relations should be in any way "upgraded", neither are there words to show that the United States executive branch has vested the power to "down-grade" the trade relations existed prior to de-recognition.

   b. Continuation of Existing International Agreements:

Prior to the termination of diplomatic ties, quite a number of bilateral agreements had been established between Taiwan and the United States. Section 4(c) of the TRA provides a legal basis for the United States to continue the agreements. It states that "[for] all purposes, including actions in any court in the United States, the Congress approves the continuation in force of all treaties and other international agreements, including multilateral conventions, entered into by the United States as the Republic of China prior to January 1, 1979, and in force between them on December 31, 1978, unless and until terminated in accordance with the law."

      c. Application of Laws:

Section 4(a) provides that "[the] absence of diplomatic relations or recognition shall not affect the application of the laws of the United States with respect to Taiwan, and the laws of the United States shall apply with respect to Taiwan in the manner that the laws of the United States applied with respect to Taiwan prior to January 1, 1979." It further provides in Sections 4(b)(1) and (3)(A) that "[w]henever the laws of the United States refer or relate to foreign countries, nations, states, governments, or similar entities, such terms shall include and such laws shall apply with respect to Taiwan"; and that "[t]he absence of diplomatic relations and recognition with respect to Taiwan shall not abrogate, infringe, modify, deny, or otherwise affect in any way any rights or obligations (including but not limited to those involving contracts, debts, or property interests of any kind) under the laws of the United States heretofore or hereafter acquired by or with respect to Taiwan."

5. A Review of the Current Relations and Possible Improvement on the Quality:

      d. Positive Aspects:

It is apparent that the TRA wants the administrative branch of the United States to deal with Taiwan "as if" it is dealing with a country, with the exception that political recognition will not be given. Thus, as mentioned above, the TRA provides that even though there is no diplomatic recognition, the application of the United States' laws with respect to Taiwan and agreements and treaties effective between the two sides will not be affected.

It appears that after the United States made the decision to switch the recognition from Taiwan to the People's Republic of China, the United States executive branch has avoided to enter into any formal-looking arrangement. The above mentioned 1978 bilateral arrangement through the exchange of letters is a typical example of this kind. The Taiwan Relations Act had changed this situation. After the enactment of the Act, formal-looking agreements were commonly concluded. The establishment of bilateral Trade and Investment Frame Work Agreement (the TIFA) indicates that formal agreement could be concluded through the channel of the Coordination Council for North American Affairs and the American Institute in Taiwan, as required by the TRA. Although the title used in this agreement is not the same as those in other TIFA concluded by the United States with other countries, the format and contents of them are basically the same. It has been the practice of the United States that there is nothing to hide from the PRC when entering into trade and economic agreements with Taiwan. This is very positive development from any perspective.

      e. Aspects Needed to Be Improved:

First, non-official relations should be reviewed: Bilateral trade relations between the United States and Taiwan are considered by government officials of both sides as very positive. There are no contentious trade issues. Government officials usually use trade volumes between two sides and the decline of trade deficit with Taiwan as indicators to show such positive relations8. However, it is apparent that Taiwan still prefers to have official relations with the United States.

6. Most people characterize bilateral relations between Taiwan and the United States as "non-official ones". The most frequently cited authorities are Sections 6(a) and 10(a) of the Act, which provides respectively that "relations conducted or carried out by ... any agency of the United States Government with respect to Taiwan shall, in the manner and to the extent directed by the President, be conducted and carried out by or through ... The American Institute in Taiwan, a nonprofit organization incorporated under the laws of the District of Columbia..." and that whenever "any agency of the United States Government is authorized or requested by or pursuant to the laws of the United States to render or provide to or to receive or accept from Taiwan, any performance, communication, assurance, undertaking, or other action, such action shall ... be rendered or provided to, or received or accepted from, an instrumentality established by Taiwan which the President determines has the necessary authority under the laws applied by the people of Taiwan to provide assurances and take other actions on behalf of Taiwan in accordance with this Act."

7. However, one could argue that diplomatic relations and official relations are legally different things. Two governments representing different territories can establish official relations through concluding agreements without diplomatic relations being established between each other. Take WTO members as an illustration: two territories can be WTO Members and thus establish treaty relations, while they may not receive diplomatic recognition from each other. Members of the WTO would be required to assume treaty obligations in the territories under their effective control in respect to the trade and customs policies. These obligations can not be carried out without the support of the governmental authority. Thus it can never be correct to say that such treaty relations are non-official ones.

8. It is clear that the diplomatic de-recognition by the United States is a deciding factor preventing the United States and Taiwan from establishing diplomatic relations. However, it is not to say that both sides can not have official relations, according to the explanation provided above. Section 6(a) of the TRA only requires that bilateral matters be conducted through the American Institute in Taiwan, in the manner and to the extent directed by the President. It does not prohibit that government agencies of respective sides to have formal or ad hoc contacts for the purpose of managing or dealing with bilateral matters. In fact, the Act authorizes the administrative branch of the United States to decide whether there would be matters or areas for which direct contact would produce more fruitful outcome. If under the administrative discretion direct interactions between governmental agencies would be more appropriate, it would be expected by the Act that the President would allow such interactions. To use the terms used in the TRA, if the President decides that if some bilateral matters are beyond the extent, such matters could be conducted not through the AIT.

9. Some might argue that the non-official arrangement did not harm the development of bilateral relations. However, even though the argument were true, we still have to say that if an official one can be established, there could be even more vibrant and mutually beneficial interactions between the two sides. If there could be official relations, government officials handling trade and other economic issues would have more effective and direct channels to enter into dialogue to solve bilateral problems and to cooperate or coordinate with each other in a more efficient way. Unnecessary efforts in coping with or evading the principle of no official relations could be greatly reduced. In sum, this paper argues that the United States government does not treat Taiwan in a way envisaged by the TRA; official relations between two sides are expected by the law when situations practically require such interactions.

10. Second, Taiwan's membership with international economic organizations should not be restricted: The Taiwan Relations Act does not set forth any restriction on the joining of

international trade or economic organizations. To the contrary, the Act implies that the United States should support Taiwan's accession to international economic organizations. As mentioned above, Section 4(c) of the TRA states that "[for] all purposes, including actions in any court in the United States, the Congress approves the continuation in force of all treaties and other international agreements, including multilateral conventions, entered into by the United States as the Republic of China prior to January 1, 1979, and in force between them on December 31, 1978, unless and until terminated in accordance with the law." Although no words in particular state that the U.S. government should support Taiwan's entry into economic organizations, it is still apparent that Taiwan's legal status should not be a problem with regard to its entry into any international economic organization. Otherwise, the law would not state that multilateral conventions entered into by both sides will still be carried on. In other words, the law implies that there should not be any problem with regard to Taiwan's status acceding to international economic organizations from the perspective of the United States.

11. However, President Clinton stated in late June 1998, when he was visiting the Chinese mainland, that the United States would not support Taiwan in joining organizations which require their members to be a state. Under the criteria set forth by President Clinton, Taiwan would virtually only be allowed to join the WTO and APEC, which do not require their members to be a state. Article XII, para. 1 of the Agreement Establishing the World Trade Organization explicitly states that: "Any State or separate customs territory possessing full autonomy in the conduct of its external commercial relations and of the other matters provided for in this Agreement and the Multilateral Trade Agreements may accede to this Agreement, on terms to be agreed between it and the WTO. Such accession shall apply to this Agreement and the Multilateral Trade Agreements annexed thereto." APEC is another international forum allowing non-country economies to be its member. In addition to these, there are very few international economic organizations which do not require their members to be a state. The OECD and IMF all require their members to be a nation. As a matter of law, Taiwan can be considered, and is considered by more than twenty countries, as a nation. But since most countries do not recognize this fact, Taiwan is not treated as it should be in regard to its legal identity. Thus if the United States decides that Taiwan should not be a member of the organizations that require their members to be a nation, then Taiwan will be in an even more difficult situation to participate in those economic organizations.

12. Membership to these organizations is very important and essential for a country to exercise its functions in dealing with economic matters. If Taiwan is excluded from being a member of international economic organizations, it will not be able to carry out its duties and to receive economically equal treatments in the same way as a member of international society should have carried and received. For instance, Taiwan's exclusion from the IMF has produced the effect that Taiwan is prevented from receiving information on international monetary matters which is essential for Taiwan to make proper and correct decisions on monetary affairs. It is also apparent that, Taiwan as an outsider to the IMF has prevented Taiwan from entering into cooperative arrangements with its trading and economic partners and thus could have adverse effect on the attainment of the purposes set forth by the IMF agreement.

13. It is true that the participation to international economic organizations is not purely bilateral matters. But it is also the very fact that United States' position toward Taiwan's participation of

international economic organizations is critical for other countries to follow; and that to establish sound bilateral relations on economic matters can not be completed without taking multilateral arrangement into operation for bilateral matters. This paper argues that (1) it is implied in the TRA that Taiwan should not be excluded as a member of international economic organizations, (2) there is no sound basis in the TRA limiting Taiwan's accession to international economic organization which require the acceding parties to be a nation, and (3) allowing Taiwan to participate in international organizations will further bilateral relationship on economic and trade matters.

14. Third, Chinese mainland's attitude and position toward Taiwan should not be a dominant factor in the policy making of the United States government on Taiwan - U.S. trade relations: There are a number of apparent examples showing that mainland China is the single most important influential factor on United States policy in regard to trade and economic matters toward Taiwan, which include matters on whether the United States would support Taiwan's accession to the WTO and the OECD. Although it has been made clear many times by U.S. government officials that Taiwan's accession to the WTO would not be linked with mainland China's accession, it is still a general perception that the United States never in fact supports the de-linkage between the two accession cases. It is understandable that the TRA does not prohibit the U.S. government from using Taiwan or mainland China as a leverage to generate most interest for the United States. But it is also clear that the TRA requires the U.S. government to conduct bilateral relations with Taiwan and mainland China separately. Any linkage established between its trade policies with Taiwan and mainland China could be considered as not in line with what the TRA has expected. The TRA provides that Taiwan should have a full status in regard to the application of U.S. laws. It is a proper interpretation that Taiwan should also be considered as a separate international entity in regard to the exercise of U.S. trade policy conducted by the executive branch.

15. To state more clearly, the Taiwan Relations Act does not provide any basis for the United States executive branch to make such conditionality. As a matter of course, the executive branch of any country would have more or less power in exercising its discretion in foreign affairs. But their discretion would have to be subject to legislation of their respective countries. In case of the United States and the Taiwan Relations Act, it is stated clearly that the maintenance of peace and security is the goal and, to attain that goal, the United States would apply the law onto Taiwan as it would apply previously to ROC and other countries. It is also made clear that the United States would support the maintenance of the membership in some international organizations. The United States government does have the discretion to decide how to achieve the goal, with certain conditions to be followed. However, if an explicit linkage between the Taiwan case and the PRC case is established by the executive branch of the United States, there could be an issue of violating the spirit of the Taiwan Relations Act.

3. Quality Improvement of Bilateral Trade Relations

There could never be "ideal" trade relations. But one can still expect to establish relations with less problems. Bilateral trade relations between Taiwan and the United States are going toward a positive direction. As mentioned above, bilateral trade ties are very close. Taiwan is the 7th largest trading partner of the United States with United States exports to Taiwan increased 10.7 percent from the previous year in 1997, while United States imports from Taiwan increased 9.1 percent.9 Having said this, a number of areas still exist on which both parties can consider to make improvement.

16. More Bilateral Arrangements Needed to Be Established:

Both sides can enhance their cooperation in several areas. In the past, some people suggested that bilateral free trade agreement could be established so as to enhance bilateral trade relationship. This proposal was not seriously discussed and in recent years, rarely mentioned. In turn, both parties are expected to have cooperation or interaction on new trade topics emerging in recent years in which both sides have great interests. There are a number of these issues for which both parties have similar positions. Competition policy is one of the areas.

There is no restriction in the establishment of comprehensive and sound bilateral economic relations under the TRA. In fact, the Act not only sets no limit in terms of quantity or areas for the United States government to establish relations, but expects the bilateral trade relations to be comprehensive. The TRA thus provides that it is enacted "to ... promote extensive, close, and friendly commercial ... and other relations between the people of the United States and the people on Taiwan."

There is an increasingly popular trend to conclude bilateral agreement on the cooperation and coordination matters of competition laws and policies between countries having close trade relations. The United States had entered into such agreements with a number of countries or regions, including Canada, Australia and the European Community. Taiwan also feels that there is a need to have such agreement with its trading partners and thus have concluded agreements with Australia and New Zealand. Under such agreements the Fair Trade Commission of Taiwan, which is in charge of the enforcement of the Fair Trade Law (Taiwan's competition law), regularly conduct bilateral consultations with its counterparts. Since Taiwan and the United States have very close trade ties and due to the fact that some potential areas for cooperation exist in order to facilitate law enforcement and to coordinate policy making, it would be practical for both sides to conclude bilateral cooperation agreement on matters related to competition policy. Such an agreement would contribute to more effective ways of dealing with an increasing number of mergers and acquisitions, international cartels, multilevel selling, as well as some unfair trade practices that affect both parties. This should also be within the expectation of the TRA.

17. Conflicts in Regard to Import Relief Can Be Reduced:

Antidumping measures adopted by the United States are one of the most frequently mentioned areas causing bilateral trade disputes. In 1998, there were at least nine cases either the measures of which are still in effect or the orders from which was issued. Following chart indicates the situation:10

Depart of Commerce Case Number	Product	Investigation Initiated	Preliminary Result	Final Decision	Date of Order
A-583-824	Polyvinyl Alcohol	04/04/95	10/10/95	03/29/96	05/14/96
A-583-825	Melamine Institutional Dinnerware	03/01/96	08/22/96	01/13/97 (02/05/97 Amended)	02/25/97
A-583-826	Collated Roofing Nails	12/20/96	05/12/97	10/01/97 (11/19/97 Amended)	11/19/97
A-583-827	Static Random Access Memory Semiconductors	03/21/97	10/01/97	02/23/98 (04/16/98 Amended)	04/16/98 (04/22/98 Amended)
A-583-828	Stainless Steel Wire Rod	08/26/97	03/05/98 (04/07/98	07/22/98 (09/15/98	09/15/98

			Amended)	Amended)	
A-583-829	Stainless Steel Round Wire	05/12/98	11/18/98	(before 04/02/99)	
A-583-830	Stainless Steel Plate in Coils	04/27/98	10/28/98	(before 03/19/99)	
A-583-831	Stainless Steel Sheet and Strip in Coils	07/13/98	12/18/98	(before 05/07/99)	
A-583-832	Dynamic Random Access Memory Semiconductors	12/13/98	(before 04/01/99)		

It is understandable that the adoption of antidumping measures is a right granted by international agreement and practices. Thus it is unrealistic to expect that any one particular country will automatically abandon the use of such measure. However, it is also apparent that the measures are in many situations misused. We understand that whether the measures are misused is an issue concerning the application of domestic trade law. But bilateral framework should be able to provide such channel to prevent or reduce the misuse of import relief. Excessive use of the measures could never promote a close and friendly commercial relationship as expected by the TRA. In this regard, the TIFA could have included the practice of antidumping duty as a priority topic in the agenda to allow both parties to conduct regular review.

18. More Substantive Works Could Be Put Forth onto the TIFA Framework:

As indicated above, TIFA provides a very useful channel for both sides to interact. However, it should be noted that there is no substantive obligation stipulated in TIFA. For this reason, TIFA can be used to serve as an effective channel for bilateral interaction, while it can also be considered as an un-necessary arrangement with only symbolic function. For the first two years after the signing of the agreement, there were two consecutive meetings held under this framework. But the third annual meeting was held two years after the second meeting (i.e. in 1998). It seems that the United States side did not have the intention to conduct their interaction under the framework on a regular basis. This paper is not to blame any side for its perspective on TIFA. However, it appears that TIFA is one of the most important frameworks established between Taiwan and the United States. If both sides do not treasure the framework, it would become less and less resorted document and could eventually become a redundant piece of paper.

It must be understood that the TRA itself can not self-fulfilling in all situations. It needs a lot of supplements to carry out the goals set forth therein. The TIFA is one of the most important supplementary legal document to fulfill TRA's goals. Both parties seems have to use the frameworks in a more systematic way.

Conclusion

As this paper mentioned, the TRA has played a very positive role in the field of bilateral trade. It provides a very solid basis for both sides to carry on their commercial relationship. As a matter of law, it is a set of domestic rules governing the government activities of the United States. However, it is in fact a law with significance influence on bilateral relations and even on Taiwan's domestic practices. Basically, the Act has been very supportive to the development of Taiwan for the last twenty years. However, we found that there is still room for further improvement on trade relations under the framework established by the TRA. Some of the problems relate to the nature that has been set forth by the practices of the United States Government and others concern the quality of the relations. The preliminary research in this paper finds that the TRA does allow and expect the executive branch of the United States to do more than what have been done today. This paper tries to provide legal persuasion for both sides to consider the enhancement of bilateral trade relations under the framework of the TRA. It also serves as a reminder that the bilateral trade ties, in terms of the nature and the quality, deserve better management under the TRA.

*Professor Changfa Lo is a professor of law at the National Taiwan University.
1 The Taiwan Relations Act (22 U.S.C. Secs. 3301-3316) was signed into law on April 10, 1979.
2 United States Assistant Secretary East Asian and Pacific Bureau of the Department of State Stanley O. Roth's presentation to The Woodrow Wilson Center and The American Institute in Taiwan, The Taiwan Relations Act at Twenty - and Beyond, cited at http://www.usia.gov/regional/ea/uschina/rothtwn.htm (visited on March 27, 1999): "I have no hesitation in declaring the TRA a resounding success. Over the past twenty years, the TRA has not only helped to preserve the substance of our relationship with Taiwan, it has contributed to the conditions which have enable the U.S., the PRC, and Taiwan to achieve a great deal more."
3 63 Stat. 1299; 25 U.N.T.S. 69.
4 The full name of the TIFA between Taiwan and the United States is the "Agreement between the American Institute in Taiwan and the Coordination Council for North American Affairs Concerning a Framework of Principles and Procedures for Consultations Regarding Trade and Investment." See Changfa Lo, On the Trade and Investment Framework Agreement between Taiwan and the United States and Its Effect on Taiwan after Taiwan's Accession to the WTO (written in Chinese language), in Sino-American Relations, 1992-1994, published by the Institute of European and American Studies, Adademia Sinica (1996).
5 Under the Agreement, Taiwan was to phase out tariffs on information technology products with its first tranche tariff cuts implemented on July 1, 1997. A second tranche was implemented on January 1, 1998. Most of the information products covered in the Agreement will be phased out by the year 2000. A handful of products will be subject to tariff elimination in the year 2002.
6 Pub. L. No. 103-465, 108 Stat. 4809 (1994).
7 For instance, Section 2(b)(3) provides that it is the policy of the United States "to make clear that the United States decision to establish diplomatic relations with the People's Republic of China rests upon the expectation that the future of Taiwan will be determined by peaceful means". This provision seems to be dealing with the security and the diplomatic problems. But similar provisions can also be applied in a way that has great relevancy with trade issues. Section 2(b)(4) provides that the United States policy is also "to consider any effort to determine the future of Taiwan by other than peaceful means, including by boycotts or embargoes, a threat to the peace and security of the Western Pacific area and of grave concern to the United States". The words "boycotts" and "embargoes" have everything to do with trade problems.
8 Kent Wiedmann, the then Deputy Assistant Secretary for East Asian and Pacific Affairs, made statement before the House International Relations Committee on August 3, 1995 indicating: "U.S. economic ties with Taiwan have grown stronger since 1979. Taiwan is our seventh-largest trading partner. It is the fifth-largest importer of U.S. agricultural products. We have a $10 billion trade deficit with Taiwan but they has declined from the high of $17 billion in 1987. Cumulative U.S. investment in Taiwan now stands at $5 billion, representing a quarter of all foreign investment there." Cited from the European and American Studies Institute of the Academia Sinica, Sino-American Relations, 1995-1997 at 268 (published in 1998).
Stanley O. Roth, Assistant Secretary East Asian and Pacific Bureau of the U.S. Department of State made a presentation to The Woodrow Wilson Center and The American Institute in Taiwan remarking: "On the economic front, the U.S. and Taiwan share a vibrant, mutually beneficial trade relationship. Taiwan is the 14th largest trading economy in the world and the seventh largest market for U.S. exports. It constitutes our fifth largest foreign agricultural market and a major market for U.S. automobiles. For our part, the U.S. absorbs one fourth of all Taiwan exports, and

our annual bilateral trade exceeds $50 billion." "The economic partnership, moreover, continues to grow. Taiwan's sophisticated economy is largest withstanding the Asian Financial Crisis and acting as a support for the region. Taipei is now pursuing an ambitious, multi-billion dollar series of infrastructure projects - projects for which U.S. firms are helping to provide professional services and equipment. Taiwan and the U.S. passed a milestone in their economic relationship last year with the successful completion of bilateral negotiations concerning Taiwan's application to the World Trade Organization. All indications are that Taiwan will continue to be an important export market for the United States."
9 Foreign Trade Barriers in Taiwan, in 1998 Foreign Trade Barriers Report by the USTR. See http://ww.usia.gov/regional/ea/uschina/taibr98.htm visited on March 27, 1999.
10 This chart is cited from *Review and Prospective of 1998 ROC-US Economic and Trade Relationship*, prepared in Chinese language by the Economic Section of the Representative Office stationed in the United States.

THE TRADE RELATIONSHIP BETWEEN TAIWAN AND THE U.S. SINCE THE TAIWAN RELATIONS ACT[7]

I. Introduction

In any international comparison of economic performance during the past four decades, Taiwan invariably stands out. Sustained high rates of economic growth transformed Taiwan from an agrarian and backward society to a thriving industrial economy. Along the way, Taiwan achieved a persistent reduction in poverty and inequality, low inflation and unemployment rates and significant improvement in almost all the social welfare indicators.

The development success story of Taiwan, which is not endowed with abundant natural resources, has drawn substantially increased attention in recent years from policy-makers and academicians in both advanced and less developed economies. Undoubtedly, the economic success is linked to the development policies followed by Taiwan. Recognizing the importance of promoting exports in the early stages of development, Taiwan switched from import substitution strategies to export-oriented strategies in the late 1950s, which have been a driving force for expansion in the decades since1.

In the global market, the U.S. was a major source of Taiwan's exports. Under the leadership of the U.S., the multilateral trading system established after World War II has substantially reduced trade barriers, especially in the industrialized countries. Taiwan has taken full advantage of these reductions to achieve remarkable economic success through an expansion of exports, especially to the United States. In fact, the U.S. market was an indispensable factor in the success of its export-oriented strategies. Taiwan's trade structure can be characterized by a high dependency upon the U.S. market, and this fact has not been influenced by the bilateral political relationship between the two countries. Accordingly, the objective of this paper is to analyze the trade relationship between Taiwan and the U.S. Following the introductory section, section II: discusses the trade structure of Taiwan, while section III: examines the bilateral trade relationship between Taiwan and the U.S. The consequences of bilateral trade between the U.S. and Taiwan is analyzed in Section IV. Finally, some concluding remarks are presented in Section V.

Section II:The Trade Structure of Taiwan

---

[7] Institute of European and American Studies Academia Sinica, Taipei, Taiwan *Da-Nien Liu, Wen-Jung Lien Chung-Hua Institution for Economic Research*

**For additional analytical, marketing, investment and business opportunities information, please contact
Global Investment & Business Center, USA
(202) 546-2103. Fax: (202) 546-3275. E-mail: rusric@erols.com**

Before analyzing the bilateral trade relationship between the U.S. and Taiwan, it is useful to have an understanding of the trade structure of Taiwan. This information can serve as a basis for understanding bilateral trade between these two economies. Hence, in this section we will first discuss the trade trends of Taiwan, and then follow it with a discussion of the bilateral trade relationship between the two countries.

Taiwan's remarkable performance in trade and the success of its export-oriented strategy are frequently cited as a model for other developing countries. The achievements can be seen from Table 1. Taiwan's exports and imports have grown much faster than gross national product (GNP), so the share of exports and imports in GNP has increased significantly. Table 1 also indicates that the growth rates of exports, imports and GNP in the export-oriented period (approximately from the 1960s to the present) have been much higher than those in the import substitution period (approximately from 1950 to 1960). It is tempting to conclude that the outstanding trade performance during the export-oriented period has played a dominant role in the success of Taiwan's economic development.

The rapid growth of Taiwan's exports during the export-oriented period was led by industrial products. This can be observed from Table 2. In 1960, approximately the year when Taiwan started undertaking its export-oriented policy, exports of industrial products accounted for about one-third of total exports. Processed agricultural products were the major exports of Taiwan at that time. The success of the export-oriented policy changed the export composition noticeably. By 1985, industrial products were responsible for nearly 94% of total exports. On the other hand, the contribution of agricultural products to exports was trivial. The trend has changed very little since then.

Table 1: The Share of Trade and Growth Rates in Taiwan

at current price, (%)

Period	Growth Rate of GNP	Growth Rate of Exports in GNP	Share of Exports in GNP	Growth Rate of Imports	Share of Imports in GNP
1952-1963	4.75	10.03	15.33 (in 1952)	6.19	16.72 (in 1952)
1963-1971	14.85	25.63	31.44 (in 1961)	22.57	28.14 (in 1961)
1971-1981	21.85	27.07	47.81 (in 1971)	27.66	44.83 (in 1971)
1981-1991	14.54	12.91	41.46 (in 1981)	11.48	34.21 (in 1981)
1991-1997	7.58	8.18	42.87 (in 1992)	10.50	40.18 (in 1992)

Source : Taiwan Statistical Data Book, Council for Economic Planning and Development, R.O.C.,1998

The structure of exports for Taiwan can be further broken down into ten SITC (Standard International Tariff Classification) categories. As Table 3 shows, we observe that the export concentration is significant. In 1980, miscellaneous manufactured articles (SITC 8), machinery and transport equipment (SITC 7) and manufactured goods classified by material (SITC 6) accounted for about 85% of total exports. The phenomenon of export concentration has even been prominent since then and the share of the three top principle products to total exports increased to almost 90% in 1997.

Table 2: Composition of Taiwan's Exports

Period	Agricultural Products	Processed Agricultural Products	Industrial Products
1955	28.1	61.5	10.4
1960	12.0	55.7	32.3
1965	23.6	30.4	46.0
1970	8.6	12.8	78.6
1975	5.6	10.8	83.6
1980	3.6	5.6	90.8
1981	2.6	4.6	92.8
1982	2.0	5.1	92.9
1983	1.9	4.8	93.3
1984	1.7	4.3	94.0
1985	1.6	4.5	93.9
1986	1.6	4.9	93.5
1987	1.3	4.8	93.9
1988	1.4	4.1	94.5
1989	0.7	3.9	95.4
1990	0.7	3.8	95.5
1991	0.7	4.0	95.3
1992	0.6	3.7	95.7
1993	0.6	3.5	95.9
1994	0.5	3.6	95.9
1995	0.4	3.4	96.2
1996	0.4	3.1	96.5
1997	0.3	1.8	97.9

Source: as in Table 1.

For additional analytical, marketing, investment and business opportunities information, please contact
Global Investment & Business Center, USA
(202) 546-2103. Fax: (202) 546-3275. E-mail: rusric@erols.com

In addition, Table 3 also reveals that machinery and transport equipment (SITC 7) has replaced miscellaneous manufactured articles (SITC 8) and become the leading exports of Taiwan. In 1997, machinery and transport equipment's share to total exports reached 52.42%, while the share of miscellaneous manufactured articles (SITC 8) dropped to only 14.09%. The changing trend

Table 3: Composition of Taiwan's Exports (by SITC Classification)

unit:%

YEAR	SITC 0 FOOD AND LIVE ANIMALS CHIEFLY FOR FOOD	SITC 1 BEVERAGES AND TOBACCO	SITC 2 CRUDE MATERIALS, INEDIBLES. EXCEPT FUELS	SITC 3 MINERAL FURLS, LUBRICANTS AND RELATED MATERIALS	SITC 4 ANIMAL AND VEGETABLE OILS, FATS AND WAXES
1980	8.55	0.07	1.67	1.49	0.02
1981	7.14	0.06	1.79	2.01	0.01
1982	6.89	0.06	2.10	1.90	0.01
1983	6.25	0.05	1.94	1.86	0.01
1984	5.43	0.03	1.64	1.82	0.03
1985	5.60	0.04	1.86	1.78	0.01
1986	5.97	0.03	1.62	1.04	0.01
1987	5.51	0.03	1.45	0.81	0.01
1988	4.90	0.05	1.68	1.62	0.01
1989	4.09	0.04	1.84	0.60	0.01
1990	3.97	0.03	1.75	0.60	0.03
1991	4.14	0.06	1.63	0.58	0.02
1992	3.76	0.06	1.59	0.65	0.02
1993	3.65	0.06	1.49	0.68	0.02
1994	3.62	0.07	1.65	0.61	0.03
1995	3.35	0.06	1.81	1.70	0.03
1996	3.06	0.03	1.64	0.90	0.04
1997	1.69	0.03	1.62	0.95	0.03

For additional analytical, marketing, investment and business opportunities information, please contact
Global Investment & Business Center, USA
(202) 546-2103. Fax: (202) 546-3275. E-mail: rusric@erols.com

SITC 5 CHEMICALS AND RELATED PRODUCTS, N.B.S.	SITC 6 MANUFACTURED GOODS CLASSIFIED CHIEFLY BY MATERIAL	SITC 7 MACHINERY AND TRANSPORT EQUIPMENT	SITC 8 MISCELLANEOUS MANUFACTURED ARTICLES	SITC 9 COMMODITIES AND TRANSACTIONS NOT CLASSIFIED ELSEWHERE
2.53	22.95	24.71	38.00	0.02
2.45	22.81	25.60	38.11	0.01
2.68	21.72	25.33	39.31	0.01
2.48	21.86	26.24	39.30	0.01
2.55	20.84	28.14	39.51	0.01
2.52	21.57	27.86	38.76	0.01
2.71	20.38	29.10	39.13	0.01
2.64	20.12	32.28	37.15	0.01
3.45	20.65	35.24	33.39	0.01
3.64	20.78	37.08	31.76	0.15
4.15	21.35	39.12	28.87	0.14
4.59	21.51	39.17	28.16	0.14
4.70	21.28	41.01	26.78	0.14
5.08	21.80	44.20	22.90	0.12
5.85	23.56	45.03	19.21	0.08
6.76	23.22	48.10	15.89	0.08
6.13	22.77	50.34	14.97	0.11
5.77	23.30	52.42	14.09	0.10

Source: Monthly Statistics of Exports and Imports, Ministry of Finance, ROC, various years

Table 4: Composition of Taiwan's Imports (by SITC classfication)

unit:%

	SITC 0	SITC1	SITC 2	SITC 3	SITC 4	SITC 7

YEAR	FOOD AND LIVE ANIMALS CHIEFLY FOR FOOD	BEVERAGES AND TOBACCO	CRUDE MATERIALS, INEDIBLE. EXCEPT FUELS	MINERAL FURLS, LUBRICANTS AND RELATED MATERIALS	ANIMAL AND VEGETABLE OILS, FATS AND WAXES	MACHINERY AND TRANSPROT EQUIPMENT
1980	6.10	0.52	13.69	25.49	0.24	27.92
1981	6.75	0.45	12.44	25.85	0.24	28.33
1982	6.57	0.63	12.79	24.34	0.34	27.96
1983	6.68	0.50	12.80	23.99	0.30	26.77
1984	6.37	0.47	13.47	21.51	0.29	28.41
1985	6.61	0.66	12.98	21.52	0.27	27.91
1986	5.51	0.43	13.19	13.01	0.23	32.40
1987	4.37	0.71	11.78	10.58	0.17	34.68
1988	4.17	0.53	9.93	7.95	0.14	32.92
1989	4.58	0.66	9.72	8.40	0.15	36.08
1990	4.62	0.54	8.12	10.88	0.18	36.96
1991	4.29	0.55	8.42	9.28	0.18	35.73
1992	4.15	0.66	7.08	7.79	0.18	39.32
1993	3.90	0.77	6.57	7.38	0.19	39.37
1994	4.05	0.81	6.68	6.92	0.20	39.04
1995	3.64	0.90	6.29	6.89	0.23	40.17
1996	4.09	0.89	6.00	8.06	0.21	39.51
1997	3.42	0.93	5.67	7.94	0.20	40.38

SITC 5	SITC 6	SITC 8	SITC 9
CHEMICALS AND RELATED PRODUCTS, N.B.S.	MANUFACTURED GOODS CLASSIFIED CHIEFLY BY MATERIAL	MISCELLANEOUS MANUFACTURED ARTICLES	COMMODITIES AND TRANSACTIONS NOT CLASSIFIED ELSEWHERE
9.45	12.25	4.16	0.18

**For additional analytical, marketing, investment and business opportunities information, please contact
Global Investment & Business Center, USA
(202) 546-2103. Fax: (202) 546-3275. E-mail: rusric@erols.com**

9.17	11.38	5.09	0.31
9.98	10.61	6.50	0.27
11.83	11.25	5.63	0.27
11.71	12.08	5.43	0.26
11.91	11.64	6.27	0.23
14.51	14.21	6.30	0.22
13.38	14.51	6.11	3.71
12.71	14.46	6.58	10.61
13.02	16.68	5.13	5.58
12.64	15.45	5.83	4.78
13.58	17.56	6.08	4.34
11.95	17.16	6.42	5.32
11.74	18.72	7.04	4.32
12.65	17.62	7.94	4.09
13.30	17.75	7.61	3.22
12.69	14.88	8.77	4.90
11.96	14.47	9.18	5.86

Source: as in Table 3

of Taiwan's exports also reflects the changing industrial structure of Taiwan. Textiles (mainly belonging to SITC 8) used to be the most important industry in Taiwan. In the early 1980 however, through the inflow of foreign capital, the electronics industry (mainly belonging to SITC 7) quickly became Taiwan's dominant industry and main exporter.

On the other hand, the composition of Taiwan's imports has not changed as much as that of exports. It can be seen from Table 4 that Taiwan's imports are more diversified than its exports. Although capital goods, such as machinery and transport equipment (SITC 7) are the most important category of imports, Taiwan also relies upon other raw materials and consumption goods, such as food and live animals (SITC 0), crude materials (SITC 2), mineral fuels (SITC 3), chemicals and related products (SITC 5), and other miscellaneous manufactured articles (SITC 8).

Furthermore, it appears that we can observe a triangular trading structure in which Taiwan imports much of its needed producer and capital goods from Japan while exporting its final manufactured products to the U.S. market. As Table 5 and Table 6 illustrate, due to historical and geographical reasons, Japan was formerly the largest trade partner of Taiwan. Exports to the U.S. increased rapidly in the 1970s and the U.S. replaced Japan as Taiwan's largest export market. This change was accompanied by a concomitant increase in imports from Japan. However, this triangle has become modified in recent years. Such a triangular trading relationship was manifested in the 1970s and 1980s, when Japan and the U.S. were responsible for some 60% of the total trade of Taiwan. Europe and East Asia (Hong Kong and ASEAN5) have since emerged as major trade partners of Taiwan. The expansion of the European market was a result of the concerted efforts of the Taiwan government and entrepreneurs to diversify Taiwan's markets. The accelerating growth of exports to East Asia can be ascribed to the rapidly growing direct trade investment of Taiwan to this

Table 5: Structure of Exports by Destination: Taiwan

Period	U.S.A.	Hong Kong	Japan	ASEAN5*	Europe	Others
1955	4.4	5.5	59.5	9.3	5.4	15.9
1960	11.5	12.6	37.7	8.7	6.0	23.5
1965	21.3	6.2	30.6	8.3	10.3	23.3
1970	38.1	9.2	14.6	8.2	10.1	19.8
1975	34.3	6.8	13.1	10.9	15.0	19.9
1980	34.1	7.8	11.0	8.0	15.8	23.3
1981	36.1	8.4	11.0	7.5	12.8	24.2
1982	39.4	7.0	10.7	7.6	11.7	23.6
1983	45.1	6.5	9.9	7.5	11.0	20.0
1984	48.8	6.9	10.5	6.2	10.1	17.5
1985	48.1	8.3	11.3	6.0	9.8	16.5
1986	47.7	7.3	11.4	5.3	12.0	16.3
1987	44.1	7.7	13.0	5.5	14.7	15.0
1988	38.7	9.2	14.5	6.7	16.3	14.6
1989	36.3	10.6	13.7	8.3	16.5	14.6
1990	32.4	12.7	12.4	10.1	18.2	14.2
1991	29.3	16.3	12.1	9.6	18.4	14.3
1992	28.9	18.9	10.9	10.1	17.1	14.1
1993	27.7	21.7	10.6	10.5	15.2	14.3
1994	26.2	22.9	11.0	11.4	13.9	14.6
1995	23.7	23.4	11.8	12.5	14.1	14.5
1996	23.2	23.1	11.8	12.2	14.6	15.1
1997	24.2	23.5	9.6	12.1	15.1	15.5

* ASEAN 5 refers to Malaysia, Thailand, Indonesia, Singapore and the Philippines.
Source: as in Table 1.

region. In 1992, Hong Kong surpassed Europe to become Taiwan's second largest export market.

In summary, the export-oriented strategy led to a prosperous Taiwan economy, narrowing the gap between developed countries and Taiwan. As

Table 6: Structure of Imports by Destination: Taiwan

Period	U.S.A.	Hong Kong	Japan	ASEAN5	Europe	Others
1955	47.5	1.5	30.5	3.7	7.0	9.8
1960	38.1	1.6	35.3	3.0	11.2	10.8
1965	31.7	1.0	39.8	4.9	8.5	14.1
1970	23.9	1.8	42.8	7.0	9.7	14.8
1975	27.8	1.3	30.6	6.2	12.7	21.4
1980	23.7	1.3	27.1	7.0	9.4	31.5
1981	24.1	1.5	28.0	6.3	9.4	30.7
1982	22.9	1.6	25.3	5.7	11.2	33.3
1983	23.0	1.5	27.5	5.7	11.2	31.1
1984	23.6	1.7	29.3	6.8	10.8	27.8
1985	22.5	1.6	27.6	7.1	12.2	29.0
1986	21.9	1.6	34.1	6.3	13.4	22.7
1987	26.2	2.2	33.8	6.3	15.1	16.4
1988	23.0	3.9	29.8	5.8	16.1	21.4
1989	23.0	4.2	30.7	6.0	16.0	20.1
1990	23.0	2.7	29.2	7.3	17.5	20.3
1991	22.4	3.1	30.0	7.8	15.9	20.8
1992	21.9	2.5	30.2	8.4	17.3	19.7
1993	21.7	2.2	30.1	8.8	17.6	19.6
1994	21.1	1.8	29.0	9.8	18.7	19.6
1995	20.1	1.8	29.2	9.9	18.1	20.9
1996	19.5	1.7	26.9	10.4	19.7	21.8
1997	20.3	1.7	25.4	11.3	18.9	22.4

ASEAN 5 refers to Malaysia, Thailand, Indonesia, Singapore and the Philippines.
Source: as in Table 1.

mentioned earlier, the trade structure of Taiwan has taken a triangular form. In the late 1980s, the triangular pattern shifted to a rectangular one in which East Asia had emerged as a new vertex. Moreover, significant industrial restructuring took place after 1987, changing Taiwan's export pattern further. In particular, direct foreign investment by Taiwan to Southeast Asia and mainland China has resulted in a reduction of exports to the United States and increased exports to Southeast Asia and mainland China.2 It is likely that such a transformation will continue as long as Taiwan's outward direct investment into these areas does not slow down.

Section III: Bilateral Trade between the U.S. and Taiwan

Table 7 shows the development of trade between the U.S. and Taiwan during the period 1961-1996. Bilateral trade has grown dramatically, from about US$132 million in 1960 to US$52,792 million in 1997, a nearly 400-fold increase over the period. This expeditious growth of total trade is due mainly to the sharp increase in exports from Taiwan to the U.S., which started to accelerate in the 1980s. On the other hand, Taiwan's imports from the U.S. did not expand as rapidly as its exports. According to Table 7, U.S. exports to Taiwan increased from US$113 million in 1960 to US$23,234 million in 1997, a 205-fold increase. During the same period, Taiwan's exports to the U.S. grew from US$19 million in 1960 to US$29,558 million in 1997, which represents a 6556-fold increase. Likewise, Table 7 also shows that the U.S. has continued to record large trade deficits, and this imbalance was getting larger before 1987. It has been pointed out that some of this trade imbalance can be attributed to the trade restrictions imposed by the the Taiwan government.

Taiwan's exports to the United States stagnated after 1987 because of the rapid and significant appreciation of its currency against the U.S. dollar. It was not until 1993 that Taiwan's exports to the United States regained their 1987 level. Taiwan imports from the United States, on the other hand, increased gradually during the same period. This resulted in a sharp decline in Taiwan's

Trade 7: Bilateral Trade Between the U.S. and Taiwan

Unit: million US$

	Exports to the U.S.	Imports from the U.S.	Total Trade Value	Trade Surplus of Taiwan
1960	19	113	132	-94
1965	96	176	272	-80
1970	564	364	928	200
1975	1,823	1,652	3,475	171
1980	6,760	4,673	11,433	2,087
1981	8,163	4,766	12,929	3,397
1982	8,759	4,563	13,322	4,196
1983	11,334	4,646	15,980	6,688
1984	14,868	5,042	19,910	9,826
1985	14,773	4,746	19,519	10,027
1986	19,014	5,433	24,447	13,581
1987	23,685	7,648	31,333	16,037
1988	23,467	13,007	36,474	10,460
1989	24,036	12,003	36,039	12,033
1990	21,746	12,612	34,358	9,134
1991	22,321	14,114	36,435	8,207
1992	23,572	15,771	39,343	7,801
1993	23,587	16,723	40,310	6,864

1994	24,338	18,043	42,381	6,295
1995	26,407	20,771	47,178	5,636
1996	26,886	19,972	46,838	6,894
1997	29,558	23,234	52,792	6,324

Source: as in Table 1.

trade surplus against the United States, falling, in 1993, to US$6,864 million, or only about half of the 1987 level.

In the meantime, export market concentration has also shifted from the United States since the 1980s (see Table 5). The U.S. market share has increased steadily since the 1970s, reaching a peak of 48.8% in 1984, after which it started to decline. In 1990, the U.S. market share dropped to 32.4%, while in 1997 its share was lowered further to 24.2%.

Another interesting feature of the two counties' bilateral trading relationship is the decline of the U.S. share of Taiwan's imports (Table 6). In 1960, the U.S. share of Taiwan's imports was 38.1%, dropping to 23.9% in 1970, and remaining fairly stable ever since. On the other hand, the Japanese share in Taiwan's imports has gradually expanded since 1970, supplanting the U.S. as Taiwan's importer.

The composition of Taiwan's exports to the U.S. and of U.S. exports to Taiwan are listed in Tables 8 and 9, respectively. We can see that Taiwan's exports to the U.S. are concentrated mainly in the area of machinery and transport equipment (SITC 7), miscellaneous manufactured articles (SITC 8) and commodities and transactions not classified elsewhere (SITC 9). As shown in Table 8, the degree of export concentration has been significant since the 1980s. Generally, Taiwan's exports to the U.S. demonstrate a quite similar pattern as its overall exports. The share of the top three products made up about 95% of Taiwan's total exports during the period. Among the top three products, machinery and transport equipment (SITC 7) has replaced miscellaneous manufactured articles (SITC 8) to become Taiwan's number one export to the United States.

As for Taiwan's imports from the United States, although machinery and transport equipment (SITC 7) is the dominant category, the concentration tendency is less significant. It should be noted that food and live animals chiefly for food (SITC 0) is also an important source of U.S. exports to Taiwan. This more or less reflects the fact that the Taiwan government has given preference to the United States in the area of the public procurement in

Table 8: The Structure of Taiwan's Exports to the U.S.

Unit: %

YEAR	SITC 0 FOOD AND LIVE ANIMALS CHIEFLY FOR FOOD	SITC 1 BEVERAGES AND TOBACCO	SITC 2 CRUDE MATERIALS INEDIBLE, EXCEPT FUELS	SITC 3 MINERAL FURLS, LUBRICANTS AND RELATED MATERIALS	SITC 4 ANIMAL AND VEGETABLE OILS, FATS AND WAXES	SITC5 CHEMICALS AND RELATED PRODUCTS, N.B.S.
1961	57.6	0	5.23	0.17	0	7.1
1965	30.75	0.01	5.47	0	0.02	3.83

Year						
1970	9.31	0.01	0.99	0	0	1.25
1975	9.89	0	0.56	0.17	0.03	0.83
1980	3.06	0	0.39	0	0.02	1.12
1981	2.56	0.01	0.28	0	0	1.25
1982	2.96	0.01	0.29	0.19	0	1.19
1983	2.45	0.01	0.23	0.18	0	1.43
1984	2.19	0.01	0.27	0.34	0	1.34
1985	2.09	0.01	0.29	0.26	0	1.19
1986	2.14	0.01	0.21	0.19	0	1.18
1987	2.13	0.01	0.23	0.05	0	1.03
1988	1.72	0.02	0.21	0.02	0	1.13
1989	1.44	0.01	0.35	0	0.01	1.43
1990	1.4	0.01	0.38	0	0.01	1.56
1991	1.3	0.03	0.39	0	0.01	1.74
1992	1.16	0.02	0.35	0	0.01	1.68
1993	1.15	0.03	0.43	0	0.01	1.62
1994	1.11	0.02	0.38	0	0.01	1.54
1995	1.01	0.02	0.4	0.01	0.01	1.41
1996	0.97	0.02	0.36	0	0.01	1.38

SITC 6	SITC 7	SITC 8	SITC 9
MANUFACTURED GOODS CLASSIFIED CHIEFLY BY MATERIAL	MACHINERY AND TRANSPORT EQUIPMENT	MISCEILANEOUS MANUFACTURED ARTICLES	COMMODITIES AND TRANSACTIONS NOT CLASSIFIED ELSEWHERE
19.67	0	8.83	1.39
32.29	4.91	21.51	1.24
15.02	26.58	45.79	1.07
12.26	26.7	47.95	1.61
15.57	27	52.42	0.42
16.17	29.28	50	0.45
14.51	29	51.34	0.5
15.65	30.44	48.99	0.62
15.36	32.36	47.63	0.51
15.61	32.11	47.5	0.95
15.7	31.88	47.71	0.98
15.55	34.19	45.88	0.92

For additional analytical, marketing, investment and business opportunities information, please contact Global Investment & Business Center, USA (202) 546-2103. Fax: (202) 546-3275. E-mail: rusric@erols.com

15.34	37.28	43.18	1.08
14.05	37.56	44.32	0.83
13.97	39.59	42.01	1.06
13.77	40.46	41.15	1.16
13.93	43.85	37.7	1.3
14.02	48.05	33.35	1.34
14.13	51.87	29.66	1.28
13.26	57.12	25.48	1.28
12.78	59.89	23.04	1.54

Table 9: The Structure of Taiwan's Imports from the U.S.

Unit: %

YEAR	SITC 0 FOOD AND LIVE ANIMALS CHIEFLY FOR FOOD	SITC 1 BEVERAGES AND TOBACCO	SITC 2 CRUDE MATERIALS INEDIBLE, EXCEPT FUELS	SITC 3 MINERAL FURLS, LUBRICANTS AND RELATED MATERIALS	SITC 4 ANIMAL AND VEGETABLE OILS, FATS AND WAXES	SITC5 CHEMICALS AND RELATED PRODUCTS, N.B.S.
1961	18.39	1.87	34.3	1.6	2.14	6.38
1965	15.67	2.31	32.75	1.65	2.8	7.79
1970	10.54	2.59	29.2	0.69	1.69	8.41
1975	11.71	1.79	26.36	0.48	0.65	8.1
1980	12.52	1.08	19.39	1.94	0.48	13.59
1981	14.26	1.67	17.06	5.12	0.28	12.91
1982	12.58	1.52	18.65	3.59	0.49	11.63
1983	16.08	1.31	19.71	4.84	0.4	16.43
1984	15.15	1.54	21.59	5.77	0.26	15.52
1985	13.73	1.53	20.41	3.97	0.3	13.07
1986	10.75	0.94	20.78	5.33	0.15	16.67
1987	8.57	2.27	18.95	4.94	0.11	17.22
1988	9.35	1.96	16.29	4.75	0.11	16.46
1989	9.2	1.58	12.34	4.77	0.11	15.88
1990	9	1.49	11.34	4.41	0.05	13.73
1991	9.04	1.29	11.01	3.47	0.03	14.43
1992	8.25	0.94	8.43	2.79	0.06	13.68
1993	8.06	0.83	8.17	2.88	0.06	12.84
1994	8.39	0.9	8.04	2.31	0.12	14.97
1995	8.65	0.71	9.23	1.63	0.15	15.93

For additional analytical, marketing, investment and business opportunities information, please contact
Global Investment & Business Center, USA
(202) 546-2103. Fax: (202) 546-3275. E-mail: rusric@erols.com

| 1996 | 11.16 | 0.73 | 9.47 | 2.19 | 0.08 | 13.64 |

SITC 6	SITC 7	SITC 8	SITC 9
MANUFACTURED GOODS CLASSIFIED CHIEFLY BY MATERIAL	MACHINERY AND TRANSPORT EQUIPMENT	MISCEILANEOUS MANUFACTURED ARTICLES	COMMODITIES AND TRANSACTIONS NOT CLASSIFIED ELSEWHERE
9.52	22.01	2.34	1.45
5.13	28.41	2.78	0.72
7.46	34.51	4.17	0.73
9.16	37.73	3.62	0.41
6.8	39.22	4.42	0.56
5.54	37.45	5.21	0.51
5.01	40.83	5.12	0.56
5.38	30.29	4.97	0.59
4.98	29.96	4.22	1
4.35	36.75	4.38	1.5
5.09	34.06	4.69	1.54
4.8	36.33	4.88	1.94
5.5	38.98	4.76	1.85
7	40.55	4.84	3.73
7.37	43.24	7.13	2.24
8.31	43.15	6.77	2.5
5.92	47.25	7.18	5.51
5.87	48.38	8.27	4.65
5.78	45.89	8.27	5.33
7.09	45.62	7.29	3.7
6.31	45.1	8.54	2.78

agricultural products of an effort to reduce the U.S. trade surplus which has been growing since the 1980s.

Section IV: Uneven Trade Bargaining between the U.S. and Taiwan

Trade relations are of central importance to the U.S.-Taiwan relationship. As the sixth-largest trading partner of the United States, Taiwan represents the second largest market for the U.S. in Asia (next to Japan), and provides significant capital investments wents as well as an expanding market for future growth. However, the close trade connections between the U.S. and Taiwan has also generated some problems and friction. This is, of course, due to the trade imbalance between the two countries. Given the success of its export-oriented policy and high dependence on the U.S. market, Taiwan has accumulated a tremendous trade surplus against the U.S. The U.S. government believes that such a trade imbalance is the result of the relatively closed Taiwan market. Accordingly, the U.S. has, since the 1970s, pushed Taiwan to open up its trade regime. Based on its security reliance and for other political reasons, Taiwan often has to accept proposals from the U.S. to open its markets.

Taiwan, then, is not only one of the most heavily trade-dependent countries in the world, but also has a considerably high degree of trade dependence on a single market, that is, the United States. By contrast, the United States is one of the least trade-dependent countries in the world and its dependency on trade with Taiwan is relatively small. The less dependent partners in a two-way trade relationship can always extract special treatment from the more dependent trade partner through trade bargaining. A trade war between the United States and Taiwan, should it occur, would inflict substantially heavier costs on Taiwan than on the United States.

This asymmetric trade relationship is further intensified by Taiwan's political reliance on the United States. The United States has long been the Taiwan's security guarantor. Even though official diplomatic relations were terminated in 1979, Taiwan has always been and is still virtually completely dependent on the United States for deterring threats from mainland China. The significance of this particular situation with respect to trade issues lies with the trade imbalance between the two sides. Consequently, the development of the trade relationship between Taiwan and the U.S. can be characterized as a "proposer-follower" type, where Taiwan has to some extent to meet US demands. In consideration of this situation, three issues come to light.

(i) Bilateral trade negotiations

In the second half of 1970s, Taiwan's trade surplus against the U.S. expanded at an unprecedented level. This fact has drawn considerable attention from the U.S. Congress and U.S. administrative departments. It is generally believed that the relatively protected Taiwan market is the most responsible for the limited amount of imports from the U.S. to Taiwan. Moreover, Taiwan has benefited from the Generalized System of Preferences (GSP) granted by the U.S.3 The situation was clearly jarring against the principle of fair trade as advocated by the U.S. Consequently, the United States aggressively began to seek greater market access to Taiwan. Bilateral trade negotiations started in 1978 under a U.S. initiative, and were to become the most important force shaping Taiwan's trade policy in the 1980s.

The U.S. set the agenda for the negotiations, focusing on market liberalization in Taiwan. Taiwan therefore had to justify its reasons for maintaining a protected market. The bargaining process was always one-sided, however with the U.S. as the dominant power. The reason why Taiwan continued to participate in these no-win negotiations year after year is obvious : the country had to maintain close ties with the U.S., both politically and economically, and it was essential to make minimum concessions to keep the U.S. satisfied and, at the same time, to lessen the harm and the adjustment costs of the domestic economy resulting from liberalization.4

The result of this uneven bargaining situation is clear: Taiwan has to accept most of the U.S. proposals. It can be seen from Table 10 that from 1978 to 1989, Taiwan and the U.S. undertook nine rounds of tariff negotiations. Overall, the U.S. has asked Taiwan to grant tariff concessions for 1,807 items, and Taiwan has granted concessions on 1,314 items in response. The overall ratio of acceptance was 73%. Particularly, in 1978, in the first round of negotiations, Taiwan has received all the U.S. requested products. While in 1986 and 1987, Taiwan accepted tariffs on 80% of the products listed by the United States.

Table 10: U.S.-Taiwan Tariff Negotiations

Year / Items	1978	1981	1984	1985	1986	1987 April	1987 August	1988	1989	Total
Items requested by the U.S.	339	49	109	174	71	66	267	174	558	1,807
Items accepted by Taiwan	339	28	59	112	58	62	239	51	336	1,314
Acceptance rate	100%	57%	54%	64%	82%	94%	90%	29%	66%	73%

Source: Ministry of Finance.

Such extensive concessions have inevitably aroused the dissatisfaction and even anger of domestic interest groups. Three groups generally put pressure on the government through legislative channels or by organizing demonstrations. As a result, the Taiwan government has sometimes hesitated on concessions, leading to trade confrontations with the U.S. and at home. The most serious domestic trade confrontation occurred in 1988, when the Taiwan government agreed to repeal the newly imposed import licensing controls on turkey meat. This decision led to demonstrations by chicken farmers which eventually turned into a bloody street riot on May 20, 1988. At this point, the Taiwan government wavered on its decision, and was immediately put on the 301 trade retaliation list by the United States, bringing the dispute into the international arena. In the end the Taiwan government was forced to meet U.S. demands and lifted the import restrictions.

(ii) Intellectual Property Rights

Intellectual Property Right (IPR) is another important issue characterizing the US-Taiwan trade relationship. Strengthening the protection of American intellectual property rights around the world through multilateral and bilateral negotiations has been at the forefront of the U.S. trade agenda since the 1980s. The importance of IPR was further increased after the enactment of the 1998 U.S. Omnibus Trade and Competitiveness Act, which included a special provision (the so-called Special 301) which would target trade partners failing to respect IPR.

Like other developing countries, Taiwan was notorious for commodity counterfeiting and other kinds of IPR abuse. Such violations of IPR were tolerated by the United States when Taiwan was an underdeveloped economy. However, the United States began to pay attention to Taiwan's infringement of IPR when Taiwan's trade surplus surged in the early 1980s. The United States perceived that the rapidly increasing trade surplus of Taiwan was in part attributable to the

Taiwan's failure to protect IPR. The United States, therefore began to pressure Taiwan to implement IPR protection measures.

The subjects covered in the U.S.-Taiwan IPR negotiations were wide-ranging. The U.S. first concern was commodity counterfeiting and patents, later shifting its attentions to textbook, computer software, motion picture, videotape and compact disk copyright issues. In response, the Taiwan government amended its relevant laws and regulations and also established the National Anti-counterfeiting Committee in order to protect IPR. The concerted efforts by the Taiwan government have considerably reduced the degree of IPR abuse in Taiwan. Given the complex nature of IPR, however, Taiwan has remained on the U.S. Special 301 list for most of the years between 1989 and 1998

(iii) The Exchange Rate

The issue of the exchange rate has also played an important role in U.S.-Taiwan trade relations. Compared to tariffs and non-tariff barriers, the exchange rate was not designed for specific industries, but the volatility of the exchange rate has a more profound impact on the domestic economy.

In the second half of the 1980s, Taiwan's trade surplus with the U.S. increased significantly. In reaction, in addition to forcing Taiwan to open its markets, the U.S. government also expressed concern about Taiwan's exchange rate policy. Several exchange rate negotiations have taken place, The U.S. government believes that the New Taiwan dollar is significantly undervalued and has urged monetary authorities to appreciate the value of the NT dollar accordingly. Taiwan's monetary authorities responded to U.S. pressure, and the NT dollar consequently appreciated more than 40% from 1985 to 1987.

The sharp appreciation of the NT dollar, together with rapidly rising wages and land prices, environmental and labor disputes, and a severe shortage of blue-collar workers, caused Taiwan's overseas direct investment to increase in leaps and bounds. Many labor intensive industries have moved their production facilities abroad. Taiwan's foreign direct investment has mainly been concentrated in Southeast Asian countries, later shifting to mainland China. As a result of these massive investments, Taiwan's trade structure has shifted toward the Asian region, and this has in turn led to a change in Taiwan's domestic industrial structure.

In summary, because of a decline in its hegemonic power, the United States has aggressively sought greater global market liberalization in order to reduce its huge trade deficit and to uphold the concept of fair trade. U.S.-Taiwan trade negotiations were initiated by the United States as a means of achieving this goal.

The nature of these negotiations is asymmetric. From the prospective of the United States, given its dominant bargaining position, it was able to fulfill most of its objectives through these negotiations. Taiwan's experience in negotiating with the United States, meanwhile, indicates that a small country with a weak bargaining position has great difficulty defending its domestic market. As a result, Taiwan was forced to open its domestic market to a considerable extent. This unexpected degree of liberalization has brought about several consequences.

First, the major accomplishment of U.S.-Taiwan negotiations is that the overall level of Taiwan's tariffs has been substantially reduced. By 1990, Taiwan's tariff rate levels were already close to those found in advanced industrialized countries, even though Taiwan had not undergone tariff negotiations through multilateral organizations (for example, GATT or WTO). In this regard, U.S. pressure helped improve the efficiency of Taiwan's markets in the long run.

Secondly, U.S.-Taiwan bilateral trade negotiations strengthened Taiwan's commitment to protecting intellectual property rights and also facilitated the modernization of the administration and enforcement of IPR. This progress has certainly led to an improvement in Taiwan's international reputation on IPR.

Unfortunately, U.S.-Taiwan trade negotiations have also generated some negative side effects. The most noticeable of these is related to the favorable trade conditions offered to the U.S. but not to other countries. As we have discussed, during U.S.-Taiwan negotiations, certain concessions made by the Taiwan government were only applicable to the United States and were not applicable at a multilateral level. The United States therefore enjoys a preferential position in Taiwan's import market. This phenomenon is particularly prevalent in the agricultural and financial sectors. When Taiwan entered into the multilateral level of negotiations (WTO and APEC) in 1990s, U.S. preferential treatment appeared to be a major problem for Taiwan. This is because concessions on a Most-Favored-Nation basis increase the adjustment costs of domestic industry, and this issue has become a major challenge for Taiwan trade negotiators.

Section V: Conclusion

This paper analyzes U.S.-Taiwan trade relations. It is generally assumed that Taiwan has benefited from the U.S. during the course of its development. In the early years, of the development of the Taiwan economy, U.S. aid was an important source of disposable domestic savings.5 Subsequently, when Taiwan shifted from import substitution to export promotion policy, the U.S. market served as a sponge for Taiwan's exports. Accordingly, trade relations intensified, and Taiwan built up a massive trade surplus to the dissatisfaction of the U.S. The U.S. government therefore started to pressure Taiwan to allow greater market access and to undertake liberalization. Through bilateral negotiation, Taiwan's market was significantly liberalized, and this has, on occasion, led to trade disputes and even confrontations between the U.S. and Taiwan.

In recent years, as the mainland China economy has undergone substantial transformation and as the Taiwan government has gradually relaxed its policy towards mainland China, bilateral trade between these two regions has began to flourish. The diversion of exports from the U.S. to mainland China has not undermined the importance of the U.S. to Taiwan's economy, however. Although Taiwanese firms have made massive investment in Southeast Asia and mainland China since late the 1980s, the U.S. market remains the most important export destination for these firms. In this regard, it is expected that the US and Taiwan will continue to maintain an intensive trade as well as economic relationship in the future.

Moreover, Taiwan has over recent years made sterling efforts to join multilateral economic and trade organizations. In January 1990, Taiwan filed an application to join the GATT, and at present it enjoys observer status at the WTO. In November 1991, Taiwan was admitted to APEC. The main reason behind Taiwan's eagerness to join various multilateral international organizations is not only a desire to increase its political visibility in the international arena, but also a desire to forge trade initiatives and commitments on a multilateral basis in order that it may start to meet the standards of free and fair trade from the viewpoint of the international community.

References

Baldwin, Robert E., T.J. Chen, and Nelson Douglas, eds. (1995), Political Economy of U.S.-Taiwan Trade, The University of Michigan Press.
Chen, T.J, ed. (1998), Taiwanese Firms in Southeast Asia Networking Across Borders, Edward Elgar, U.K.

Jacoby, Neil H.(1966), U.S. Aid to Taiwan: A Study of Foreign Aid, Self Help, and Development, New York: Frederick A. Praeger Publishers.
Kuo, Shirley W.Y. (1983), The Taiwan Economy in Transition, Boulder Westview Press.
, Economic Policies: The Taiwan Experience 1945-1995, Hwa-Tai Publishing Company of Taiwan.
1 For more details regarding the contribution of exports to economic development in Taiwan, see Kuo (1983).
2 See Chen, ed. (1998).
3 In 1989, along with Korea, Hong Kong and Singapore, Taiwan graduated from the U.S. GSP.
4 See Baldwin, Chen and Nelson, eds (1995), ch4.
5 See Jacoby (1966) and Kuo

THE NATIONAL COMMITTEE ON AMERICAN FOREIGN POLICY'S PROJECT ON U.S.-CHINA POLICY AND CROSS-STRAIT RELATIONS[8]

In the aftermath of the Cold War, the United States has a huge stake in the maintenance of peace and stability in the East Asia/Pacific region. Yet the unresolved "Taiwan problem," if not wisely managed on all sides could lead to a new cold war in the region and a growing danger of major military conflict between China and Taiwan that will almost certainly involve the United States and Japan as well.

The dangers inherent in the situation were clearly revealed in the events of 1995-96 when, after a visit to the United States by Taiwan's president Lee Teng-hui, a visit interpreted by Beijing as one of a series of steps taken by the United States that violated Washington's "one China" policy, Beijing launched a series of military exercises and missiles tests in the waters off Taiwan. The United States responded by sending two aircraft carriers to the region, a development that led to the most serious military confrontation between the United States and China in a quarter century. U.S.-China and China-Taiwan relations have improved somewhat in the four years that have passed since this crisis, but the underlying dangers and dilemmas remain.

The future status of Taiwan still stands as the single most important, most difficult, and most dangerous issue in U.S.-China relations and there are as yet few signs that the PRC and Taiwan, even after a resumption of their quasi-official dialogue broken off in the aftermath of the crisis, are close to a mutual accommodation that would provide a basis for a new kind of political relationship that would reassociate Taiwan with the mainland on terms acceptable to both.

Although the U.S. government is extremely worried about the volatile relationship between Beijing and Taipei, it has made it clear that it has no intention of mediating the dispute between them and that any arrangements concluded between the two parties should be on a mutually acceptable basis. Nevertheless, the United States has too much at stake in the dispute between Beijing and Taipei to simply stand by and remain passive about trends that could drift toward a dangerous new crisis.

It is for this reason that private organizations such as the National Committee on American Foreign Policy can be quite helpful. The Committee has been sponsoring a Roundtable on U.S.-China Policy and Cross-Strait Relations for the past two years. We believe that the NCAFP, as well as other private organizations and individuals in the United States, can play an important role in facilitating dialogue between Beijing and Taipei, and in encouraging some kind of modus vivendi between them. The participants in the NCAFP's roundtable have been a small group of

---

[8] By Donald S. Zagoria Institute of European and American Studies Academia Sinica, Taipei, Taiwan

scholars, former government officials, and influential individuals from the United States, China and Taiwan. There have been four meetings of the roundtable, all in New York City, and a fifth meeting will take place in June l999.

To encourage a candid exchange of views, the roundtable has not been open to the press and all the participants have been assured that the proceedings are not for attribution, unless otherwise indicated. A summary of the discussions has been made available to the participants and to a few policy makers in all three governments. In preparing for the roundtables, participants have been briefed by government officials and some government officials have been invited to address the roundtables and to answer questions. But the NCAFP is a private organization and it does not speak for the American government.

In sum, the roundtables have sought to encourage frank exchanges among the participants and to provide a sheltered arena in which ideas can be aired and through which trust can be nurtured. The NCAFP has no illusions about the difficulties involved in finding solutions to the problems and it may not even be possible to find such solutions, but we believe that the act of seeking common ground is itself constructive and that such a dialogue is bound to clarify the situation and to keep all three sides well informed about the perspectives of the other two. We also believe that the roundtable proceedings are taken very seriously by all three governments and we have been told by one high-ranking American official that the NCAFP roundtable is "the most important (unofficial) forum for cross-strait dialogue."

Finally, it is our intention to make public an interim report on the cross-strait issue sometime in the fall of 1999. This report will analyze the policies and perceptions of all three sides -- Beijing, Taipei and Washington -- and it will offer some policy recommendations for easing tensions and increasing stability.

In the essay that follows, I will first discuss some of the recent developments in cross-strait relations; then I will highlight what seem to be the strategies of the two sides that have been developed to deal with each other. I will close with some comments on the U.S. role and some suggestions for policy makers. I would like to make clear that although I draw on the insights of all the participants in the roundtables the views that I express are my own and do not necessarily reflect the views of other participants or of the U.S. government.

Recent Developments in Cross-Strait Relations

The two senior negotiators, Koo Chen-fu from Taiwan and Wang Dao-han from China, met in China in mid-October 1998 and Wang is scheduled to pay a return visit to Taipei sometime in the fall of 1999. As a result of the resumption of these talks, which were suspended following the crisis of 1995-96, the atmosphere of cross-strait relations has improved somewhat. But the two sides are still divided on fundamental political issues, especially the vexed issue of reunification. Nor can the two sides agree an how to define "one China" and there remains a deep and pervasive sense of mutual mistrust. Beijing believes that Taiwan is drifting towards independence. Taiwan believes that mainland China is seeking to strangle it diplomatically by seeking to cut off its remaining diplomatic ties and its entry into international organizations. Finally, the military situation in the Taiwan Strait is taking a turn for the worse. According to a recent Pentagon report, Beijing is stationing 150 to 200 missiles in southern China opposite Taiwan and it is planning to increase that number to 650 over the next few years. Beijing evidently believes that by threatening Taiwan with missiles, it is deterring Taiwan from moving towards independence. All this suggests that relations between China and Taiwan are unstable and that mainland China's political and strategic outlook is beginning to harden.

What accounts for this instability? The basic problem is that Beijing views Taiwan as a renegade province of China that, under the leadership of Taiwan's President Lee Teng-hui, is moving increasingly towards independence even while it continues to pay lip service to the principle of "one-China." The PRC says that the eventual reunification of Taiwan with the mainland should take place in accordance with its "one country, two systems" formula, a formula that has virtually no takers in Taiwan. And China also condemns Taipei's activities at broadening its international recognition, including its bid to join the United Nations, as part and parcel of its campaign to establish its independence from the mainland. Beijing's suspicions that Taipei is moving towards separatism are reenforced by some of the statements of the tough-talking KMT president of Taiwan and other Taiwanese officials who assert that Taiwan is already an independent, sovereign state even though it has no intention of declaring de jure independence Beijing's suspicions are also heightened by the fact that while the Taiwanese are keen to talk to the mainland about practical issues such as illegal immigration and investment, they are reluctant to enter into dialogue about the major political issues.

The KMT government of Taiwan insists that it cannot enter such negotiations until the PRC accepts the reality that China is a divided nation under two separate political entities and begins to deal with Taiwan on an equal basis and not as a mere renegade province.

Lying at the heart of the matter is the basic issue of sovereignty. For Beijing there is no such issue. In Beijing's view, there is only one China, that China is the PRC, and Taiwan is part of the PRC.

Taiwan, however, is reluctant to enter into any negotiations that will jeopardize its own claim to be a sovereign entity. On this basic matter, both the ruling Kuomintang (KMT) party and the main opposition Democratic Progressive Party (DPP) are in agreement. The DPP goes even further in the direction of independence than the KMT. The DPP charter calls for an independent "Republic of Taiwan" and the popular former mayor of Taipei, Chen Shui~bian, who is likely to be the DPP candidate for president in the elections scheduled for the year 2000, has recently issued a three point program in which he says that Taiwan is "an independent, sovereign state independent of the PRC and not part of the PRC" and that Taiwan and the PRC are two "mutually exclusive and independent ethnic Chinese states." Moreover says Chen, in a veiled warning to the KMT, any change in the status quo of Taiwan must be approved by the Taiwanese people and not decided by one political party or leader unilaterally. In short, the DPP will oppose any negotiations by the KMT with Beijing on reunification, even if the KMT were so inclined to enter into such negotiations.

In sum, Beijing and Taipei have taken up what would seem to be completely irreconcilable positions on the basic issues of sovereignty and reunification. Beijing insists that Taiwan is a part of China and that the matter of reunification cannot be postponed indefinitely, especially now that Hong Kong and Macao have been recovered. The KMT government of Taiwan, for its part, while not ruling out the eventual possibility of reunification, insists that this issue must await the day when China becomes a democracy and achieves a much higher standard of living than it has now. And the DPP opposition party in Taiwan insists that there is no question of reunification with mainland China because Taiwan and the PRC are two "mutually exclusive and independent states."

These fundamental political differences, moreover, strike highly emotional chords on both sides. The PRC cannot accept a permanent separation of Taiwan that appears to violate China's sovereignty and territorial integrity. China's modern history of being victimized by imperialist powers, including Japan which seized Taiwan from China in the late nineteenth century, makes these issues ones of extraordinary sensitivity. But the majority of the people of Taiwan have a strong sense of Taiwanese identity; Taiwan's government and opposition views its long history of independent rule since 1949 as justifying its claim to being a sovereign entity; and the majority of the people in Taiwan reject a posture of subordination to the PRC central government.

Under such circumstances, the potential for misunderstanding and miscalculation is very high. And there have already been serious miscalculations on both sides. On the Taiwan side, President Lee Teng-hui and some of his advisors now concede that the PRC reaction to Lee's visit to Cornell in 1995 -- the visit that triggered the military crisis during the following year and a half -- was stronger than they anticipated. On the Beijing side, many PRC leaders, especially in the military, appear to believe that increasing military pressure on Taiwan will deter the independence movement on the island. Yet while there may be a germ of truth in this idea, the fact is that public opinion polls on Taiwan show convincingly that, as a result of that pressure, few Taiwanese any longer have confidence and trust in the PRC. Given the absence of trust, it is difficult to imagine that a substantial number of Taiwanese would be in favor of reunification at any time in the foreseeable future.

The PRC's recent missile buildup along the coast opposite Taiwan is likely to increase the potential for miscalculation. Taiwan may react to the PRC's missile buildup by seeking technology and weapons systems from the United States in order to improve its missile defense systems and Taiwan may seek to engage the United States closer in the defense of the island. If the United States goes along with these requests at some point it is likely to convince the suspicious PRC that it is reactivating the U.S.-Taiwan defense relationship which was terminated when the United States recognized the PRC in 1979. Such developments in all likelihood would be met with an escalation in tension between the PRC and Taiwan and between the PRC and the United States.

PRC and Taiwan Strategies for Dealing with Cross-Strait Relations 2

In recent years, both the PRC and Taiwan have developed what seem to be comprehensive strategies for dealing with each other and with the United States. The PRC strategy is designed to deter Taiwan from seeking independence, to enlist U.S. support in this effort and to encourage Taiwan to enter into negotiations with the mainland on reunification. The PRC strategy contains the following elements:

1) induce the United States, Japan and Russia to commit themselves to the PRC's "one-China" policy in order to ensure that Taiwan cannot hope realistically to gain support for de jure independence;

2) gradually reduce the number of states that recognize Taipei (it is now 28) and exclude Taiwan from international organizations;

3) develop a military posture, including the deployment of mobile missiles opposite Taiwan, that reminds the Taiwanese people that China has the capabilities to inflict heavy costs on Taiwan for pursuing an independent course;

4) seek to increase trade and investment relations with Taiwan so that the Taiwan business community develop an ever larger stake in cooperative relations with the mainland;

5) increase Taiwan's sense of insecurity by working to exclude it from the region of coverage of the U.S.-Japan security relationship.

For its part, Taipei has also developed a comprehensive strategy for dealing with the PRC and Washington. That strategy includes the following elements.

1) seek practical talks with Beijing on issues such as trade and investment, illegal immigrants, fishing disputes, cultural exchanges, etc., while avoiding any discussion of basic political issues that involve the questions of sovereignty or reunification; 2) get Beijing to stop treating Taipei as a political subordinate and to recognize it as a political equal;

3) talk about eventual reunification but fashion preconditions such as democracy and equalization of wealth that are sufficiently remote so as to nullify any possibility for reunification for a very long time;

4) maintain a vigorous but limited economic relationship with the PRC so that China will be reluctant to antagonize the Taiwan business community, but at the same time ensure that Taiwan's economy does not become excessively dependent on trade with the mainland;

5) make it clear to the U.S. executive branch that if it goes too far in accommodating PRC concerns, Taipei can and will play the "Congress card";

6) use the PRC's missile buildup to justify more weapons purchases from the United States and to get the United States progressively more involved in the island's security;

7) continue to try to expand Taiwan's diplomatic relations and to enter international organizations, including the United Nations and the World Trade Organization.

In sum, the existing status quo is highly unstable. Although the cross-strait dialogue has resumed, there is no agreement on the fundamental issues that divide the two sides and there is a high degree of mutual suspicion.

The Role of the United States

As a result of history, the United States is inextricably involved in the dispute between Beijing and Taipei. Until 1979, when the United States officially recognized Beijing as the legitimate government of China and ceased recognition of Taiwan, the United States had a defense treaty with Taiwan and the island state was one of its most loyal allies during the Cold War against communism. After 1979, the United States developed an unofficial relationship with Taiwan that was codified in the Taiwan Relations Act which was passed by the U.S. Congress and enshrined in U.S. domestic law.

This unique piece of legislation dictates that the United States has a vital stake in the security of Taiwan and in a peaceful resolution of the impasse between the mainland and Taiwan. It also mandates that the United States continue to sell "defensive arms" to Taiwan. This legislation appears to conflict with the Communiqué of 1982 with the PRC which calls for a steady reduction in U.S. arms sales to Taiwan, but the contradictions in these documents have never been reconciled. The. United States now manages its relations with Taiwan through an "unofficial" organization called the American Institute on Taiwan which has offices both in Taipei and in Washington. Over the years while maneuvering in the framework which includes both the TRA and the Three Communiqués, the United States has managed to develop a relatively cooperative relationship with Beijing while continuing to maintain an equally cooperative relationship with Taiwan. U.S. trade with both mainland China and with Taiwan has flourished and Taiwan has shed its authoritarian past and become a thriving free-market democracy with a free press, a popularly elected president and legislature, and several opposition parties. Six American presidents have managed the ambiguities inherent in this triangular relationship to the considerable advantage of all three sides. Still, the uncertainties remain. Among the most prominent of these are the following. What will be the future status of Taiwan? Will it reunify with the mainland? Will it simply maintain its existing ambiguous status as a de facto state which does not declare de jure independence? Or will it at some time in the future formally declare independence? The PRC has on numerous occasions declared that if Taiwan does formally declare independence, it will go to war. And the PRC has never given up the right to use force in order to recover what it regards as its rightful territory. Meanwhile with U.S. assistance Taiwan has developed a substantial modern army and air force designed to deter the PRC.

Although it is debatable whether Taiwan in and of itself is of vital strategic significance to the United States (the U.S. Joint Chiefs were prepared to abandon Taiwan in 1949 after the Chinese Communists took control of the mainland), there can be little doubt but that the United States now has a substantial stake in a peaceful resolution of the differences between Beijing and Taipei. If Beijing were to forcefully subjugate Taiwan in contravention of U.S. insistence that the dispute must be resolved peacefully, this fact would have a disastrous impact on the U.S. alliance system in East Asia, especially the key security relationship with Japan.

To put it another way, all of America's interests in East Asia -- and they are substantial -- would be promoted by a peaceful resolution of the differences between Taipei and Beijing. And all of America's interests in East Asia would by jeopardized by a military conflict between the two. That is why, in recent years, the United States has seen its role in the cross-strait issue as: deterring the use of force by the PRC; warning Taiwan against moving toward de jure independence; and urging both parties to enter into a meaningful dialogue that could eventually lead to a mutually acceptable settlement.

Although there has been much debate among American academics about whether or not President Clinton's recent statement on the "Three No's" when he visited China in late June 1998, constituted a change in policy on the cross-strait issue, subsequent developments suggest that this was not the case. The President's statement in China, along with other developments such as the beginning of visits by former Secretary of Defense William Perry to the PRC and Taiwan, have to be assessed against the background of the 1995-96 Taiwan Strait military confrontation. As a result of that crisis, during which the United States sent two aircraft carriers to the waters near. Taiwan, many American academics, members of Congress, and some key policy makers concluded that the Taiwan Strait was one place in East Asia -- along with the Korean peninsula -- where events could easily spin out of control. There was also lingering resentment, especially in the U.S. State Department that Taiwan had not been mindful of American interests in the first half of 1994 when it had gone around the executive branch and played the "Congress card" to obtain a visa for President Lee Teng-hui to visit Cornell University.

Put bluntly, the U.S. administration, which initially said it was not going to grant a visa to President Lee and so informed Beijing, was pushed down a road it preferred not to have traveled. The sense of festering resentment fed into an increasing sense of danger. And many in the U.S. government were intent on reminding Taiwan that sending U.S. aircraft carriers to the seas off Taiwan in March 1996 was not intended to constitute a blank security check for Taipei to engage in provocative behavior towards Beijing that would destabilize the situation and draw in the United States unnecessarily. In sum, Taiwanese officials and politicians need to consider U.S. interests, as well as their own.

But it should be noted that President William J. Clinton, although he publicly endorsed the "Three Nos" during his visit to China, did not give in to the most extensive set of Chinese demands vis-à-vis Taiwan. There was no "fourth communiqué," no joint statement, no agreement on a timetable for reducing arms sales to Taiwan, and no commitment as to whether the United States will eventually provide theater missile defense to Taiwan. Also the President specifically referred to the Taiwan Relations Act while in China, the first time that this has been done.

Also, in November 1998, Secretary of Energy Bill Richardson traveled to Taipei despite PRC objections to any cabinet level visit to the island. The trip had several objectives, one of which was to reassure those in Congress who wondered whether American policy was changing fundamentally following President Clinton's visit to China. Richardson's trip was a signal by the American government that American policy was not changing in any fundamental way.

In short, there has been no change in official U.S. policy on the cross-strait issue. The United States is committed to a peaceful resolution; it welcomes the resumption of the cross-strait dialogue; and it seeks to reconcile its commitments as contained in the three communiqués with the PRC and the legal requirements imposed by the Taiwan Relations Act. On the other hand, what has changed is the growing awareness in the U.S. administration, Congress and American policy circles that the cross-strait situation is inherently unstable and extremely dangerous and that it needs to be managed carefully.

Reducing Tensions: Some Suggestions

Suggestions for reducing tension between the PRC and Taiwan and for bringing greater stability to cross-strait relations can be divided into five categories: "small steps" to build trust; military "confidence building measures (CBMs)" to reduce the risk of accidental conflict; exploiting economic interdependence; "interim agreements" of various kinds designed to freeze the status quo for a long period of time; and suggestions for reassociating mainland China and Taiwan in a "confederation" or "commonwealth." I will discuss each of these in turn.

Small Steps

The "small step" approach would probably be the easiest way to begin easing tensions. According to this idea, there are now on the table between the mainland and Taiwan a number of "practical" issues which demand resolution. These include the problems of illegal immigrants, fisheries disputes and hijacking, and the potential for agricultural cooperation. The two sides are already close to agreement on an accord to stop hijacking and the PRC has responded positively to an overture by Taiwan to increase agricultural cooperation. Another area in which the mainland and Taiwan might find common ground is in the realm of institutionalizing cross-strait dialogue. Taiwan's President Lee Teng-hui, in a speech to the National Unification Council on April 8, called on the two sides of the Taiwan Strait to establish a "mechanism for peace and stability through institutionalized consultations." Some PRC analysts have expressed similar sentiments. At a recent meeting of the NCAFP Roundtable, one PRC analyst suggested that the Straits Exchange Foundation (SEF) and the Association for Relations Across the Taiwan Strait (ARATS) establish working subcommittees to explore difficult issues. How to institutionalize the cross-strait dialogue would seem to be a useful topic of discussion for the two sides when Wang Dao-han visits Taiwan this fall.

Military CBMs

A number of analysts also have recently suggested a variety of military "confidence building measures" which would include; establishing a "hot line" between Beijing and Taipei, prenotification of military exercises, invitations to the military on the other side of the Strait to attend military exercises, etc. Some believe that the United States should encourage the establishment of a military buffer zone between Taiwan and the PRC in order to avoid incidents in the air and at sea. Taiwan is reportedly now studying a variety of such ideas.

The Importance of Economic Interdependence

Yet another promising path towards easing tension between the two sides would be to exploit the growing economic interdependence between Taiwan and the PRC.

One of the most critical factors in Taiwan-PRC relations in future years is bound to be the growing trade and investment links between the two sides of the Taiwan Strait. Taiwan is mainland China's third largest outside investor, having pumped around $40 billion into the mainland economy. About half of Taiwan's listed companies now have investments on the mainland and Taiwan businessmen are finding the mainland even more attractive after suffering huge losses in Southeast Asia due to the economic crisis of recent years. Trade relations are also growing despite the absence of direct trade links. Analysts attribute more than seventy percent of the growth in the U.S. trade deficit with mainland China to exports from mainland China by Taiwanese firms operating there.

But Taiwan's increasingly intimate economic relations with the mainland are a cause of concern for the Taiwan government. Taipei officials fear that Beijing could use growing economic links between the two sides of the Strait as political leverage to force the opening of direct cross-strait trade and communication links which would then increase even more the degree of Taiwanese dependence on the mainland economy. For Taipei, the limiting of direct cross-strait trade and communications links is an important bargaining chip in its struggle to attain equal political status at the negotiation table and is not to be abandoned lightly.

The Taipei government's "go slow" policy on economic relations with the mainland has, however, run into opposition from certain important sectors of the Taiwan business community. The chairman of the Formosa Plastics Group, Taiwan's largest business conglomerate, openly opposes the government's "go slow" policy. This is an indication that some sectors of the Taiwan business community find the huge potential of the mainland market an alluring and almost irresistible attraction if the Taiwan economy is to remain competitive and to transform itself into a technology-intensive island. (See King Rong-yung, "New Models Eyed as Asia Struggles in Difficult Times," The Free China Journal, April 1, 1999).

All this raises the question of whether Taiwan might find it advantageous to ease restriction on investment into the mainland, which are now limited to projects involving less than $50 million in capital, in exchange for some political quid pro quos from the mainland. For example, there have been intermittent proposals from both sides for an agreement on cessation of hostilities and the mainland is very anxious to reach such an agreement. Might it not be in Taiwan's interest to trade an easing of restrictions on its "go slow" policy in exchange for a mutually acceptable agreement on cessation of hostilities?

Interim Arrangements

Some suggestions for stabilizing cross-strait relations are more ambitious. Recently, several American scholars have suggested a variety of interim agreements to stabilize the cross-strait situation for a long period of time. Joseph Nye, former Assistant Secretary of Defense for International Security Affairs, writing in the Washington Post of March 8, 1998, stressed three points which he claimed could bridge the gap between Beijing and Taipei. Nye said:

1) The United States should state plainly that its policy is "one China" and no use of force. In addition the United States should say that if Taiwan were to declare independence the United States would not recognize or defend it. Moreover the United States should work hard to discourage other countries from recognizing Taiwan's independence. At the same time the United States would repeat that it will not accept the use of force, since nothing would change as the result of any abortive declaration of independence by Taiwan;

2) the PRC should say that if Taiwan decisively rejected the idea of declaring independence, Beijing would not oppose the idea of more international living space for Taiwan and would broaden the "one country, two systems" formula to "one country, three systems," thereby recognizing the differences between Hong Kong and Taiwan.

3) Taipei would explicitly express its decision to foreswear any steps towards independence, intensify the cross-strait dialogue and stimulate greater flows of investment and exchanges of people across the Strait.

Still another proposal for an "interim agreement" between the two sides was advanced by Dr. Kenneth Lieberthal in February 1998. Dr. Lieberthal. who is now the National Security Council's senior advisor on Asia, was a professor of government at the University of Michigan when he advanced his ideas publicly in Taiwan. These ideas included the following:

1) The two sides would agree to establish an interim arrangement to govern the cross-strait situation for a period of decades, at the end of which time, and on a negotiated date, formal talks to discuss political unification of the country would begin. The interim period might be about fifty years.

2) The two sides would agree that during this interim period both Taiwan and the PRC exist within "one China" but that the relationship between them would not be that between sovereign entities or between a central government and a province.

3) Taiwan would explicitly agree that it is a part of China and that it will not claim de jure independence.

4) The PRC would explicitly agree not to use force against Taiwan.

5) The two sides would agree that for the interim period each side will be in charge of its domestic affairs and foreign policy.

6) The two sides would agree to undertake regular talks at a high political level to reduce areas of conflict and to enhance mutual confidence.

7) The two sides could discuss the possibility of further reducing tension by changing the names of the PRC to "China" and changing the name of the Republic of China to "Taiwan, China."

There are a number of problems with proposals such as Nye's and Lieberthal's. First, it seems unlikely that the Taiwan government will agree to a formulation that there is only one China and that Taiwan is part of it. Both the KMT and the DPP now say that Taiwan is already an independent sovereign entity and that the sovereignty issue should not be part of any official negotiation with the PRC. It is highly unlikely that any Taiwanese government will renounce its claim to sovereignty. Second, domestic politics both in Taiwan and the PRC could seriously complicate any effort to reach such an agreement. On Taiwan, both the KMT and the DPP would have to agree to such an arrangement so that it would not become a political football during elections. And on the mainland, too, it might be extremely difficult for any Chinese leader to agree to put off a resolution of the Taiwan issue for fifty years, particularly now that President Jiang Zemin has said that this issue cannot be postponed indefinitely. Third, negotiations between the PRC and Taiwan are still in a very early stage and it is doubtful that those negotiations have reached the stage where the two sides could talk seriously about such fundamental issues. Finally, a number of Taiwanese academics and political analysts argue that such an agreement would be merely a "scrap of paper" unless there is some way of monitoring and enforcing it.

Confederation or Commonwealth

Other long-term solutions involve the idea of creating a "confederation" or a "commonwealth" which would link mainland China and Taiwan. David Dean, a former State Department official, advanced a proposal for a "confederation" in 1994. He argued that a compromise which will accommodate Beijing's requirement for reunification while doing the same for Taiwan's status as a political entity with international responsibilities is "not beyond reach." A confederation would give Taiwan its own government, political, economic, military, and social system. It would also provide for two seats for China in the UN General Assembly, one for Beijing and one for Taipei, like the multiple representation of the former Soviet Union. Taipei also would have the right to conduct its own relations with other nations.

The confederation idea would have many advantages for both Beijing and Taipei. For Beijing it would mean an end to irritation and worry about Taiwan's drift towards independence. Such an agreement would mean highly profitable direct cross-strait trade, more Taiwanese investment in China, and full use by the PRC of Taiwan's large pool of technicians, managers, educators, scientists, and doctors. This approach would also lead to improved relations between China and the United States and between China and other countries in Asia and Western Europe.

For Taiwan, the benefits are equally clear: peace and stability, reduced military spending, direct travel and trade, international representation, and membership in the United Nations. More recently, the "confederation" idea has been taken up by prominent individuals in Taiwan. In 1994 Mr. Yu Chi-chung, publisher of the China Times, advocated the formation of a Chinese confederation. In early 1998, the former DPP Chairman, Mr. Shih Ming-teh, proposed the creation of a Greater Chinese Commonwealth similar to the British Commonwealth of nations.

Most advocates of confederation or commonwealth status envisage Taiwan as part of a Chinese Republic but keeping the separate, democratic government it now enjoys and its own military as well as membership in the UN (two seats for the Chinese Republic) and international representation.

A "confederation" or "commonwealth" solution to the Taiwan issue would also be very much in the U.S. interest. Many Americans have forged strong bonds of friendship with Chinese in Taiwan and are concerned about their future. The U.S. government is also committed to a peaceful solution and hopes that any agreement with Beijing will guarantee the political freedom and security of the Chinese people on Taiwan. At the same time, the United States has a strong interest in maintaining a stable, cooperative, and peaceful relationship with the PRC.

Conclusion

The United States is now at a critical juncture in its relationship with the PRC. According to former Secretary of Defense William J. Perry, there has never been a time in recent history when he was more concerned about the U.S.-China relationship based on what is going on in Washington today.

As Perry says, if Washington insists on treating China as a future enemy, it will surely become one. Since the 1996 Taiwan Strait crisis, when the United States and China came close to a military confrontation, the Clinton Administration has sought to develop a constructive relationship with China. Although the Administration had unrealistic expectations in seeking to build a "strategic partnership," and despite the fact that the United States and China remain divided over numerous issues, significant progress is being made. After the recent visit to the United States of China's Prime Minister, Zhu Rongji, China and the United States are very close to a final agreement on China' s entry into the World Trade Organization. Once China is admitted to the WTO, Taiwan will follow. This very fact will greatly facilitate economic relationships between China and Taiwan and it will integrate China more closely into the global community.

The United States has several policy options vis-à-vis China and the cross-strait issue. First, it can abandon the policy of engagement with China, treat that policy as a failure,.and upgrade its relations with Taiwan. This policy would be extremely dangerous. A new Cold War with China, which would likely follow such a course of action, would necessitate a substantial rise in the U.S. defense budget and -- especially if such a new Cold War was widely believed to have been caused mainly by the United States -- it would alienate most of America's allies in Asia, including Japan. Few, if any, of those allies would join the United States in a premature effort to contain China. A second policy option would be for the United States to try to broker a grand bargain between China and Taiwan along the lines suggested by Lieberthal, Nye, and others. Under present circumstances, however, such a policy is unlikely to be successful because of the enormous lack of trust between the two sides and because of domestic politics in Taipei, Beijing, and Washington.

The third policy option, which the NCAFP endorses, is to continue with some adjustments, current U.S. policy on the cross-strait issue. The United States should continue to deter the use of force by Beijing, reject de jure independence for Taiwan, and encourage the two sides to continue, and to institutionalize, the cross-strait dialogue, and to increase economic and cultural relations. The United States should not abandon the delicate framework it has developed during the past twenty years to manage the cross-strait issue. Over the longer run, the best hope is that as a result of increased contacts and trade, the two sides will themselves work out a mutually acceptable arrangement to govern the relationship for an extended period of time. The United States can best seek to ensure such an outcome by continuing to maintain a peaceful environment in the Taiwan Strait and in East Asia.

**For additional analytical, marketing, investment and business opportunities information, please contact
Global Investment & Business Center, USA
(202) 546-2103. Fax: (202) 546-3275. E-mail: rusric@erols.com**

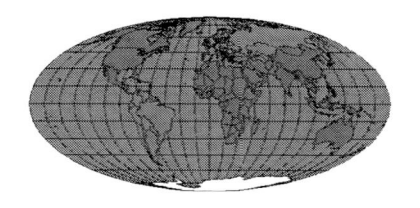

WORLD DIPLOMATIC AND CUSTOMS GUIDE LIBRARY
2006

Price: $99.95 Each

TITLE	ISBN 1
1. Afghanistan Customs, Trade Regulations and Procedures Handbook	0739757075
2. Afghanistan Diplomatic Handbook	0739757032
3. Africa Countries Mineral Industry Handbook	0739757083
4. Africa Telecom & Internet Business Opportunities Handbook	0739757091
5. Albania Customs, Trade Regulations and Procedures Handbook	0739757109
6. Albania Diplomatic Handbook	0739757040
7. Albania Fishing Industry Business and Investment Opportunities Handbook	0739757113
8. Albania National Defense and Armed Forces Handbook	0739757121
9. Algeria Customs, Trade Regulations and Procedures Handbook	073975713X
10. Algeria Diplomatic Handbook	0739757059
11. Angola Customs, Trade Regulations and Procedures Handbook	0739757148
12. Angola Diplomatic Handbook	0739757067
13. Anti-Globalizm Movement Handbook	0739757156
14. Antigua and Barbuda Customs, Trade Regulations and Procedures Handbook	0739757164
15. Antilles (Netherlands) Customs, Trade Regulations and Procedures Handbook	0739757172
16. Antilles (Netherlands) Diplomatic Handbook	0739757180
17. Argentina Customs, Trade Regulations and Procedures Handbook	0739757199
18. Argentina Diplomatic Handbook	0739757202
19. Armenia Customs, Trade Regulations and Procedures Handbook	0739757210
20. Armenia Diplomatic Handbook	0739755781
21. Aruba Customs, Trade Regulations and Procedures Handbook	0739757229
22. Australia Army, National Security and Defense Policy Handbook	0739757237
23. Australia Customs, Trade Regulations and Procedures Handbook	0739757245
24. Australia Diplomatic Handbook	073975579X
25. Austria Customs, Trade Regulations and Procedures Handbook	0739757253
26. Austria Diplomatic Handbook	0739757261
27. Azerbaijan Customs, Trade Regulations and Procedures Handbook	073975727X

For additional analytical, business and investment opportunities information, please contact Global Investment & Business Center, USA at (202) 546-2103. Fax: (202) 546-3275. E-mail: rusric@erols.com

TITLE	ISBN 1
28. Azerbaijan Diplomatic Handbook	0739757288
29. Bahamas Customs, Trade Regulations and Procedures Handbook	0739757296
30. Bahamas Diplomatic Handbook	073975730X
31. Bahrain Customs, Trade Regulations and Procedures Handbook	0739757318
32. Bahrain Diplomatic Handbook	0739757326
33. Baltics Countries (Estonia, Latvia, Lithuania) Mineral Industry Handbook	0739757334
34. Bangladesh Army, National Security and Defense Policy Handbook	0739757342
35. Bangladesh Customs, Trade Regulations and Procedures Handbook	0739757350
36. Bangladesh Diplomatic Handbook	0739757369
37. Barbados Customs, Trade Regulations and Procedures Handbook	0739757377
38. Belarus Customs, Trade Regulations and Procedures Handbook	0739757385
39. Belarus Diplomatic Handbook	0739757393
40. Belgium Customs, Trade Regulations and Procedures Handbook	0739757407
41. Belgium Diplomatic Handbook	0739757415
42. Belize Customs, Trade Regulations and Procedures Handbook	0739757423
43. Belize Diplomatic Handbook	0739757431
44. Benin Customs, Trade Regulations and Procedures Handbook	073975744X
45. Benin Diplomatic Handbook	0739757458
46. Bermuda Customs, Trade Regulations and Procedures Handbook	0739757466
47. Bermuda E-Commerce Guide	0739757474
48. Bermuda Investment and Business Contacts Directory	0739757482
49. Bhutan Customs, Trade Regulations and Procedures Handbook	0739757490
50. Bhutan Diplomatic Handbook	0739757504
51. Bolivia Customs, Trade Regulations and Procedures Handbook	0739757512
52. Bolivia Diplomatic Handbook	0739757520
53. Bosnia and Herzegovina Customs, Trade Regulations and Procedures Handbook	0739757539
54. Bosnia and Herzegovina Diplomatic Handbook	0739757547
55. Botswana Customs, Trade Regulations and Procedures Handbook	0739757555
56. Botswana Diplomatic Handbook	0739757563
57. Botswana Telecom Industry Investment and Business Opportunities Handbook	0739757571
58. Botswana Telecom Industry Laws and Regulations Handbook	073975758X
59. Brazil Customs, Trade Regulations and Procedures Handbook	0739757598
60. Brazil Diplomatic Handbook	0739757601
61. Brunei Customs, Trade Regulations and Procedures Handbook	073975761X
62. Brunei Diplomatic Handbook	0739757628
63. Bulgaria Customs, Trade Regulations and Procedures Handbook	0739757636
64. Bulgaria Diplomatic Handbook	0739757644

For additional analytical, business and investment opportunities information, please contact Global Investment & Business Center, USA at (202) 546-2103. Fax: (202) 546-3275. E-mail: rusric@erols.com

TITLE	ISBN 1
65. Burkina Faso Customs, Trade Regulations and Procedures Handbook	0739757652
66. Burkina Faso Diplomatic Handbook	0739757660
67. Burundi Diplomatic Handbook	0739757687
68. Burundi Peace Agreements Handbook	0739757695
69. Cambodia Customs, Trade Regulations and Procedures Handbook	0739757679
70. Cambodia Diplomatic Handbook	0739757709
71. Cambodia Tax Guide	0739757717
72. Cameroon Customs, Trade Regulations and Procedures Handbook	0739757725
73. Cameroon Diplomatic Handbook	0739757733
74. Canada Customs, Trade Regulations and Procedures Handbook	0739757741
75. Canada Diplomatic Handbook	073975775X
76. Cape Verde Diplomatic Handbook	0739757768
77. Caribbean Countries Mineral Industry Handbook	0739757776
78. Caribbean Development Bank Handbook	0739757784
79. Cayman Islands Diplomatic Handbook	0739757792
80. Central African Republic Diplomatic Handbook	0739757806
81. Central America Mineral Industry Handbook	07397577814
82. Central European Countries Mineral Industry Handbook	0739757822
83. Chad Diplomatic Handbook	0739757830
84. Chile Customs, Trade Regulations and Procedures Handbook	0739757849
85. Chile Diplomatic Handbook	0739757857
86. China Army, National Security and Defense Policy Handbook	0739756818
87. China Customs, Trade Regulations and Procedures Handbook	0739757865
88. China Diplomatic Handbook	0739757873
89. Colombia Customs, Trade Regulations and Procedures Handbook	0739757881
90. Colombia Diplomatic Handbook	073975789X
91. Commonwealth of Independent States (CIS) Handbook	0739757903
92. Comoros Customs, Trade Regulations and Procedures Handbook	0739757911
93. Comoros Diplomatic Handbook	073975792X
94. Congo Diplomatic Handbook	0739757938
95. Congo, Democratic Republic Diplomatic Handbook	0739757946
96. Cook Islands Diplomatic Handbook	0739757954
97. Costa Rica Customs, Trade Regulations and Procedures Handbook	0739757942
98. Costa Rica Diplomatic Handbook	0739757970
99. Costa Rica Ecological and Nature Protection Handbook	0739757989
100. Costa Rica Trade Policy Handbook	0739757997
101. Cote d'Ivoire Diplomatic Handbook	0739756001
102. Croatia Customs, Trade Regulations and Procedures Handbook	073975601X

For additional analytical, business and investment opportunities information, please contact Global Investment & Business Center, USA at (202) 546-2103. Fax: (202) 546-3275. E-mail: rusric@erols.com

TITLE	ISBN 1
103. Croatia Diplomatic Handbook	0739756028
104. Croatia Financial & Banking Law and Regulations Handbook	0739756036
105. Cuba Army, National Security and Defense Policy Handbook	0739756826
106. Cuba Customs, Trade Regulations and Procedures Handbook	0739756044
107. Cuba Diplomatic Handbook	0739756052
108. Cuba Export-Import and Business Directory	0739756060
109. Cyprus Customs, Trade Regulations and Procedures Handbook	0739756079
110. Cyprus Diplomatic Handbook	0739756087
111. Cyprus Financial Market Investment and Business Opportunities Yearbook	0739756095
112. Cyprus Parliament Guide	0739756109
113. Czech Republic Customs, Trade Regulations and Procedures Handbook	0739756117
114. Czech Republic Diplomatic Handbook	0739756125
115. Czech Republic Army, National Security and Defense Policy Handbook	0739756133
116. Denmark Customs, Trade Regulations and Procedures Handbook	0739756141
117. Denmark Diplomatic Handbook	073975615X
118. Djibouti Diplomatic Handbook	0739756166
119. Dominica Diplomatic Handbook	0739756176
120. Dominican Republic Diplomatic Handbook	0739756184
121. Dubai Customs, Trade Regulations and Procedures Handbook	0739756192
122. Dubai Export-Import and Business Directory	0739756206
123. Dubai Jebel Ali Free Zone Business Opportunities and Regulations Handbook	0739756214
124. Ecuador Customs, Trade Regulations and Procedures Handbook	0739756222
125. Ecuador Diplomatic Handbook	0739756230
126. Egypt Customs, Trade Regulations and Procedures Handbook	0739756249
127. Egypt Diplomatic Handbook	0739756257
128. El Salvador Customs, Trade Regulations and Procedures Handbook	0739756265
129. El Salvador Diplomatic Handbook	0739756273
130. Equatorial Guinea Diplomatic Handbook	0739756281
131. Eritrea Diplomatic Handbook	073975629X
132. Eastern European Countries Mineral Industry Handbook	0739756303
133. Estonia Army, National Security and Defense Policy Handbook	0739756311
134. Estonia Customs, Trade Regulations and Procedures Handbook	073975632X
135. Estonia Diplomatic Handbook	0739756338
136. Ethiopia Diplomatic Handbook	0739756346
137. Falkland Islands Diplomatic Handbook	0739756354

For additional analytical, business and investment opportunities information, please contact Global Investment & Business Center, USA at (202) 546-2103. Fax: (202) 546-3275. E-mail: rusric@erols.com

	TITLE	ISBN 1
138.	Faroes Diplomatic Handbook	0739756362
139.	Fiji Customs, Trade Regulations and Procedures Handbook	0739756370
140.	Fiji Diplomatic Handbook	0739756389
141.	Finland Army, National Security and Defense Policy Handbook	0739756397
142.	Finland Customs, Trade Regulations and Procedures Handbook	0739756400
143.	Finland Diplomatic Handbook	0739756419
144.	France Army, National Security and Defense Policy Handbook	0739756427
145.	France Customs, Trade Regulations and Procedures Handbook	0739756435
146.	France Diplomatic Handbook	0739756443
147.	France Senate Handbook	0739756451
148.	Gabon Diplomatic Handbook	073975646X
149.	Gambia Diplomatic Handbook	0739756478
150.	Georgia (Republic) Customs, Trade Regulations and Procedures Handbook	0739756486
151.	Georgia Diplomatic Handbook	0739756494
152.	Germany Army, National Security and Defense Policy Handbook	0739756508
153.	Germany Customs, Trade Regulations and Procedures Handbook	0739756516
154.	Germany Diplomatic Handbook	0739756524
155.	Ghana Banking and Financial Sector Business and Investment Opportunities Handbook	0739756532
156.	Ghana Customs, Trade Regulations and Procedures Handbook	0739756540
157.	Ghana Diplomatic Handbook	0739756559
158.	Ghana Financial Market Business Opportunities and Regulations Handbook	0739756567
159.	Gibraltar Diplomatic Handbook	0739756583
160.	Gibraltar Offshore & Customs, Trade Regulations and Procedures Handbook	0739756575
161.	Global Aviation Industry Handbook	0739756605
162.	Global E-Commerce Laws and Regulations Handbook	0739756753
163.	Global Embassy Contacts Directory	0739756613
164.	Global Leather Exporters & Importers Directory	0739756621
165.	Global Mining, Oil and Gas Industry Directory	073975663X
166.	Global Mobile & Cellular Communications Industry Directory	0739756648
167.	Global National Libraries Directory: EUROPE	0739756656
168.	Global Non Profit Organizations Directory	0739756664
169.	Global Offshore Financial Services Providers Directory	0739756672
170.	Global Oil & Gas Industry Directory	0739756680
171.	Global Pharmaceutical Industry Directory	0739756699
172.	Global Privatization Handbook	0739756702

**For additional analytical, business and investment opportunities information,
please contact Global Investment & Business Center, USA
at (202) 546-2103. Fax: (202) 546-3275. E-mail: rusric@erols.com**

	TITLE	ISBN 1
173.	Global Sea Food Industry Directory	0739756718
174.	Global Senate Handbook	0739756729
175.	Global Shipbuilding Industry Directory	0739756737
176.	Global Telecom Industry Handbook: Regulations and Contacts	0739756745
177.	Global Transpiration Contacts Directory	0739756761
178.	Greece Customs, Trade Regulations and Procedures Handbook	073975677X
179.	Greece Diplomatic Handbook	0739756788
180.	Greenland Diplomatic Handbook	0739756796
181.	Grenada Diplomatic Handbook	073975680X
182.	Guatemala Diplomatic Handbook	0739756834
183.	Guernsey Diplomatic Handbook	07397566842
184.	Guinea Diplomatic Handbook	0739756850
185.	Guinea-Bissau Diplomatic Handbook	0739756869
186.	Guyana Diplomatic Handbook	0739756877
187.	Guyana President BHARRAT JAGDEO Handbook	0739756885
188.	Haiti Customs, Trade Regulations and Procedures Handbook	0739756893
189.	Haiti Diplomatic Handbook	0739756907
190.	Honduras Customs, Trade Regulations and Procedures Handbook	0739756915
191.	Honduras Diplomatic Handbook	0739756923
192.	Hungary Army, National Security and Defense Policy Handbook	0739756931
193.	Hungary Customs, Trade Regulations and Procedures Handbook	073975694X
194.	Hungary Diplomatic Handbook	0739756958
195.	Iceland Customs, Trade Regulations and Procedures Handbook	0739756966
196.	Iceland Diplomatic Handbook	0739756974
197.	India Army, National Security and Defense Policy Handbook	0739756982
198.	India Customs, Trade Regulations and Procedures Handbook	0739756990
199.	India Diplomatic Handbook	0739755005
200.	Indonesia Customs, Trade Regulations and Procedures Handbook	0739755013
201.	Indonesia Diplomatic Handbook	0739755021
202.	International Telecommunication Union Handbook	073975503X
203.	Iran Customs, Trade Regulations and Procedures Handbook	0739755048
204.	Iran Diplomatic Handbook	0739755056
205.	Iraq Diplomatic Handbook	0739755064
206.	Iraq Economic Sanctions, Customs, Trade Regulations and Procedures Handbook	0739755072
207.	Ireland Army, National Security and Defense Policy Handbook	0739754440
208.	Ireland Customs, Trade Regulations and Procedures Handbook	0739755080
209.	Ireland Diplomatic Handbook	0739755099

For additional analytical, business and investment opportunities information, please contact Global Investment & Business Center, USA at (202) 546-2103. Fax: (202) 546-3275. E-mail: rusric@erols.com

	TITLE	ISBN 1
210.	Israel Army, National Security and Defense Policy Handbook	0739755110
211.	Israel Customs, Trade Regulations and Procedures Handbook	0739755102
212.	Israel Diplomatic Handbook	0739755129
213.	Italy Customs, Trade Regulations and Procedures Handbook	0739755137
214.	Italy Diplomatic Handbook	0739755145
215.	Jamaica Diplomatic Handbook	0739755161
216.	Jamaica Offshore Customs, Trade Regulations and Procedures Handbook	0739755153
217.	Japan Army, National Security and Defense Policy Handbook	073975517X
218.	Japan Customs, Trade Regulations and Procedures Handbook	0739755188
219.	Japan Diplomatic Handbook	0739755196
220.	Jordan Customs, Trade Regulations and Procedures Handbook	073975520X
221.	Jordan Diplomatic Handbook	0739755218
222.	Kazakhstan Customs, Trade Regulations and Procedures Handbook	0739755226
223.	Kazakhstan Diplomatic Handbook	0739755234
224.	Kenya Customs, Trade Regulations and Procedures Handbook	0739755242
225.	Kenya Diplomatic Handbook	0739755250
226.	Korea North Army, National Security and Defense Policy Handbook	0739755307
227.	Korea South Army, National Security and Defense Policy Handbook	0739755315
228.	Korea, North Customs, Trade Regulations and Procedures Handbook	0739755269
229.	Korea, North Diplomatic Handbook	0739755277
230.	Korea, South Customs, Trade Regulations and Procedures Handbook	0739755285
231.	Korea, South Diplomatic Handbook	0739755323
232.	Kuwait Customs, Trade Regulations and Procedures Handbook	0739755331
233.	Kuwait Diplomatic Handbook	073975534X
234.	Kyrgyzstan Customs, Trade Regulations and Procedures Handbook	0739755358
235.	Kyrgyzstan Diplomatic Handbook	0739755366
236.	Laos Customs, Trade Regulations and Procedures Handbook	0739755374
237.	Laos Diplomatic Handbook	0739755382
238.	Latvia Army, National Security and Defense Policy Handbook	0739755390
239.	Latvia Customs, Trade Regulations and Procedures Handbook	07397554404
240.	Latvia Diplomatic Handbook	0739755412
241.	Lebanon Army, National Security and Defense Policy Handbook	0739755420
242.	Lebanon Customs, Trade Regulations and Procedures Handbook	0739755439
243.	Lebanon Diplomatic Handbook	0739755447
244.	Lesotho Diplomatic Handbook	0739755455
245.	Liberia Diplomatic Handbook	0739755463
246.	Libya Customs, Trade Regulations and Procedures Handbook	0739755471

For additional analytical, business and investment opportunities information, please contact Global Investment & Business Center, USA at (202) 546-2103. Fax: (202) 546-3275. E-mail: rusric@erols.com

	TITLE	ISBN 1
247.	Libya Diplomatic Handbook	073975548X
248.	Liechtenstein Diplomatic Handbook	0739755498
249.	Lithuania Army, National Security and Defense Policy Handbook	0739755501
250.	Lithuania Customs, Trade Regulations and Procedures Handbook	073975551X
251.	Lithuania Diplomatic Handbook	0739755528
252.	Luxembourg Diplomatic Handbook	0739755536
253.	Macao Customs, Trade Regulations and Procedures Handbook	0739755544
254.	Macau Diplomatic Handbook	0739755552
255.	Macedonia Customs, Trade Regulations and Procedures Handbook	0739755587
256.	Macedonia Diplomatic Handbook	0739755595
257.	Macedonia National Security, Army and Defense Policy Handbook	0739755560
258.	Macedonia Parliament and Legislative Activities Handbook	0739755579
259.	Madagascar Customs, Trade Regulations and Procedures Handbook	0739755609
260.	Madagascar Diplomatic Handbook	0739755617
261.	Malawi Diplomatic Handbook	0739752625
262.	Malaysia Army, National Security and Defense Policy Handbook	073975565X
263.	Malaysia Customs, Trade Regulations and Procedures Handbook	0739755633
264.	Malaysia Diplomatic Handbook	0739755641
265.	Maldives Diplomatic Handbook	0739755668
266.	Mali Diplomatic Handbook	0739755676
267.	Malta Customs, Trade Regulations and Procedures Handbook	0739755684
268.	Malta Diplomatic Handbook	0739755692
269.	Man Diplomatic Handbook	0739755706
270.	Marshall Islands Diplomatic Handbook	0739755714
271.	Mauritania Diplomatic Handbook	0739755722
272.	Mauritius Customs, Trade Regulations and Procedures Handbook	0739755730
273.	Mauritius Diplomatic Handbook	0739756749
274.	Mexico Customs, Trade Regulations and Procedures Handbook	0739755757
275.	Mexico Diplomatic Handbook	07397557675
276.	Micronesia Diplomatic Handbook	0739755773
277.	Middle East and Arabic Countries Copyright Law Handbook	0739755811
278.	Middle East Countries Mineral Industry Handbook	0739755803
279.	Middle East and Arabic Countries Design Law Handbook	073975582X
280.	Middle East and Arabic Countries Patent Law Handbook	0739755838
281.	Middle East and Arabic Countries Trademark Law Handbook	0739755846
282.	Moldova Customs, Trade Regulations and Procedures Handbook	0739755854
283.	Moldova Diplomatic Handbook	0739755862
284.	Monaco Diplomatic Handbook	0739755870

For additional analytical, business and investment opportunities information, please contact Global Investment & Business Center, USA at (202) 546-2103. Fax: (202) 546-3275. E-mail: rusric@erols.com

	TITLE	ISBN 1
285.	Mongolia Customs, Trade Regulations and Procedures Handbook	0739755889
286.	Mongolia Diplomatic Handbook	0739755897
287.	Morocco Customs, Trade Regulations and Procedures Handbook	0739755900
288.	Morocco Diplomatic Handbook	0739755919
289.	Mozambique Diplomatic Handbook	0739755927
290.	Myanmar (Burma) Energy Sector Business Opportunities Handbook	0739755935
291.	Myanmar Army, National Security and Defense Policy Handbook	0739754041
292.	Myanmar Customs, Trade Regulations and Procedures Handbook	0739755943
293.	Myanmar Diplomatic Handbook	0739755951
294.	Namibia Diplomatic Handbook	073975596X
295.	NATO Enlargement Handbook	0739755978
296.	Nepal Customs, Trade Regulations and Procedures Handbook	0739755986
297.	Nepal Diplomatic Handbook	0739755994
298.	Netherlands Customs, Trade Regulations and Procedures Handbook	0739754009
299.	Netherlands Diplomatic Handbook	0739754017
300.	New Zealand Army, National Security and Defense Policy Handbook	073975405X
301.	New Zealand Customs, Trade Regulations and Procedures Handbook	0739754025
302.	New Zealand Diplomatic Handbook	0739754033
303.	Nicaragua Customs, Trade Regulations and Procedures Handbook	0739754068
304.	Nicaragua Diplomatic Handbook	0739754076
305.	Niger Diplomatic Handbook	0739754084
306.	Nigeria Customs, Trade Regulations and Procedures Handbook	0739754091
307.	Nigeria Diplomatic Handbook	0739754106
308.	North America Mineral Industry Handbook	0739754114
309.	Norway Army, National Security and Defense Policy Handbook	0739754122
310.	Norway Customs, Trade Regulations and Procedures Handbook	0739754130
311.	Norway Diplomatic Handbook	0739754149
312.	Norway Tax Treaties with Foreign Countries Handbook	0739754157
313.	Oman Customs, Trade Regulations and Procedures Handbook	0739754165
314.	Oman Diplomatic Handbook	0739754173
315.	Oman Royal Police Handbook	0739754181
316.	Pacific Countries Mineral Industry Handbook	073975419X
317.	Pakistan Army, National Security and Defense Policy Handbook	0739754203
318.	Pakistan Customs, Trade Regulations and Procedures Handbook	0739754211
319.	Pakistan Diplomatic Handbook	073975422X
320.	Palestine Diplomatic Handbook	0739754238
321.	Panama Customs, Trade Regulations and Procedures Handbook	0739754246

For additional analytical, business and investment opportunities information, please contact Global Investment & Business Center, USA at (202) 546-2103. Fax: (202) 546-3275. E-mail: rusric@erols.com

	TITLE	ISBN 1
322.	Panama Diplomatic Handbook	0739754254
323.	Papua New Guinea Diplomatic Handbook	0739754262
324.	Paraguay Diplomatic Handbook	0739754270
325.	Peru Customs, Trade Regulations and Procedures Handbook	0739754289
326.	Peru Diplomatic Handbook	0739754297
327.	Philippines Agricultural Sector Business Opportunities Handbook	0739754300
328.	Philippines Army, National Security and Defense Policy Handbook	0739754319
329.	Philippines Customs, Trade Regulations and Procedures Handbook	0739754327
330.	Philippines Diplomatic Handbook	0739754335
331.	Philippines Financial Market Business Opportunities Handbook	0739754343
332.	Philippines National Police Force Handbook	0739754386
333.	Philippines Science and Technology Policy Handbook	0739754351
334.	Philippines Trade Policy Handbook	073975436X
335.	Philippines Transportation and Communication Policy Handbook	0739754378
336.	Poland Army, National Security and Defense Policy Handbook	0739754394
337.	Poland Customs, Trade Regulations and Procedures Handbook	0739754408
338.	Poland Diplomatic Handbook	0739754416
339.	Portugal Customs, Trade Regulations and Procedures Handbook	0739754424
340.	Portugal Diplomatic Handbook	0739754432
341.	Qatar Customs, Trade Regulations and Procedures Handbook	0739754467
342.	Qatar Diplomatic Handbook	0739754475
343.	Romania Army, National Security and Defense Policy Handbook	0739754483
344.	Romania Customs, Trade Regulations and Procedures Handbook	0739754491
345.	Romania Diplomatic Handbook	0739754609
346.	Russia and NIS Central Eurasia) Mineral Industry Handbook	0739754513
347.	Russia Army, National Security and Defense Policy Handbook	0739754521
348.	Russia Customs, Trade Regulations and Procedures Handbook	073975453X
349.	Russia Diplomatic Handbook	0739754548
350.	Russian KGB Handbook: Past and Present	0739754556
351.	Russian Navy Handbook: History and Modern Situation	0739754564
352.	Russia-NATO Cooperation Handbook	0739754572
353.	Rwanda Diplomatic Handbook	0739754580
354.	Samoa (Western) Diplomatic Handbook	0739754599
355.	Saudi Arabia Customs, Trade Regulations and Procedures Handbook	0739754602
356.	Saudi Arabia Diplomatic Handbook	0739754610

For additional analytical, business and investment opportunities information,
please contact Global Investment & Business Center, USA
at (202) 546-2103. Fax: (202) 546-3275. E-mail: rusric@erols.com

TITLE		ISBN 1
357.	Scotland Central Police Handbook	0739754645
358.	Scotland Customs, Trade Regulations and Procedures Handbook	0739754629
359.	Scotland Diplomatic Handbook	0739754637
360.	Senegal Diplomatic Handbook	0739754661
361.	Seychelles Diplomatic Handbook	0739754653
362.	Sierra Leone Diplomatic Handbook	073975467X
363.	Singapore Government Encyclopedic Directory	0739754688
364.	Singapore Army, National Security and Defense Policy Handbook	0739754459
365.	Singapore Customs, Trade Regulations and Procedures Handbook	0739754696
366.	Singapore Diplomatic Handbook	0739754718
367.	Slovak Republic Army, National Security and Defense Policy Handbook	0739754742
368.	Slovak Republic Customs, Trade Regulations and Procedures Handbook	0739754750
369.	Slovak Republic Customs, Trade Regulations and Procedures Handbook	0739754726
370.	Slovak Republic Diplomatic Handbook	0739754769
371.	Slovak Republic Diplomatic Handbook	0739754734
372.	Solomon Islands Diplomatic Handbook	0739754777
373.	Somalia Diplomatic Handbook	0739754785
374.	South Africa Army, National Security and Defense Policy Handbook	0739754797
375.	South Africa Customs, Trade Regulations and Procedures Handbook	0739754807
376.	South Africa Diplomatic Handbook	0739754815
377.	South Africa Environmental Business Opportunities Handbook	0739754831
378.	South America Mineral Industry Handbook	073975484X
379.	South America Police Handbook	0739754823
380.	Spain Customs, Trade Regulations and Procedures Handbook	0739754858
381.	Spain Diplomatic Handbook	0739754866
382.	Sri Lanka Army, National Security and Defense Policy Handbook	0739754890
383.	Sri Lanka Customs, Trade Regulations and Procedures Handbook	0739754874
384.	Sri Lanka Diplomatic Handbook	0739754882
385.	Sri Lanka National Police Handbook	0739754904
386.	Sudan Customs, Trade Regulations and Procedures Handbook	0739754912
387.	Sudan Diplomatic Handbook	0739754920
388.	Suriname Customs, Trade Regulations and Procedures Handbook	0739754939
389.	Suriname Diplomatic Handbook	0739754947
390.	Swaziland Diplomatic Handbook	0739754955
391.	Sweden Customs, Trade Regulations and Procedures Handbook	0739754963
392.	Sweden Diplomatic Handbook	0739754971

For additional analytical, business and investment opportunities information, please contact Global Investment & Business Center, USA at (202) 546-2103. Fax: (202) 546-3275. E-mail: rusric@erols.com

	TITLE	ISBN 1
393.	Switzerland Army, National Security and Defense Policy Handbook	073975498X
394.	Switzerland Customs, Trade Regulations and Procedures Handbook	0739754998
395.	Switzerland Diplomatic Handbook	0739759000
396.	Syria Customs, Trade Regulations and Procedures Handbook	0739759019
397.	Syria Diplomatic Handbook	0739759027
398.	Taiwan Army, National Security and Defense Policy Handbook	0739759035
399.	Taiwan Customs, Trade Regulations and Procedures Handbook	0739759043
400.	Taiwan Diplomatic Handbook	0739759051
401.	Taiwan National Police Handbook	073975906X
402.	Taiwan President Chen Shui-bian Handbook	0739758978
403.	Tajikistan Customs, Trade Regulations and Procedures Handbook	0739759086
404.	Tajikistan Diplomatic Handbook	0739759094
405.	Tanzania Diplomatic Handbook	0739759108
406.	Thailand Customs, Trade Regulations and Procedures Handbook	0739759116
407.	Thailand Diplomatic Handbook	0739759124
408.	Thailand Royal Army, National Security and Defense Policy Handbook	0739759132
409.	Thailand Royal Police Handbook	0739759140
410.	Togo Diplomatic Handbook	0739759159
411.	Tunisia Customs, Trade Regulations and Procedures Handbook	0739759167
412.	Tunisia Diplomatic Handbook	0739759175
413.	Turkey Army, National Security and Defense Policy Handbook	0739759205
414.	Turkey Customs, Trade Regulations and Procedures Handbook	0739759183
415.	Turkey Diplomatic Handbook	0739759191
416.	Turkey National Intelligence Organization and Policy Handbook	0739759213
417.	Turkmenistan Customs, Trade Regulations and Procedures Handbook	0739759221
418.	Turkmenistan Diplomatic Handbook	073975923X
419.	Uganda Diplomatic Handbook	0739759248
420.	UK Bank of England Handbook	0739759337
421.	UK British Monarchy Handbook	0739759345
422.	UK Department for International Development (DfID) Handbook	0739759353
423.	UK Department for Transport, Local Government and the Regions (DTLR) Handbook	0739759361
424.	UK Department of Trade and Industry (DTI) Handbook	073975937X
425.	UK Foreign and Commonwealth Office (FCO) Handbook	0739759388
426.	UK Her Majesty's Treasury (HMT) Handbook	0739759396
427.	UK Immigration and Nationality Policy Handbook	073975940X
428.	UK Intelligence & Counterintelligence Handbook	073975470X

For additional analytical, business and investment opportunities information, please contact Global Investment & Business Center, USA at (202) 546-2103. Fax: (202) 546-3275. E-mail: rusric@erols.com

	TITLE	ISBN 1
429.	UK Intelligence and Security Policy Handbook	0739755418
430.	UK National Intelligence Service Handbook	0739759426
431.	UK National Police Handbook	0739759442
432.	UK Northern Ireland Office (NIO) Handbook	0739759434
433.	UK Royal Air force Handbook	0739759450
434.	UK Royal Army Handbook	0739759469
435.	UK Royal Navy Handbook	0739759477
436.	Ukraine Army, National Security and Defense Policy Handbook	0739759256
437.	Ukraine Customs, Trade Regulations and Procedures Handbook	0739759264
438.	Ukraine Diplomatic Handbook	0739759272
439.	United Arab Emirates Customs, Trade Regulations and Procedures Handbook	0739755280
440.	United Arab Emirates Diplomatic Handbook	0739759299
441.	United Kingdom Army, National Security and Defense Policy Handbook	0739759302
442.	United Kingdom Customs, Trade Regulations and Procedures Handbook	0739759310
443.	United Kingdom Diplomatic Handbook	0739759329
444.	United States Customs, Trade Regulations and Procedures Handbook	0739759485
445.	United States Diplomatic Handbook	0739759493
446.	Uruguay Diplomatic Handbook	0739759507
447.	US Arms Sales to Foreign Countries Handbook	0739759515
448.	US Defense Policy Handbook	0739759523
449.	US Economic and Political Assistance to Macedonia Handbook	0739759531
450.	US Federal Depository Libraries Directory	073975954X
451.	US Federal Government Directory	0739759558
452.	US Federal Grant Management Handbook	0739759666
453.	US Immigration Policy and Programs Handbook	0739759574
454.	US Ocean Transportation Companies Directory	0739759582
455.	US War Against Iraq Handbook: Political Strategy and Operations	0739750655
456.	US-Russia Cooperation Against Terrorism Handbook	0739759590
457.	US-Russia Economic & Financial Cooperation Handbook	0739759604
458.	US-Russia Military Cooperation Handbook	0739759612
459.	US-Russia Political Cooperation Handbook	0739759620
460.	US-Russia Scientific & Technological Cooperation Handbook	0739759639
461.	US-Russia Space Cooperation Handbook	0739759647
462.	Uzbekistan Customs, Trade Regulations and Procedures Handbook	0739759663
463.	Uzbekistan Diplomatic Handbook	0739759671

For additional analytical, business and investment opportunities information, please contact Global Investment & Business Center, USA at (202) 546-2103. Fax: (202) 546-3275. E-mail: rusric@erols.com

	TITLE	ISBN 1
464.	Venezuela Diplomatic Handbook	073975968X
465.	Vietnam Diplomatic Handbook	0739759698
466.	Vietnam Financial and Trade Policy Handbook	0739759779
467.	Western European Countries Mineral Industry Handbook	073975971X
468.	World Trade Organization Handbook	0739759701
469.	Yemen Diplomatic Handbook	0739759728
470.	Yugoslavia Customs, Trade Regulations and Procedures Handbook	0739759736
471.	Yugoslavia Diplomatic Handbook	0739759744
472.	Zambia Diplomatic Handbook	0739759752
473.	Zimbabwe Diplomatic Handbook	0739759760

For additional analytical, business and investment opportunities information, please contact Global Investment & Business Center, USA at (202) 546-2103. Fax: (202) 546-3275. E-mail: rusric@erols.com

GLOBAL US ECONOMIC AND POLITICAL COOPERATION HANDBOOK LIBRARY
(PRICE $99.95)

Ultimate handbook on US economic and political cooperation with respected countries. Assistance, political support, strategy and more...

TITLE
1. US – Argentina Economic and Political Cooperation Handbook
2. US -- Armenia Economic and Political Cooperation Handbook
3. US – Australia Economic and Political Cooperation Handbook
4. US – Austria Economic and Political Cooperation Handbook
5. US – Azerbaijan Economic and Political Cooperation Handbook
6. US – Belgium Economic and Political Cooperation Handbook
7. US – Bosnia & Herzegovina Economic and Political Cooperation Handbook
8. US – Brazil Economic and Political Cooperation Handbook
9. US – Bulgaria Economic and Political Cooperation Handbook
10. US – Canada Economic and Political Cooperation Handbook
11. US – Chile Economic and Political Cooperation Handbook
12. US – China Economic and Political Cooperation Handbook
13. US – Costa Rica Economic and Political Cooperation Handbook
14. US – Croatia Economic and Political Cooperation Handbook
15. US – Cuba Political and Economic Relations Handbook
16. US – Czech Republic Economic and Political Cooperation Handbook
17. US – Egypt Economic and Political Cooperation Handbook
18. US – El Salvador Economic and Political Cooperation Handbook
19. US -- Estonia Economic and Political Cooperation Handbook
20. US – Finland Economic and Political Cooperation Handbook
21. US – France Economic and Political Cooperation Handbook
22. US – Georgia Economic and Political Cooperation Handbook
23. US – Germany Economic and Political Cooperation Handbook
24. US – Greece Economic and Political Cooperation Handbook
25. US – Hungary Economic and Political Cooperation Handbook
26. US – India Economic and Political Cooperation Handbook

To order and for additional analytical and marketing information, please contacrt
International Business Publications, USA at:
P.O. Box 15343, Washington, DC 20003, USA. Phone: (202) 546-2103. Fax: (202) 546-3275.
E-mail: rusric@erols.com

27.	US – Indonesia Economic and Political Cooperation Handbook
28.	US – Iran Political & Economic Relations Handbook
29.	US – Iraq Political & Economic Relations Handbook
30.	US – Israel Economic and Political Cooperation Handbook
31.	US – Italy Economic and Political Cooperation Handbook
32.	US – Japan Economic and Political Cooperation Handbook
33.	US – Kazakhstan Economic and Political Cooperation Handbook
34.	US – Kuwait Economic and Political Cooperation Handbook
35.	US – Kyrgyzstan Economic and Political Cooperation Handbook
36.	US – Latvia Economic and Political Cooperation Handbook
37.	US – Lithuania Economic and Political Cooperation Handbook
38.	US – Mexico Economic and Political Cooperation Handbook
39.	US – Moldova Economic and Political Cooperation Handbook
40.	US -- New Zealand Economic and Political Cooperation Handbook
41.	US – Norway Economic and Political Cooperation Handbook
42.	US – Norway Economic and Political Cooperation Handbook
43.	US -- Peru Economic and Political Cooperation Handbook
44.	US – Philippines Economic and Political Cooperation Handbook
45.	US – Poland Economic and Political Cooperation Handbook
46.	US – Portugal Economic and Political Cooperation Handbook
47.	US – Russia Economic and Political Cooperation Handbook
48.	US – Saudi Arabia Economic and Political Cooperation Handbook
49.	US – South Africa Economic and Political Cooperation Handbook
50.	US – South Korea Economic and Political Cooperation Handbook
51.	US – Spain Economic and Political Cooperation Handbook
52.	US – Sri Lanka Economic and Political Cooperation Handbook
53.	US – Sweden Economic and Political Cooperation Handbook
54.	US – Switzerland Economic and Political Cooperation Handbook
55.	US – Taiwan Economic and Political Cooperation Handbook
56.	US -- Turkey Economic and Political Cooperation Handbook
57.	US – Turkmenistan Economic and Political Cooperation Handbook
58.	US – UK Economic and Political Cooperation Handbook
59.	US – Ukraine Economic and Political Cooperation Handbook
60.	US – Uruguay Economic and Political Cooperation Handbook
61.	US – Uzbekistan Economic and Political Cooperation Handbook
62.	US -- Venezuela Economic and Political Cooperation Handbook
63.	US – Vietnam Economic and Political Cooperation Handbook
64.	US – Yugoslavia Economic and Political Cooperation Handbook

**To order and for additional analytical and marketing information, please contacrt
International Business Publications, USA at:
P.O. Box 15343, Washington, DC 20003, USA. Phone: (202) 546-2103. Fax: (202) 546-3275.
E-mail: rusric@erols.com**

NEW! GLOBAL US DIPLOMATIC AND POLITICAL RELATIONS HANDBOOK LIBRARY (PRICE $99.95)

Ultimate handbook on US diplomatic and political relations with respected countries. History, foreign policy guidelines, issues, treaties and agreements, diplomatic and political contacts and more...

TITLE
1. US – ARGENTINA Diplomatic and Political Relations Handbook
2. US – ARMENIA Diplomatic and Political Relations Handbook
3. US – AUSTRALIA Diplomatic and Political Relations Handbook
4. US – AUSTRIA Diplomatic and Political Relations Handbook
5. US – AZERBAIJAN Diplomatic and Political Relations Handbook
6. US – BELGIUM Diplomatic and Political Relations Handbook
7. US – BOSNIA & HERZEGOVINA Diplomatic and Political Relations Handbook
8. US – BRAZIL Diplomatic and Political Relations Handbook
9. US – BULGARIA Diplomatic and Political Relations Handbook
10. US – CANADA Diplomatic and Political Relations Handbook
11. US – CHILE Diplomatic and Political Relations Handbook
12. US – CHINA Diplomatic and Political Relations Handbook
13. US – COSTA RICA Diplomatic and Political Relations Handbook
14. US – CROATIA Diplomatic and Political Relations Handbook
15. US – CUBA Diplomatic and Political Relations Handbook
16. US – CZECH REPUBLIC Diplomatic and Political Relations Handbook
17. US – EGYPT Diplomatic and Political Relations Handbook
18. US – EL SALVADOR Diplomatic and Political Relations Handbook
19. US – ESTONIA Diplomatic and Political Relations Handbook
20. US – FINLAND Diplomatic and Political Relations Handbook
21. US – FRANCE Diplomatic and Political Relations Handbook
22. US – GEORGIA Diplomatic and Political Relations Handbook
23. US – GERMANY Diplomatic and Political Relations Handbook
24. US – GREECE Diplomatic and Political Relations Handbook
25. US – HUNGARY Diplomatic and Political Relations Handbook
26. US – INDIA Diplomatic and Political Relations Handbook
27. US – INDONESIA Diplomatic and Political Relations Handbook
28. US – IRAN Diplomatic and Political Relations Handbook
29. US – IRAQ Diplomatic and Political Relations Handbook
30. US – ISRAEL Diplomatic and Political Relations Handbook
31. US – ITALY Diplomatic and Political Relations Handbook
32. US – JAPAN Diplomatic and Political Relations Handbook
33. US – KAZAKHSTAN Diplomatic and Political Relations Handbook

To order and for additional analytical and marketing information, please contacrt International Business Publications, USA at:
P.O. Box 15343, Washington, DC 20003, USA. Phone: (202) 546-2103. Fax: (202) 546-3275.
E-mail: rusric@erols.com

34.	US – KOREA NORTH Diplomatic and Political Relations Handbook
35.	US – KOREA SOUTH Diplomatic and Political Relations Handbook
36.	US – KUWAIT Diplomatic and Political Relations Handbook
37.	US – KYRGYZSTAN Diplomatic and Political Relations Handbook
38.	US – LATVIA Diplomatic and Political Relations Handbook
39.	US – LITHUANIA Diplomatic and Political Relations Handbook
40.	US – MEXICO Diplomatic and Political Relations Handbook
41.	US – MOLDOVA Diplomatic and Political Relations Handbook
42.	US – NEW ZEALAND Diplomatic and Political Relations Handbook
43.	US – NORWAY Diplomatic and Political Relations Handbook
44.	US – PERU Diplomatic and Political Relations Handbook
45.	US – PHILIPPINES Diplomatic and Political Relations Handbook
46.	US – POLAND Diplomatic and Political Relations Handbook
47.	US – PORTUGAL Diplomatic and Political Relations Handbook
48.	US – RUSSIA Diplomatic and Political Relations Handbook
49.	US – SAUDI ARABIA Diplomatic and Political Relations Handbook
50.	US – SOUTH AFRICA Diplomatic and Political Relations Handbook
51.	US – SPAIN Diplomatic and Political Relations Handbook
52.	US – SRI LANKA Diplomatic and Political Relations Handbook
53.	US – SWEDEN Diplomatic and Political Relations Handbook
54.	US – SWITZERLAND Diplomatic and Political Relations Handbook
55.	US – TAIWAN Diplomatic and Political Relations Handbook
56.	US – TURKEY Diplomatic and Political Relations Handbook
57.	US – TURKMENISTAN Diplomatic and Political Relations Handbook
58.	US – UKRAINE Diplomatic and Political Relations Handbook
59.	US – UNITED KINGDOM Diplomatic and Political Relations Handbook
60.	US – URUGUAY Diplomatic and Political Relations Handbook
61.	US – UZBEKISTAN Diplomatic and Political Relations Handbook
62.	US – VENEZUELA Diplomatic and Political Relations Handbook
63.	US – VIETNAM Diplomatic and Political Relations Handbook
64.	US – YUGOSLAVIA Diplomatic and Political Relations Handbook

To order and for additional analytical and marketing information, please contacrt
International Business Publications, USA at:
P.O. Box 15343, Washington, DC 20003, USA. Phone: (202) 546-2103. Fax: (202) 546-3275.
E-mail: rusric@erols.com